HIP PRIE.

The Story of Mark E. Smith and The Fall

Simon Ford is a regular contributor to *The Wire*, *Art Monthly* and *Mute*. His other books include *The Realization and Suppression of the Situationist International* and *Wreckers of Civilization: The Story of COUM Transmissions and Throbbing Gristle*. He lives and works in Brixton, London, and can be contacted at hippriestauthor@hotmail.com

HIP PRIEST

The Story of Mark E. Smith and The Fall

SIMON FORD

QUARTET BOOKS

First published by Jeremy Beale and Stella Kane
at Quartet Books Limited
A member of the Namara Group
27 Goodge Street
London W1T 2LD

ISBN 0 7043 81672
Typeset by Antony Gray
Printed and bound in Great Britain
by Creative Print and Design Group

Contents

Acknowledgements

First I'd like to thank those closest to the band for all the help they've given: Una Baines, Martin Bramah, Dave Bush, Kay Carroll, Michael Clark, Tony Friel, Anthony Frost, Steve Hanley, Pascal Le Gras, Julia Nagle, Yvonne Pawlett, Marc Riley, Craig Scanlon, Marcia Schofield, Grant Showbiz, Brix Smith and Richard Thomas. Next up for thanks are all the many people that have helped in both large and small ways to make this book possible: Darren Andrews, Merlin Carpenter, Graham Coleman, Anthony Davies, Christian Flamm, Jeremy Glogan, John Godbert, Alun Graves, Chris Bohn and Tony Herrington and *The Wire*, Matthew Higgs, Stewart Home, Stella Kane, Rich Kidd, Martin Madron, Steve Parkin, Barney Perkins, Jo Pryde, Pauline van Mourik Broekman, Simon Worthington and Josephine Berry of *Mute* magazine, Julie Taylor, Howard Slater, Rob Waite, Antek Walczak, Trevor Wishart, and Dick Witts. Thanks also to all the staff at the National Art Library, Victoria and Albert Museum, The British Library, the Lending Division of the BL at Boston Spa, Manchester Central Library and the Family Record Centre. The Fall has been particularly well served by a dedicated group of enthusiasts on the Internet who have selflessly collated and published masses of useful information. All of this can be accessed via The Fall website at www.visi.com/fall. Specifically, though, this book would have been poorer and taken much longer to write without the work of first Rich Kidd and then Stefan Cooke on the Fall News website. Much use was also made of the online Gigography and Jeff Higgott's Discography and Conway Paton's Lyrics Parade. Thanks also to all the people on the Fallnet discussion list for providing me with daily doses of Fall-related information, comment and humour. Outside of the Internet, the highest respect is due to Graham Coleman and Rob Waite, the editors of the essential and late-lamented Fall fanzine *The Biggest Library Yet* (*TBLY*). My pen-ultimate thanks go to all the journalists who have sat for hours in pubs interviewing Mark E. Smith so I didn't have too. My final thanks go to Dinah Winch, who not only made countless and priceless suggestions for improving the text, but also, as a companion, has made the years working on the book the best years of my life.

Lyrics from the following works are reproduced by kind permission of Minder Music Ltd:

'Repetition' – Mark E. Smith, Karl Burns, Una Baines, Anthony Friel, Mark Beddington

'C 'n' C's Mithering' – Mark E. Smith, Marc Riley, Craig Scanlon, Stephen Hanley

'Impression Of J. Temperance' – Mark E. Smith, Mark Riley, Craig Scanlon

'In The Park' – Mark E. Smith

'Prole Art Threat' – Mark E. Smith, Marc Riley

'Slates, Slags, Etc.' – Mark E. Smith, Marc Riley, Craig Scanlon, Stephen Hanley, Paul Hanley

'Iceland' – Mark E. Smith, Marc Riley, Craig Scanlon, Stephen Hanley

'The Classical' – Mark E. Smith, Marc Riley, Craig Scanlon, Stephen Hanley, Paul Hanley, Karl Burns

'And This Day' – Mark E. Smith, Marc Riley, Craig Hanlon, Stephen Hanley, Paul Hanley, Karl Burns

'Hip Priest' – Mark E. Smith, Marc Riley, Craig Scanlon, Stephen Hanley, Paul Hanley

'Fortress' – Mark E. Smith, Marc Riley, Craig Scanlon, Karl Burns

'Deer Park' – Mark E. Smith, Marc Riley, Craig Scanlon, Karl Burns

'Mere Pseud Mag. Ed.' – Mark E. Smith, Marc Riley

'Just Step S'ways' – Mark E. Smith

'Who Makes The Nazis?' – Mark E. Smith

'Look, Know' – Mark E. Smith, Marc Riley, Stephen Hanley, Karl Burns, Kay Carroll

'Neighbourbood Of Infinity' – Mark E. Smith, Marc Riley, Craig Scanlon, Stephen Hanley, Karl Burns

'Garden' – Mark E. Smith, Craig Scanlon, Stephen Hanley, Paul Hanley, Karl Burns

ACKNOWLEDGEMENTS

'Hexen Definitive/ Strife Knot' – Mark E. Smith, Karl Burns, Craig
   Scanlon

'Elves' – Mark E. Smith, Brix Smith

'Craigness' – Mark E. Smith, Craig Scanlon

'Bombast' – Mark E. Smith, Stephen Hanley

'Paintwork' – Mark E. Smith, Craig Scanlon, Simon Rogers

'Living Too Late' – Mark E. Smith

Introduction

> I was watching The Fall and they were all stood with their backs to the audience. Then they turned around and Mark's got this outfit on that's made up of 60-watt light bulbs. He looked just like a lizard with a great big long tail. The highlight of the evening was when all these light bulbs lit up.[1]

In the 1988 song 'Twister', Mark E. Smith sings about dictating his autobiography to his biographer. His title for the book is *Renegade Genius*. Although an obvious cliché, and dosed here with Smith's heavy irony, the phrase is entirely fitting: renegade genius, an exceptional creative talent who refuses to be enslaved by another's system. It's an attitude that, over the past twenty-five years, has helped create a musical phenomenon with few equals in terms of both durability and cultural impact. From Smith's early days playing in an attic in Prestwich to his performance at the Royal Festival Hall in London, the Smith position remains: 'A record should be a mark, a statement, it should be everything, an encapsulation of life.'[2] This story is as much about that attitude as it is about Smith and The Fall.

As everybody knows Smith is the commonest name in Britain. The word means someone who works with metal, and probably derives from the Anglo-Saxon word 'smitan', meaning 'to strike'. It's a fitting name for someone renowned for both his conspicuous ordinariness and his inclination indiscriminately to hit out. But Smith's character remains much more complex than this neat formula suggests. For all his reputation, it's difficult to find somebody with a bad word to say about him. Grant Showbiz's comments are representative: 'What doesn't come over in most of the stuff you read is that he's a loveable, wonderful guy, not a curmudgeonly old git who sits in the pub and rambles on about how much he hates everything!'[3]

---

1 Una Baines describing the dream that inspired her song 'Lizard Man'. Interview with author. All quotes in the book without references come from interviews with the author conducted between 1999 and 2002.
2 Mark E. Smith, 'Interview', *Printed Noises*, no. 4, 1980
3 *The Unutterable* press release, 2000

This book documents the many sides of Smith's character, from the lyricist of penetrating insight to the bad-tempered despot. As he himself admitted, the range of his possible personas has led to wildly varying assessments of his worth: 'Every artist wants credibility. A couple of years ago, I read a poll on the hundred best artists of all time. The Fall was in there between Mozart and Puccini. I was very proud of that. Of course, the next day I can pick up a paper and be the guy with no teeth who beats everybody up.'[4] It's a schizophrenic characterization that he has encouraged not just in his contrary and unpredictable behaviour but also through the many *alter egos* adopted and abandoned over the years, including Roman Totale, Fiery Jack, The Man Whose Head Expanded, Carrier-Bag Man, Riddler, The Crying Marshal and the Hip Priest. It is a characteristic that can also be applied to The Fall: 'There's been about ten different Falls,' said Smith, 'line-up wise and attitude wise.'[5]

Hanging over this ever-changing cast of diverse characters is Smith's almost occult policy of secrecy and concealment: 'I'll tell you one thing about me. I don't give away my secrets.'[6] This strategy includes deflecting speculation about his obviously deep sense of identification with The Fall. When asked by a hapless journalist if The Fall was an extension of his personality, Smith's reply was typically confrontational: 'Dunno, you're the one sitting there in your round glasses and trendy leather jacket. You tell me what you think it's an extension of . . . I enjoy saying this to journalists. But for every bloke pulling a pint, there's about ten thousand journalists writing an article about it.'[7] The continuing enigma of The Fall is perhaps Smith's greatest achievement: that despite all the interviews, reviews and analysis, The Fall still defies explanation. And Smith remains determined to keep it that way. He even writes notes to himself saying: 'Do not go round explaining yourself.'[8] The Fall exists and he thinks that's enough: 'I know what The Fall is and I don't think there is much you can do to explain it.'[9]

---

4 Lisa Verrico, 'Are You Talking to Me?', *Dazed & Confused*, December 1998
5 George Kay, 'Mancunian Caustic', *Rip It Up*, no. 215, July 1995
6 Tom Cox, 'Just Who Does Mr Grumpy Think He Is?', *The Times*, 24 November 2000
7 John Robinson, 'The E Regeneration', *NME*, 5 September 1998
8 Mark E. Smith, 'Musical Influence in Great Britain on Big-head here', in Chris Roberts (ed.), *Idle Worship*, London: HarperCollins, 1994
9 Smith in Charles Neal, *Tape Delay*, Wembley: SAF Publishing, 1987

Despite such statements, something approaching a doctrine can be pieced together from the various interviews Smith has conducted over the years. First, the project is continually to strip rock back to its basics: 'If it doesn't sound good on a little cassette recorder, then forget it.'[10] Second, never stop: 'Everyone wants to settle down and get comfy. I mean, OK, get a wife and kids, but don't just stop! You've gotta *produce*. What are we here for? If you don't produce you're just an animal – a pig in a poke!'[11] Third, in order to survive in the music business live in the now, never look back or too far forward: 'I never stop and reflect on what I've just done, and I don't think more than three months ahead . . . I make LPs, I listen to them once to see they're all right, and that's it. I can look at all that shit when I'm like sixty or something.'[12] And the final lesson for today – know what you like: 'I've got a layman's ear. If it sounds rubbish to me, it's rubbish.'[13]

Some, of course, have passed similar judgement on The Fall and many have been mystified at the band's appeal and ridiculed the extraordinary devotion of its followers. For the latter, though, The Fall makes music that in many ways renders all other music somehow impossible. After The Fall there's not much left to say, as Smith explained: 'The Fall is similar to somebody who writes books about how books aren't necessary.'[14] My relationship with the band started in 1982 when I bought my first album, *Hex Enduction Hour*. I was seventeen, living in the seaside resort of Paignton, and I had to order it through my local record shop, Soundz. I can't remember why I went to the trouble. It was probably a combination of reviews and interviews in the music press and hearing some tracks on John Peel's radio show. Anyway, it arrived, I took it home and played it non-stop until I bought my next record by The Fall, and the next, and . . . the rest is history, the rest is basically this book.

To be a Fall fan is to live at least part of your life in a parallel universe, a universe inhabited by containers and their drivers, bingo-masters, city hobgoblins, male slags and chiselers, a universe

10   Mark E. Smith, in an interview on VPRO-Radio, broadcast 13 May 1993
11   Johnny Cigarettes, 'One Man and his Grog', *NME*, 7 May 1994
12   Simon Price, 'Counter Culture', *Melody Maker*, 18 December 1993
13   Mark E. Smith, interviewed by Mark Radcliffe for BBC Radio Five, *Hit the North*, broadcast 23 April 1991; transcript published in *TBLY*, no. 6, July 1996
14   Bob Giddens, 'Hobgoblins on the Loose', *Zig-Zag*, June 1980

where everything can be correlated to a song by The Fall. Give me any subject and I can run it through my Fall-addled mind and come up with something relevant: from Accrington to Xanadu, from Martin Amis to Colin Wilson, from aphids to squids. The Fall has been more than a soundtrack to many people's lives, its also provided the voice-over and the subtitles. The Fall becomes the very language you think through. Its corpus provides an inexhaustible stream of neologisms and buzz-words, trigger phrases that you just can't shake off: 'eat yourself fitter', 'totally wired', 'just step sideways', 'a Jew on a motorbike', even 'Hey! Hey! Hey! Hey!' Maybe these voices are a sign I've been listening to The Fall and working on this book for too long. Or maybe it's because The Fall, more than any other band, provides a key to understanding, or at least describing, the wonderful and frightening world we live in at the end of the twentieth century and the beginning of the twenty-first.

To date there has been just one other book on The Fall, Brian Edge's 1989 *Paintwork: A Portrait of The Fall*. This slim Omnibus Press publication came at the height of the band's pop acceptability. The departure of Brix, however, just before the book was published gave it an instantly dated appearance. Dave Jennings in *Melody Maker* criticized the book for side-stepping Smith's reactionary views, for overlooking his drug-taking and for failing to find out why Mark E. Smith ultimately seems to drive everyone, even his wife, out of his life.[15] Mat Snow added that after reading the book he was still nowhere nearer to knowing, 'What makes him tick?'[16] Perhaps this book might help, but I doubt it. I suspect the answer to this question is beyond anybody, even Smith. And if he did know he definitely wouldn't tell us.

Given such a concern for privacy, it is not surprising that Smith declined my requests for an interview. This has meant that I've drawn extensively on the many interviews that already exist in the music press. Such a muting and distancing of Smith's presence in this book has resulted in at least one positive effect: it has enabled me to bring forward into the light the experiences and recollections of other people associated with the group. Given the potential numbers involved (around forty people have played in The Fall), I'm very

15 Dave Jennings, '*Paintwork*', *Melody Maker*, 9 September 1989
16 Mat Snow, '*Paintwork*', *Q*, no. 38, November 1989

aware that this book offers only a partial account of the people that have entered and exited its gravitational pull over the past quarter of a century. A book is a finite thing and to encapsulate a moving target the size and complexity of The Fall is something no single author will ever achieve.

For an indication of the difficulties involved you only have to look at what happened during the year 2002, when the bulk of this book was written. In this one year alone, The Fall released one single, one live album, five compilation albums, one spoken-word album, one picture disc, played thirty-two live gigs (including organizing and cancelling two American tours), released eight reissues of earlier albums, contributed to three various-artists compilations and provided the soundtrack for a Vauxhall Corsa television advertisement. For a band repeatedly dismissed throughout the years as well past its sell-by date, that's quite impressive form.

Simon Ford
Brixton, January 2003

1

Stranger in Paradise, 1957–1976

> Being a Smith, you tend to get confused with everybody else. It's the greatest strength you can have. People don't take you seriously and people never fuckin' rate you, and I like that. You're always observing. I like to be anonymous. I don't like the limelight, never have.[1]

It was Tuesday 5 March 1957 and Tony Bennett singing 'Hold my hand, I'm a stranger in paradise' drifted through the rooms of a semi-detached house in Sedgley Park, Greater Manchester. In the house was Irene Smith, her enjoyment of the music tempered somewhat by labour pains. Later that day, her first child, Mark Edward, was born at Crumpsall Hospital.[2] Irene and John Edward Smith had moved up the Bury New Road to Sedgley Park after their marriage in 1955 at St James's Church in Higher Broughton, Salford. Soon there were three sisters, Caroline, Suzanne and Barbara, to keep the young Mark company.

Like many families of his generation, Smith's family had been deeply affected by the experience of the Second World War. His grandfather on his mother's side, James Brownhill, had been part of the British army that fought bravely against the Nazis in France. Smith later listed him amongst his heroes: 'He took on the Waffen-SS with his bare hands in 1940 at Dunkirk because his rifle jammed, which was a pretty brave thing to do, but then the infantry had no choice, they had to stand and fight. All the officers had scarpered, so my grandad and his lot had to stick around to enable those buggers to get away. Dirty work, but he was dead modest about it, a dead nice bloke. And dead little too. That's the funny thing because he was only four foot eleven! That's tiny, isn't it! Far too small to be taking on the whole of Nazi Germany, but he did all right. He

---

1 David Cavanagh, 'The Fall', *Volume*, no. 4, September 1992
2 'Born to the strains of "Stranger in Paradise" ', in Mark E. Smith, *The Fall Lyrik & Texte*, Berlin: Lough Press, 1985

never got any medals or anything but his house was covered with daggers and iron crosses, which I suppose were all the decorations he needed.'[3]

Smith's father was too young to fight during the Second World War but he joined the army as soon as he was able. According to Smith, he was involved in some clandestine post-war vigilante-ism: 'I can only talk about this now because he's dead. He was attached to the Black Watch Regiment, who had twelve of their number murdered in a concentration camp. Anyway, he and his mates found out who was responsible, and hunted them down after the war. They found one guy who was a scientist or something, and so was being guarded by American troops. So they had to somehow get rid of the guards, kill the guy, then leg it back to the British sector.'[4] Smith also claimed two uncles who were captured and tortured in Japanese prisoner-of-war camps. They survived but died shortly before they could claim compensation in 1995.[5] After leaving the army John E. Smith returned home to become a plumber and general building contractor, working with his father, Frederick Smith, in the family plumbing business. Smith's mother, Irene, worked in the local post office as a clerk.

Smith's family home is in a quiet leafy avenue in Sedgley Park, just on the southern edge of Prestwich, a village wrapped around the Bury New Road that links Manchester to the market town of Bury. It sits on the north bank of the valley that descends down to the River Irwell, and is overlooked by the area's parish church, St Mary's. The word 'Prestwich' derives from the Old English words 'preost' and 'wic' meaning 'priest's retreat' or 'the dwelling of a priest' – a fitting lair for the future Hip Priest of legend. Sedgley Park is so named because for much of its history it was marshy and thus the favoured environment for the grass-like plant, sedge. The population of Prestwich expanded significantly when the Bury New Road, following roughly the route of an old Roman road, was completed in 1828. Between 1801 and 1951 the population rose from 1,800 to 34,500. The area was home to one of the largest Jewish communities in the

3 Ted Kessler, 'Mark E. Smith: Heroes & Villains', *NME*, 11 December 1993
4 Roger Sabin, 'People Talking: M. E. Smith', *Speak*, 1996
5 Mark Sutherland, 'We Have Ways of Making You Talk: The Fall', *NME*, 25 March 1995

country, with its own cemetery established in the village as early as 1840.[6] In 1897, Prestwich became an urban district with its own council. The locals were an independent breed, constantly fighting off pressure to join one of their larger surrounding neighbours, Salford, Manchester or Bury. It was not until April 1974 that Prestwich finally succumbed and became part of the new Metropolitan District of Bury.

Growing up and remaining close to his roots in his 'priest's retreat', Smith benefited from both a close proximity to one of the most vibrant, stimulating and cosmopolitan cultural centres in Europe and the ability to hole up and live anonymously amongst the curtain twitchers of Prestwich. An indication of Smith's love of the area and its local mythology is the number of Prestwich buildings featured on early record covers by The Fall. Unfortunately, much that Smith appreciated about the area – particularly its older, often decrepit, semi-derelict buildings – was being systematically demolished. 'Every building I ever have from Prestwich on the back of my covers gets fucking pulled down,' he noted disgustedly. 'The church on *Grotesque* is probably one of the few photographs left of the thing. Like the building on 'Elastic Man' was pulled down, the building on *Hex Enduction Hour* was pulled down, the building on *Dragnet* was pulled down [laughs], it's unbelievable. All these places I cherish are pulled down.'[7]

The Anoraked Brat

In 1998, the *NME* asked Smith what his earliest memory was: 'Getting washed by my mother the day before school when I was about four,' he replied. 'I don't know what happened the previous four years; I was probably locked up in a closet.'[8] The year was 1961 and Smith was on his way to Sedgley Park Primary School. He was a bright kid, passed his eleven-plus and gained a place at Stand Grammar School, a mile or so up the Bury New Road in Whitefield.

6 C. E. Makepeace, *Prestwich: A Brief History*. Prestwich: Prestwich Borough Council, 1973

7 Michael Lang, 'The Fall – Mark E. Smith Interview', *BravEar*, vol. 3, no. 5, Fall/Winter 1986

8 Mark E. Smith, 'On the Couch: Mark E. Smith, The Fall', *NME*, 12 December 1998

Each day for the next five years he would cross the M62, the noisy concrete boundary that separated Prestwich from Whitefield. Smith's memories of the area – his schooldays, his cadet training and the hours spent running cross-country – meant he avoided returning for years until a couple of gigs in 1998. 'Going up there now, it's quite nice,' he said. 'Places I hated I now like. The attitude of the people is quite funny in Whitefield, they're completely unhip.'[9]

The most famous 'Old Standian' was Lord Clive of Plassey (1725–74), famous for his role in the expansion of the British Empire in India. The school itself was built at Stand towards the end of the seventeenth century on land made available by the bequest of Henry Siddall, a tailor from Radcliffe Bridge. By 1958 there were six hundred boys crammed into its redbrick buildings. By 2001, however, another part of Smith's childhood lay in ruins as the local authority closed down the school and demolished it to make way for a new housing development. Fellow pupil, Jeremy Adelman, remembered the schoolboy Smith as 'quite quiet and moody'. Another classmate, Alan Engmann, recalled Smith as a 'tall spindly guy, long hair, drop-out attitude, not too good at sport (although I think that may have changed later on)'. Lack of enthusiasm for sport brought Smith to the attention of 'Haggis' (Mr Hargreaves), the sports master 'cum-geologist, cum-sadist', said Engmann. Haggis was the archetypal sadistic PE teacher, infamous for hosing down under-performing school-kids with cold water. Engmann and Smith were in Siddall House, named after the school's founder. The other houses were Clive, Philips and Raglan, all named after various explorers and aristocrats associated with the history of the school and the local area. The classes were organized according to ability and Smith, thought Engmann, was 'definitely not at the top. I would have said middle.'

Although a few years younger than Smith, fellow Old Standian Ian Levine remembered Smith as being a bit 'severe': ' . . . he looked like a snapper. I guess it's because he was physically unassuming – even then very thin and anaemic looking – so it was his defence against bigger lads picking on him. He really looked like the sort of guy who could tear you off a new arsehole just with words – very, very verbally pugnacious – a real chip on his shoulder – and something of

9 Smith, interviewed by Tony Herrington, London, April 1999, transcript posted on Fallnet

a loner! To me he was an older boy I'd pass on the corridors between lessons. We wouldn't say anything to him because he looked like he'd twat you if you gave him any lip.'

Smith's strong sense of individuality and his refusal to conform with received opinion quickly set him apart from the rest of his class. One time he was learning about graphs and the class was asked to vote for the Beatles, the Rolling Stones, the Monkees or John Fred and the Playboys. The graph showed a stack of votes for the first three and just one, Smith's, for the Playboys: 'They said who do you like, Beatles or the Stones? and I said I like the mad one and they're going, "What about the Monkees, Smith?" and I'm going I don't know them we don't have a record player in our house and my dad doesn't allow the radio on and they were going, "Must be mad." They started calling me a freak. It was like *Lord of the Flies*.'[10]

Smith's contrary taste in pop music was not the only thing that set him apart from his schoolmates. His working-class values plus a broad Mancunian accent provoked relentless derision: 'The teachers couldn't understand a word I said . . . they used to laugh at me, and stand me up in front of the class and make me read something and made out that was exactly how not to speak. But I come top of the class two fucking years in English.'[11]

Outside of school Smith followed closely the fortunes of Manchester City. It was a good time to be a fan. In 1966, under Joe Mercer and the extrovert Malcolm Allison, City won the Division Two championship and in the 1967/8 season, the First Division Championship. In the next season the thirteen-year-old Smith would have boasted to his schoolmates about his team's winning of both the FA Cup and the European Cup Winners' Cup. Smith's favourite player was Tony Coleman, a maverick left-winger who played for the club between 1967 and 1970. Smith's choice of idol was typically idiosyncratic. 'He was the wild man of City – the Keith Moon of soccer – completely ungovernable,' Smith enthused. 'He used to vomit before every game because he was so nervous. His kit was always dirty, he used to have big boils over his face, but he was the only one who scored any goals . . . United had millions of pounds and City had to buy blokes from Doncaster Rovers. They were a joke, but the championship was

10   James Brown, 'Rebellious Jukebox', *NME*, 29 July 1989
11   David Stubbs, 'The Indelible Prinz', *Melody Maker*, 12 November 1988

ours. All Mancunians support City – only outsiders support United (joke). When I was at school, there were only ever three City fans and thousands of United fans. Every City game I watch I think is great, but watching Coleman [in 1968] unhinge the United defence when we beat them 3–1 at Old Trafford was brilliant.'[12]

When not fantasizing about Manchester City winning the cup, Smith might have day-dreamed about the Belle Vue Aces, one of the premier speedway clubs in the world. 'His school blazer had loads and loads of speedway badges on it!' recalled Ian Levine. 'We used to take the piss behind his back that the weight of his lapels with all those metal badges on it made him stoop like a hunchback! He was a serious speedway head.' During the sixties and early seventies, the club and world champion Ivan Mauger would draw thousands of spectators to its midweek night meetings. On the inner sleeve of *Dragnet* you can see Smith peering through the stadium gates at Belle Vue, doubtlessly thinking back to the days when he used to watch the Aces from its wooden stands.

Smith's other extra-curricular experiences were not always so innocent: 'I come from a class of burglars,' he once boasted. 'Oh yeah. I used to do some myself. Yeah. I used to do all sorts of things.'[13] In 1981 he wrote a short story for *City Fun*, 'Incident from the Early Life of the Anoraked Brat', that centred on the aftermath of a raid on a local 'alcohol warehouse'. Smith and his friends escaped with bottles of whisky and cans of beer stuffed into their *Manchester Evening News* paper-boy canvas bags. 'We hid the drink in a bush off a big sports pitch,' Smith wrote. 'That night was the first time I ever drank a lot of beer, laughed on the grass . . . we got away. "School holidays'll be great." '[14] Smith started drinking when he was just thirteen and would often accompany his dad and grandad to the pub. 'I mean, it was different then,' he said. 'I'm quite a light drinker. They were serious about it.'[15]

One of Smith's friends was 'Thomas', a half-Irish, half-English boy a couple of years older than Smith who shared his absurd sense of

12 Mark E. Smith, 'Heroes', *Melody Maker*, 27 September 1986
13 Jonh Wilde, 'The Mouth that Roared', *Melody Maker*, 5 March 1988
14 Mark E. Smith, 'Incident from the Early Life of the Anoraked Brat', *City Fun*, 9–22 January 1981
15 Roy Wilkinson, 'The Hardcore Pub Fella', *Select*, September 1996

humour and vivid imagination. Thomas also helped develop Smith's individualistic personality by encouraging his disdain for fashion, convention and the local 'gang' mentality: 'Me and Thomas would always go from gang to gang, and always could,' Smith said. 'So if we joined one we'd get attacked by the other. So they'd have us tied up against lamp-posts and they'd be hitting us with sticks. And Thomas would be going, "Oh, where did you get them jeans from?" or, "That bloody haircut you've got, it's fantastic." And you just had to laugh because they didn't even know he was taking the piss. And they'd go, "Oh, you're just mad you are." And you'd be crying and they thought it was because they were hitting you but it was with laughter, they were that stupid.' Another trick they used to play was going to synagogue youth clubs and pretending to be Jewish: 'He'd have like a suit jacket on, with fucking big lapels on, and a tie, and a rotten shirt which had a fucking big hole in it, and pants that were falling to bits, but he'd carry it off. And he'd go, "I've just come back from the Casino, won a hundred pounds," and all these rich Jewish kids would be totally taken in by it.'[16]

Whereas most of Smith's schoolmates did what their parents told them to do, Thomas and his Irish friends were different: 'They'd always take the piss out of kids who really had nice clothes and stuff . . . it made me more secure in myself. I had great parents, but Thomas was one of those guys who could reduce you to tears and laughter just by talking. That's why I had a really nice childhood, because of Thomas.'[17] After Smith left school he drifted apart from Thomas: 'Apparently he never goes out of the house much now, but he was always like that. Even later on when I'd go round and ask him if he was coming to the pub he'd say: "Yeah, I'll just go and change me socks," and he'd be up there an hour. Then he'd come back and he'd have two different socks on.'[18]

16 James Brown, 'Drunken Driver Causes Chaos – in a JCB!', NME, 31 October 1987
17 Lang, op. cit., Fall/Winter 1986
18 Brown, op. cit., 31 October 1987

Pink Floyd? Crap!

It was not until Smith reached fourteen that his father allowed a record player into the house. Up to that time all he could listen to was BBC Radio Two. However, he quickly developed an interest in music, especially as it became another way to challenge conformity: 'I went through it all, really quick: Pink Floyd? Crap! T.Rex? Rubbish! Paul McCartney? Urrgh! Black Sabbath, "Paranoid"? Great! Know what I mean? That was the first single I bought! Everybody else was into Emerson, Lake & Palmer, Greenslade, Pink Floyd, sixth-form crap, and I just didn't get into it. I was a late starter, but I got into it really quickly when I did.'[19] Smith's first experience of live rock music came at a gig by the Groundhogs in 1971 at the Free Trade Hall, Manchester. 'I remember that they were very good,' Smith said. 'At the time I didn't like weirdo music, y'know weirdo long hair stuff. It was at the time of the LP *Split*, they were sort of like John Lee Hooker on acid.'[20] Another band that Smith caught at the Free Trade Hall was Van der Graaf Generator with its eccentric leader, Peter Hammill. 'They were better than The Doors if you ask me,' Smith enthused. 'Peter Hammill came on in jackboots and they didn't have a guitarist and it was like the second concert I'd ever seen and it was just the best thing I'd ever seen in my life.'[21]

Smith's year at school was the first to 'enjoy' an extra year of schooling when the school-leaving age was extended to sixteen. Many of his classmates stayed on and studied for A levels before going on to university. Smith was, of course, different. He left Stand as soon as he could and continued his education at a local college. His parents put him under no pressure to pass exams and stay on at school. The opposite, in fact, as Smith explained: 'My father used to say to me, "What're you reading a book for? There's something wrong with you," and stuff like that. It's real good 'cause it encourages you, it makes it exciting. I mean my parents got me out of school as fast as possible which I didn't like at the time but it's sort of brought out the self-education sort of idea in me. And I feel better for it.'[22]

19   Andy Gill, 'Mark E. Smith's Record Collection', *Q*, no. 49, October 1990
20   Mark E. Smith, 'My First Gig: Groundhogs', *Melody Maker*, 5 December 1998
21   Mark E. Smith, on *Mark Goodier's Evening Session*, BBC Radio One, broadcast 7 May 1992
22   Scott Brecker, 'Wordsmith', *Option Magazine*, July/August 1986

There was also pressure on Smith to join the family's plumbing business, a practical trade that Smith, looking back, thought would have come in handy: 'I really wish I'd done a plumber's apprentice,' he said laughing. 'It'd be great to be able to do your art and have that back up. Plumbers make fortunes. They never used to when I was a kid . . . But I just don't have it in my hands, you gotta have it. I can't even change a plug now, it's real hard.'[23]

So Smith said good riddance to Stand in the summer of 1973 and enrolled as an A level student at St John's College, along with his girlfriend Una Baines. The two had met earlier that summer at a fair in Heaton Park: 'He just asked me for a light and I didn't smoke,' Baines recalled, 'and then we got talking about music and how we didn't like fairs, just really got on. Me and my friend had to remember his phone number. She had to remember one half of it and I had to remember the other. Luckily we remembered and a couple of days later I rang him up and it all started from there.' Baines was exactly a month younger than Smith, and from the Collyhurst area of Manchester, where her family shared a terraced house. 'It was like Coronation Street,' she said, 'but they knocked it down and we moved two hundred yards across the road to the new council estate. It was a very deprived area. My mum was Irish and my dad was from Manchester, both from big families. When I met Mark I was still wearing my black satin Marc Bolan jacket and was into Bowie and stuff like that. But it was like I was outgrowing that sort of stuff, the glam scene had become just too commercial. Mark introduced me to the Velvet Underground.'

Smith and Baines stayed on for just three months at St John's College. Baines's dad was made redundant and she felt obliged to get a job: 'I worked in offices, including a company that had asbestos mines in South Africa. I always wanted to copy the incriminating files and send them to the *Evening News* to get published.' Discontented with office work, Baines enrolled as a student psychiatric nurse at Prestwich Hospital. She left home and rented a flat nearby on Kingswood Road. At the time the hospital was the largest employer in the area and cared for 2,600 patients, some of whom could be found walking the streets of Prestwich and sneaking pints in the local pubs ('care in the community', Manchester style).

---

23   Lang, op. cit., Fall/Winter 1986

Smith like Baines also came under pressure to start bringing money into the household. Although difficult to stomach at the time, he later appreciated his father's refusal to help fund his education: 'My dad had never given me money. I wanted to go to college when I was sixteen, so I did for a short while, but he gave me no money. So my ribs would be sticking out. I'd hate the bastard. I'd go, "You bastard. Other kids are getting money." But when I thought about it I didn't really like college anyway. I educated myself a lot better.' The experience stood him in good stead for the uncertain and erratic rewards of the music industry: 'I don't have any real money problems, I never have. I've been in real bad debt with tax due to the group. But I've always been able to live on anything. Some kids go through life and because their parents gave them a lot of money they are in a permanent state of debt and personal insecurity. My father always said to me, "Look, if you've got five pounds in your pocket on Friday, your life's made," which is great. That's the ideal. That's a real English working-class attitude. They were brought up during the Blitz. They don't throw anything away.'[24]

So Smith left further education and entered the job market. It was never his ambition, however, to make a career out of the clerical work he was offered: 'My ambition was to get a flat on the dole and take drugs and avoid work at all costs!'[25] It was not the best time to be looking for work. The post-war 'Golden Age' was well and truly ended and talk of 'crisis' dominated the newspapers. While Smith studied at St John's College in October 1973 the price of petrol quadrupled as the Arab-Israeli war began to disrupt the world's oil supply. In November, the National Union of Miners implemented an overtime ban in support of a pay claim. On 13 November the Conservative Prime Minister, Edward Heath, declared a state of emergency in an attempt to deal with the growing fuel crisis. Smith's first experience of work coincided with the 'three-day week' of January 1974. In February Heath called a general election but was defeated by his Labour rival, Harold Wilson. Despite cuts in public spending and what amounted to a compulsory wages policy, the new government did little to revive the economy as it drifted closer to

24 ibid.
25 Ian Gittins, 'The Fall: Funfair for the Common Man', *Melody Maker*, 3 March 1990

recession. It was no wonder then that school leavers showed little optimism or expectation of a bright future of full employment. 'When I was at school they tried to get you into shit jobs,' Smith said. 'They'd try and get you behind the counter at Lewis's for about £9 a week. I got fired from my first job after three months and I went home dancing!'[26] This first job was at a Louis Edwards's meat factory where Smith was paid just £8.50 per week and offered a season ticket to watch Manchester United.[27]

His second job was as a poorly paid clerk at an importing and exporting business in Manchester Docks. In many ways the job was ideal; it was regular work with a steady income at a time when unemployment was on the rise. His desk job also provided cover for his writing and he took full advantage of his breaks to use the office typewriters. The job also brought him into contact with lorry drivers from all corners of the world: 'I used to love it, me. Get home about six-thirty, then straight down the pub.'[28] By the mid-seventies, however, the docks were in terminal decline. A series of dock strikes during 1971 and 1972 lead to many firms moving away or closing down. More disastrously, the number of ships coming to Manchester began to decline as dock facilities suitable for the newer and larger container ships were built at Ellesmere Port near Liverpool. It was not until the eighties and the Salford Quays Development Plan that investment began to flow back into the docks area. And this time the emphasis would be on culture rather than industry. Little could Smith have guessed that twenty years after he left the docks he would be back there performing on stage at The Lowry, a futuristic arts centre, accompanying a ballet dancer.[29]

Stooges to Stockhausen

With his new job, Smith needed little further encouragement to leave home and move in with Baines on Kingswood Road: 'I never really liked my dad, I used to hate him, that's why I left. I used to get on

26 Ron Rom, 'Semi-detached Suburban Mr Smith', *Sounds*, 19 July 1986

27 Mark E. Smith, 'Embarrassing Moments', *When Saturday Comes*, no. 35, 1990; also in *TBLY*, no. 11, 1998, p. 35

28 Rom, op. cit., 19 July 1986

29 Smith appeared with Michael Clark, 19–20 May 2000, The Lowry, Salford Quays.

really well with my mother, but apart from that I couldn't wait to get out of the house. Other kids used to get a fiver for passing their eleven-plus, all my dad did was call me a bookworm.'[30] Both Smith and Baines were impatient for their independence and eager to experiment with new friends, music, books and drugs. The two-bedroom flat was on two floors with a private staircase entrance. With no central heating and just one electric fire, it froze during the winter, but it was theirs. 'Everybody else was living at home,' recalled Baines. 'It was all wallpapered with photocopies of the Velvet Underground.'

In the flat Smith found it much easier to listen to music and read whatever he liked. His interest in reading started when he was just five and he discovered *Batman* comics. 'We hadn't any books in the house,' he recalled. 'We had an encyclopaedia and a map, that was all. So I went to the public library. Reading wasn't much encouraged at the school I went to. I enjoyed Hardy and *Macbeth*. Very much. But then they tried to make us read Jane Austen. Terrible. I read Nietzsche at fifteen because it was good. It was wild. I used to read a lot of Wilfred Owen's poetry.'[31]

Leaving school helped his education immensely: 'It's amazing how much you want to read a book when you're out of the education system. That's one bad thing, forcing people to read *Jane Eyre* and irrelevant shit like that.'[32] As befitted his autodidactic sensibilities, Smith's taste in books was suitably idiosyncratic. If a general pattern to Smith's reading interests can be discerned it follows the off-beat *noir* of non-mainstream genre fiction: spy, detective and science fiction by the likes of John Le Carré, George V. Higgins, Edgar Allan Poe, Raymond Chandler and Kurt Vonnegut. Smith also devoured ghost and horror stories by authors such as M. R. James, Algernon Blackwood and Arthur Machen. In literary fiction, Smith has acknowledged the influence of Louis-Ferdinand Céline, Wyndham Lewis, Malcolm Lowry and William Burroughs. However, the two writers who figured most strongly as influences on the young Smith were H. P. Lovecraft and Philip K. Dick.

Lovecraft was an American writer in the tradition of Edgar Allan Poe and Algernon Blackwood. Although predominantly working in

30 Rom, op. cit., 19 July 1986
31 Mark E. Smith, 'An Early Liking for Nietzsche', *Independent*, 6 May 1993
32 Stubbs, op. cit., 12 November 1988

the horror genre, his stories, published in pulp magazines like *Weird Tales*, often strayed into the genres of fantasy and science fiction. He was a neglected figure during his lifetime and it was not until the sixties that interest in his work began to grow. Smith was an early advocate of his work, seeing countless parallels to his own environment and writing. In particular, both believed that beneath the surface of a supposedly banal material world there lay a world of myths and supernatural forces. Vampires and castles in Transylvania were unnecessary; the streets of Prestwich could be examined to yield plenty of horrors for the receptive soul.

The science-fiction writer Philip K. Dick was born in Chicago but lived most of his life in California. Like Lovecraft, Dick and his work also suffered from neglect during his lifetime. The filming of his 1968 novel *Do Androids Dream of Electric Sheep?* as *Blade Runner* came just too late as he died of a heart attack just a few weeks before its première in 1982. Dick was also an expert at looking below the surface of the most ordinary of everyday situations for traces of significance and conspiracy. The paranoia suffered by Dick's characters can also be seen in some of Smith's later creations, like the harassed author in 'How I Wrote Elastic Man' and the man followed by soap-opera writers in 'The Man Whose Head Expanded' (note also the quintessentially Dicksian titles). Smith was also a big fan of American television crime dramas, such as *Dragnet* and, his favourite, *The Untouchables*, which was hosted by the distinctive narrator Walter Winchell. Another favourite from this period was the original series of *The Twilight Zone*, with its titles and plots consistently finding their way into Smith's lyrics over the years.

Alongside books and television, Smith was now able to indulge his musical interests. With his first week's wages he bought his favourite Stooges album, *The Stooges*, produced in 1969 by John Cale with its classic versions of 'I Wanna Be Your Dog' and 'No Fun'. 'I only bought it for the cover,' Smith later explained. 'When I went into Virgin Records in Manchester they all sneered at me from the counter so I knew I must be on to something good. I remember playing it and thinking it sounded exactly like the Rolling Stones, only miles better.'[33] Between 1974 and 1976 Smith discovered a wide range of cult and experimental bands to add to his collection of Black Sabbath,

33 Smith, op. cit., 27 September 1986

Peter Hammill and Iggy Pop records. There was the inimitable Velvet Underground and Captain Beefheart, kraut rock by Can and Faust, trash proto-punk from the New York Dolls, old rockabilly by Gene Vincent, blues by John Lee Hooker, reggae by Lee 'Scratch' Perry and even classical music by Karlheinz Stockhausen.

Despite Smith's obvious love of their music, none of these artists would have a direct influence on his vocal and writing style: 'The problem was I knew I could never be like any of them . . . I admired Iggy Pop, but he was too American rock and roll to influence me. I liked his music, but at the same time it felt alien to me.'[34] As a vocalist Smith refused all prior models except perhaps one: 'I used to like Lou Reed a lot as a kid. Saw him a couple of times and I think I picked up a couple of his mannerisms.'[35] One of these mannerisms was a reputation for being 'difficult'. Smith was one of the few people to buy Reed's *Metal Machine Music* in 1975 and like it: 'I was buying it when everybody else was taking it back.'[36]

We were all writing poetry

The next step in the evolution of The Fall occurred one day, probably in 1975, when Smith and Baines were relaxing on the couch at Smith's parents' house, listening to the Velvet Underground and The Doors. The front door opened and in came Smith's sister, Barbara, with two new friends, Martin Bramah and Tony Friel. Bramah, born September 1957 in Manchester, and Friel, born 4 May 1958 in Birkenhead, had first met at Heys Boys' Secondary School. Bramah remembered Friel as 'a very eccentric boy. He got picked on a lot, but he had this wild imagination. I was drawn to him because he was full of mad ideas and tall tales.' Bramah left school with just one O level, in art: 'We were really just factory fodder. It was a boys' school, very military in attitude, so we just tried to avoid it as much as we could. We would wander into town and do shop-lifting. To be honest, most of the instruments we used to start The Fall were

---

34 Lisa Verrico, 'Are You Talking to Me?' *Dazed & Confused*, December 1998
35 George Kay, 'The Fall of Slick, Mark E. Smith's Enduction Hour', *Rip It Up*, September 1982
36 Edwin Pouncey, 'Invisible Jukebox: Mark E. Smith', *The Wire*, no. 203, January 2001

stolen.' Like Smith and Baines, Bramah lasted just three months in further education. His teacher at Radcliffe Further Education College described trying to teach him as 'pissing against the wind'.

Friel dropped out of school without any qualifications but was determined to make his way as a musician: 'I always had an interest in art and music,' he said. 'The first record I bought was the Rolling Stones' "Get Off My Cloud". At the age eleven or twelve, I really got into Marc Bolan and he inspired me to play guitar.' Meeting Smith helped accelerate Friel's musical education: 'Mark and I shared an interest in music, and would spend many evenings listening to records. Mark had an interesting collection, lots of bands I never listened to before, like Can, and sixties US punk bands.' It was not long before Friel, Bramah, Smith and Baines were meeting regularly at Kingswood Road to take drugs (LSD, speed and magic mushrooms), play music and talk about what they wanted to do with their lives. 'We were totally wrapped up in music,' Bramah said, 'it meant a lot to us. The bands we loved, we loved dearly; it was our escape from what the world was offering us. Every weekend we were getting out of our faces. But we didn't see it as a nihilistic thing because to us it was a quest for knowledge; we were hungry to see different ways of being. We were all writing poetry.'

The four of them became a gang that often left the flat for forays into the night seeking people to antagonize: 'I used to take acid and go round clubs wearing swastika armbands,' Smith later confessed. 'We used to try and cause fights with heavy metal gangs and get bands to play proper music and real heavy stuff like that.'[37] What united them all was a love of music and the desire to form a band. At first Bramah was going to be the singer, with Smith on guitar, Friel on bass and Baines on drums, just like Moe Tucker in the Velvet Underground. It soon became apparent, however, that Smith had little aptitude for the guitar and he swapped roles with Bramah. Baines was also unlikely to be able to afford a drum-kit and instead she started saving up for a keyboard. Despite their enthusiasm, they still might have taken it no further if it had not been for the visit to Manchester's Lesser Free Trade Hall on Friday 4 June 1976 of the Sex Pistols. They decided to go only after reading a reference to the Stooges in Neil

37 Barney Hoskyns, 'Hip Priest: The Mark Smith Interview', NME, 14 November 1981

Spencer's legendary *NME* review of an early Sex Pistols show. In the small audience that night were many of the instigators of the next twenty years of the Manchester music scene, including soon-to-be manager of the Buzzcocks, Richard Boon, Joy Division's Bernard Sumner and Peter Hook, and Steven Patrick Morrissey later of The Smiths.

Even when Smith and his friends met up in nearby Cox's Bar, it was still touch and go whether they could be bothered to see the band. 'We were all going, shall we go, shan't we go?' Smith remembered. 'Sounds a bit naff to me, it's from London. It had to be American for us. Malcolm McLaren walked into the pub – into the vault – and he had this leather suit on, big ginger hair, winkle pickers. Pretty unusual in those days. He came over to us and said, "Are you coming over to see the band?" It really impressed me – a good management style that. Impressive. So we decided to go. And it was good.'[38] Bramah's expectations were also low: 'We'd heard about them already through the music press, just as a group that did Stooges cover versions. There was a photo of a guy with short hair and I was wondering what these "skinheads" were doing covering Stooges' songs, I wasn't really into the idea. I went along thinking I could heckle or something but I was really bowled over. I got my hair cut soon after. I could see something was happening.'[39]

Just over a month later, on Tuesday 20 July, the Sex Pistols returned to the Lesser Free Trade Hall. This time they were supported by Slaughter and the Dogs, a local band with glam-rock roots, and Buzzcocks with Pete Shelley and Howard Devoto, the promoters of both shows, this time joining their heroes on stage. By this time tales of anarchy, chaos and the Sex Pistols filled the scandal-hungry music press. Not surprisingly the gig was a sell out with approximately four hundred people paying the one-pound entrance fee. It was this second gig, more than the first, which helped form a community of sorts in Manchester. The 'punks' were beginning to distinguish themselves from the rest of the audience. But it was not just the clothes that mattered, it was the commitment to making music and singing lyrics

38 David Nolan, *I Swear I Was There: Sex Pistols and the Shape of Rock*, Manchester: Milo Books, 2001
39 Martin Bramah, 'Simply Blue: Martin Bramah Interviewed', *The Hell With Poverty*, no. 4, Autumn 1985

that cut through pop's worthless platitudes. 'The Pistols put you in a context where it's possible to understand more,' said John Cooper Clarke. 'I mean, it's probably a cliché now, but words like fascist and fascism jumped out. Things like that just weren't in pop songs.' It was a movement that borrowed from a century of avant-garde shock-tactics, but this time it was working-class kids delivering the *épater les bourgeois*. Clarke went on to describe the New Wave as 'the nearest thing that there's ever been to the working classes going into areas like surrealism and Dada. Until now they've been the domain of the middle classes.'[40]

For many observers that night seeing the Sex Pistols and Buzzcocks was an empowering experience. 'If they could do it, so could I,' many thought, Smith included: 'I remember seeing the Buzzcocks and thinking, "Bloody hell! I could do better than that!" It's a cliché now, but that honestly was the attitude at the time, anyone can do it. Up until I saw the Pistols doing stuff like "Stepping Stone" and other garage songs, the idea of us playing in public was pure fantasy.'[41] At that time the music scene was very different. 'People didn't start bands in Manchester,' said Bramah. 'The gigs were all at big venues and bands came from out of town and half of them were American. You didn't think you could really do it, until the punk thing happened.' For Smith it had a practical effect: 'We had been messing around for about two months previous with songs, etc. But never thought we could do it in public, i.e. playing – the Pistols motivated us into thinking we could do it, that if you wanted to play you didn't have to hire the Opera House or the Rainbow.'[42]

Over the summer the punk movement continued to grow, fuelled by sensationalist reporting in the tabloids and enthusiastic feature articles in *NME, Melody Maker* and *Sounds*. September saw the 100 Club Punk Festival in London and in November the first Sex Pistols single, 'Anarchy in the UK', was released. Media interest turned into full-scale moral panic at the beginning of December when the Sex Pistols swore on live television. At the height of the frenzy, on 9 December, the Sex Pistols stormed through a set at Manchester's

---

40 Steve Clarke, 'Cooper Clarke's in the Kitchen Mixin' Up the Medicine', *NME*, 28 January 1978
41 Barry McIlheney, 'Entertaining Mr Smith', *Melody Maker*, 12 October 1985
42 Mark E. Smith, 'Interview', *There Go Those Martian Martians*, February 1979

Electric Circus as part of their disintegrating 'Anarchy Tour'. Again the Buzzcocks supported in what would be their last gig with Howard Devoto on vocals. Years later Smith joked: 'I would have a marvellous job in shipping if it weren't for the Sex Pistols. I'd probably have my own shipping company, worldwide! Many times I've cursed the Sex Pistols!'[43]

With the nucleus of the band already in place and a sense of urgency and direction provided by the nascent punk movement, one vital ingredient was still missing: a name for the band. According to Bramah, Smith's initial suggestions included Master Race and the Death's Heads and the less inflammatory, the Shades. For a while the band called itself The Outsiders, after a book (*L'Étranger*) by the French novelist and existentialist philosopher Albert Camus. When they discovered another group was already using that name, Friel suggested The Fall, the title of another book by Camus (*La Chute*). At a draft stage entitled 'A Puritan of Our Time', *La Chute* tells the story of Jean-Baptiste Clamence, a successful Parisian barrister who realizes his bourgeois existence is a sham and exiles himself to Amsterdam where he becomes a self-styled 'judge penitent', prosecutor of himself and all those he meets. The book is written in the form of a mono-logue that takes place in a bar in a seedy waterfront area of Amsterdam (analogous in many ways to Smith's countless bar-room interviews). It was a perfect name for the new group: simple, distinc-tive and evocative of the withering social and moral critiques that would come to define Smith's lyric writing. The name also placed the band in a different league from the countless bands forming on the cusp of punk's first wave. The high-brow literary connections in-stantly set the group apart from the many bands with joke and ephemeral 'punk' names such as the Vibrators and Manchester's Ed Banger and the Nosebleeds. Considering it just as important as being separate from the punk bands, The Fall was also at pains to escape classification as a self-consciously artistic and experimental band. As Smith declared: 'It was about time a fairly intelligent roots working-class band did something as opposed to art-school types.'[44] The Fall, according to Smith, identified a whole swathe of the population not

43 Nolan, op. cit., 2001
44 Mark E. Smith, 'Interview', *Vsign*, no. 2, 1979

being catered for, or addressed, by the music industry: 'There were no groups around that I thought represented people like me or my mates. No one was speaking to the clerks and the dockers. If I wanted to be anything, it was a voice for those people. I wanted The Fall to be the band for people who didn't have bands.'[45]

45 Verrico, op. cit., 1998

2

Stepping Out, 1977

There's not a band in the whole of London fit to lick the plectrums of the virtually unknown The Fall.[1]

At the beginning of 1977 there was little to suggest that Manchester might become a centre of innovation, a catalyst for a 'new wave' explosion in music. The consequences of the Sex Pistols' appearances in 1976 inevitably took some time to filter through to bands that were scarcely proficient enough to play live, let alone record. A harbinger of what was to come could be heard on 29 January when the Buzzcocks' *Spiral Scratch* EP was released on their own New Hormones label. Over the next six months it sold 16,000 copies, unprecedented for a do-it-yourself effort. Punk continued its progress from underground to overground and April saw the release of *The Clash* and the first Stranglers album, *Rattus Norvegicus*. Both groups were closely associated with the London music scene which remained the focus of media attention. The obsession with London enabled places like Manchester and Liverpool to develop out of the public eye. For Manchester this obscurity ended in May when *Melody Maker* ran a report: 'New Wave Devolution: Manchester Waits for the World to Listen'. In the article Tosh Ryan of Rabid Records provided a succinct description of Manchester's volatile combination of poverty and self-determination: 'The area is so neglected, so economically deprived and full of massive housing complexes, that the mood of the place was right and ready for a new movement in music with a markedly different criteria of success. What has developed is peculiar to Manchester and I can only hope that instead of going to London for future deals, the agents and record companies will come here.'[2]

According to the article, the three leading bands were the

---

1 Tony Parsons, 'Buzzcocks', *NME*, 3 December 1977
2 News Background, 'New Wave Devolution: Manchester Waits for the World to Listen', *Melody Maker*, 14 May 1977

Buzzcocks, the Drones and Slaughter and the Dogs. The Drones were managed by Paul Morley and signed to the Ohm label. Slaughter and the Dogs were on Rabid, a label started by Tosh Ryan, Lawrence Beedle and Martin Hannett. From the start The Fall particularly loathed Slaughter, chiefly because they appeared to be jumping on the new-wave bandwagon. 'They were all like fucking dicks who'd been playing "Smoke On The Water" for years,' Smith explained, 'and then they saw a bit of money there. It was good actually because it kicked me into starting thinking really y'know, that's horrible! We could do that, and we can't even play.'[3] The feeling of animosity between the two bands was mutual. Slaughter's vocalist Wayne Barrett once described The Fall to Gary Bushell as 'music to play to your fridge . . . The fucking Fall. They're about as much use as tits on a nun, balls on a bishop and Edward Heath's promises.'[4] Smith replied in kind, describing Slaughter as a 'spineless' band, purveyors of 'beergut and peroxide and "wock 'n' woll"' and coming on all mean, ha ha!' He felt sorry for Bushell who 'must have a really hard time interviewing all these bands who have nothing to say'.[5]

An important component of the 'new movement in music' not mentioned in the *Melody Maker* article was the Manchester Musicians' Collective, established at the beginning of the year by Dick Witts and Trevor Wishart. Witts promoted concerts of contemporary classical music using money earned as a percussionist for the Hallé Orchestra. Wishart was a composer-in-residence at North-West Arts. He had a long-standing interest in musicians organizing themselves into co-operatives and collectives and it was his idea to set up a collective in Manchester to share equipment and promote gigs. 'We wanted to know how these kids made music when they were musically illiterate,' Witts explained. 'This was fascinating because we were over-burdened with knowledge about music, we were just playing other people's stuff and here were these kids coming along playing something from nowhere.'

North-West Arts occupied an office, shop and a basement café on King Street, one of the most exclusive streets in Manchester city

---

3 Mark E. Smith, on Grant Showbiz's 'Falling through Time: Part 2', Resonance Radio, broadcast June 1998
4 Gary Bushell, 'The Boot Boys are Back in Town', *Sounds*, 22 September 1979
5 Ian Penman, 'All Fall Down', *NME*, 5 January 1980

centre. Witts persuaded the organization to let out the basement on Monday nights to the Collective. From The Fall it was Friel that first made contact with Witts and the Collective: 'It had quite an impact on me personally,' Friel said. 'I met lots of interesting people and it turned me on to "new music" which has been an interest ever since.' Friel convinced the other members of The Fall to come along to meetings, and eventually the group was offered the chance to play. There was one problem: The Fall didn't have a drummer. 'I was lucky I had a job,' Smith recalled, 'but anybody you'd meet was on the dole, so getting anybody with a drum-kit who would be all right was totally out of the question.'[6] Through an advertisement they found 'Dave', a bald, car-coat-wearing insurance salesman and rabid Tory whose one attempt at song-writing was entitled 'Landslide Victory'.[7] He wasn't perfect but for the moment he had to do. Another problem was Baines's keyboard. Her bank loan was still being processed so with no keyboard she had to watch the first gig from the audience. Unfortunately no one can recall the date of the gig other than that it was in May, but Witts remembered the venue as being 'like a fashionable restaurant in the late-seventies with everything white. It was done out like a small white cave. We just took the tables and chairs out. Mark and Martin, who were taller than the others, had to bend down because of the low ceiling. It wasn't really public, the audience was just a group of other musicians sitting around listening.'

This included local heroes, the Buzzcocks. 'The first gig was recorded so somebody might have a tape somewhere,' said Bramah. 'It was a small room and Mark just let fly with such venom from day one. I remember he just sort of reached into the audience and virtually poked his finger up Howard Devoto's nose.' For Friel the gig was the opportunity he'd been waiting for: 'As you'd expect it was a bit rough – just right! We were really pleased to have a chance to play outside the bedsit! People were kind and it was very encouraging.' What hit the small audience immediately was the intensity of the band, especially Smith who, according to Witts, 'howled the place down'. Later Baines told him: 'I don't know what the fuck he was

---

6 Mark E. Smith, 'Interview Transcript', *TBLY*, no. 6, July 1996 (from the Australian *Fast Forward* tapezine, August 1982)
7 Martin Bramah, 'Simply Blue: Martin Bramah Interviewed', *The Hell With Poverty*, no. 4, Autumn 1985

doing. I've never heard him do that before, it scared me!' Bramah was not so surprised: 'It was just welling up inside us all. That was the way we were living, that was the way we felt and that was the way Mark was. I mean if you went out to a club with Mark he'd pick a fight with someone. But that was just Mark: irrational and erratic. He didn't practise it, he didn't plan it, he was just like that.'

Belief in their own creativity dictated against The Fall playing any cover versions that night. Instead the set was all original and ranged from political rants like 'Hey! Fascist' and 'Race Hatred' (with its 'What yer gonna do about it?' chorus) through to the adrenalin rush of 'Psycho Mafia'. The set ended with an extended two-chord dirge entitled 'Repetition'. The song was almost a manifesto for the new group, albeit one laced with a heavy dose of sarcasm, with Smith prophetically announcing: 'Repetition in the music and we're never gonna lose it.' Years later Smith reminisced about the gig to Sylvia Patterson. 'It was in a basement with about twenty-odd peope there. We played with a socialist brass band and a guy who made symphonies out of bird noises.' The latter probably referred to a work by avant-garde composer Wishart, either *Red Bird* or *Menagerie*, the latter of which featured Tony Blackburn introducing recordings of disasters. Unfazed by the competition, Smith described the night as 'great, totally surreal. They thought we were great 'cos we were the first group who played continually in the chord of E. Wasn't exactly the Beatles heheh. Weren't even headlining, it was the bird noises, then us, then the brass band.'[8]

The sound was poor and the musicianship rudimentary but the commitment, ambition and charisma were there for all to see. It was a phenomenal début but before the group could move on it needed a drummer who shared at least some of the group's ethos. The answer was close to hand. Prior to The Fall, Bramah had been a member of a putative group called Nuclear Angel with someone he'd known since he was twelve years old: 'I first met Karl Burns on the street. He had this picture of Hitler and two of his henchmen and one had a ring round his head and Karl was insisting this was his father. That was my first meeting with Karl Burns, this mad kid claiming his dad was a Nazi.' Burns was a natural musician on guitar and drums.

8 Sylvia Patterson, 'Git Pop Now!', *NME*, 3 February 1996

Nuclear Angel never performed live but rehearsed in the cellar of a shoe shop off Deansgate (in Manchester city centre) owned by the bass player's dad. Here they would thrash out New York Dolls and Stooges covers – until one night they got carried away and trashed all their equipment. When Bramah invited him to join The Fall, Burns had long hair and was into heavy metal but Bramah was persuasive and convinced him to give the new group a chance. Dave the drummer shouldn't be forgotten though. He will always hold the dubious honour of being the first of many members to be sacked from The Fall.

Hey! Fascist

The Fall's second gig took place on 3 June 1977 at a 'Stuff the Jubilee' festival in a space known as The Squat on Devas Street in Manchester. Earlier the group had attended an anti-Jubilee demo. 'There was about twelve of us,' Baines recalled. 'Someone tried to unfurl this banner with "Stuff the Jubilee" on it and the police came along and said "Put that banner down." He refused saying it was his democratic right to protest and they just pulled him into the back of a police van and kicked his head in. So that was the end of the demo.'

The Squat was situated in a decrepit building that had, in better days, been the home of the Royal Manchester College of Music. When the college revealed plans to demolish the building to make way for a car park it was occupied by students who then successfully campaigned for it to be turned into a live music venue.[9] Mick Middles recalled it as an 'evocative box of floorboards and dust, complete with a precarious ramshackle stage, a bar that seemed to have been stolen, plank for plank, from a hostelry in Trenchtown, Jamaica, and a set of toilets into which only the brave, the stupid and the desperate – that's four pints of Newcy Brown desperate – would dare to enter.'[10] Deborah Curtis described The Squat as 'the worst venue – the surrounding landscape had already been flattened and The Squat stood lonely, waiting for its fate, yet bands flocked to play there. The first

9   Dave Haslam, *Manchester, England: The Story of the Pop Cult City*, London: Fourth Estate, 1999
10 Mick Middles, *Ian McCullough: King of Cool.* London: Independent Music Press, 1998

time I went there, I didn't believe anyone would be able to perform because I was convinced that the power wasn't even connected.'[11] Chris Brazier recalled its walls were covered with intellectual graffiti – 'Eschew Obfuscation' and 'Mass Communication is the first necessity of revolution' – that immediately linked it to the student politics of the time.[12]

Other local groups appearing at 'Stuff the Jubilee' were the Drones, Warsaw (who would soon rename themselves Joy Division), The Worst and the Negatives (which included writer Paul Morley on guitar and photographer Kevin Cummins on drums). Baines, who now had her own keyboard, remembers the night well: 'I played the national anthem with all these explosion sounds from my new keyboard. It was called a Snoopy and the week after I bought it, it got reviewed in *Sounds* or *Melody Maker* as the worst keyboard you could get – totally slated. It was just the cheapest, but even so I never did pay off the loan.' In the audience that night was Mick Middles, who described the moment The Fall took to the stage: 'Four males and one female lift themselves from the crowd and assembly on the stage. They look, with the exception of the female, like a Tarmac gang. Even in this slovenly environment, the band's dress sense seems stunningly drab. The music they begin to produce completes the scene. A clumsy rock base is topped by a tinkly and wildly out-of-tune keyboard. But there's something about that singer, something exquisitely menacing. "THE PSYCHIATRIST MUST BE KILLED," he spits, with charismatic menace. Instantly I forgive him for wearing the most horrendous pink silk shirt known to man.'[13]

Later the same month, The Fall played a Rock Against Racism benefit supporting the Buzzcocks and the Verbals at North-East London Polytechnic. The political context of the gig suited the band well. In these early days its set was dominated by songs like 'Race Hatred', 'Dresden Dolls' and 'Hey! Fascist'. But as Bramah explained, although there was a strong left-wing element in the group, they were wary of too close an association with organizations like the Socialist Workers' Party: 'The core of that left-wing attitude was

11 Deborah Curtis, *Touching from a Distance: Ian Curtis and Joy Division*. London: Faber & Faber, 1995

12 Chris Brazier, 'Out, Racists, Out!', *Melody Maker*, 5 November 1977

13 Mick Middles, 'The North Will Rise', *Underground*, no. 8, November 1987

working-class struggle and that's what we related to. Una was a very strong feminist and would be prepared to strike up an argument in a pub with any man who said anything remotely sexist. Tony Friel was a member of the local Communist Party.' These were politically polarized times. A month later, in August, there were violent clashes as demonstrators tried to halt a National Front march in Lewisham, South London. One early gig by the band at the Squat was shared with local reggae group Exodus, and took place just a day before a demonstration against the National Front in Manchester.[14] Chris Brazier wrote that the predominantly white audience revelled in both the reggae rhythm of Exodus and the 'new wave challenge' of The Fall. All in all 'perfect preparations for facing the National Front on the streets the following day'.[15]

Smith's political ideas were forged by his working-class upbringing and his experiences working on the docks. He was attracted to extremist ideologies, and although appreciating the exposure Rock Against Racism gigs gave the band, Smith found the populist and sloganeering attitude of the organizers ideologically limiting. 'I was disillusioned very quickly,' he said in 1978. 'I'd always equated left-wing politics with revolution . . . What happens is before you go on they say, "Will you hold this poster up?" – and it's a picture of Belsen, "DON'T LET IT HAPPEN AGAIN." And I would say – we're a political *band*, that's what we *sing* about. But they want you to make announcements between songs; they see you as an entertainment – you might as well be singing Country and Western.'[16] Smith later elaborated on his problems with these benefit gigs: 'I thought, rock against racism, I'm sort of for that, but it's a revolution, right, so if you're going to have a revolution against racism, you want a revolutionary music, which didn't HAPPEN. It didn't matter what the entertainment was, as long as the proletariat was there. Which is not what our fuckin' attitude is.'[17]

Between 1977 and 1978, The Fall's reputation as a political band continued to grow and attracted the attention of two young music

14 Brazier, op. cit., 5 November 1977
15 Chris Brazier, 'United We Stand . . . ', *Melody Maker*, 22 October 1977
16 Ian Penman, 'Between Innocence & Forbidden Knowledge . . . Comes The Fall', *NME*, 19 August 1978
17 Mark E. Smith, 'Interview', *Cool*, no. 2, February 1980

journalists, Tony Parsons and Julie Burchill, looking for a suitable figurehead to lead the *NME*'s battle against the National Front. The Fall seemed to fit the bill and Smith was invited down to the *NME* offices. Smith takes up the story: 'We went in and Tony and Julie were sniffing coke on the table and lying there necking y'know. We got talking and I could see very clearly that they were going to use this band, y'know, chew 'em up, spit 'em out. We were also turning down a lot of record companies at the time because of the way they wanted to push us. It was all about we had this song "Hey! Fascist", y'know. They were talking about bricking people over the head, things like that, so much garbage. I thought Parsons was all right, but Burchill was a hysterical woman. She was going on about the work-ing class, and I was trying to catch her out, saying what about these National Front skinheads that are working class. She's going . . . "You fucking liberal . . . you fucking liberal." It was crazy, we just got on the coach and went home.'[18] Most bands would have jumped at the chance to appear on the front cover of the *NME*, even if it was to be with the slogan, as reported, of 'The band that stands against the National Front'.

Before any of this happened Smith and Baines had contributed to a music and politics summit at the offices of *New Manchester Review*. The question put to the gathering was: 'What's wrong with music?' Was it capitalism, the star system, the class system, too much reliance on technology, not enough creativity or exploitative record companies? When the latter, in the form of CBS's Penn Roberts, suggested that any of the musicians present in the room would accept a £150,000 contract to produce three albums and six singles, Smith disagreed: 'No we wouldn't accept it. The worst bit is being told how much music to produce. If all you want is money then you might as well just go and get a job. Why should record companies always be dictating the terms?' Smith thought one of the major issues facing music was the dominance of 'sophisticated' musicians: 'People, especially working-class kids, are inhibited from trying to play because of the expertise of music-college groups like the Pink Floyd. But punk rock has shown that they can do it.' Baines added to Smith's comments saying: 'The potential is in everyone to have a go; not just to talk about music.

18   Simon Dudfield, 'The Man in the High Castle', *NME*, 17 October 1988

Whether it's good or bad music is not the point. But records don't encourage people to think they can have a go.'

The discussion then moved on to examine what was considered the proper subject matter of songs. Baines thought songs about love were 'all part of the way in which society sells sex'. The new wave was an opportunity to move away from this romantic escapism, although she recognized that no particular position on sexism had yet been taken: 'It's changed by absence,' she observed, 'they haven't said anything sexist or anti-sexist. It's just that they don't have a line on it yet.' Paul Morley wanted to know why Baines could not be more optimistic. She replied: 'But what about the Stranglers, they're supposed to be anti-establishment but by being sexist they're just perpetuating the same fucking myths that society stands on anyway.'

Harpoon's bass player, John Levinson, showed how much he was off the pace of the conversation when he butted in and said: 'There is nothing political expressed in music because there's nothing to say in music. There may have been with Bob Dylan ten years ago.' Baines was having none of that: 'Why isn't there? There's nothing that relates to the working class . . . lyrics are generally written by men and they are very sexist . . . In a socialist society music would be another way for people to express themselves, available to everyone.'[19] The summit was interesting on a number of levels: not only did it show that in Manchester, at least, music was seen as inextricably political, but it also revealed the strong voice that Baines had within the band and what a key role she played in its early political orientation.

Entertainment for radicals

In July, one of Smith's favourite bands came to play at the Electric Circus. All the way from Australia, the Saints were promoting their latest single 'This Perfect Day'. The tour included an appearance on *Top of the Pops*, where Smith and the band must have been impressed by the group's nonchalant performance. Decidedly not dressed for the occasion – with his open-neck shirt, jeans and long hair – lead singer Chris Bailey went through the pantomime of miming with little emotion. In an uncanny precognition of Smith's later performance,

19 Anon., 'A Look inside the Music Machine', *New Manchester Review*, no. 40, 26 August–22 September 1977

Bailey ended the song by struggling to get the microphone out of its stand and almost fumbled it to the ground.

The Fall's exploits in London included a support slot with the Buzzcocks at the opening of the Vortex in Wardour Street in Soho. Completing the bill was John Cooper Clarke and, although not advertised, Johnny Thunders and the Heartbreakers, who played a couple of numbers. Allan Jones described the interior decoration at the Vortex as 'a brewery executive's ideal of contemporary good taste: ubiquitous Formica and violently coloured plastic fittings. Unbelievably, the walls are decorated with Pirelli calendar pin-ups, Art Nouveau prints and Tudor wall hangings.' The audience looked like 'weekend punks, whose sense of style and dress has been informed by the wayward imaginations of picture editors on the *Sunday People* and the *Sun*. Affluence has stylized out of existence the bizarre individuality of that early punk army.'[20] Smith largely concurred: 'Fuckin' terrible. The audience totally ignored us, so fuckin' cool. No one reacted in any way. Everyone just stood there posin'. We were the scruffiest people in the place and we had no money for drinks or 'owt. An' there's all these street kids in bondage suits sippin' vodka and orange. It freaked us out.'[21] The Fall also suffered the fate of many support acts when *Sounds* reporter Angela Ripper turned up too late to see their act: 'The Fall came on earlier than expected and I only caught their last number.'[22] Still it was a start at least: the band's first mention in the national music press outside of the gig guides.

One fanzine editor had the audacity to criticize the band's set for being 'too slow and too long and a bit too deadly serious'. Smith wrote back in uncompromising terms: ' . . . your criticisms are very common, i.e. we've had them before. As to the speed question, the original concept of the group was a musical vehicle for the lyrics – maybe that has/will change. Anyway, we would not like to compromise on any terms, be they "old" or "new" wave, and surely the whole idea of what's going down now is to change things both musically and environment, "fashion" wise, etc., both within the

20 Allan Jones, 'Vortex: Hot Rail to Hell', *Melody Maker*, 6 August 1977

21 Malcolm Heyhoe, 'Why The Fall Must Rise', *NME*, 18 March 1978

22 Angela Ripper, 'Heartbreakers / Buzzcocks / John Cooper Clarke / The Fall : Vortex', *Sounds*, 16 July 1977

movement and out of it – the minute we have to speed up/slow down/cut out ANYTHING is the minute we pack it in.'[23]

Far from packing anything in, The Fall was about to get even stronger. During the summer a new figure appeared on the scene. Kay Carroll (born Kay Sullivan on 27 December 1948) spent her first fifteen years living in North Manchester, first in West Gorton then Ardwick. As a teenager, she was a regular visitor to the Apollo Theatre and saw some of the most important bands of the sixties, including the Beatles, Stones, Zombies and Them. Due to Manchester's slum-clearance programme, her family was eventually shifted out to Whitefield. By her early twenties, Carroll was married with two children. Her marriage, however, was not happy and she left her husband to begin a career in nursing, studying at Prestwich Hospital. 'Leaving my children was the biggest and one of the few regrets of my life,' Carroll said. 'It still haunts me, but I was such a selfish bastard when I think about it. If I could turn back the clock and change it, I don't think I would though, because then everything that has happened to me in the last twenty-six years would also have to change.'

Carroll hooked up with a staff nurse at the hospital called Jim, a 'spiritual guy' who enjoyed 'wandering the countryside, talking to trees, smoking grass and being at one with the universe'. In the spring of 1977 she was introduced to Una Baines, through a mutual friend called Dennis. Carroll had confided to Dennis that she would love to try some acid. 'I felt I'd missed out in the sixties due to domesticity. He said he knew where he could get some, that happened to be Ms Baines. I liked Una a lot, she was a militant feminist and fearless hell raiser.' So one evening Carroll and Dennis went round to Kingswood Road for an acid trip. Just as they were peaking Smith walked in the door. 'He'd just got home from work,' Carroll recalled. 'He dropped a tab and not long after that, Friel, Bramah and Burns showed up. I had no idea at this point how they were connected to Una. She introduced Mark as her boyfriend, the rest as friends. The trip was weird, but wasn't a bad one by any stretch of the imagination. However, Friel and I took an immediate dislike to one another.'

Carroll and Jim's relationship broke down and she spent most of

23   Mark E. Smith, 'Race Hatred', *Jolt*, 1977

her spare time hanging out with Baines and Smith at the flat: 'Una would go on for hours about the band they had formed,' Carroll recalled, 'and how they were going to be big one day. I didn't pay much attention. The punk and new-wave thing hadn't filtered down to me yet, I was still into Pink Floyd, Can and Hawkwind, but Una and Mark started turning me on to Lou Reed, The Doors and Iggy. I loved that stuff.' Carroll confessed to Baines that she wanted to leave Jim, and Baines suggested she move in with them, into their spare bedroom. Not soon afterwards Carroll experienced her first gig by The Fall: 'When I heard the band it blew me away. I wasn't expecting it at all, I wasn't expecting anything to tell you the truth but their sound was so hypnotic, they had a sound like Can, and Mark's poetry was – and still is – just pure genius. I was hooked!'

At the end of July, a feature article on the Manchester scene by Paul Morley appeared in the *NME* with a cover title that ran 'Manchester: The Truth Behind the Bizarre Cult Sweeping a City's Youth'. Its main focus was the Buzzcocks, Howard Devoto, Slaughter and the Dogs and the Drones, with The Fall situated – alongside Warsaw, Ed Banger and the Nosebleeds and The Worst – as interesting newcomers. Morley spoke about how The Fall often prompted comments such as, 'I thought the Clash were political until I saw you.' Overall he thought the band's approach was 'perhaps too serious' and described Smith as an 'angry concerned narrator'. The lyrics were 'clipped ideologies, entertainment for radicals maybe', which he likened to a Henry Cow approach.[24] The band was probably divided over the merit of being compared to seventies' art-rockers Henry Cow. Friel might have appreciated Morley spotting the avant-garde jazz-rock fusion influences, but Smith was probably aghast at comparisons with what the music press labelled 'Canterbury Rock'. Both, though, would have appreciated Henry Cow's intransigent anti-commercialism and Morley's recognition of the experimental edge to their music.

Short Circuit – Live at the Electric Circus

The Fall's prospects continued to be intertwined with those of the ever-popular Buzzcocks, who, in August, signed to United Artists for

24 Paul Morley, 'They Mean It, Ma–a–a–nchester: From the UK Roots', *NME*, 30 July 1977

what sounded like a fortune at the time, £75,000. The Fall celebrated with the group with more support slots, all useful preparation for The Fall's most important gig to date, a two-day festival marking the closure of the Electric Circus. The weekend of the 1-2 October was important for a number of reasons. It was the first opportunity for a collective show of strength for the nascent Manchester music scene. It was also an opportunity for the bands to assess each other's progress and at the same time attract the attention of the national music press. The immediate reason for the gig was to ensure the Electric Circus closed with a bang and not a whimper. Situated two miles to the north of the city centre, the ex-Bingo hall faced closure because of numerous breaches of fire regulations. Like many Manchester venues it had seen better days, but its youth club atmosphere was perfect for the enthusiastic bands and their young fans. In fact, it was the popularity of local groups that had led to the club's downfall. The Electric Circus had a legal capacity of 280, but the Buzzcocks and other bands were regularly attracting audiences of 500 or more. The manager, Alan Robinson, could not afford the improvements that would make the hall safe so the venue had to close. As a gesture to community spirit, it was decided that all profits from the gig would go to the cancer research department of Manchester Hospital. True to their word five months later the Buzzcocks presented a £75 cheque to the hospital.[25]

The line-up for the first night of the festival included Manicured Noise, the Swords, Big in Japan, Steel Pulse and the Drones. The second night opened with Warsaw, followed by The Prefects, The Worst, The Fall, the début of Howard Devoto's new group Magazine and finally the Buzzcocks. At the end of the night there was a stage invasion and, as was the case with many Manchester gigs, John the Postman came on to sing a version of 'Louie Louie'. Both nights were recorded by Virgin and selected tracks were released on a ten-inch album, *Short Circuit*, in June 1978. The two songs by The Fall – 'Stepping Out' and 'Last Orders' – represented the group's first appearance on vinyl.

Jon Savage was at the gig for *Sounds*, and was not impressed by The Fall, describing them as 'competent but uninspiring'.[26] The Fall

25 Anon., 'News', *Melody Maker*, 18 February 1978
26 Jon Savage, 'Power Cut at the Electric Circus', *Sounds*, 15 October 1977

probably forgave *Sounds* – just – because the article was accompanied by the first published photograph of the band. The next week brought more good news when Paul Morley's review in *NME* provided particularly fulsome praise for The Fall: 'A potentially great group . . . relay their messages amidst semi-complex, if surprisingly catchy, structures. They are angry, committed and genuine. They play long sets; they have so many strong songs they're almost too much to take in one sitting.'[27]

The Electric Circus weekend also provided a good excuse for another 'focus on Manchester' feature. Together with the Buzzcocks, Magazine and John Cooper Clarke, The Fall and The Worst were highlighted in Chris Brazier's 'United We Stand' article for *Melody Maker*. Brazier, a committed leftist writer, realized The Fall had more to offer than a sharp line in political slogans: 'They are fiercely committed to a Leftist opposition of injustice,' he wrote, 'but that neither blinkers them to other aspects of experience, nor does it reduce their musical power. Like Magazine, they make genuinely progressive music, and, despite their idiosyncrasies (like the ambitiously tuneless vocal), they have no real limits, having the right attitude as well as the requisite ability.'[28]

Despite his appreciation of The Fall, Brazier thought it was The Worst that exemplified the real strengths of the Manchester scene (although they actually came from just outside Preston). Accompanying Brazier's article was a photograph of the band – Allan Deaves on guitar and vocals, Ian Hodges on drums and Woody on bass (later replaced by 'Robin') – dressed in torn black leather biker jackets, a look that would later be taken up by hardcore punk acts like GBH and Discharge. Smith repeatedly sang their praises – literally in the line, 'The Worst died for you,' in 'It's The New Thing' – and Carroll described them as 'the craziest MFs you could ever meet, like the Three Stooges meet the Velvet Underground'. The Worst couldn't play and were proud of it. Each gig was a mad improvisation, so on-punk-message they were unsignable, totally incorruptible: 'A lot of people don't think we mean it,' said Deaves, 'but we've said between us that we'll never sign up. Never. We're not in it for the money – all we want is to get up there and enjoy

27 Paul Morley, 'The Last Days of the Electric Circus', *NME*, 22 October 1977
28 Brazier, op. cit., 22 October 1977

ourselves, help the kids enjoy themselves, and express ourselves.'[29] The Worst was nominally managed by barman and fanzine editor Steve Shy and although closely associated with New Hormones never quite made it on to vinyl (witness their tragic omission from Virgin's *Short Circuit*). Thus all that remains of songs such as 'Vim', 'LSD', 'Pass Me The Vaseline' and 'Gimme The Money', is just that, the titles.[30] They eventually disbanded in early 1978 with Deaves declaring they enjoyed playing in his garage more than playing gigs, because 'with a gig you have to please the audience'.[31]

A self-operative unit

The Fall continued to grow in confidence and productivity, but because it was still loosely organized as a collective, decision-making became increasingly complex. In an attempt to help out with these problems, Kay Carroll was invited to act as manager of the group. By this time the domestic arrangements at Kingswood Road had changed considerably. 'Una and Mark were having problems and I became mediator and would listen to both of them,' recalled Carroll. 'It would get quite freaky at times, with lots of amphetamine going around.' The result was that Baines and Smith split up and soon afterwards Smith and Carroll became lovers. As more of Smith's time was devoted to The Fall, his absences from work became increasingly difficult to excuse, and he left to sign on the dole. He was soon joined by Carroll, who used part of her last pay cheque from the hospital to pay for a phone to be installed at the flat. This meant she would no longer have to use the public phone box across the road to book gigs and haggle with record companies.

At the end of October, the Buzzcocks released 'Orgasm Addict', their first single on United Artists, and set off on a UK tour. Among the support acts were The Worst, The Flys and The Fall. It was during this tour that Steve Garvey, a close friend of Bramah, joined the Buzzcocks as bass guitarist. Garvey prepared for his audition by accompanying Bramah on a trawl for suitable clothes through the

29 ibid.
30 Morley, op. cit., 22 October 1977
31 A.M. Waring-Hushpuppies, 'If I had a Time Machine I'd go to a Worst Gig in it', *Zig-Zag*, no. 90, December 1978

second-hand shops of Prestwich, a favourite haunt also for Smith.[32] Richard Boon, the Buzzcocks' manager, remained supportive of The Fall and the following month put up the money for its first studio session. On Wednesday 9 November, the group piled into Manchester's Indigo Studios on Gartside Street and quickly recorded four songs, 'Bingo-Master', 'Psycho Mafia', 'Repetition' and a version of 'Frightened'. The plan was for all the tracks to be released by Boon on either New Hormones or United Artists as a seventeen-minute EP, but interest waned as Boon's time was increasingly taken up with managing the Buzzcocks' burgeoning career. The tapes were returned to the group and hawked around various labels, but no one in 1977 was able to deal with The Fall's uncompromising attitude and desire to control all aspects of its music, from recording to distribution. The group thought about releasing the EP themselves, but as they could barely afford their own phone this was never really feasible.

All they could do was carry on gigging and developing a solid fan base in places like Liverpool, where The Fall débuted at Eric's in November, playing between the Toilets and the Buzzcocks. There were many links between the Liverpool and Manchester scenes, not least a shared distrust of the London scene. The main force behind Eric's was Roger Eagle, supported by local *habitués* who went on to make names for themselves in the music industry, including Jayne Casey, Pete Burns, Pete Wylie, Holly Johnson and Bill Drummond. It may have been at this Liverpool gig that The Fall first made the acquaintance of other Eric's regulars, Ian McCulloch (later of Echo and the Bunnymen) and Julian Cope (of Teardrop Explodes). Carroll remembered them as loyal fans and close friends of The Fall: 'God they were a lot of fun to be with. If we were playing within forty miles of Liverpool those guys would turn up. It's hard to appreciate what a small, connected clique we belonged to back then. Ian and Julian were really good friends more than sycophants. Guys would just start helping us with the gear without me even asking sometimes, although I would always check them out. It was really powerful especially at gig time, when they would appear from everywhere. Mark always made out they were our roadies, adds to

32   Tony McGartland, *Buzzcocks: The Complete History*, London: Independent Music Press, 1995

the myth I suppose, but I think they just wanted to hang around and touch the magic. Thing was I always appreciated theirs too.'

McCulloch remembers vividly the first time he saw The Fall: 'I had never seen a band like The Fall, they changed everything for me. I mean, there was something incredibly poetic about them. There was such power in Mark's words, the way he would spit them across and totally disregard his audience. It was endlessly fascinating especially as these gigs were very small. You just knew it was a big talent in a small hall, which is a rare thing. I learnt so much . . . It was The Fall who really, truly opened my eyes to the possibilities. Sure, the Pistols and the Clash were great, and I was well into all that, but Mark and the band seemed to take things a step further. They were also the first band that I knew personally, so it was fascinating to see how it worked from the inside. And Mark was just so smart.'[33] As well as musical ideas, McCulloch also borrowed Smith's overcoat, and never gave it back. The coat was later the inspiration for the ubiquitous 'raincoat brigade', shoe-gazing followers of Echo and the Bunnymen and Joy Division. Before going their separate ways, McCulloch, Cope and Wylie formed the Crucial Three, and included in their repertoire was The Fall-inspired 'You Don't Notice Time On The Bury New Road'.

By the end of the year the Manchester Musicians' Collective moved to the Band on the Wall in Swan Street, in the Ancoats area of Manchester. Three bands would play each week, with the takings, after expenses, being distributed equally among the musicians. The Fall first played there on Sunday 13 November along with Trevor Wishart and Pride. Mick Middles reviewed the gig for the magazine *Trick* and described the venue as a 'Manchester jazz club, filled from wall to bar with the beard 'n' glasses/real ale/student/ Ivor Cutler intellectual sect'. The Fall's set at this time included 'Hey! Fascist', 'Psycho Mafia', 'Dresden Dolls', 'Bingo-Master' and 'Industrial Estate'. Middles appreciated the band's uncompromising attitude, describing them as 'your alternative to the Clash registers'. He described Smith's 'casual sneer', Baines' 'fresh suffragette looks' and Bramah's 'slash guitar' style. As was often the case with early gigs, the night climaxed with what Middles was already calling 'The

---

33   Middles, op. cit., 1998

Fall's classic', 'Repetition', which Smith prefaced on this occasion with the warning: 'This song's gonna last for three hours.'[34]

Also at the gig was *Sounds* journalist Ian Wood, another early convert: 'There's an indefinable buzz in Manchester about this band,' he wrote, 'yet little is known about them. All that can reliably be said is that The Fall avoid the current commercial clichés of the band-wagon, and disown the poseurs that inhabit Manchester's hipper gigs. They look totally nondescript, clean cut even. Probably why their impact surprises so much. You might not enjoy them, but you can't ignore The Fall.' He ended his report explaining that, 'Their sole aim is to be a self-operative unit.'[35]

The following Thursday, The Fall played Katie's in Beeston, just outside Nottingham. It was now the *NME*'s turn to check out this hot new band, with Malcolm Heyhoe reporting that The Fall 'delivered a curious set earmarked for mayhem and discord. Visually odd and angry, their songs are short sharp summaries.' Towards the end, just as Smith was about to launch into 'Bingo-Master', the power was cut and the club plunged into darkness. 'From the stage rose embittered voices,' wrote Heyhoe, ' "We'll get Robin Hood . . . " ' [36]

The press attention helped to secure more vitally needed gigs. Despite December being a busy period for the group, Burns, Friel and Bramah still found time to moonlight as musical advisors and stage extras in a 'punk musical' entitled *The Story of Frank Confessions*. The play toured various Manchester youth clubs and was directed by Warren Hooper of the Contact Theatre.[37] It presented a cautionary tale of a young punk rocker called Frank Confessions whose dubious talents makes him a target for manipulation by the music business. The Fall guys played his backing band, The Runs. 'We originally were a cabaret band in a strip club,' Bramah said, 'and this punk manageress comes in and says we're great and she has this protégé, Frank Confessions, who was like a Johnny Rotten character, and we're the backing band she needs for her star. We're then dressed like London punks, we rocket to fame and then he pisses on the

34 Mick Middles, 'No Hip–ocrisy, No Clash Registers: The Fall, Band on the Wall, Manchester', *Trick*, December 1977
35 Ian Wood, 'The Fall, Manchester', *Sounds*, 3 December 1977
36 Malcolm Heyhoe, 'The Fall: Katie's, Nottingham', *NME*, 10 December 1977
37 Anon., 'Frank Confession', *New Manchester Review*, no. 46, 2–15 December 1977

amps and electrocutes himself and dies. Then it switches to the future and we're in this job centre and he comes back from the dead in this hideous mask and there's another song and that's the end. So it was like Ziggy Stardust meets the Sex Pistols. The kids loved it. The music must have been very much like The Fall, basically because it was the same band, although I can't remember us reusing any of it. I remember Mark and Una came to see it and Mark was furious. It was the first sign we weren't all going to get on. Mark really thought it was treacherous to do this pastiche of punk rock.'

Friel leaves

The year ended for The Fall with a Rock Against Racism benefit on 23 December at Stretford Civic Centre. The Fall topped a bill that included John Cooper Clarke and The Worst, plus an unscheduled encore by John the Postman. An ultra lo-fi recording of The Fall's set was released in 2000 as *Live 1977* by Cog Sinister/Voiceprint. It was a significant gig for Friel, because, as Bramah announced to the audience, 'It's the bass player's last gig. It's like losing your left leg.' The main reason for Friel's departure was his disapproval of Carroll's growing managerial control. Carroll later suspected Smith of manipulating the situation to help remove Friel from the band: 'I knew, much later, that Mark knew Friel would leave if he brought me in. Mark is very astute, incredibly manipulative when he wants things to happen without confrontation for himself. I saw this behaviour over and over again and, don't get me wrong, it's not a complaint, it's one of Smith's more enigmatic qualities that intrigued me. Well, it did until it happened to me.' Bramah and Baines were also concerned about Carroll's growing influence and how it was changing the balance of the band. 'When Mark and Kay became a team,' Bramah said, 'it became a bit of a dictatorship and that changed the band because we'd started as all equal friends. Kay was his enforcer, his strength and his mouthpiece within the band. We all recognized his talent and just put up with things, but I think Kay made it harder to be in the band. Especially for Tony who thought The Fall was as much his vehicle as Mark's. He'd thought of the name and was the primary musician within the band.'

Almost immediately upon leaving The Fall, Friel formed a new band, The Passage, with Lorraine 'Lol' Hilton on keyboards and Dick

Witts on drums. Over the next couple of years the group played countless local gigs and signed to Steve Solamar's Object Music label, releasing just a couple of EPs, 'New Love Songs' and 'About Time' before Friel left in November 1979. His next band, Contact, formed with Duncan Prestbury, also signed to Object Music and released just one EP, 'Future/Past', in early 1980.

Despite the departure of Friel, the year ended on a high note for the group with a feature article by Chris Brazier in *Melody Maker*. Brazier emphasized the group's nondescript image – 'when's the last time you saw a new waver wearing a sweater' – and described Smith's singing as 'intensely cynical' and 'deliberately tuneless'. Brazier quizzed Bramah and Smith about their characterization as a political band, provoking Bramah to point out there was more to the band than its political opinions: 'People try to tie us down too much – we've got other things besides the political angle. We're not in this band to put over the beliefs of any political party, or even our own political ideas exclusively, though in our political songs we mean what we say – we didn't form as a political band.' To which Smith added: 'You're not a very good songwriter if you can only write about one dimension of life. You have to write what you feel. One day you might be particularly angry at fascism, have a real gut-reaction like you do when you go on pickets like we do. But there again, it's difficult to feel things when you're away from the original situation, it feels a little forced. Like "Race Hatred", another of our songs – this lot want to rehearse it but I can't sing about racial hatred again and again till I get it right because I'd lose all feeling for it. And as lyrics they don't stand up on their own: the song only works when it's full of live feeling.'[38]

Looking back in 1998, Smith recalled his ambitions in 1977 quite clearly. All he wanted to do was 'say what I wanted' the aim being 'to make the songs very fuckin' odd and particularly English. I wanted them to be a mish-mash of all sorts, particularly a lot of garage groups of the mid-sixties. I used to go to all sorts of different clubs in Manchester, which was why The Fall had to appeal to someone who was into cheap soul as much as someone who liked avant-garde groups like Stockhausen. I even wanted the Gary Glitter fans.'[39]

38 Chris Brazier, 'United They Fall', *Melody Maker*, 31 December 1977
39 Lisa Verrico, 'Are You Talking to Me?' *Dazed & Confused*, December 1998

3

Bingo-Master's Break-Out!, 1978

> I used to always be in the *NME* saying, 'Ah, The Fall! I discovered two groups, Shalamar and The Fall.' I still can't stop saying, 'I discovered them, gave them to the world.' And one day I received this letter and it was from Mark E. Smith himself. Inside there was a ten-pence piece sellotaped to a sheet of paper. It said, 'Dear Dan, here's ten pence, now we're even, shut up.'[1]

Danny Baker did not, of course, discover The Fall. The basis for his conceit was a gig in January 1978 at Huddersfield Polytechnic where he saw The Fall supporting Jimmy Pursey's Sham 69. Bowled over by what he saw, he persuaded the editor of *Zig-Zag* magazine to let him write a feature on the band. The article included the first testimony of 'Roman Totale', full name Roman Totale XVII: 'We are opposed to compromise, fascists, rich revolutionaries and cars. Our message is not contrived nor preached, it just comes out that way! We think ninety per cent of the New Wave is crap, though we don't like to adopt a superior attitude.'[2] The fictional Totale provided Smith with an *alter ego* that the band could communicate through. In 1980 he provided Totale with the following mythical biography: 'Roman Totale XVII was born in a coal shed under the buzz of a defective street lamp. From birth he roamed Britain as a self-proclaimed professor of speed speech. In the summer of 1979 he fled from Lancashire and settled in the Welsh mountains until an encounter with F. Jack forced him into withdrawal from the world. He is the mental manifestation of The Fall camp, and dwells underground while above him trends grind on slowly and sickly.'[3]

Another new recruit to the band was Jonnie Brown, Friel's replacement on bass guitar. Originally from Rotherham, Brown was then an

---

1 Danny Baker, speaking on BBC Greater London Radio, broadcast 10 November 1996
2 Danny Baker, 'The Fall', *Zig-Zag*, February/March 1978
3 *Totale's Turns* press release, 1980

in Manchester. In answer to an advertisement in
ttended an audition and was recruited. Brown
s before the Huddersfield gig but he was sacked
eks. At the audition he and Baines felt an instant
e embarrassing,' remembered Baines, 'because I
d I'd only known him for two days.' She soon
at Brown was a heroin addict. 'When I moved
taking it because I had this idea of people who
vn and out and living on the street, you don't
rently clean-living art student. After I'd been
a week or two, he told me that there was
lit us up if I didn't get involved in it. And I
Brown soon turned out to be unreliable and
d found out why they sacked him. Baines
le of months before she finally left him. In
massive nervous breakdown that took her
year to recover from. At first she tried to continue with the
band and moved back to Kingswood Road with Carroll and Smith,
but it was not a good time for her.

The band quickly replaced Brown with Eric McGann (real name
Anthony McGann, also known as Echo and Rick Goldstraw). McGann
had previously been in John Cooper Clarke's backing band, the Curious Yellows. 'He lived just down the road in Prestwich,' Bramah
recalled, 'we didn't know him at all, but he became a big influence on
us. He was from a different generation and as far as Prestwich was
concerned he was the musical intelligentsia.' McGann's first gig with
The Fall took place in March at Rafters in Manchester. It was The
Fall's first hometown gig for three months. Reviewer Ian Wood described Smith dedicating songs to the promoters and turning a strobe
light on the audience. New numbers included 'Futures and Pasts',
'Rebellious Jukebox' and 'Mother Sister'. Wood was also intrigued by
the 'ridiculous rumours' surrounding the band, including: 'they hate
each other, they're in a mental hospital, they're splitting up'.[4]

The amount of press attention on The Fall was astonishing considering the group had still to release a single or even record a John Peel
session. A distinguishing characteristic of these early articles was the
emphasis journalists put on Prestwich as a context for understanding

4 Ian Wood, 'The Fall Stumble into the Void', *Sounds*, 8 April 1978

The Fall. Smith, it seemed, refused to leave the area for interviews, and journalists were required to trek up the Bury New Road to meet him. From the start, though, Smith proved to be an intelligent and highly quotable interviewee. In March, Malcolm Heyhoe asked him about The Fall's reputation for being too serious and always arguing. 'There's never a common agreement within the band,' Smith replied. 'Instead there's a tension that makes us stronger.' What kept The Fall together? 'We've never been signed up. It's a big help – we're independent and that's how we want it. We're not continually repayin' agents and promoters for PA. The songs we sing are just personal experiences. If you identify with them, that's fine.'[5]

One person finding it difficult to identify with anything at this time was Una Baines. 'I left the band to recover,' she said. 'I just couldn't do it. The worst of it was I absolutely loved the new songs Martin was writing and really wanted to play them but I literally couldn't. I just couldn't do it, my head was in bits. Eric would just keep ringing up and say, "Go on, just one more gig." And I'd go, "Oh all right then." I remember the last one I did which was particularly horrendous, although it got a brilliant write up, and I just stood there looking at my keyboards. I think people thought it was just part of The Fall.' Baines's departure marked a significant moment for the band. She had stood beside Smith when he first picked up a microphone and sang into a tape recorder and was instrumental in shaping the band's political stance. 'She was relentless and fearless when it came to her feminist views,' recalled Carroll. 'The guys, with the exception of Burns, on the surface, were very supportive and outspoken about women's issues. She may have felt some of the material and the process of choosing each song leaned towards the more patriarchal side of the band. Una appeared to get really paranoid at times, and that definitely gave way also to the feelings of darkness in her keyboard music. Things could get really black for her.'

In order to make a clean break from The Fall, Baines left Kingswood Road and moved in with old friend and nurse at Prestwich, Steve Toyne, then living in a shared house in Whitefield. 'I was literally the mad woman in the attic,' Baines said. 'I used to do things like get up a three o' clock in the morning and bake bread for everybody and make cups of tea. I was just on another planet. I used

5 Malcolm Heyhoe, 'Why The Fall Must Rise', *NME*, 18 March 1978

to get up and listen to "Kill City". Iggy Pop's lyrics were one of the few things that really made sense at that time.'

Just before she left, Baines and The Fall were filmed by Granada Television performing 'Industrial Estate' and 'Psycho Mafia'. The recording captures Smith's singing style at this time – very animated, with his head nodding energetically to the beat as he restlessly paced the small studio. At the end there was a brief interview with Smith acting as the spokesman: 'We're not offensive, we're not offensive people, but the music is offensive to a lot of people. Coming from the North you've got this inoffensive cap-touching attitude which we're trying to break out of. A lot of people appreciate the stance, appreciate the communication.'

Musical chairs

To help find a replacement for Baines, The Fall placed an advertisement in the *NME*. Yvonne Pawlett – a young fan particularly smitten with Karl Burns – answered and was invited along for an audition. Pawlett was born on 23 May 1959 in Rotherham, although most of her childhood and school years were spent in Doncaster. Her interest in music began when she was given her grandmother's old piano. Although she was encouraged to take formal music lessons, other interests soon took over. 'I'd been given a beautiful German shepherd puppy when I was five,' Pawlett said, 'and she was all I was interested in. My main recollection from my childhood is being out playing with my dog Sindy and my friends and their dogs. We lived on a housing estate which backed on to an area of woodland, fields and old stone quarries and I was always out with my dog. I can hardly remember being in the house at all. My main interests were dogs and horses and anything to do with nature, trees, flowers, birds, fish and clouds.'

At school Pawlett demonstrated a talent for art and successfully applied for a place on a foundation course at Doncaster Art College. The creative environment reignited her interest in music, and she became obsessed with Nico, the Velvet Underground, and The Doors. She had just finished the course when she applied for the keyboards job in The Fall. 'Her dad drove her to the audition,' Bramah recalled. 'She immediately got the job because she had that look. Anyway she couldn't play any better than Una. I couldn't play the keyboards either, but I wrote the keyboard lines after working them out on the guitar. She used to improvise as well, but at that time I was the main musical arranger. Yvonne was great, she was a lovely girl. She was very stressed out by the dynamic of The Fall. We were already a known band and she still used to live with her parents and then she suddenly was right in the middle of this mad scene.'

For some of her time in the group, Pawlett stayed with Smith and Carroll at Kingswood Road. 'It was OK really,' she said, 'I thought we got along pretty well really, considering at first we were complete strangers and not friends.' Her first gig came in early May and couldn't have been more daunting – supporting Siouxsie and the Banshees at the Greyhound in Croydon. The Fall and the Banshees were worlds apart in both music and style. 'We were always like the drips and the pullovers,' Smith recalled, 'and they were walking around with this regalia. We'd be tripping them up and going, "art students!", pushing them and shit. It's a British tradition, they basically are art students. They're all art students. They come from nice families, and they put on this fucking rebellious, fucking socialist, fucking, you know, con, and they all pretend they are working class and it's all real funny.'[6]

The Fall returned to London a week later to play a gig with The Passage, John Cooper Clarke and Patrick Fitzgerald at Goldsmiths' College. Geoff Hill almost missed the show: 'I was in the bar downstairs when they came on and I thought a Boeing had crash-landed upstairs, shiver me timbers. I shoved my earplugs in and struggled up the stairs against the hurricane-like wall of sound to get my weekly quid's worth of Saturday-night Armageddon.' What Hill saw stretched his powers of description: 'vocals that make Arthur Mullard sound like Julie Andrews', was the best he could muster.[7]

At the time The Fall was preparing for its first appearance on John Peel's BBC Radio One show. The show's producer, John Walters, had seen The Fall at Croydon. Liking what he heard, he wrote to the band and the first of what would become twenty-odd John Peel sessions was arranged for the end of May and broadcast on 15 June. The four tracks recorded – 'Futures and Pasts', 'Mother Sister',

6 Michael Lang, 'The Fall – Mark E. Smith Interview', *BravEar*, vol. 3, no. 5, Fall/Winter 1986

7 Geoff Hill, 'John Cooper Clarke / The Fall / The Passage: Goldsmiths' College', *NME*, 27 May 1978

'Rebellious Jukebox' and 'Industrial Estate' – featured Smith, Bramah, Pawlett and Burns, with congas supplied by van driver, Led Zeppelin fan and insurance salesman, Steve Davies. The bass player, McGann, resigned just before the band set out for London. 'Eric hated Steve Davies because he thought his style was wrong for the band,' explained Bramah. 'Steve was going to drive us, but he also brought his congas to play on the session. Eric saw these congas in the back of the van and took one look at Steve's Hawaiian shirt and said, "I'm not getting in the van." So we said, "Right, see you." He thought he understood what The Fall was all about and because he was older than us, he had to steer us in the right direction. He was quite right that Steve Davies was wrong, but he didn't get the point that doing what was wrong was also part of Mark's vision. So we now had to find a bass guitar. Tony Friel was still friendly with me so we drove round to Tony's and asked him if we could borrow his bass. Luckily he said OK and I played the bass on the session.'

On their return, the band offered the vacant post of bass player to their sixteen-year-old roadie, Marc Riley. Unfortunately Riley had no bass so he borrowed one from his best friend and fellow roadie, Steve Hanley. Both, along with Craig Scanlon, had been pupils at St Gregory's, a Catholic grammar school. The three of them, plus Steve Murray on vocals and a long-forgotten drummer, formed the Sirens: 'We did one gig,' Hanley recalled. 'It was mostly our own stuff plus we did "I'm Waiting For My Man" and "I'm Down" by the Beatles. We got together, rehearsed, did one gig and then the singer left.'

The Sirens rehearsed at T. J. Davidson's, the same studio and rehearsal complex used by Joy Division and many other Manchester bands. They were briefly joined by The Fall who up to 1978 had been rehearsing at St Margaret's youth centre near Heaton Park. Carroll remembers the Sirens as keen fans of The Fall: 'Steve, Craig and Marc would stand at the back of our rehearsal room in Davidson's when The Fall was doing their "shit" and one day I invited them to come and help us load and unload the equipment (big of me eh!). After that they just ended up coming to lots of gigs at my invitation and they would roadie. We couldn't pay them much, other than a few beers and, of course, free gigs, but God did they work hard for us.'

Riley joined The Fall at a good time. In addition to the Peel-session broadcast, the band was also celebrating its first documentation on vinyl: the release of *Short Circuit – Live at the Electric Circus*, a ten-inch limited edition EP on Virgin Records. Accompanying The Fall's 'Stepping Out' and 'Last Orders', were tracks from the Drones, Warsaw, John Cooper Clarke, Steel Pulse and the Buzzcocks. Virgin delayed production and distribution of the record because it was reluctant to take attention away from the imminent release of Magazine's first album *Real Life*. Smith also delayed the release when he demanded revisions to The Fall's contract because it was different from the one sent to the Buzzcocks and Magazine.[8]

'Stepping Out' was an appropriately jaunty track to launch a career and 'Last Orders' followed with an equally defiant cry against anybody trying to restrain the group, with Smith declaring he'd been given his 'last orders'. The reviews for the record as a whole were mixed but The Fall escaped any criticism. Jon Savage thought the record a 'disgustingly shoddy testament', but picked out 'Stepping Out' as the best track with its 'muscular modern dance' and 'hypnotic time, electric piano fills and growled lyrics'. Meanwhile, 'Last Orders' showed 'the signs of greatness to come, in its formative stages'.[9] Adrian Thrills agreed: 'The two most interesting tracks here have to be those that mark the vinyl début of The Fall – intense, promising and defiant.'[10] And Chris Brazier praised Smith's 'compelling vocal delivery, a strange suggestion of cynicism and effervescence'.[11]

Politics remained high on the group's agenda, and when a by-election was held in July in Manchester and a National Front candidate stood, The Fall volunteered to take part in a three-day Manchester Carnival in Moss Side's Alexandra Park organized by the Anti-Nazi League and Rock Against Racism. The organizers invited The Fall to play on the first night but they forgot to tell the council and the gig was at first cancelled then allowed to go on as a 'rehearsal', with just Graham Parker and the Smirks as the only performers.[12]

To compensate its fans, The Fall played a hastily arranged gig at UMIST the next day as support to the Rich Kids. Proceedings were

8 Heyhoe, op. cit., 18 March 1978
9 Jon Savage, 'Conurbation Rock', *Sounds*, 24 June 1978
10 Adrian Thrills, 'Various: Short Circuit', *NME*, 22 July 1978
11 Chris Brazier, 'Circus Clowns', *Melody Maker*, 1 July 1978
12 Anon., 'Fall Out', *Sounds*, 22 July 1978

delayed as The Fall refused to go on before their biggest fan, John the Postman, arrived (which he did at just after nine). John had started out as a Buzzcocks fan, infamous for his impromptu a cappella 'Louie Louie' encores. But he soon grew tired of them and became a fan of The Fall: 'The Buzzcocks didn't seem to be progressing at all,' he said, 'and I'd seen it all, unlike The Fall who were always different. I've seen The Fall about a hundred and twenty-five times, about ninety of those between about 1977 and 1981. Most of them were an occasion; they were always special, I thought.'[13] Also in the audience was Paul Morley, who described The Fall as 'hard and primitive' and 'innovators, performing a kind of bleached disco music, relentlessly repetitive, a metallic dub music'.[14] It's debatable what impact the gigs had on the by-election, but the National Front candidate, a business-studies teacher at Bramhill High School, Mr H. Andrew, received just over 600 votes, coming in fourth behind the Liberals, Conservatives, and the Labour Party, which held the seat.

Just over a week later, on 22 July, The Fall took part in its first outdoor festival, the Deeply Vale People's Free Festival. Hanging out with the other bands, Smith formed a friendship with Here & Now and their sound man Grant Showbiz. Showbiz was born Grant Cunliffe in 1956 in Hemel Hempstead. He had recently dropped out of university to work as Steve Hillage's guitar roadie and had quickly picked up the basics of sound engineering. Now he was part of the Here & Now travelling circus: 'I was their general manager and dogsbody as well as sound man. For our national tour I turned up with a briefcase which was promptly thrown from the tour bus on to the motorway. They called me Showbiz after that. It's a great name for me; it stops me being too serious and sums me up.'[15]

Step Forward

Miles Copeland III was the son of Miles Copeland Jr (at one time a key CIA agent) and brother of Stewart Copeland (drummer for the Police). He started the Step Forward label with *Sniffin' Glue* fanzine

13 Dave Haslam, *Manchester, England: The Story of the Pop Cult City*, London: Fourth Estate, 1999
14 Paul Morley, 'Chaos & Concern', *NME*, 22 July 1978
15 Graham Coleman, 'Grant Showbiz', *TBLY*, no. 9, August 1997

stalwarts Mark Perry and Harry Murlowski. Copeland had been involved in the music industry for many years before punk arrived. He already owned the BTM label and was renowned for producing albums by bands such as Wishbone Ash and Renaissance. Step Forward was his entrée into what he hoped would be the profitable world of new wave. The label's first single appeared in June 1977 with 'Fascist Dictator' by the Cortinas, this was closely followed by 'Right To Work' by Chelsea. The Fall finally signed to Step Forward in the middle of 1978, after Carroll negotiated clauses that meant full artistic control stayed with the group: 'I refused large amounts of money up front from any record contracts,' she recalled. 'I didn't want to be beholden to anyone. The trade-off for me was total creative control for The Fall, which included the music, producers, studios, even who cut the vinyl. It also included the artwork, posters and newspaper advertisements.' Their main point of contact at Step Forward was Nick Jones, whom Carroll remembered fondly: 'He was so supportive and incredibly protective, regardless of what Miles Copeland did or thought, and was invaluable in my naïve early days. He was a wealth of information and pro-artist too.'

The money received through signing the contract was just enough to enable the group to come off the dole in time for Christmas 1978, paying them around ten pounds per week. With the band's growing workload, Carroll's behind-the-scenes managerial influence also grew. Along with the record company, there were also meetings with lawyers, publicists, accountants and publishers to organize. Although in many ways naïve, Carroll quickly grasped the importance of publishing agreements and made certain that the record companies they signed with never owned any of the songs, instead they were leased for a fixed number of years, before reverting back to the group. Like the rest of the band, however, she had no personal contract: 'I worked for them because I believed in them and not for the money; we were all paid the same. I just wanted the band to stay in control and for us to stay out of the red. I never wanted us to be put in a position of desperation, that's when sell-outs can occur and that was never an option for me. I'm very proud of that.'

When Carroll caught the coach down to London to speak to Virgin and Step Forward it was her first ever visit to the capital. The band had initially offered the 'Bingo-Master' session tapes to Martin Hannett at Rabid Records but he wanted to re-record it and add more guitars.

'Fuckin' . . . up yer arse,' was Smith's response.[16] The more they delayed, the more dated and unrepresentative of The Fall the recording became. After rejection from Virgin, next stop was Step Forward where Copeland thought it sounded 'a bit 1977', 'That's because it bleedin' is!' Smith exclaimed.[17] Smith was determined to release the EP, even though they had plenty of offers to record new material. It was important, he felt, to have this early document of The Fall on general release. Eventually Step Forward relented and on Friday 11 August, The Fall released the first piece of vinyl it could call its own.

The EP *Bingo-Master's Break-Out!* included the tracks 'Psycho Mafia', 'Bingo-Master' and 'Repetition'. It was very much a document of its time, with both Baines and Friel having long departed. Ex-bass player Jonnie Brown supplied the cover drawing of a crazed bingo-master restrained under lock and key. The title and 'The Fall' with its crooked second 'l' were written in schoolroom felt-tip pen in Smith's soon-to-be-familiar spidery scrawl. With its slow thumping bass-drum intro, 'Bingo-Master' tells the tale of a man who realizes the meaninglessness of his life and ends it 'with wine and pills'. It was written after a visit to a bingo hall with Smith's parents. 'It was incredible,' he said. 'There was this guy there with these balls going. It wasn't like a place you'd go for your leisure, it was a glorified works canteen. And the people were going there straight from work.'[18] Journalists were sent a press release which 'explained' each of the songs. 'Bingo-Master' was apparently written 'out of actual stoned experience, composed about a month before recording. The only number which is a 2nd take – the mis/tuned guitar being a deliberate rejection of the 1st take which was much more melodic. Martin's guitar did not sound the same before or after. The tension in the band was at an all time peak and this shows through.'

'Psycho Mafia', the punkiest track on the EP, was distinguished by its quirky electric piano and Smith's vocalization, which lay somewhere between singing and ordinary speech. The sound he produced would never be musical in the conventional sense, but could be described as an instrument in its own right, especially during moments of abstracted outburst and rhythmic stress. The track

16 Mark E. Smith, 'Radio Interview Transcripts', *TBLY*, no. 6, July 1996
17 ibid.
18 Wood, op. cit., 8 April 1978

established at the outset a classic Smith-ism with the rhyming of 'mafia' and 'love-ah'. Smith's trademark 'ah' at the end of some words, as well as its use as an occasional rhyming and rhythmic device, gave added emphasis to the lyrics. It also coincided with those places where he needed to draw breath, a trait that can be disguised by trained singers. For Smith this extra syllable came naturally and was not an artificial embellishment. 'I can't grasp that "Ah" thing,' he later complained. 'It's just having a go at me for my accent. That's easy, that's lazy.'[19] According to the press release, 'Psycho Mafia' began 'as a tribute to a local street-gang, but on completion of the lyrics it took on a sinister aura – an aura of oppression, a sort of subconscious manifestation of events which were happening around the writer at the time. The music, strangely enough, is a sort of tribute to the new R'n'B bands which were the only thing happening at the time of writing, i.e. early '76.'

On 'Repetition', Bramah's guitar is well to the fore and Smith's lyrics range widely across international politics, simultaneous suicides and mental hospitals where 'they put electrodes in your brain and you're never the same'. The press release reported that the 'Repetition' recorded was 'an early version and one of the shortest. This is how "Repetition" was on the day – now it is much more different and we're on about the twentieth version. The possibilities are endless. Played live, it is an instant converter – there is a point in the song where everybody gets into it, a turning point from non-interest to mass hypnosis. Has been criticized for its non-humour, which couldn't be further from the truth.'

The press release as much as the record – in its off-beat tone and truncated language – signalled that The Fall had no desire to follow the industry standard. Colin Irwin in *Melody Maker* described the EP as 'amazing' and The Fall as a band 'with the musical intensity of Suicide coupled with a truly inspired feel for the quirky'.[20] Paul Rambali made 'Hong Kong Garden' by Siouxsie and the Banshees his Single of the Week in the *NME*, but The Fall was commended for its 'rampant symbolism' and its 'off-beat' music played by 'eager, inspired amateurs'.[21] Vivien Goldman in *Sounds* saw in 'Repetition' a

19 Mark Sutherland, 'We Have Ways of Making You Talk', *NME*, 25 March 1995
20 Colin Irwin, 'Rise of The Fall', *Melody Maker*, 12 August 1978
21 Paul Rambali, '*Bingo-Master's Break-Out!*', *NME*, 19 August 1978

convenient opportunity effortlessly to fulfil his word quota for the review: 'They did repetition, they did repetition, they did repetition, they did repetition, they did repetition, they did repetition, they did repetition (that's the B-side that I like, the A-side's a stone killer if you like hideous sounds, which I don't).'[22]

Imagine if Johnny Rotten met Eddie Waring and lived

With the release of the EP came more offers of gigs and yet more music press attention. Ian Penman, in a *NME* feature article, observed that the band wore the same clothes off stage as on: 'They are shabby, ordinary, have no "image" but unlike certain other image-less people do not osmose any kind of urban-commando tout-suite street chic. In other words they do not exploit their background.'[23] The band's 'Northern' roots were often an issue, especially – surprise, surprise – when they played in London. Reporting on a gig supporting Penetration at the Lyceum in August, Adrian Thrills described The Fall as a northern version of Subway Sect. 'Imagine if Johnny Rotten met Eddie Waring and lived,' he wrote, 'that'll give you some idea of Mark Smith's vocals. Every song title is finished with a drawled 'aaa' (as in 'ups and under-aaa').'[24] Waring was then every southerner's idea of a northern character, made famous first though his rugby league commentary and later as a compère on the popular television show *It's a Knockout*. Allan Jones was also at the Lyceum and described a set that included the lyrically ambitious new song 'Various Times', with Smith's lyrics 'fragmented word patterns, acerbic but fully evocative of a threatening future and a present that is no less turbulent'. Bramah's guitar sounded like 'broken glass being ground on to concrete or sheet metal beneath heavy boot heels'. The music was 'sparse' and 'almost psychotically lean on melody'. Jones summed up his report by saying that although they were still 'technically inadequate', he graciously admitted The Fall could eventually 'mature into an authentically inter-esting group'.[25] It was left to Gary Bushell in *Sounds* to put the verbal

---

22 Vivien Goldman, '*Bingo-Master's Break-Out!*', *Sounds*, 12 August 1978
23 Ian Penman, 'Between Innocence & Forbidden Knowledge . . . Comes The Fall', *NME*, 19 August 1978
24 Adrian Thrills, 'Penetration Envy', *NME*, 26 August 1978
25 Allan Jones, 'Fall-out Menace', *Melody Maker*, 26 August 1978

boot in by describing The Fall as 'bleak, monotonous and pretentious' and 'characterized by the worst vocalist I've ever heard, Mark Smith, who insisted on ending everyah wordah with "ah" '.[26]

On the two days following the heady glamour of the 'Harvey Gold-smith presents' Lyceum show, The Fall played support slots for Here & Now at the Tower Club in Oldham and Mr Pickwick's in Liverpool.[27] The headliners were a straggling bunch of musicians-cum-proto-travellers, currently in the middle of what they billed a 'free tour', where the takings each night consisted only of donations. All they required was enough money to cover the running-costs of a red single-decker bus and the living expenses of fifteen adults, two babies and a dog. For the rest of the tour they were supported by Mark Perry and his band Alternative TV. Smith thought the real reason why Here & Now played free gigs was because 'nobody'd pay to see them'.[28]

Another milestone was reached on 8 September when The Fall played their first London gig as headliners, at the Marquee in Wardour Street with Bristol group Gardez Darkx as support. Paul Morley, reporting for the *NME*, highlighted Smith's already established anti-stage act: 'The singer covers his hesitancy and unsureness with cynical superiority. He performs reluctantly. This doesn't necessarily mean he has no commitment, it just means he doesn't like to show off.'[29] The gig was combined with a visit the following day to Surrey Sound studios to record the band's next single. In this great period of firsts, The Fall also played its first gigs in Belfast in September, with two nights at the Harp Lounge, supported by local band Protex. The band was there at the invitation of Good Vibes and the fanzine *Alternative Ulster*, to which Smith was a regular contributor. The zine reported that Smith opened the set with, 'We're The Fall . . . As in eternally untogether . . . As in national murder . . . As in from heaven.' Later Smith wrote that the trip was 'the best holiday I've had for years', but advised his Irish readers, 'Don't go to England. It's blown.'[30]

---

26 Gary Bushell, 'Penetration', *Sounds*, 26 August 1978
27 The latter set was released in 2001 as *Live in Liverpool '78* on Cog Sinister/ Voiceprint.
28 Mark E. Smith, 'Interview', *Vsign*, no. 2, 1979
29 Paul Morley, 'The Fall, Marquee, London', *NME*, 16 September 1978
30 Mark E. Smith, 'The Mark Smith Page', *Alternative Ulster*, *c.* 1978, undated cutting in Yvonne Pawlett's scrapbook

Smith's pessimistic view of England was partly based on his Manchester experiences. Riding high in the national charts was local anti-hero Jilted John (real name, Graham Fellows) with his eponymously titled 'Jilted John' single, popularly remembered for its 'Gordon is a moron' chorus. As for live music venues, although Rafters had recently closed down it had been replaced by Travolta's and an exciting new venue had opened in May at the Russell Club. The Factory, hosted by local television presenter Tony Wilson and his friend Alan Erasmus, soon became the vital link between the punk and the new-wave scene in Manchester. At the end of the year they released the *Factory Sampler*, two seven-inch singles made up of tracks by Joy Division, John Dowie, Cabaret Voltaire and Durutti Column. The Fall's first appearance there was as support to Chelsea on 28 September. Over the next couple of months, The Fall exhausted nearly all the local venues, playing at Kelly's, Manchester Polytechnic, Band on the Wall and, most bizarrely of all, Prestwich Hospital. The latter gig was attended by a recuperating Baines, but she was left disappointed, thinking they should have played for the patients rather than the staff.

The latest journalist to trek out to Prestwich was Dave McCullough of *Sounds*. The main topic of conversation was the band's relationship with the music industry: 'We're not into being uncommercial,' Smith explained. 'That's silly. That's middle-class. But we saw what a load of crap the new wave was. I mean, we used to be really into it, y'know, hey! The Revolution! ... When you leave work to concentrate on rock and roll you're really swapping one trap for another, only at least at work you get a wage. You have unions and that. When you sell your soul to a factory you at least get bread for it. The music industry is the most medieval system there is.' The last word was left to Carroll: 'The time clock of The Fall is very slow,' Kay reflected. 'If we'd been signed up last year we wouldn't be together now. I mean, when two members leave a band in a short space of time the record company rushes you into getting quick replacements who probably aren't into the band at all. Anyway, you don't sign to a record company, you sign to the whole bureaucracy, to the clerks and PR men who need you to survive. The only thing that matters is the music and these days that's the very thing that's thought of last, even after the fucking sleeves and

31 Dave McCullough, 'The Last Great Band Not in Captivity', *Sounds*, 4 November 1978

the colour of the fucking vinyl.'[31] As this quote makes apparent, Carroll soon developed a fearsome reputation within the Manchester music scene for her outspoken views on musical integrity. One of her targets for criticism, John Cooper Clarke, described her as a 'teenage Hilda Ogden', with 'sell out' her favourite phrase. 'She says it in her sleep, y'know – "sell out, sell out". Like she saw me a week ago walking down Salford High Street wearing me red Annello & Davide boots, and the first thing she said was, "Ah, he's sold out! Not the John Cooper Clarke I used to know!" '[32]

It's The New Thing

Carroll's relentless assault on a complacent and self-indulgent music industry carried over into The Fall's music and featured strongly in the band's second single 'It's The New Thing' with the B-side 'Various Times'. The front-cover photograph by Steve Lyons showed the band lined up against a whitewashed brick wall, striking a self-consciously cheesy pose with a raised fist salute. The clothes were a discordant miscellany of T-shirts, tatty jeans, black leather jackets and Riley's 'Booze is the only answer' sweatshirt and were meant as a parody of the self-important posturing of bands like the Clash. Through the lyrics to 'It's The New Thing', Smith rails against the music industry's fascination with the latest 'new thing', whereas The Fall, he proudly proclaims, has 'never sold out' or tried to become a 'clever act'. The B-side, 'Various Times', is less self-referential, slower and more musically complex, with three sections – past, present and future – providing a ominous musical backdrop to Smith's description of camp guards, drop-outs living their roots and people with heads full of lead and stomachs awash with weak beer.

In the *NME*, Ian Penman predicted it would be Single of the Week everywhere and that Smith rendered 'all previous spokesmen redundant'.[33] Chris Westwood concurred, also making it Single of the Week for *Record Mirror* and writing: 'It rocks, plunders, amuses, startles with its musical incongruities, brings out laughter and sweat

---

32 Nick Kent, 'This Year's Esperanto', *NME*, 11 November 1978
33 Ian Penman, 'The Fall: "It's The New Thing" ', *NME*, 18 November 1978
34 Chris Westwood, 'The Fall: "It's The New Thing" ', *Record Mirror*, 18 November 1978

simultaneously . . . The Fall are no chic, they are the real thing.'[34] Ian Birch in *Melody Maker* was the one dissenting voice. He described the single as 'a marginal improvement on the grossly overrated *Bingo-Master's Break-Out! EP*' and sees it as a slightly more accessible move. Nevertheless, it's little more than a big, thrashing beat with instruments colliding and everyone getting drunk.'[35] *Melody Maker* compensated for the bad review by providing in the same issue a feature article on the group by Oliver Lowenstein. He stressed their uncompromising attitude as the only band of Manchester's first wave 'who haven't passed up on their initial ideals'. Again the journalist travelled up to Prestwich where he was invited into Smith and Carroll's flat: 'Books are on the floor and records too. Much played, and ill-kept. On the mantelpiece a postcard is noticed, a portrait of D.H. Lawrence.' Smith talked about the new environment he operated in, the music scene. No longer could he write material like 'Stepping Out', which was originally based on his resentment at working down on the docks: 'The music scene is just as stimulating as any other average working environment. The possibilities are endless, I thought I'd find it difficult, but . . . ' Along with this new source of subject matter, Smith's main concern was how to fit the lyrics to the music: 'I'm pulled two ways. I don't agree with Tom Robinson singing anti-sexist songs against stale old Chuck Berry riffs. That's farcical. But I also don't agree with Henry Cow singing political tracts in front of quasi-classical avant-garde music, even though I enjoy it. It's very obscurist.'[36] The Fall's path lay somewhere between the two: continuing with serious lyrics plus musical experimentation but never losing sight of an upbeat rhythm and a catchy tune.

After the single was released and another Peel session recorded, The Fall once again joined Here & Now for a 'free tour', this time taking in many Scottish venues. Smith was keen to join the tour so he could reach his growing Scottish fan base. He was not particularly keen, however, on free gigs: 'I mean, it's economically impossible for us. We're working lads . . . How can it work for anybody? How can you work for nothing? Do you work for nothing? I mean. I

35 Ian Birch, 'The Fall: "It's The New Thing" ', *Melody Maker*, 18 November 1978
36 Oliver Lowenstein, 'A New Career in a New Town', *Melody Maker*, 18 November 1978

don't. Our fucking band's been on the dole for two years, we're just starting to make a living. I think people should pay for what they fucking get, anyway. We do this 'cos we like Here & Now, that's all. I dunno, I just wanna make a living out of the band, you know. I want independence, which we've got. We fight for it. [Pause] Is the bar open?'[37]

Immediately after the tour, the group was scheduled to go into Camden Town Suite for five days to record its début album. But the exhausted, sick and half-starved band missed the first three days and was left with just two, 15–16 December, to record and mix everything. 'Mark was ill with a "psychosomatic voice",' said Bramah. 'He'd gone to the doctors because he'd lost his voice, he had a sore throat and it was swollen and the doctor said it was psycho–somatic. Which meant there was nothing wrong with him, he was just nervous.' Smith recovered just in time to record the album and end the week with a headline gig at the Marquee. Next up were two more gigs, at the Electric Ballroom, London and the Venue in Manchester, then Karl Burns decided he didn't want to be a member of The Fall any more.

It was another potentially catastrophic moment for the band, but more than that it was personally distressing, for Carroll at least: 'He came by one evening and announced he was leaving, he didn't really give a concrete reason. I had the feeling that things weren't happening fast enough for him. It came like a bolt out of the blue. I just burst into tears and the look on his face told me he had no idea how much I cared for him and respected him.' Burns's chief complaint was Smith's apparent lack of appreciation and respect for him. He was also constantly riled by Smith's last-minute changes to the set list, a ritual designed to make each gig unique and keep the musicians in a state of tension: 'So there would be the guys in the dressing-room,' Carroll remembered, 'going bonkers, asking for the set list and Mark, I think, getting some sadistic pleasure from withholding it from them, until he was ready.'

Bramah thought Smith was frustrated by Burns's drumming style: 'Karl was all over the kit. Mark only missed him after the event but at the time he was like, "Stop playing those tom-toms, just play straight beat." Burns left because he was just sick of us. He thought we were

37   Graham Lock, 'A Guided Tour of Here & Now', *NME*, 13 January 1979

crap and he wanted to be in a band that could play again. He thought he could do better and fair enough, he tried.' Carroll was certain the band was going to miss him dearly. 'In my estimation he was one of the greatest drummers not only to come out of that old New Wave era but previous and subsequent ones too. Karl was so different; he wasn't into all the posturing and élitism that was so rampant back then. He loved the accolades that the scene produced but it was sex and drugs and rock 'n' roll all the way for Karl. He drummed hard and played the same way. You got what you saw, heard and paid for with Karl, it was that simple.' Smith's summation of the high turnover of band members – Friel, Baines and Burns – was succinct to the point of cruelty: 'Xmas '77 – He wants to be a musician + study music sheets. He quit. Easter '77 – She quit – freak-out. Xmas '78 – he wants to be a musician + get crowd reaction. He quit – dog shit.'[38]

38 Mark E. Smith, 'The Mark Smith Page', *Alternative Ulster*, no. 9, *c.* 1979, undated cutting in Yvonne Pawlett's scrapbook

4

Er, What's This Song About? Er, Nothing, 1979

> People can't understand us, we're experimental, but our musical
> priority is rock 'n' roll, the whole stale thing.[1]

At the beginning of 1979, a simple advertisement appeared in the
music press: 'The Fall require drummer – 061 798 9874.'[2] There were
few responses so Smith was grateful when his sister recommended
a drummer from a recently deceased rockabilly band, the Velvet
Collars. Teetotaller Mike Leigh later appeared at a rehearsal, decked
out in velvet-trimmed drape, drainpipes and brothel creepers and
driving a very useful van. 'He came along expecting a rockabilly
band,' said Bramah, 'but he was also up for a gig where he'd get paid.
He didn't really know what the hell he'd got into, but he became
very loyal.' Leigh was not the only candidate; Smith had first asked
The Worst's drummer, Ian Hodges, but he declined. There was some
initial resistance to Leigh's joining but Smith's will prevailed: 'Mike
was like the strength we needed, we always needed . . . there was a
lot of opposition, 'cos Mike doesn't play conventionally, he plays his
drums, he doesn't knock shit out of them.'[3]

Leigh's first appearance was a Valentine's Day gig at Altringham
Bowden Vale Social Club. 'We were doing cabaret circuits at the
time, just to earn money,' said Smith. 'Fuckin' godawful! Fuckin'
terrible! Good though. It toughened you up. They'd be throwing
glasses – proper glasses, like – and spitting at you. I see a lot of groups
today, and they don't know they're born. But touch wood nobody
ever walks out of a Fall concert. You've got to keep the fuckers in
there. That's how we got half our following. You fuckin' win them

---

1 Smith, quoted in Ian Wood, 'An Experimental Sore Thumb', *New Manchester
Review*, no. 72, 12–25 January 1979
2 Unidentified press cutting in Yvonne Pawlett's scrapbook
3 Ian Penman, 'All Fall Down', *NME*, 5 January 1980

over and get their respect. They still come now. Miners from Wakefield and Newcastle.'[4]

From his days with the Velvet Collars, Leigh was not fazed by this type of audience. More of a challenge came with his second gig on 19 February, facing the students of Manchester Polytechnic. Given the tribal subcultures of the times, Leigh's Teddy Boy attire affronted both the punks and the nouveau mods in the audience. Smith, with obvious glee, recalled that people in the audience 'wanted to kill him!'[5] A similar response occurred later in February at the Lyceum in London, where the youthful audience waiting for Generation X obviously did not appreciate the bedraggled rockabilly of The Fall with its drummer dressed in a cap, bow tie and waistcoat.[6] Harry George in the *NME* blamed the tense atmosphere on Smith for throwing cans at the audience.[7] Smith later said of the incident: 'George thought we were throwing cans indiscriminately at the audience, but we could see the guy who was doing it – he'd been canning us throughout the set.'[8] Smith always enjoyed the challenge of getting through to a new audience: 'People always say to us why don't we do those pseudy bloody bills like – Pop Group / Scritti / T. Gristle / Fireball XL, etc., but what's the point of playing to mid-twenties intellectuals HUH?!!?!'[9]

Northern white crap that talks back

Step Forward finally released The Fall's first album, *Live At The Witch Trials*, on 16 March. The front cover reproduced a pencil drawing of some trees in a landscape by 'John Wriothesley', a pseudonym for John Godbert, a friend of the band. It was a difficult cover to print and mistakes meant the release was delayed by a week. Altogether the album cost just £3,700 to put out, and that included the petrol money needed for the vans to distribute it. The contract meant that The Fall and Step Forward shared fifty-fifty in both the costs and the

4   David Cavanagh, 'The Fall', *Volume*, no. 4, September 1992
5   Gary Hopkins, 'Free FALL', *One Two Testing*, June 1986
6   Anon., 'Jaws', *Sounds*, 3 March 1979
7   Harry George, 'Generation X, Lyceum', *NME*, 10 March 1979
8   Graham Lock, 'Stopping, Starting, and Falling All Over Again', *NME*, 7 April 1979
9   Mark E. Smith, 'Interview', *Vsign*, no. 2, 1979

profits.[10] It went on sale at Rough Trade in London for £3.20 and over the next year sold a very respectable 10,000 copies. The Fall celebrated by upping its wages to £15 a week.[11]

The album had been recorded on a single day, 15 December 1978, and mixed the next (by Bob Sargeant and engineer Alvin Clark – 'scientific but terrific' as the sleeve says). It brought together a combination of the old and the new. Already trying to distance themselves from a too obviously political image, three songs from the band's live set – 'Hey! Fascist', 'Race Hatred' and 'Dresden Dolls' – were excluded. Instead the album concentrated on Smith's cryptic and fantastic tales of psycho-drama and scrapbook imagery. It opened with 'Frightened', an old song that Smith wrote when he was just sixteen. Next up was 'Crap Rap 2' with its notorious statement of intent: 'We are The Fall! Northern white crap that talks back.' After 'Like To Blow' and 'Rebellious Jukebox' came 'No Xmas For John Quays', an anti-heroin song, sung perhaps with Baines's recent experiences in mind. 'Mother-Sister!' opened with the immortal question and answer: 'Er, what's this song about? Er, nothing.' The last track on side one was the autobiographical 'Industrial Estate', surely the first song ever to celebrate these hinterlands of the post-industrial urban landscape?

Side two opened with 'Underground Medicin'', one of many songs on the album riddled with drug references, as was the next track 'Two Steps Back'. The third track, 'Live At The Witch Trials', had Smith confessing: 'I still believe in the R 'n' R dream, R 'n' R as primal scream.' The album ended with 'Music Scene', an eight-minute harangue against envy and success in the music business. It was the most avant-garde track on the album, with its use of cut-up cassette recordings and its dramatization of the battle between the band and the studio with the latter's periodic time announcements – 'six minutes!', 'six forty!' – as the band refused to stop.

As a début album, it was provocatively arrogant in its ambitions, combining a ramshackle avant-gardism with irrepressible moments of punk enthusiasm. Graham Lock, in *NME*, thought as music it possessed 'true rock energy', but you could also dance to it and 'pretend

10 ibid.
11 Penman, op. cit., 5 January 1980

it's avant-garde.'[12] Allan Jones in *Melody Maker* was more critical of the 'amateurism' of the musicianship and thought Smith's voice rarely shone through the 'shallow' production.[13] Less critical was Chris Westwood in *Record Mirror* who gave the album five stars and chose to interpret the musicianship as 'rehearsed incompetence'. Dave McCullough in *Sounds* could hardly control his enthusiasm: 'An album of staggeringly rich, mature music, inner questioning hand in hand with rock and roll at its fiercest, its dirtiest, its freshest, its finest, its most honest, rock and roll (you remember the phrase) at its naked, most stimulating prime.'[14]

We see YOU as The Enemy

To coincide with the release of the album, the band went on a nation-wide tour, interrupted briefly by a support slot for the Buzzcocks at the King's Hall, Belle Vue, in front of four thousand people.[15] A smaller and more volatile audience greeted them on 25 March for a return visit to the Lyceum. It was billed by promoters Straight Music as 'The Gig of the Century' and had The Fall appearing alongside up-and-coming bands of the moment Stiff Little Fingers, Gang of Four, Human League, the Mekons and the Good Missionaries (featuring Mark Perry). Second on the bill, The Fall faced a continual hail of gob, cans and plastic glasses. One punk even leapt on to the stage, appropriately as Smith sang, 'A figure walks behind you,' and punched him in the face. Before anyone could react, the attacker jumped back into the audience and disappeared. Smith quickly recovered and was able to continue.

After the gig he told Graham Lock: 'It was the same guy who'd canned us at the Gen X gig. I don't wanna give him any publicity, he's just a psycho.' Lock thought that the audience reaction stemmed from The Fall's refusal to pander to the audience with 'old crowd-pleasers'.[16] One person unlikely ever to be pleased was Gary Bushell of *Sounds*: 'This was doomy, dreary, tuneless and dull fare garnished

12 Graham Lock, 'The Fall Land on Their Feet', *NME*, 24 March 1979
13 Allan Jones, 'The Fall: Exposing Contradictions', *Melody Maker*, 24 March 1979
14 Dave McCullough, 'Music for The Man Who Has Everything (and Wants It All on One Album)', *Sounds*, 24 March 1979
15 Penman, op. cit., 5 January 1980
16 Lock, op. cit., 7 April 1979

by Smith's cretinous sub-Devoto vocal ramblings making for a sound which at least one prominent barbed-up Scottish drunkard likened to early Pink Floyd.'[17] More supportive was Charles Shaar Murray in the *NME*. The Fall's music was 'difficult' and 'arty' and 'threatening', but not in the conventional sense. The band were threatening 'in that they tell you stuff that you may not want to hear in a manner to which you are not accustomed'. All Bramah's 'licks' sounded 'upside-down' and Smith in his 'Prince Valiant' haircut and maroon shirt possessed 'an indomitably accusing voice and more personal courage than anybody else in the hall that night'. Pawlett looked 'shit-feared, as well she might be', and her playing he described as 'misty and pervasive, gauzy and stinging'. Murray summed up the gig as 'a watershed between the seventies and the eighties'.[18]

For Smith the gig proved that The Fall had outgrown the punk and new-wave scene. 'I think we're on our own now,' he explained. 'There's no one else.' The Lyceum gig clarified exactly what The Fall was for and what it was against. 'I felt really good,' he said. 'Yeah, I was pleased. I thought we were the only ones who represented what the whole thing was supposed to be. The band got a lot of strength out of it.' The audience reaction showed how far the original punk and new-wave scene had codified into an exclusive subculture with little room for individual and original bands like The Fall. Smith compared it to the 'witch trials' of the sixteenth and seventeenth centuries: 'We thought, y'know, we've been here since 1977, don't insult us by telling us what we are . . . how DARE you throw cans at us! We see YOU as The Enemy.'[19]

The Fall refused to be fitted into any existing category and this meant it was attacked, or Smith perceived it was attacked, from all sides: 'Intellectuals didn't like us because we weren't, like, college. Longhairs didn't like us 'cos we didn't sound like heavy rock. Punks didn't like us 'cos we didn't have safety pins.'[20] In an industry obsessed with image, Smith's appearance was always going to make him stand out. His was a furry-collared-parka look, put together from the charity and second-hand shops of Prestwich and Bury. It

17 Gary Bushell, 'Future Now', *Sounds*, 31 March 1979
18 Charles Shaar Murray, 'Coping with the '80s', *NME*, 31 March 1979
19 Dave McCullough, 'The Famous Five Fight On', *Sounds*, 21 April 1979
20 Cavanagh, op. cit., September 1992

smacked of exaggerated ordinariness, tailor-made for a character slouched comfortably into the plainness of his name. Smith's legendary bad taste in shirts, jumpers and anoraks acted as the sartorial equivalent of his splenetic lyrics – they were clothes that swore. Smith never could see why people made such a fuss: 'I was working in the docks and couldn't give a fuck about getting a Union Jack T-shirt and spiky hair.'

Of course, later, his non-style became iconic and much-imitated, most obviously by Jarvis Cocker of Pulp. 'Now people are actually wearing parkas as a fashion statement, and these horrible V-necks. It's like Pulp and the stuff he wears. He pays loads of money for crap my mam bought me second hand for 10p.'[21] One design duo, Fraser Moss and Jimmy Collins of YMC (You Must Create), even created a Mark E. Smith jacket. It went on sale in Selfridges during the summer of 1999 at a cost of £200. 'It's a bit of hero worship really,' said Fraser Moss. 'It's that early-'80s anti-fashion look Mark had, when he looked like he was wearing a Burton's suit all the time. I just liked the idea of that and thought he deserves a jacket named after him for that.'[22] The biggest advantage of Smith's look, in distinction from his late-seventies safety-pinned foes, was that it enabled him to roam the streets and pubs of Prestwich and talk to anybody, young or old, without being instantly dismissed as a punk or troublemaker. 'I've figured out why I don't dress weird,' Smith said. 'I don't dress weird 'cos people won't talk to you when you dress weird. I have this strong suspicion that only people who are very, very straight dress weird.'[23]

Personal and musical differences

Kay Carroll's maiden name was Sullivan and she sometimes added the prefix 'O', signing letters 'KO'S'. With the critical success of *Live At The Witch Trials*, relentless press attention, a growing fan base and countless gigs to organize, Carroll's job had become increasingly chaotic: 'I was always the guardian of the camp, nothing and no one got by me. I was like the bouncer meets the triage doctor.' While Smith and the band had the final say on musical content, it was

---

21 Bill Dunn, 'Old Peculiar', *Esquire*, December 1997
22 Fraser Moss, quoted in Anon., 'Q&A', Q, September 1999
23 Mat Snow, 'Before and After The Fall', *NME*, 3 November 1984

Carroll who dealt with record companies, booking agents, public relations, lighting and sound engineers, producers and studios. Her aim was to protect the band members from anything that distracted them from what they did best. 'All my focus,' she said, 'was always on keeping the bullshit from the band, especially Mark, so that they could do their shtick unhindered. I was a tough mother, literally, always in protective mode, but I never really felt like a manager, I felt I was an extension of the band.'

A major test for Carroll was organizing the band's first proper promotional tour during March and April 1979. It started on familiar territory at Eric's in Liverpool with Dave McCullough there to describe The Fall at sound-check for posterity. Bramah 'picks a dizzy path through his crazy upside-down instrument'. Riley 'stands solid, a big-boned husky sixteen-year-old'. Pawlett 'crouches humbly, a shockingly sussed young lady from Doncaster and another erstwhile Fan. She looks like Sue from *The Sooty Show.*' Leigh, 'resplendent in sequined waistcoat and loud jacket, sits silent, like a great proud rock and rolling walrus'.[24]

During a break in the tour, on 20 April at an Iggy Pop gig at the Factory, Bramah announced he wanted to leave the band. The decision could not have come at a worse time. Carroll was immediately forced to cancel dates in Retford, Sheffield, Derby, Newport, Manchester, Dudley and Norwich. Despite these cancellations the news still took some time to filter through to the music press. When it did, the inevitable 'personal and musical differences' were cited as the main cause.[25] The split could actually be traced back to Christmas 1978 when Baines and Bramah started seeing each other: 'What happened was I sent a card to Martin at Christmas and he came round to see me at New Year, I think he bought me a Patti Smith album. And we got back together again and got a flat.'

Through early 1979 Baines would often accompany Bramah to gigs. One night at the Beehive in Blackburn was particularly memorable. 'It was a bikers' dive,' recalled Bramah, 'and at that time in the late seventies there were a lot of bikers and Hell's Angels. We'd sound-checked and the band was up in the dressing-room and me and Una went down into the bar to have a pint. The pub was filled

24 McCullough, op. cit., 21 April 1979
25 Anon., 'A Fall Out!' *NME*, 12 May 1979

with these bikers, the Windsor Chapter of the Hell's Angels. We had a couple of pints and as we walked through this gang of bikers – I was walking ahead and Una was behind – one of them grabbed Una's arse. She had a pint in her hand and she poured it over his head. I turned round and just saw this biker standing up with his long curly hair dripping in beer and he just seemed to rise and rise and rise. I thought I'd better walk over and talk our way out of this. So as I walked towards him somebody behind me just smacked me round the back of my head. Then they all stood up as a gang and laid into me and all I could do under that kind of onslaught was curl up in a ball on the floor. The guy who'd had the pint poured over him smashed me over the head with his dimpled pint glass. I remember one of them had his arm missing and he was hitting me on the head with his stump. I was getting badly beaten up but I was able to crawl into this stairway and then I came to myself and stood up and my hands were covered in blood and my head was dripping with blood, and I just stood up and went, "That's enough," and stared at them. I think they were quite shocked at how much blood there was, so they stopped and at that moment the bouncers came and broke it up.' Amazingly the gig went ahead. 'I have no idea how he was able to play,' said Carroll, 'but he insisted. His stuff that night was awesome.'

Travelling with The Fall, Baines got to know the roadies, Craig Scanlon and Steve Hanley, and briefly joined their band, Staff 9. When Yvonne Pawlett was unable to make a gig on 4 April at the Newport Stowaway Club, Baines stepped in and helped out on keyboards: 'That was the day before my birthday,' she recalled, 'it was really special actually. It felt like I was welcomed back, it was really nice.' The welcome, however, proved to be short lived. Adding to her breakdown problems, Baines had now developed asthma. One attack meant that Bramah missed a rehearsal so he could take her to hospital for checks. Later Carroll visited Baines when she was alone and was furious, accusing her of ruining the band: 'I told her what had happened but she wouldn't listen,' said Baines. 'Anyway I told Martin later what had happened and he said, "Right, that's it, I'm leaving." It was the straw that broke the camel's back. I was begging him that he shouldn't leave on my account, because that's just what they wanted, that was the ammunition they wanted: "Look, she came along and ruined Martin's career" sort of thing. But he'd had enough.'

That night Iggy Pop played at the Factory with Bramah and Eric

McGann moonlighting as stage security. It was a poignant moment to leave the band: 'The first time I saw Iggy Pop was the *Lust For Life* tour,' said Bramah, 'when David Bowie was playing keyboards at Manchester Apollo. We were all at that, Mark included. Iggy Pop was very important to all of us as an inspiration. I left The Fall because of the way that Kay was treating Una. Kay hated the fact that Una got hooked up with me, because Una was a big threat to her because Mark really loved Una, and if she wanted to, Una could have got him back.' With the departure of Bramah all the founding members of the band had now been removed. Smith was in total control, just the way he liked it. But he still needed a guitarist and fortunately standing in the wings, literally at most gigs, were two, Hanley and Scanlon.

Steve Hanley was born in Dublin on 20 May 1959 but left for England with his parents at just a few months old. 'I don't really feel Irish,' he confessed. 'Working-class really, me dad came over looking for a job. He worked for Dunlops then eventually he had a sandwich shop in Wythenshawe. That's where I grew up, a big estate in Wythenshawe.' Hanley's dad was friends with Marc Riley's dad and both of the children went to the same primary school and local grammar school. Hanley didn't enjoy school: 'It was a grammar school but we didn't do Latin or anything like that. It was basically where you went if you just about passed your eleven-plus. It was more technical – metalwork – that kind of thing, sending kids out as apprentices, working for the gas board. People from St Gregory's generally didn't go to university.'

Riley and Hanley shared an interest in music, in particular T-Rex and Mott the Hoople. The budding music enthusiasts were joined at school by a Mancunian Captain Beefheart fanatic, Craig Scanlon (born 7 December 1960). The three also followed local band Slaughter and the Dogs and saw them support the Sex Pistols at the Lesser Free Trade Hall. It wasn't long before they started their own band, the Sirens: 'It was probably Marc who was the main influence,' Hanley remembers. 'I was going to be the drummer, but I bought a motorbike instead. I was about eighteen or nineteen and at South Trafford College studying hotel management.' When Riley joined The Fall, this spurred Hanley and Scanlon to form another band, Staff 9. 'We had a singer called Graham and a drummer whose name was Bernie Cox,' said Hanley. 'He was going out with a girl at the time, Heather, who eventually ended up as my missus! We did about ten gigs altogether, supporting The Fall about six or seven times, including Eric's and one in London.'

With Bramah's departure, Scanlon and Hanley were well placed to step in when needed. The day after the Iggy Pop gig, Smith and Carroll called them up and invited them to Prestwich for a chat. Hanley thought Scanlon would simply replace Bramah, but both were recruited. Hanley modestly remembered it as making little difference from being a roadie: 'The bass player is a glorified roadie anyway. That was the end of Staff 9. We knew most of the tracks already. They weren't that hard, let's face it, it was fairly simple stuff. From the minute I joined it was professional. I stopped signing on and we were getting paid mostly through money from gigs. We were playing all the time, B&Bs and transit vans. The rest of the time I was living at home with my folks.'

Hanley and Scanlon's first gig was on 9 May at the Music Hall, Aberdeen. 'A total disaster,' Hanley recalled. 'The PA packed in and we ended up playing instrumentals.'[26] The tour continued relatively smoothly and ended on 18 May with a support slot with Penetration at the Manchester Apollo. The Fall's next Manchester date was on 20 July with Echo and the Bunnymen as support at the Factory. Nigel Bagley was booking the venue at this time and he could always rely on The Fall to draw a crowd of around four hundred and fifty, making them the third biggest Manchester band behind Buzzcocks and Magazine.[27] The only real competition was Joy Division, whose début album *Unknown Pleasures* had just been released on Factory Records.

Not something you'd do for life

The self-styled 'Stuff the Superstars Funhouse Special Festival' on Saturday 28 July at the Mayflower Club, Gorton, was organized by Andy Zero of *City Fun*, a magazine he founded a year before. Described by Middles as a 'street community magazine', *City Fun* operated an open editorial policy, with all contributions welcome.[28]

26 Mark Kendall, 'Hello, Goodbye: Steve Hanley and The Fall', *Mojo*, no. 75, February 2000
27 Figures from Mark Johnson, *An Ideal for Living: A History of Joy Division*, London: Proteus Books, 1984
28 Mick Middles, 'Truth, Justice and the Mancunian Way', *Sounds*, 11 August 1979

Published fortnightly, its circulation at one time ran to 1,300 copies. 'It was incredibly militant,' Carroll said, 'totally anti-police and gay rights motivated, ahead of its time when I think about it, although it came over a little immature and whiney. They had a writer who would bug Mark and the band all the time, his name was Mick Hucknall. I really liked him. He was a bit of a sycophant though and Mark couldn't stand him. Really weird, after I split from the band, years later, I'm watching the Academy Awards on television and who appears on it but Mick and Simply Red. You could have knocked me down with a feather. The last time I saw him he had this little pseudo-punk band, the Frantic Elevators. They were really terrible, not a smattering of soul to be heard! Life is strange and sometimes surprising.'

The Fall, as Zero's favourite band, naturally took the headline spot. The other bands formed a roll call of the Manchester music scene at that time: the Hamsters, the Frantic Elevators, Joy Division, Ludus, the Liggers, the Distractions and John the Postman. Middles described the festival as 'hedonistic' and not confined to the Mayflower: 'The bands, the audience, the journalists and the road crews spilled, rather dangerously, into the local pubs, staggering along Hyde Road. In the Rock Tavern at 2 p.m., for instance, it was possible to see Mark E. Smith holding court before assembled inebriated hordes, including the *NME*'s Ian Penman.'[29]

'Stuff the Superstars' proved to be Yvonne Pawlett's final appearance for The Fall. Her reason for leaving was refreshingly unique: she jacked in life as a rock 'n' roll star to look after her sick dog. 'Manchester wasn't my hometown,' she explained, 'and I didn't really know anyone when I moved there. The group wasn't making much money at the time and I couldn't afford a place of my own. Ideally I would have liked to have brought my dog over to live with me but she needed regular veterinary care by then. She was between thirteen and fourteen when I was in The Fall and had hip problems. I would have needed to have rented somewhere with a garden for her to potter about in.'

It was an awkward time to leave the band as they were just about to go into the studio and record the next album. But there was little

29 Mick Middles, *From Joy Division to New Order: The Factory Story*, London: Virgin, 1996

animosity: 'Yvonne was so unassuming,' Carroll said, 'and seemed quite happy just to play the keyboard. She laughed a lot and her knowledge of music was tremendous. I remember at interviews she was never assertive and I never could quite figure out whether she was shy, nervous or really didn't give a shit, maybe a combination of each.' Pawlett, for her part, also bore no grudges and had few bad memories of her time in the group: 'The group wasn't something I felt a part of for many and various reasons, it was just one of those things. Not something you'd do for life, one of those transient things you do when you're about eighteen or nineteen, spirit of the times and all that, especially during punk. It's very hard to remain excited about it though. It's nothing like you think it's going to be until you've done it full time.'

So Pawlett returned to Doncaster and three years later joined another band, Shy Tots. Along with Pawlett, there was Dennis Hardcastle (guitar), Colin Rocks (drums), Tim Bradley (bass) and Simon Walsworth (vocals). The Shy Tots released just one EP, distributed by Red Rhino and the Cartel and featuring the tracks 'Gallery', 'Babble' and The Fall-like 'English Industrial Estates'. The band fell apart though when the lead singer finished his degree. Later, rumours circulated that Pawlett was working for a radio station somewhere in Poland, but the truth was less prosaic: 'I'd always found the sciences the easiest subjects at school and it was where my interests lay,' she said. 'I eventually did a master's degree in a branch of horticultural and environmental science, sponsored through work. I've always worked within the framework of investigative biology, ecology and earth sciences for various companies over the years. I have two children, Nicholas and Alexandria, and another German shepherd dog that I'm hoping to start breeding from, when I have the time.'

Pawlett's leaving and the fresh injection of Scanlon and Hanley's raw talent opened up an opportunity for Smith to edge the band away from any lingering remnants of art-school rock. With little or no keyboards, The Fall, he hoped, would alienate an undesirable element of its audience, specifically, 'Eno-orientated crapheads'.[30] Minus Pawlett, *Dragnet* was recorded in just three days in August at Cargo Studios in Rochdale. At the controls was Here & Now sound

30   Smith, quoted in Penman, op. cit., 5 January 1980

man Grant Showbiz plus the owner of Cargo, John Brierley. Show-biz's only prior recording experience was a live performance by Alternative TV. 'Grant was totally useless in a way, but it worked out well,' said Smith. 'He was always floundering, which brought a lot of good things out, like quick fades. We just bullied him into everything.'[31]

Speaking to the Manchester fanzine *Printed Noises*, Scanlon offered an insight into how some of the songs on *Dragnet* were written: 'We have this team like Lennon and McCartney – me and Marc Riley. We usually get together and write the music, or maybe Mark's got an idea on his guitar and we build on that, or take away from it . . . All the songs on *Dragnet* have got tunes, but not all of them are intentional. I have a little piece, Marc'll have a little piece, we'll put them together and they'll just fit. It's a big coincidence, all the music fitting to-gether.'[32] As Scanlon mentioned, Smith was not averse at the time to picking up a guitar and strumming a few notes: 'I think I've got an advantage over musicians,' he explained, 'in that I know nothing about music and suspect I'm tone deaf. I have a plastic four-string guitar which I do a lot of writing on (e.g. 'No Xmas For John Quays'). So simplicity doesn't embarrass me.'[33]

Rowche Rumble

Just before the release of *Dragnet* came The Fall's third single, the double A-side, 'Rowche Rumble' and 'In My Area'. Both tracks were recorded before Pawlett left on 11 June at Cargo, with John Brierley as engineer and Oz McCormick and The Fall as producers. By this time the press releases had become works of literature in themselves. Smith described 'Rowche Rumble' as 'a great dance number and combines a cheek-in-tongue put down of a popular sweetie with The Fall's tribute to Racey. Dig it.' 'In My Area': 'The most difficult song they attempt, the mistakes are glorious. Smith almost sings on it.' The press release also found space for concise pen-portraits of the all-new line-up. Scanlon was 'the bookworm of the group. His genius is still in formation. Plays cranky lead that flows.' Riley was

31 Bob Giddens, 'Hobgoblins on the Loose', *Zig-Zag*, June 1980
32 Mark E. Smith, 'Interview', *Printed Noises*, no. 4, 1980
33 Smith, op. cit., *Vsign*, 1979

'very popular with younger Fall-fans, gets letters asking for guitar lessons, etc.' Hanley was a 'giant in stature and mind. Not many people have heard him talk.' Leigh was 'straight but great, ex-rock 'n' roll revival band. Plays standing up sometimes. Big man but big heart. Ex-bouncer and is serving penance with The Fall.' And finally Smith: 'Called a dictator by many. Audiences love him ha ha. Has problems at dry cleaners, viz; "How did your coat get like that, Mr Smith?" "What do you do for a living!" "I hang around old buildings for hours and get very dirty in one hour." '

The single came in a plain white sleeve, with just the name of the band and the song titles scrawled across the front cover. The track and personnel information on the back cover was typed and gave the impression that it was designed one evening on a kitchen table. It was anti-design design, seemingly effortless but almost impossible to imitate; an aesthetic totally in tune with The Fall's music. 'Rowche Rumble' referred back to Smith's shipping-clerk days, when he did business with the Roche Chemical Company. One day, due to a clerical error, Smith found himself with piles of barbiturates that he attempted to hide in stores across Manchester and in the bottom drawer of his desk at work.[34] Would he get rumbled? Against a simple drummed intro, Smith chants the song's title before the rest of the band crashes in and drives on at a reckless tempo, till the end when the introduction is repeated. The slower tempo of 'In My Area' gave Smith more room for his observational lyrics and spot-on aphorisms, while Pawlett's off-kilter electric piano provides an aural equivalent of madness.

The single was well-received, making John Hamblett's joint Single of the Week in the *NME* along with Disco Spectacular's cover of 'Aquarius'.[35] It also made Dave McCullough's joint Single of the Week, this time with Racey's 'Boy Oh Boy'.[36] Elsewhere, Ian Birch of *Melody Maker* was finally won over: 'Brimming with well-meaning wryness, it careers along in entirely its own way, independent of all fashions and alert to every possibility. Improves with every play.'[37]

---

34 Dave Haslam, 'Hip, Hip, Hip, Hip Priest', *City Life*, 18 July 1986
35 John Hamblett, 'Champagne 'n' Valium', *NME*, 18 August 1979
36 Dave McCullough, ' "Rowche Rumble" ', *Sounds*, 11 August 1979
37 Ian Birch, ' "Rowche Rumble" ', *Melody Maker*, 11 August 1979

Yog Sothoth rape me Lord

Step Forward released The Fall's second album on 26 October, accompanied by music-press adverts (claiming, 'The hero is no spaz . . . ') and a Totale-authored press release: 'This is not the spineless usual. It's Original Article. Not romantic not sub-intellectual not "tough" recycled cabaret glam three-chord big boots.' *Dragnet*, he claimed, 'is white crap let loose in a studio but still in control. Sung in natural accents in front of unaffected music.' The stark black and white cover design by Tina Prior showed a butterfly caught in a spider's web.

The album opens with a shout of, 'Is there anybody there?', to which the band shouts back, 'Yeah!' The first two tracks, 'Psykick Dancehall' and 'A Figure Walks', share a supernatural theme, as does much of the album. During his adolescence, Smith had been particularly interested in all things ghostly and later half-joked, 'I used to be psychic, but I drank my way out of it.'[38] It was an interest he shared with Carroll, who also possessed psychic gifts and had attended seances at the Whitefield Spiritual Church with her mother, a practising medium. In the early seventies, Carroll's mother opened a psychic centre on the corner of Gardner Road and Bury New Road in Prestwich. 'It was over a row of shops that consisted of a bakery, hairdresser's and a shoe shop,' Carroll explained. 'It had originally been a dance studio, you know tap, ballroom dancing, things of that nature. *Voilà* "Psykick Dancehall"! It's still open to my knowledge.'

Part of the inspiration behind the next track, 'Printhead', was a review of 'It's The New Thing' by Ian Birch, with his, 'Nevertheless, it's little more than a big, thrashing beat with instruments colliding and everyone getting drunk,'[39] becoming in Smith's version, 'The band little more than a big crashing beat, instruments collide and we all get drunk.' Smith dedicates 'Dice Man' to all ex-band members, while 'Before The Moon Falls' portrays The Fall as private detectives just back from a 'musical pilgrimage' and operating out of a secluded office. 'Your Heart Out' provides an anti-sentimental discourse on love and the lack of it and the effects of too much speed.

Side two opens with the exuberant 'Muzorewi's Daughter', co-written with Carroll. Smith's vocal performance is as peculiar as his obscure subject matter: imagine being the daughter of Bishop

38 Tony Herrington, 'Mancunian Candidate', *The Wire*, no. 151, September 1996
39 Ian Birch, ' "It's The New Thing" ', *Melody Maker*, 18 November 1978

Muzorewa of Rhodesia. 'Flat of Angles' tells the tale of a man trapped and hiding in a flat after killing his wife. When he eventually goes out he thinks the streets are 'full of mercenary eyes'. 'Choc-stock', with music by Scanlon, forms another anti-music-biz rant. Next up is the stand-out track on the album, 'Spectre vs Rector'. The Fall recorded the first section in an old warehouse and Smith later overdubbed the vocals in such a way that it created an eerie echo effect. The lyrics revel in Smith's love of the Lovecraftian horror-story genre, with him chanting, 'M. R. James be born be born / Yog Sothoth rape me lord,' and telling the story of a rector from Hampshire and a spectre from Chorazina. Part one is spectre versus rector. Part two has the inspector visiting the rector. Part three sees the spectre possess the rector. Part four is the inspector versus the rector possessed by the spectre. In the fifth part the 'hero' appears, his soul 'possessed a thousand times'. In the final part the spectre enters the hero 'but the possession is ineffectual'. The album ends light-heartedly with 'Put Away', notable for the first appearance of a kazoo on a Fall recording.

In his review, Dave McCullough concentrated on the extraordinary 'flattened and narrow' production of the album, which created an atmosphere disturbing enough to make it 'similar in feeling, if not in the fineries of sound, to early Doors and Velvets material'.[40] Paul Du Noyer thought it was 'irresistible and unique, a happy, challenging music of unforced energy and simple vision, just everyday inspiration, seized in the instant before it vanishes'.[41] Allan Jones considered the album flawed by occasional moments of 'breast-beating' and 'self-righteousness' but insisted The Fall should be 'taken seriously as an important voice for the next decade'.[42]

With this praise ringing in their ears the band started a promotional tour of England, and in the process provided the bulk of material for the following year's live album, *Totale's Turns*. Journalists who caught The Fall on this tour focused on Smith and his unique stage presence: 'The most disturbing part is the voice,' wrote Penny Kiley, 'the arrogance of that nagging monotone lightened only by the occasional scream.' Smith was 'the focal point of the group. Hunched, awkward, he typifies the poet as misfit . . . the anti-hero, with his back to the

---

40 Dave McCullough, 'Sounds of Reality', *Sounds*, 10 November 1979
41 Paul Du Noyer, 'Cryptic', *NME*, 10 November 1979
42 Allan Jones, 'Falling into the Eighties', *Melody Maker*, 17 November 1979

audience.'[43] Pete Scott was equally obsessed with Smith's anti-cha-risma: 'Hey, I bet when you were at school there was a scruffy kid in your class who smelled bad, right? Well now that he's grown up a bit, he calls himself Mark Smith and sings with The Fall.'[44] At least some of Smith's attitude to performing can be traced to his respect for the American anti-establishment comedian, Lenny Bruce. 'He just kept on talking,' Smith explained. 'That's what I thought was good about Bruce, the way he used to insult his audience almost.'[45]

Smith soon had his own opportunity to insult American audiences when Copeland's American distribution company IRS invited The Fall over. The first gig took place on 1 December at the Palladium Theatre, New York, with The Fall supporting the Buzzcocks. A reviewer for *Variety*, although appreciative, obviously had problems understanding Smith's accent: '[The Fall] seem capable of gaining a cult, [but] the quintet was hampered by a lack of clarity by lead singer Mark Edward Smith. The material was more declarative than straight rock, which seemed out of place on the rock evening.'[46] The high-light of the tour was a support slot for Iggy Pop in San Diego. 'It was like a big Talk of the Town,' Riley remembered, 'all these couples sat around tables, drinking wine, and just a couple of people stood there at the front, looking at you. Really weird! Like a cabaret, really.' After all those years listening to the Stooges in Prestwich, this new context was truly surreal for Smith: ' . . . he was doing the whole stuff, the cut bit and everything, and there were all these check shirts, coked out of their heads, with tans . . . at the back of the club was this big window, you could see a bit of beach, with palm trees on it.'[47] After the gig The Fall returned to their hotel room to watch television. 'Then there was a knock on the door,' said Riley, 'and this guy said, "Iggy's having a party, do you want to come?" "Er, no thanks." You can spot ex-Fall members because they're often seen on street corners, kicking themselves.'[48]

---

43 Penny Kiley, 'The Fall, Eric's, Liverpool', *Melody Maker*, 17 November 1979
44 Pete Scott, 'Messages of Nihilism to Post-punk Mutants: The Fall, Retford', *Sounds*, 1 December 1979
45 Penman, op. cit., 5 January 1980
46 Kirb, 'Buzzcocks, Fall, Sports', *Variety*, 5 December 1979
47 Andy Gill, 'The Wit and Wisdom of Mark Smith', *NME*, 10 January 1981
48 Will Hodgkinson, 'Home Entertainment: Mark Radcliffe and Marc Riley', *Guardian*, Friday Review, 9 March 2001

For Smith the tour reinforced his hatred of the music industry. IRS he described as a 'bunch of fools' who didn't really know what they were doing. But playing to Americans was an enlightening experience, 'they view their rock differently, it's like going for a meal, everyone sits around eating'. The best part for the band was partying in Los Angeles with Claude Bessy and the *Slash* magazine underground crowd. Most importantly, though, Smith found lots of material for new lyrics: 'I got a lot of songs out of it. It's a very evil place.' The reason they'd gone to America was because they felt they were being taken for granted back home. The tour was useful but had its drawbacks: 'America put The Fall back about four months, we went there and played to audiences that were like aliens.' The culture shock went both ways, with Smith being asked to tone his accent down. Apparently this wasn't such a problem for London bands, 'they could just about understand cockney,' said Smith, 'but can't quite grasp Mancunian.' So was it worth it? 'Well it took a while to get over it, put it that way.'[49]

49   Giddens, op. cit., June 1980

5

Grotesque, 1980

The Fall is an institution. It's my life, but I'm not The Fall. This band, now, threatens me, which is how it should have been all along. This is great, this is the first Fall where I can drop out and not feel embarrassed about it.[1]

The new decade started for The Fall with a two-page splash in the *NME* courtesy of Ian Penman. The interview took place in a pub near Carroll and Smith's new flat in a large redbrick Victorian house on Glebelands Road. The area was spoilt for pubs: in the early eighties one local brewery alone, Holts, owned ninety in a fifteen-mile radius. Carroll and Smith's favourite was the Forresters on Bury New Road. Another regular there was Ian Levine: 'Basically, the Forresters' posse was exclusively male, except for Kay, who could drink anyone under the table and beat them at pool with one hand tied behind her back.' Along with pool, Carroll also played on the women's darts team. The pub was Carroll and Smith's escape from the music business. 'The crowd in there really had no idea what we were doing,' said Carroll, 'and the ones that did, didn't give a shit, so it was cool: we were barflys.' Other pubs they frequented were the White Horse, the Red Lion, the Wilton, the Grapes and the Church, an old coaching inn on Church Lane. Conveniently, The Fall's new rehearsal room and office were also nearby.

The band had not lasted long at Davidson's rehearsal studio. Not only was the rent about to increase, but security was poor and privacy non-existent, with band practice often interrupted by fans or other musicians. So Carroll was pleased to find a two-roomed office at 429b Bury New Road, near Strangeways Prison: one room for rehearsals and the other for Carroll's office. The office was busier than the rehearsal room as the band would sometimes go for weeks without rehearsing. Smith often preferred gigs over rehearsals for trying out

---

1   Smith, in Ian Penman, 'All Fall Down', *NME*, 5 January 1980

and developing new material: 'I think the only place you can rehearse genuinely is on stage,' he said. 'That's one of the only reasons we play you know. Because no matter what anyone says, you can't get any work of great merit out of just staying in a shed for years and not going outside. I've written lots of stuff on stage.'[2] Hanley remembers the band trying various ways to write new material, including round each other's houses: 'We were never a band for rehearsing anyway, only when we had to, like the day before the tour. When we did an album some of the tracks we rehearsed on tour, but others we made up on the spot. Some we played once then never did them again, it depended on the songs.'

All of the songs on The Fall's next single – 'Fiery Jack', '2nd Dark Age' and 'Psykick Dancehall #2' – were established live favourites by the time they were recorded at Foel Studios in Wales. On the single's cover Suzanne Smith's pencil sketch of 'Fiery Jack' portrayed him as a wino-type figure casting a devil-shaped shadow. In the song he was a forty-five-year-old man, too fast to work and write, he just burned. Smith saw him as a self-fulfilling prophesy: 'In a mystical way, Fiery Jack is the sort of guy I can see myself as in twenty years.'[3] The back cover carried the Lovecraft-influenced last testament of Roman Totale: 'The events which I am about to relate concern the thing that rests alongside me. This "master-tape" is the result of experiments which took place in the remote Welsh hills one autumn . . . (here the document is illegible) . . . I have not long left now but I urge the finder of this "master-tape" never to unleash it on humanity! – Ah! already the evil Deit–y Ri–Kol is clawing at my brain! – If it is unleashed – The Fall is here, the ectoplasm exorcized and Humanity Can Either Eat That Grenade Or Face The Second Dark Age!'

Totale's warnings went unheeded and the single was released at the end of January, eventually reaching number four in the newly created independent charts. Reviewers such as Adrian Thrills immediately picked up on the new rockabilly sound: 'someone somewhere has been applying some drastic surgery to their musical sensibilities with the result that Mark Smith's impenetrable lyrics are now intoned over an uncharacteristic bopping high-school backdrop.'[4] Mick Middles

2 Smith, on KPFA, San Francisco, broadcast 10 July 1981
3 Dave McCullough, 'Totale Turnaround', *Sounds*, 21 June 1980
4 Adrian Thrills, 'Singles: "Fiery Jack" ', *NME*, 2 February 1980

made 'Fiery Jack' his Single of the Week[5] and Chris Bohn added his plaudits: 'A great subversive country and western shuffle tune, warped to fit Mark E. Smith's offbeat words and snarl, makes this The Fall's most attractive single to date.'[6]

We didn't want to be A&M trailers

March saw The Fall embark on an ill-starred mini-tour of the UK accompanied by the Cramps, a bunch of hybrid rockabilly punks from New York. They were visiting England to promote their latest album, *Songs The Lord Taught Us* on Illegal records, and consisted of Bryan Gregory, Lux Interior, Nick Knox and Ivy Rorschach. Illegal formed part of Miles Copeland's label empire and it was his brilliant idea to showcase his star alternative bands together. Unfortunately the bands were incompatible in style and attitude and this, added to the usual disputes over which was the headline act, made for a bad-tempered tour. At the first date on 7 March at King's College, London, the audience started boisterously and just got worse: it was their Rag Ball, a traditional time for students to behave badly. The Fall were not impressed and Steve Taylor noted Smith's seeming lack of interest in the audience: 'The Fall indulged in some PIL-style backs-to-the-audience self-absorption. With a musical lack of style three years out of date, Mark E. Smith's Lydonesque grumblings and a backing resembling a working-men's-club version of punk sounded badly adrift, sadly drained of tension.'[7]

Another witness at the gig was Roland S. Howard, recently arrived from Australia with his band The Birthday Party. He described the two bands as 'anathema' to each other with The Fall's aim 'to be completely unpretentious' and the Cramps' 'to be Aliens'. One incident involved Smith and Carroll hauling Lux Interior in front of a mirror and telling him to 'look at yourself, you look fuckin' ridiculous!' What Lux saw was a 'huge quiff, naked torso, gold leather hipsters and winkle-picker ankle boots. Dead Elvis. What's not to like?' The rest of Howard's memory of the night was

---

5 Mick Middles, ' "Fiery Jack" ', *Sounds*, 23 February 1980
6 Chris Bohn, ' "Fiery Jack"/"2nd Dark Age" ', *Melody Maker*, 9 February 1980
7 Steve Taylor, 'Trash: Cramps/The Fall, King's College, London', *Melody Maker*, 15 March 1980

dominated by a chaotic Cramps set that ended with a stage invasion: 'Ivy chews gum, ice-maiden style, Lux jams the microphone into his screaming mouth, Bryan Gregory wiggles his skinny ass and shoots members of the crowd with a plastic gun loaded with ping-pong balls, Nick Knox decides that he is now superfluous and leaves his domain to the amateur. Panic! Panic! Panic! This is now, officially, a riot.'[8] The next night the two bands played Eric's in Liverpool (incidentally, one of the last gigs at the seminal venue before the local authorities closed it because of licence problems). Dates followed in Leeds, Scotland and Birmingham before the two bands said their farewells in London at the Electric Ballroom.

The whole experience proved too much for Mike Leigh and he resigned. Leigh found it hard to survive on the money and left for more regular work, rumoured to be either in insurance or as a drummer in a cabaret band on a cruise ship. The mismatched tour with the Cramps may also have helped convince Smith and Carroll that Step Forward was not the best label to be on. Royalties were also slow to materialize and the group was continually sidelined in favour of Copeland's other bands, the Police and Squeeze. Despite these problems, Smith remained appreciative of Copeland's early support for The Fall when other labels wouldn't touch them. The work they did on *Dragnet* especially impressed him: 'They got it out, the promo was really good, they got the press sussed out without creeping, but the money wasn't there to back it up. We weren't getting our royalties and because they were so into action all the time we found we were being left behind. And with a band like us we need some kind of security because we don't operate along the same lines. Like the other bands they had, like Squeeze and Police, it was OK for them because one day they were going to get signed up. But we didn't want to be A&M trailers and we were skint all the time.'[9]

Smith and Carroll had got to know Rough Trade's Geoff Travis during the recording of 'Fiery Jack', which he produced with Mayo Thompson. Travis was five years older than Smith and came from Finchley, North London, the son of a Jewish insurance broker. His specialist record shop, Rough Trade, opened on Kensington Park Road just in time to catch the punk and reggae boom of 1977.

8 Roland S. Howard, 'Gimme Danger', *World Art*, no. 19, 1997
9 Paolo Hewitt, 'Rise of The Fall', *Melody Maker*, 29 November 1980

Inspired by the punk ethic, Travis saw an opportunity to work with the new, small and independent labels. His shop sold hundreds of the Buzzcocks' *Spiral Scratch* EP and this led him to realize how much poor distribution held back independent labels. 'We always saw distribution as a political thing,' he told Jon Savage. 'If you only have W.H. Smith selling books, then you only get a certain kind of book. If you set up a viable system that sells other kinds of literature, then you give people a chance to decide for themselves.'[10]

Alongside a distribution company, Travis set up Rough Trade Records with Richard Scott and operated special profit-sharing agreements which saw recording costs shared fifty-fifty with bands. This ensured low recording budgets and equally restrained marketing and advertising campaigns. The quality of the product was intended to be its best advertisement. Travis convinced Smith and Carroll that Rough Trade could do a better job for them than Step Forward. 'Miles was pretty pissed at us when we left,' Carroll recalled. 'Geoff, though, was a great guy, lots of fun and totally on the artist's side. I just negotiated a one-record deal at a time with him.' For a while it proved to be a promising arrangement between an innovative record company, its maverick talent-spotter and a fiercely independent band. It impressed Dave McCullough so much he described the union as 'a dream come true, like two sources of the same river joining'.[11]

Will you fucking get it together instead of showing off?

The Fall's response to the challenge of the 'difficult third album' was *Totale's Turns (It's Now Or Never)*, a hybrid mixture of live tracks and lo-fi recordings. Released in May 1980 on Rough Trade, the sleeve was amateur to the point of genius, no expense spent. Beneath the rubber stamped 'The Fall' was the felt-tipped title and the hilariously underwelming tour itinerary: 'Doncaster! Bradford! Preston! Prestwich!' Roman Totale typed an introduction for the back cover. Side one, he wrote, was 'recorded in front of an 80% disco weekend mating audience, but we never liked preaching to the converted anyway.' Totale ended with this qualified endorsement: 'I don't

10 Travis, in Jon Savage, *England's Dreaming: Sex Pistols and Punk Rock*, London: Faber and Faber, 1999
11 Dave McCullough, 'Society's Scourge', *Sounds*, 17 May 1980

particularly like the person singing on this LP. That said, I marvel at his guts. This is probably the most accurate document of The Fall ever released.'

Releasing a live album made sense in a number of ways. First, it was the best way to document what Smith considered to be a first-rate line-up in its prime. Second, the band needed to earn some money and a live album could be put together quickly and cheaply (it was mastered, the press release proudly announced, from commercial cassette recordings). Intended to be sold at a budget price of £2.50, *Totale's Turns* was never a total cash-in even though some shops decided to sell the album at full price. Sales were good and the album became The Fall's first independent chart number one, staying there for five weeks before being knocked off top spot by Toyah Wilcox's *The Blue Meaning*.

The album further established Smith's reputation as a cantankerous performer, with its inclusion of such endearments to the audience as, 'The difference between you and us is that we have brains.' Not to see them excluded, Smith later turned on his own band: 'Will you fucking get it together instead of showing off?' he exclaimed during 'No Xmas For John Quays'. Alongside live versions of previously released tracks such as 'Fiery Jack' and 'In My Area', three new songs were included: 'Cary Grant's Wedding', 'New Puritan' (recorded 'at home during which said home was attacked by a drunk, which accounts for the tension on that track') and 'That Man', a song about phoney new-wave preachers.

As with many recordings by The Fall, by the time Rough Trade released the record the list of personnel was already out of date. To replace Mike Leigh, Smith recruited Steve Hanley's younger brother, Paul. Also accompanying the group on selected live dates was clarinettist Dave Tucker and conga player Steve Davies. The latter was particularly useful when The Fall visited the Netherlands for a mini-tour in early June because Paul Hanley remained stuck at home sitting his O levels. 'I played eleven gigs in fourteen nights,' said Davies, 'but I don't think I really considered myself a member of The Fall. I was more of a friend of the band really.' At this time Davies was also in another band called Mushroom Tango, which specialized in Gong and Can covers. His other band was called Victor Draygo, 'a bunch of wannabe posers from Rossendale. We were all in relationships, married with kids even, trying to rekindle something through the punk stuff.' When Smith asked Davies to do the Dutch tour, he knew he was taking a risk in more than one sense: 'I also had a seven-seater estate car that came in handy for transporting them around! I almost crashed the car within half an hour of setting out too. Some numbers I played the congas and others I played the kit. I didn't have any of the stops and starts, and I had to listen to the music, watching Marc Riley and Steve Hanley to keep the timing going.'[12]

The group reverted to its usual line up with Paul Hanley for a gig at the ICA in mid-June. Sold out weeks in advance, it was part of 'Rock Week', a prestigious showcase in front of London's self-regarding cultural élite. Paul Du Noyer characterized Smith as sounding like 'Eddie Waring toasting' and the band as 'all surface un-attraction but quickly addictive'.[13] Describing a subsequent gig in Edinburgh, Johnny Waller was also struck by the power of the band, despite various deliberately thrown spanners in the works, such as 'wailing kazoo and keyboard cacophony'.[14] Such anti-musical devices could easily have degenerated into aimless pranks, but The Fall used them to jolt and hold the listener's concentration. Gill Smith thought the band members looked so 'engrossed and dedicated' during a two-night stint at the Marquee that the crowd must have wondered whether they were actually enjoying themselves.[15] Steve Hanley explained: 'Our attitude was very professional. It was like a matter of life or death, a good gig: post-mortems and everything.'

You don't have to be weird to be weird[16]

Paul Hanley's first appearance on vinyl was on the July double-A-side release 'How I Wrote Elastic Man' and 'City Hobgoblins', produced once more by Travis and Thompson. 'How I Wrote Elastic Man' self-referentially details the story of a writer whose 'art' is destroyed by success and celebrity, a process Smith might have been experiencing at the time. Paul Hanley bashes the drums with

12   Tim Wesley, 'Where are they now? Steve Davies', *TBLY*, January 1999
13   Paul Du Noyer, 'The Fall, Ludus', *NME*, 28 June 1980
14   Johnny Waller, 'The Fall: Edinburgh', *Sounds*, 19 July 1980
15   Gill Smith, 'The Fall, Marquee, London', *Melody Maker*, 2 August 1980
16   Captain Beefheart phrase from a press campaign of April 1974 promoting the album *Unconditionally Guaranteed*

more gusto than finesse and the main guitar riff is relentlessly repetitious, but combined with the intelligent lyrics and a catchy chorus the result is infectious. 'City Hobgoblins', meanwhile, dwells in familiar territory, under floorboards and in cupboards where inner-city demons ('ten times my age, one tenth my height') reside. The warped production and Smith's paranoid vocals just add to the Hammer House of Horror atmospherics.

Gary Bushell reviewed the single in *Sounds*, saying it was 'punk with the stuffing knocked out of it, embellished by the worst singing voice in the world (sort of Max Bygraves crossed with a donkey with hiccups).'[17] Bushell's choice for Single of the Week was Angelic Upstarts' 'Last Night Another Soldier'. Relating to this, a letter from Smith appeared in the magazine a couple of weeks later, asking why Bushell was so paranoid about the army, 'Surely you're too short and too old to be conscripted?' A provoked Bushell replied: 'I'm six foot tall and twenty-four-years-old and next time I meet Mark Smiff or any of you tediously self-important ineffectual hippies I intend to demonstrate a revolutionary interpretation of square-bashing.'[18] Despite Bushell's bluster the single sold well and rose to number two in the independent charts, beaten only by Joy Division's 'Love Will Tear Us Apart' – a record laden with the significant burden of Ian Curtis's recent suicide.

Rough Trade released The Fall's next single, 'Totally Wired', at the beginning of September. With Kay Carroll and John Brierley at the controls, Paul Hanley's drumming is by now much more assured and the full potential of his brother's bass playing is finally realized. Add to this Smith's most compelling vocal performance to date, with its twist of northern sour, plus lyrics that added new life to a perennial rock 'n' roll tale of drugged excess, and you have a decade-defining single. Even the cover design, with its hastily scribbled grimacing face, is a masterpiece of restrained graffiti.

The single once again peaked at number two in the independent charts, pipped to the number one spot by Zounds, anarcho-punks on the Crass label. Madness's 'Baggy Trousers' was Danny Baker's Single of the Week in *NME*. 'Totally Wired' he thought was 'ugly' and poorly produced: 'I can't see there's an audience for The Fall's

---

17   Gary Bushell, 'The Fall: "How I Wrote Elastic Man" ', *Sounds*, 19 July 1980
18   Joe Totale, Letter, *Sounds*, 9 August 1980

constant verbal battering. There's too much on folk's minds these days to want to carry a slice of someone else's. This is the age of The Fact not The Opinion.'[19]

The song celebrated The Fall's preferred drug at the time: 'We took speed but it was just like having a cup of coffee really,' said Steve Hanley. 'When you've been in the pub or on the bus all day and you've got a gig it was just something to get you going. At times there was a lot of it but it was never a big thing.' Despite Hanley's casualness, speed played quite a large part in the story of The Fall. Speed (or amphetamines) amplifies, or seems to amplify, both the mental and physical capacities of the user, resulting in a feeling of self-confidence and euphoria. Although made illegal in 1964, it remained the drug of choice for the mods, the Northern Soul fanatics and the punks. In contrast to the decadent 'high society' image of cocaine, speed was seen as a cheap proletarian drug. In 1981 Smith was well aware of the downside of its use: 'You do get rain, of course, especially when you're taking a lot of speed and that, you start looking in mirrors and getting ulcers.'[20] Use over a number of years could result in exhaustion, depression, wakefulness, nervousness, violent mood swings, impotence, skin rashes, auditory hallucinations, paranoia and anxiety. Physically the drug suppresses the appetite, which can lead to chronic weight loss and malnourishment, and it also destroys dentine, causing tooth rot. Researchers have also noticed what they call the 'McGyver effect' where users are consumed by a tremendous urge to take things apart and put them back together again (amazingly The Fall's line-up changes played no part in this research).[21]

We're the most hated group in Britain

In September, The Fall played its third session for John Peel's radio show, recording 'Jawbone And The Air-Rifle', 'New Face In Hell' and the definitive versions of 'Container Drivers' and 'New Puritan'.[22] Something about these sessions seemed to bring out the best in the

19 Danny Baker, 'The Fall: "Totally Wired" ', *NME*, 6 September 1980
20 Barney Hoskyns, 'Hip Priest: The Mark Smith Interview', *NME*, 14 November 1981
21 Miriam Joseph, *Speed*, London: Carlton Books, 2000
22 Both of the latter appeared on 'Kicker Conspiracy' in 1983.

band. 'The thing about recording a John Peel session,' said Riley, 'is that you get in the van in the morning, in our case you drive two hundred miles, get out, unload the gear, and record everything in a pretty quick time. I mean you would do four songs for a session. Now normally, even for bands like The Fall, you would take two or three days to record four tunes. In this case you'd have to have it all done and dusted by ten o'clock at night. So you would get into the studio, wheel everything down into the catacombs in Maida Vale, set up and do the deed. And I remember, I think it was the third session we did, we recorded the first track, made a right old racket, as we did, went in to start listening back to it, make sure we were happy with it, and I turned round to look at the producer [John Sparrow], and his pipe had gone out. This is the truth, his pipe had actually gone out, and he was asleep.'[23]

Just over a week after the session, The Fall played at Tatton Community Centre, Chorley. Mick Middles thought the small community centre was a perfect place to see The Fall. The local youth may not have been particularly big fans of the group but they appreciated the effort. This did not, of course, mean Smith returned any compliments. He concluded the set sarcastically, 'Thank you for being a simply wonderful audience. We'll certainly never play here again.'[24] In an interview at the time, Carroll elaborated on The Fall's attitude to its fans: 'We expect nothing from our audience, and in the same vein they, if they are a Fall audience, should not expect anything from us. It's a matter of, "I want to go there, I want to hear it, I want to go home," and that's all it should be about. There's too many people in audiences that just want escape, they want people up there to live out their fantasies and you just can't give it 'em.'[25]

Hatred was a theme occupying much of Smith's mind at the time. A few days after Chorley, at Manchester Polytechnic, he introduced the band with: 'Good evening, you know who we are. We're the most hated group in Britain.' In an interview broadcast on Irish radio he explained: 'I'm very interested in cultivating The Fall as the most hated band in the music scene because we prick a lot of thorns in

23 Riley, on BBC Radio 4's 'Front Row', broadcast on 29 January 1999
24 Mick Middles, 'The Fine Art of Insulting Audiences: The Fall, Chorley', *Sounds*, 4 October 1980
25 Mark E. Smith, 'Interview', *Printed Noises*, no. 4, 1980

people's sides.' The band wanted to be heard but it wouldn't compromise to achieve success: 'I'm saying what I want to say and I don't kiss anybody's arse when I'm doing it.' This also applied to his band, over which he operated a form of dictatorship. Democracy had no place in The Fall because, Smith claimed, it produced 'a mediocre average'. When it came to band members Smith was adamant: 'I'm pretty fascist.' The Fall was too important to leave to the musicians. There was also only one 'right' side of the cultural divide: 'You know, there's entertainment and there's culture, and we're on the cultural side of the line.'[26] Despite Smith's attempts at inviting hatred and alienating potential audiences, The Fall's next album shot to number one in the independent charts and stayed there for three weeks before being overtaken by a Christmas surge to buy UB40's *Signing Off*.

The Fall's fourth album, *Grotesque (After The Gramme)*, was produced by Geoff Travis, Mayo Thompson, Grant Showbiz and The Fall and recorded at Cargo, Rochdale, with trusted engineer John Brierley and Street Level, London. It was rumoured to have cost just three hundred pounds and much of that went on the full-colour sleeve with its 'grotesque peasants' painting by Suzanne Smith.[27] The back cover carried informal portraits of the band, plus a shot of Smith in his flat next to a large Pickwick records stall proudly displaying his Elvis records. Also in a quote on the back cover – edited by J. Totale, his 'vicious son' – R. Totale (deceased) announced, 'C 'n' N Music is born!' Country and Northern was Smith's term for the mutant genre The Fall was inventing.

From the first track, the belligerent 'Pay Your Rates', the casual listener immediately realizes this is not going to be easy listening. The British class system comes under scrutiny in 'English Scheme', while 'New Face in Hell' tells the story of a wireless enthusiast who discovers government secrets and is then framed for the murder of his neighbour.[28] 'C'n'C's Mithering' is an extended whine about things that annoyed Smith, including boils, dirty socks, collapsed

---

26 Smith, on Dave Fanning's radio show, RTE (Ireland), broadcast 18 October 1980
27 Ian Pye, 'The Fall: *Grotesque (After The Gramme)*', *Melody Maker*, 22 November 1980
28 This plot bears no relation to that found in the 1977 *New Face in Hell* by Roger Busby, no. 6 in the Fleetway Thriller Library series.

ceilings, loud lawn-mowers on a Sunday morning, and his upstairs neighbour's constant hoovering. It was probably this song that prompted Smith's publisher – more used to hackneyed love songs – to exclaim, 'What's this – your entry for the Nobel Prize for Literature?'[29]

The one song bearing a slight resemblance to a three-minute pop song is 'The Container Drivers', The Fall's contribution to the hyper-specialized trucking genre. Smith had written 'Impression of J. Temperance' the year before 'in a bed and breakfast in Retford miles from anywhere when the locals got suspiciously friendly and there was a huge man-sized one-eyed teddy bear on the landing'.[30] The song details the birth of the 'hideous replica' of J. Temperance with its 'brown sockets and purple eyes'. 'In The Park' offers an unromantic look at casual sex in awkward locations. The lo-fi nature of 'WMC-Blob 59' was openly celebrated by the band, who in a press release teased equipment fetishists with a list of tools used: '1 x Shure microphone (B-roke); 1 x 'Schitti' 15w amp; 1 x 1964 Red 'New Beat' plastic guitar; 1 x model no. 90000 AC Lewis's tape recorder with special 'Hopeless' black-grey mike. This is a very funny track. It's a pity you can't hear what's going on.'[31] 'Gramme Friday' is yet another drug song, this time narrated by the appropriately named Robertson Speedo.

The most innovative aspect of the album is the combination of Smith's finely observed yet almost free-form spiel with music that knows when to be unobtrusive and when to raise the hackles, a blend that peaks with the final track 'The N.W.R.A.' (The North Will Rise Again). The dramatic narrative is dictated by R. Totale's son, Joe, and describes the United Kingdom as it descends into riotous turmoil after a Northern uprising. The song was later misread as a pro-Northern 'rebel' song, but Smith's intentions were more subtle: 'The way I wrote it was from a few dreams I had after playing up north a lot,' he explained. 'It's purely fantasy, science-fiction stuff. But of course, everybody's gonna go, "Huh! The North! Here we go again – Smith talking about flat caps," and all that clichéd rubbish. Actually, the message in it is that if the North did rise again, they would fuck it up.

29 Statement-cum-handout for *Grotesque (After The Gramme)*, 1980
30 Excerpt from Fall Foundation Handout, *c.* 1980, reproduced in *TBLY*, no. 16, 1999
31 ibid.

Not that they ever rose before . . . It's just like a sort of document of a revolution that could happen – like somebody writing a book about what would have happened if the Nazis had invaded Britain.'[32]

During November The Fall went on the road to promote *Grotesque* (although typically the set was dominated by new material not on the album). The last two dates of the year took place at Acklam Hall in Notting Hill on 11–12 December, supported by Furious Pigs and the Hamsters. The first night's performance was recorded and later issued in 1982 by Chaos Tapes as *The Fall Live In London 1980* (aka *Live At Acklam Hall*), a cassette-only release limited to four thousand copies. Based in East Anglia, Chaos Tapes had already released live tapes of 'Punk's not dead' bands like Discharge, Anti-Pasti and Vice Squad. 'They said they wanted to put it out and we thought it was the second night, the good night, and said yeah,' said Smith, 'but it was the first night.' Smith admitted it was unpolished: 'Yeah, it's raw but it's a good laugh. We were trying out the stuff from *Slates* for the first time so it is rough. Like, that's the idea of this – to break the backs of all these twats who tape new numbers at our gigs. 'Cos we play new stuff into our set quick it doesn't take 'em long to realize they can tape a gig and put them out before the album's released.'[33]

The gigs were a good way to end a productive year. The band came tenth in the Best Group readers' poll in *NME* (top was the Jam, second was Joy Division) and had four tracks in John Peel's Festive Fifty.[34] Signs of a new professionalism can be read into Smith and Carroll's decision to hire a professional publicist for the first time, namely Versa Manos, and her public relations company Vice Versa. Perhaps it was Manos who secured Smith a commission to write an end-of-the-year piece for *NME*. Smith's subject matter included Dexys Midnight Runners and their quest for the 'young soul rebels' ('This was the year the precincts filled up with young crims who hate the Dexys even though they're the people being searched for'); New Romantic fashions ('The toughs now dress like '30s faggots'); being outspoken in 'hard times' ('This was the year of SHUT YOUR RAP LAD DONT YOU KNOW THESE ARE HARD TIMES?!?'); and the proliferating number of youth cults ('Middlesboro, Saturday night – five hundred

32 Andy Gill, 'The Wit and Wisdom of Mark Smith', *NME*, 10 January 1981
33 X. Moore, 'After the "Gram" ', *NME*, 3 April 1982
34 Anon., 'Readers' Poll '80', 24 January 1981

people and ten fashions from football fans to students, no applause, the audience was arguing within their own cults'). Smith also confessed to starting an A level English course and discovering people he didn't know existed: 'The drinking of the cursed classes kept us clever asses sneering at the literate classes! Go see 'em!'[35]

However, despite the band's high profile in the music press and four critically acclaimed albums, the band was still taking home just £30 a week. Smith not surprisingly remained disillusioned about the record industry: 'You can't attack the system by opting out of it, which is what earlier members of the band did. When it wasn't going their way they just copped out. Not because they hated playing the guitar any more, which is what it's all about, but they'd rather play the guitar at home, than get into all these hassles.' The Fall opted in but on its own terms and Smith was smart enough to see that there was room for mavericks, indeed the music industry needed people like Smith to keep it from stagnating: 'The record industry needs The Fall like it needs oil, it needs us a lot more than it needs the streamlined bands.'[36]

35   Mark E. Smith, 'Message From The Fall', *NME*, 20 December 1980
36   Bob Giddens, 'Hobgoblins on the Loose', *Zig-Zag*, June 1980

6

Male Slags, Slates and Tapes, 1981

Early this year, things were too gruesome to behold for this writer –
The Fall had been diluted into part of an almost Betrayal environment; anti-fashion schtick, backs to the audience mate, pass us the
hair dye wack – Mere Grubby Pseuds making capital out of The Fall
sweat and pre-cog.[1]

By 1981, the effects of Margaret Thatcher's first term as prime
minister, with her policies of monetarism and cut-backs in public-
sector spending, meant that unemployment grew at an alarming rate
(from 5.7 per cent in 1979 to 13.4 per cent in 1982). Meanwhile in
America President Ronald Reagan pumped millions of dollars into the
military as nuclear war with Russia once again became a distinct
possibility. Throughout Britain, musicians such as Paul Weller and
the Stranglers, vocally supported anti-nuclear demonstrations
organized by the Campaign for Nuclear Disarmament (CND). In
the summer of 1981, the first of what would become an annual
pilgrimage to the Glastonbury Festival began. Political issues featured
regularly in the music press and teenagers and their music became
increasingly politicized. Interviewers often questioned musicians
about their political beliefs and Smith was no exception. Speaking to
Andy Gill, he expounded on the effects of the recession (then termed
'hard times') and what he thought was the necessary response: 'I *want*
to be didactic. I *want* to be opinionated. I don't think because we're
having a fucking hard time everybody should stop having opinions
and start getting into good-time stuff. I think people in hard times
need brain stimulation more than at *any* time.'[2]

As 1981 unfolded, its politically transitional nature became apparent
and residual leftist attitudes from the seventies were overtaken by the
new eighties' creed of possessive individualism: in cinema, the realism

---

1   Smith's sleeve notes for 'Lie Dream Of A Casino Soul', released November 1981
2   Andy Gill, 'The Wit and Wisdom of Mark Smith', *NME*, 10 January 1981

of *The Long Good Friday* became the nostalgia of *Chariots of Fire* and on television the cynical leftism of *The History Man* became the fetishization of wealth and privilege in *Brideshead Revisited*. The pop tarts of the New Romantic movement – Depeche Mode, Japan, Duran Duran, Spandau Ballet – encapsulated the increasingly dominant escapist spirit of the times. By the summer of 1981 the charts reverberated with the synthesized sound of Soft Cell's 'Tainted Love' and the Human League's breakthrough hit 'Love Action' (followed in October by the phenomenally successful album, *Dare*). Even Scritti Politti, a previously hard-core political band, dumbfounded its loyal fan base and embarked on a journey to chart success with 'The "Sweetest Girl" '. Rearguard action, but hardly effective, came in the form of Heaven 17's '(We Don't Need This) Fascist Groove Thang', a political message scatter-gunned over the heads of a heaving dance floor. Smith's political opinions, as represented in countless music press interviews, remained intentionally provocative. In 1981, he declared an élitist belief that the intellectual minority should be subsidized by the masses – 'I'm a firm believer in the 80% subsidizing the 20%' – and it was perfectly clear on which side of the equation Smith saw himself.[3] In many ways he conformed to the stereotype of the working-class Tory supporter; someone who hated Thatcher and yet admired her 'guts' and who had difficulty identifying with a Labour party led by the well-meaning but ineffective Michael Foot.

The Fall started this tempestuous year on 15 January with a gig at the reopened Rafters in Manchester. The set was notable for the first appearance of 'Winter', a slow-tempo'd meditative song that showcased the band's growing fluency. A few days after the gig, Edwin Pouncey visited Smith and Carroll at their 'creaking flat' in Prestwich. Smith, in an upbeat mood, spoke confidently about his band's abilities: 'The Fall could go out without me and just play instrumentals and it would still be fucking good.' Carroll thought the band's potential was so great it was difficult to know what to do next: 'It's like trying to find your own personal vein when you've got twenty-five million of them, which one to choose? The Fall are getting very spiritual to me at the moment, very Third Ear Bandist.'[4]

3 ibid.
4 Edwin Pouncey, 'The Prestwich Horror and Other Strange Stories', *Sounds*, 31 January 1981

The link to the early seventies acoustic improvisers probably meant nothing to the hundreds of young post-punk fans that followed The Fall on its January and February tour. For some, though, familiarity was beginning to breed contempt. Kirsty McNeill warned that with his 'safe, cult following' and regular indie chart success, Smith was 'dangerously close to making a career out of this routine'.[5] A bootleg video of the band playing on 17 March at Leeds University reveals Smith spending much of the gig with his back to the audience, singing to the drums, hunched over various lyric sheets, chewing gum and shaking the mike like it was a maraca. The gig's high point is the première of 'Hip Priest', a talismanic song containing a description of an *alter ego* that in various forms – later as 'Big New Priest' – would accompany Smith throughout his career.

Prole Art Threat

Although scheduled for release in mid-April, distribution of *Slates* was delayed until the start of May. The production team almost outnumbered the band, with assistance at the mixing desk from Adrian Sherwood, Geoff Travis and Grant Showbiz. Smith's plan was to stay one step ahead of imitators by allowing a more polished production of The Fall sound to emerge: 'It's the first time I've ever let anyone else do the production.'[6] The intention was to cut just two tracks but the band's productivity at this time proved untameable and six tracks were recorded. The resulting ten-inch record resided unhappily somewhere between a maxi-single and a mini-album. According to the BPI, the record industry's governing body, to qualify as a single a record could not contain more than four tracks and to qualify as an album it must retail above a minimum of £2.49. With its six tracks and retailing at, as the cover said, 'two pounds only u skinny rats', *Slates* as a format effectively did not exist and would not appear in the official charts.[7] It did, however, appear in *Record Business*'s independent singles chart, reaching number three, a creditable position considering it was competing with records half its price.

5   Kirsty McNeill, 'The Fall, Glasgow', *NME*, 7 March 1981
6   Barney Hoskyns, 'Hip Priest: The Mark Smith Interview', *NME*, 14 November 1981
7   Paolo Hewitt, 'All Fall Down in the Charts', *Melody Maker*, 2 May 1981

Smith labelled side one 'OBJ' and side two 'SUBJ'. He intended the former as an objective report on reality and the latter as a subjective and personal vision of an inner world. It's difficult, though, to take these demarcations seriously as Smith's writing style remained elliptical throughout, collating realistic elements, such as snippets of overheard conversation, with surreal characters, like the 'Man With Chip' in 'Prole Art Threat'. The subject of the opening track, 'Middle Mass', was equally ambiguous: partly a disquisition on the increasing power of the middle classes – 'evil is not in extremes, it's in the middle mass' – and partly a piss-take of Marc Riley. Riley later confronted Smith about the lyrics: 'It's a great song, but it does cut through me when I listen to it. I went up to him one day in the studio and said it's about me this song, isn't it? And he started fumbling and said, "Oh no, it's about somebody else called Marc." My respect for him went right down. I always stand by what I write. Having said all that, Smith is one of the best lyricists that I've ever encountered.'[8] 'Older Lover', with its insistent rhythm and simple guitar riff, creates a minimal foundation upon which Smith sings about tiring of older lovers. 'Prole Art Threat' refers to working-class culture and its supposed threat to the 'wet lib' type who rides 'third class on a one-class train'. Smith later explained that the song started out as a play about a commuter who 'flips out on leftism and gets caught up with MI5 and all that. I just compressed it and made more of a joke about it.'

Side two, the subjective side, opens with the bright and breezy 'Fit And Working Again' but is followed by the more strenuous work-out, 'Slates, Slags, Etc.', a bitter listing of all that's wrong and bad in the Smith universe, from 'plagarization' to 'academic thingys' who 'ream off names of books and bands'. The final track, 'Leave The Capitol', on one level apparently 'relates time warps and encounters in Victorian Vampiric London', but is more obviously a distillation of Smith's hatred of London.[9] Smith never did like the capital: 'I think it's a secret fear that I wouldn't be as good if I was living in London. I don't get as hassled up in Manchester as I do there. When I'm in London I feel like how a madman would feel. Like there's people whispering behind me back all the time when I go out. They never come up to me.'[10]

8   Jimmy Dare, 'Riley', *Debris*, no. 6, January 1985
9   Smith, in press release for US tour, summer 1981
10 Ron Rom, 'Semi-detached Suburban Mr Smith', *Sounds*, 19 July 1986

The predominantly London-based music press didn't take it personally and continued to shower the band with praise. Ian Pye thought *Slates* was 'six tracks of hectoring madness',[11] while Andy Gill memorably described Smith's subject as 'mini-operas, maybe, small scenarios of life confused with fantasy, rough-hewn, sore and scabby blocks of narrative, comment, invective and the like, scrambled up and spat out in gobs'.[12] Amazingly it was Smith's own record company, Rough Trade, that provided the most persistent and unwelcome criticism. 'They'd go, Er, the tea boy doesn't like the fact that you've slagged off Wah! Heat on this number,' recalled Smith. 'And fuckin' . . . the girl who cooks the fuckin' rice in the canteen doesn't like the fact that you've used the word "slags". They had a whole meeting over the fact that we mentioned guns in one song. Y'know . . . it is not the policy of Rough Trade to be supporting fuckin' . . . And I'd go, What the fuck has it got to do with you? Just fuckin' sell the record you fuckin' hippy.'[13]

Smith was justly proud of *Slates* and thought it could have been a much more influential record, because of its innovative format and content, if Rough Trade had promoted it more forcefully.[14] Smith also claimed that Rough Trade could not handle the band's success, had 'no fuckin' taste' and was 'just a bunch of, like, commune people'.[15] They would never press enough records, distribution was poor and the marketing strategy dictated against sending review copies to daily newspapers in favour of obscure left-wing magazines. When he complained, they accused him of selling out: 'If they'd been a big label and gave me £50,000 then I might've let them have a say.'[16] But they were not and so the band left Rough Trade and signed to a fresh start-up label, Kamera, run by Saul Galpern, better known later as managing director of Suede's label, Nude. Kamera was a completely unknown quantity but given the sparsity of its roster, Galpern could at least guarantee The Fall his full attention.

11 Ian Pye, 'The Fall: *Slates*', *Melody Maker*, 2 May 1981
12 Andy Gill, 'Gruff, Tumble and Fall Boys', *NME*, 2 May 1981
13 David Cavanagh, 'The Fall', *Volume*, no. 4, September 1992
14 Edwin Pouncey, 'Rough Justice', *Sounds*, 9 June 1984
15 Smith, interviewed on 2 December 1982 for *Allied Propaganda*, reproduced in *TBLY*, no. 19, 2000
16 George Kay, 'The Fall of Slick, Mark E. Smith's Enduction Hour', *Rip It Up*, September 1982

'Mark and I went to Saul's home and hung out with him,' said Carroll. 'I think Versa introduced him to me. We were his first band on the Kamera label and although he appeared to be a bit of a "Jack the Lad" character I remember Mark liked him.'

With a new label confirmed, The Fall embarked on its first proper European tour, taking in the Netherlands and Germany, and a substantial American tour. Once again Paul Hanley stayed at home, primarily to work on his A levels but also because of American work-permit complications. In his place, The Fall's prodigal son, Karl Burns, returned. Since the end of 1978 Burns had practised his trade in a variety of bands. The first was the Teardrops, a group which included in its various line-ups the Buzzcocks' Steve Garvey and ex-bass player with The Fall, Eric McGann. In January 1979, the Teardrops released a twelve-inch EP, *In And Out Of Fashion*, on Bok Bok Records.[17] The band's one album, appropriately entitled *Final Vinyl*, was released in June 1980 on Illuminated, with Dave Price on vocals, Garvey on guitar and Burns on drums. Later in June, the same trio, renamed Bok Bok but still playing its Buzzcocks-inspired power pop, released a single 'Come Back To Me'. Along with turning out for the Tear-drops, Burns also briefly joined The Passage and, even more briefly, Public Image, staying just long enough to record one track with them, the B-side 'And No Birds Do Sing', on the June 1979 single 'Death Disco'. Rumour has it he left the band after John Lydon and Keith Levene set fire to his shirt with lighter fuel while he was asleep.[18] Next stop for Burns was touring with John Cooper Clarke and playing drums on his excellent 1980 album *Snap, Crackle and Bop*. Despite these diversions, Burns's spiritual home remained The Fall and the prospect of almost three months of touring fun and mayhem proved just too good an opportunity to miss.

The European leg of the tour went smoothly and The Fall opened in America on 31 May in Oklahoma City. Over the next month and a half the band followed a tough schedule playing approximately thirty gigs. Some tracks were captured on the live album *A Part of America Therein, 1981* released on the US Cottage label in 1982. The back-cover photograph commemorated a personal highlight for

---

17 Ian Wood, 'Record News', *New Manchester Review*, no. 73, 26 January–8 February 1979
18 Barry Lazell, 'Info Riot', *Sounds*, 23 March 1985

Carroll and Smith, a visit to The King's house at Graceland. On reflection the tour pleased Smith, the only downside being a support slot with the Clash in New York. The two bands represented for Smith 'the real and the plastic'. The Fall's set ended when the Clash, disliking what they heard and sensing the audience's, they thought, misplaced enthusiasm, ordered that the PA be turned off. Afterwards, Joe Strummer came up to Smith: 'Hi, you're Mark Smith, you can't stand to talk to me, can you?' Smith felt sorry for him: 'He's a nice bloke but just irresponsible.' Strummer, according to Smith, was perpetrating a major crime by selling out his country: 'England is where all the real art in the world comes from but I don't want this to come from all these rich English bands pretending to be cockneys, it's not on. The Clash were really selling this plastic England, they looked like English minstrels it was just embarrassing.'[19]

Smith was particularly proud of the way The Fall handled audiences in out-of-the-way places. 'Those kids in the Midwest have got no preconceptions,' Smith said, 'so you're taken on your true worth. We got a lot of cat calls, but it was like starting all over again. It was great.'[20] Inevitably, some in the audience were bemused by the lyrics. 'Sometimes we'd get really straight guys,' said Smith, 'businessmen in Hawaiian shirts and they'd be standing there and really listening and I'd be singing about Wigan Casino or something.'[21] Whereas on the last trip Smith had hooked up with the LA underground, on this trip he enjoyed the company of the Memphis scene and more specifically the Panther Burns led by Tav Falco and ex-Big Star guitarist Alex Chilton.

One song played most nights during the tour was 'N.W.R.A.'. It became particularly relevant as news filtered through about the riots taking place back home in England. Reading the American press, Smith was convinced that England was on the brink of revolution: 'They went over the top as usual and I just panicked. I thought, "Christ, the North has risen at last and here's me sitting in Atlanta." I ran out to find the nearest paper shop but in America it was like six miles away.'[22] At Chicago the compère warmed up the audience by

19 Mick Middles, 'Back from the Slates', *Sounds*, 5 September 1981
20 Hoskyns, op. cit., 14 November 1981
21 Middles, op. cit., 5 September 1981
22 ibid.

ostentatiously introducing The Fall as being 'from the riot-torn streets of Manchester, England'.

This particular spate of civil unrest started in April when major rioting broke out in Brixton, London, after a particularly provocative police initiative called 'Operation Swamp' which involved large numbers of police randomly stopping and searching predominantly young black men. In July, while The Fall was in America, riots started in Toxteth, Liverpool and Southall, West London. Inspired by television coverage and similar complaints against violent policing methods and deteriorating social conditions, rioting took place throughout the country, including Moss Side, Manchester. Smith's opinions on the upheavals were broadcast on KPFA, a San Francisco radio station: 'I think it's pretty good, especially where I'm from, Manchester, it's great. It should have happened a hundred years ago as far as I'm concerned.' He singled out Thatcher as the main instigator: ' . . . she's an antagonist, that's where she's good really. But people voted her in for their own greed, all looking at rewards.'[23] On return to England he expected to find the country in a state of emergency, but instead the moment of crisis had passed, for the time being at least: 'I was really disappointed but really the rioting has eased a lot of tension in Manchester. It was horrible just before we went away but now everyone seems loose.'[24]

It's not the Dylan part that matters – it's the truck part

With Burns once again back in the band, The Fall had a problem. Who would be kept on as drummer: him or Paul Hanley? Smith's unconventional solution was to keep them both on, with Burns's technical ability complementing Paul Hanley's self-taught style (he later stated his main drumming influences as Ringo Starr, Topper Headon, Karl Burns and Stoker, drummer for Dexys Midnight Runners).[25] There were precedents for two-drummer line-ups, including Gary Glitter and more recently Adam and the Ants. In midsummer, the new line-up headed off on a three-date trip to

23 Smith, on KPFA, San Francisco, broadcast 10 July 1981
24 Middles, op. cit., 5 September 1981
25 Mark Prindle. 'Paul Hanley – 2002', email interview from: http://www.mark prindle.com/hanley-i.htm

Reykjavik in Iceland supported by Purkurr Pilnikk. It was here that Smith heard about Megas Jonsson and fell down flat in the Café Iol. In Hljorite, Reykjavik, the band recorded 'Look, Know', 'Hip Priest' and 'Iceland', the latter written from scratch in the studio. Following the group was Colin Irwin of *Melody Maker* and he later described how 'Iceland' was recorded. 'Is he going to sing?' asked the engineer, Tony Sutcliffe. Grant Showbiz went off to look for Smith. On his return he said: 'He's going to play a cassette first, and then he's going to sing.' The tape of whistling wind started up and Smith began his vocals: 'A plate steel object was fired and I did not feel for my compatriots.' Later Riley was ecstatic about the results. 'No, we didn't know what he was going to do either,' he explained to Irwin. 'He just said he needed a tune, something Dylanish, and we knocked around on the piano in the studio and came up with that. But we hadn't heard the words until he suddenly did them.'[26]

Smith's fame continued to grow and in August he contributed to the *NME*'s 'Portrait of the Artist as a Consumer'.[27] The feature had started earlier in the year and had already included Siouxsie Sioux and Bono (favourite book? – 'The Bible'). As would be expected from an autodidact, Smith's list proved wilfully diverse and at times obscure. His favourite fiction included *A Small Town in Germany* by John Le Carré, *A Scanner Darkly* by Philip K. Dick, *The Sirens of Titan* by Kurt Vonnegut Jr, *The Deer Park* by Norman Mailer, *The Black Room* and *Ritual in the Dark* by Colin Wilson, *Cogan's Trade* by George V. Higgins and *At the Mountains of Madness* by H.P. Lovecraft. Non-fiction favourites included *Gulcher* by Richard Meltzer, *Beyond Good and Evil* by Frederick Nietzsche, *US Civil War Handbook* by William H. Price, *True Crime Weekly* and *Private Eye*. Two fictional books were also included: ' "How I Created Modern Music", D. McCullough (a weekly serial)' and ' "Fibs About M. E. Smith" by J. Cope (a pamphlet)'.

As 'artists' he appreciated Wyndham Lewis, Malcolm Allison (the recently sacked manager of Manchester City), Virgin Prunes and 'The Worst live, Manchester, Dec. '77.' His selected films were surprisingly high-brow and included Visconti's *The Damned*, Polanski's *Macbeth* (with soundtrack by Third Ear Band) and Fellini's

26   Colin Irwin, 'The Decline and Fall in Iceland', *Melody Maker*, 26 September 1981
27   Mark E. Smith, 'Portrait of the Artist as a Consumer', *NME*, 15 August 1981

Roma. More mainstream selections were Ray Milland's *The Man with X-Ray Eyes* and *The Lost Weekend*, Jack Lemmon's *Days of Wine and Roses*, Albert Finney's *Charlie Bubbles* and Mel Brooks's *High Anxiety*. Television favourites were just the Aussie drama *Bluey* and John Cleese advertisements.

His favourite music included works by Peter Hammill, Johnny Cash, Der Plan (a Berlin-based group with lead vocalist Moritz Rrr), Alternative TV, the Los Angeles group Fear and the Panther Burns. Albums worthy of mention were *Take No Prisoners* by Lou Reed, *God Save The Queen* by the Sex Pistols, *Raw And Alive* by the Seeds, *Radio City* by Philip Johnson and *We're Only In It For The Money* by the Mothers of Invention. Smith was also a fan of Greg Shaw's *Pebbles* series of compilation albums (a not-to-distant descendent of the original *Nuggets* series that featured American mid-sixties psychedelic garage bands). *Nuggets* and *Pebbles* would eventually come to provide the blueprint for The Fall's 'garage' sound of the eighties and nineties. From these records you could get to hear original versions of 'Mr Pharmacist' by the Other Half, 'Incense and Peppermints' by Strawberry Alarm Clock and 'Strychnine' by the Sonics, plus tracks by the Seeds, the Monks, the Third Bardo and the Driving Stupid. One cassette Smith never went anywhere without was his *16 Greatest Truck Driver Hits*, with its classic tracks 'How Fast Them Trucks Can Go' by Claude Gray, 'Widow Maker' by Jimmy Martin and 'Truck Drivin' Man' by Hylo Brown. Meltzer, at least, was impressed by Smith's enthusiasm for trucker music: 'He played me a cassette of songs about trucks by some actual trucker trying hard to sound like Dylan ("It's not the Dylan part that matters – it's the truck part").'[28]

His favourite comedians were Lenny Bruce, Bernard Manning, 'all Ian Curtis derivatives' and Alan Pellay. As a drag queen, Pellay (aka Alana Pellay and Lana Pellay) was probably the last person you would expect to find as part of The Fall's entourage at this time. But Smith and Carroll had befriended him after seeing his act at the Devonshire Hotel, Ardwick, with his friend Andy Zero. 'We were expecting some punk poet or musician,' recalled Carroll. 'Andy didn't really say what his act was. Well, when Alan hit the stage we found out – he was a drag queen and a female impersonator and he was awesome.

28   Richard Meltzer, *A Whore Just Like All the Rest: The Music Writings of Richard Meltzer*, USA: De Capo Press, 2000

After the show, the make up and wigs came off and he came over and had a drink with us. He was obviously gay and way out of the closet. I adored Alan, he was incredibly funny and didn't give a shit what people thought of him.' Pellay described Smith at this time as a 'young lad with greasy hair, a few spots and a carrier bag. There was something very endearing about him, an aura. We cultivated a friendship.'[29] Pellay's independent mind and lifestyle endeared him to Smith and Carroll and he was occasionally invited to open for The Fall with his camped-up Shirley Bassey-style performances. 'The audience and the media didn't know what to make of it,' said Carroll, 'but that was the intention, we wanted to push their posingness into their faces, and Alan certainly did achieve that for us, I think.'

Pellay had been part of the Ranch scene in 1977 where he met Foo Foo Lamarr and Andy Zero: 'It wasn't unusual,' Carroll said, 'to see those "Dresden dolls" dancing next to transvestites and/or drag queens. Without Foo Foo I don't think the Manchester scene would have been so creatively strong and lasting.' In the eighties, Pellay moved down to London to further his acting career, most notably as part of the Comic Strip team. The last time Carroll saw him, he helped her prepare for a meeting with Geoff Travis by making her up to look like Bette Davis: 'Alan was a genius with make-up. Yeah, I really did look like Bette. When I walked into Rough Trade, nobody recognized me and when they did it was shock and disbelief. I really think they thought I had lost it, but I stayed in character and the meeting went fine.'

In October, The Fall embarked on another UK tour. After warm-up gigs at Fagin's, Manchester and North London Polytechnic, it began properly at the New Regent in Brighton and ventured up as far north as Edinburgh and as far south as Plymouth before finishing on 6 November at the Imperial Cinema, Birmingham, co-headlining with ex-Velvets starlet Nico. New songs introduced on this tour included 'Just Step S'ways', 'Session Musician' and 'Stars on 45', a medley of 'I'm into CB', 'Fiery Jack' and the kazoo riff from 'New Face In Hell'. The bulk of the material came from recent and forthcoming singles, *Slates* and unrecorded tracks that would eventually appear on *Hex Enduction Hour.*

29 Cath Carroll, 'Silicone Chip', *NME*, 22 June 1985

Also in November Smith received what for some would have represented the ultimate accolade, the absolute incontrovertible evidence of finally 'making it': he was the cover star of the *NME*. The photograph by Anton Corbijn of Smith, with his floppy fringe, sallow cheeks and bulging eyes, was captioned, 'The Fall, the rise of Citizen Smith'. Barney Hoskyns wrote the feature article as a follow-up to an extensive and insightful review of a recent gig at North London Polytechnic. In this Hoskyns had written that The Fall had re-invented the clichés of Northern and working-class culture and now revelled in 'the *shit* of proletarianism'. A Fall concert was inescapably political not because Smith wrote *about* particular subjects and issues but because he dramatized them: cultural contradictions were highlighted rather than ignored or glossed over. Smith's subject, according to Hoskyns, was nothing less than the 'death of the working class and the destruction of the "traditions" it has maintained to justify the wrongs it has suffered'.[30]

The subsequent feature article provided Hoskyns with more space to expand on these themes. This was the early eighties and rock journalism was, for some at least, an intellectual vocation. Hoskyns opened with a quote from the French philosopher Jacques Derrida talking about the need for an 'implacable sobriety in the work of destruction'. Sober, however, would never be a word to describe anything about The Fall. More successful was Hoskyns's comparison of The Fall's 'prole pop' with folk music's oral tradition and narrative structure. For Hoskyns it was mostly a question of authenticity: 'They show up virtually the whole of the rest of rock as a gross, illusory hype.'[31]

The Fall's authenticity was in full working order for the mid-November release of 'Lie Dream Of A Casino Soul', the first single for the Kamera label. You only have to compare it to the contemporary romanticism of Dexys Midnight Runners' *Searching for the Young Soul Rebels* to see what Hoskyns meant. With production by Richard Mazda and the two-drummer line-up, The Fall sound had gained the weight and momentum of an articulated lorry. 'Lie Dream' dated from the beginning of the year but had taken on added poignancy in

---

30 Barney Hoskyns, 'Anti-social Workers: The Fall, North London Poly', *NME*, 31 October 1981

31 Hoskyns, op. cit., 14 November 1981

September when the spiritual centre of British Northern Soul, Wigan Casino, closed down. Rather than being a straightforward critique of the fanatical Northern soul scene, the song actually grew out of Smith's admiration for the all-nighters. 'It was just the story of one person growing out of that thing,' said Smith. 'Some felt that I was slagging that whole attitude which it wasn't at all. It's a great shame that it needs an interview to explain that.'[32] Smith had been brought up on a diet of Northern soul and many of his most loyal fans were soul boys. 'There are actually a lot of old soul boys who like The Fall,' Smith said, 'because that music was always offbeat and it gives them a feeling for the sort of wackiness that you find in our music. It's really funny because Dexys bust a gut trying to attract that audience and never even got close. All the kids I know just thought it was pathetic 'cause they were wearing the clothes they'd been wearing six years ago and ripping off all these horn riffs that they knew off by heart from the originals.'[33]

At the end of the year there was plenty of evidence of the band's growing popularity. Four tracks made Peel's Festive Fifty and the band came fourth in the 'Best Group' category in the *NME*'s readers' poll, behind the Jam, Echo and the Bunnymen and Human League.[34] The Fall's last gig of the year took place on 7 December at the Venue, London, supported by the up-and-coming Welsh band, the Alarm. One particular song premièred that night was 'The Classical'. Over the next few days the band retreated to the Regal Cinema in Hitchen, to record what for many is still considered The Fall's masterpiece album.

32 John Wilde, 'The Fall Guy', *Zig-Zag*, November 1983
33 Don Watson, 'Looking at The Fall Guise', *NME*, 1 October 1983
34 Anon., 'NME Readers' Poll 1981', *NME*, 30 January 1982

Who Makes the Nazis? 1982

I'm proud of me nationality, yeah, and proud to be Mancunian, and if something was threatening either of these issues I'd bloody well do something about it.[1]

From the opening line of 'The Classical' – 'There is no culture is my brag' – to the 'no fucking respite' of 'And This Day', *Hex Enduction Hour* grabs you and just doesn't let you go. Released in March 1982, it was produced by Richard Mazda and Grant Showbiz, with Smith throwing his usual spanner into the works. 'I was trying to rough it up,' he said. 'It worked well. What I'm going for is a well-produced noise thing. Not like bringing out the obvious things, but bringing out everything, bringing out the distortion and producing it well.'[2] *Hex Enduction Hour* brought out everything, everything that was great about The Fall. The press release highlighted the band's satirical intent, but beyond that did little to explain what the songs were about ('have a bleedin' guess', as the album cover says). Just as Smith intended, it was more than advertising copy, it was more like 'a piece of writing in itself'.[3] Smith's cover art for *Hex Enduction Hour* took the graffiti idea to its logical conclusion with its cackling one-liners: 'Suits off, jeans on', 'Chummy lifestyle', 'Hail Sainsbury's!', 'Nukey Boers', etc. 'I like the cover to reflect what's inside,' Smith said. 'I think rock artwork has gone right down the drain – I do all my own. Like, I love all those misspelt posters – a graphic designer would never get it right in years! My attitude to the sleeve is the same as my attitude to music.'[4]

On the opening track, 'The Classical', Smith tells us there is no culture, makes a reference to 'obligatory niggers' and shouts accusingly, 'Hey there, fuckface!' twice. Then it's straight into 'Jawbone and the Air-Rifle', a song about a rabbit-killer who out hunting one night 'lets out a misplaced shot' and takes on the curse (or hex) of the Broken

1 Helen Fitzgerald, 'The Fall', *Masterbag*, no. 18, Autumn 1982
2 Smith, talking to Richard Skinner on *Rock On* for BBC Radio One 1982, transcript in *TBLY*, no. 6, July 1996
3 Edwin Pouncey, 'Creek Show', *Sounds*, 28 September 1985
4 Sandy Robertson, 'Hex Education', *Sounds*, 8 May 1982

Brothers Pentacle Church. The economy with which Smith describes the rabbit-killer and the woe in his life is characterization of the highest order. The tempo then slows for 'Hip Priest', a Smith *alter ego* down to his 'last clean dirty shirt' and fed up with not being 'appreciated'.[5] 'Fortress' describes doing time with 'four left-wing kids' in a BBC studio, here described as a 'Nazi Fortress'. In 'Deer Park', Smith transferred Norman Mailer's tale of corruption in the American film industry to the London music scene, dismissed here as 'Subculture, art-dealer jerk off' while in 'Mere Pseud Mag. Ed.' he vilifies someone whose 'brain was in his arse'. In the press release, Smith described 'Winter' as 'a tale concerning an insane child who is taken over by a spirit from the mind of a cooped-up alcoholic'. 'Just Step S'ways' offers advice on escaping 'this futurist world today' and answers, 'Who Makes the Nazis?' with a list that includes 'Intellectual half-wits' and 'Buffalo lips on toast, smiling'. 'Iceland' provides a melancholic calm before the crashing waves of 'And This Day', an epic onslaught of trouncing drum and fairground organ shards topped by the whipped-up spume of Smith's vitriol. It had been twenty-five minutes long but was edited down to the ten minutes needed to make the album exactly one hour long – the *Hex Enduction Hour*.

The album could hardly have been better received. Colin Irwin in *Melody Maker* thought it was 'incredibly exciting and utterly compelling'[6] and Richard Cook in *NME* considered it 'their masterpiece to date'.[7] One listener, Mark Storace of heavy-metal band Krokus, was not so impressed: 'The whole album is just one long downer . . . Giving this album to me to review is like giving a watch-repairer a guitar and expecting him to be able to do something with it.'[8] The review was part of a feature in *Flexipop!* magazine where musicians reviewed each other's albums. Smith's reading of Krokus's *One Vice At A Time* showed slightly more sympathy: 'If strapped down, gimme this any day, as opposed to more Sheffield synth Puffs, self-pitying punks or the latest blonde girl Proving Her Point.'[9] Despite Storace's

---

5 'Hip Priest' later featured on the soundtrack of the film *The Silence of the Lambs*.

6 Colin Irwin, 'The Manic Maze', *Melody Maker*, 6 March 1982

7 Richard Cook, 'These Fallish Things: The Fall, *Hex Enduction Hour*', *NME*, 13 March 1982

8 Mark E. Smith and Mark Storace, 'View from the Top', *Flexipop!*, no. 17, March 1982

9 ibid.

criticism, *Hex Enduction Hour* became the first album by The Fall to get into the mainstream chart, reaching the dizzy heights of number 71. It fared better in the indie chart, but was kept off the number one spot by the soul/funk sextet Pigbag's first album *Dr Heckle and Mr Jive*.

Do y'know what you look like before you go out?

The Fall promoted the album with a two-month tour, starting in mid-March at Bristol Polytechnic. One stand-out gig took place at Hammersmith Palais with support from the energetic Nick Cave and his band The Birthday Party. The Fall's productivity remained un-diminished and new songs written and test-driven during the tour were 'Solicitor In Studio', 'Kicker Conspiracy', 'Backdrop' and 'Tempo House'. The Britain they toured suffered from debilitating unemployment, with the three million mark being passed in January. This was the year of the ground-breaking television drama *Boys from the Blackstuff* and the founding of the peace camps at Greenham Common and Molesworth. Support for Thatcher and her Conserv-ative government was being severely tested, not least by the recently founded Social Democratic party and its alliance with the Liberals. These domestic problems were temporarily swept aside, however, when on 2 April, General Galtieri of Argentina launched an invasion of the Falkland Islands. By the time his forces surrendered in mid-June, 255 British and 720 Argentine troops had lost their lives.

With all this social strife and international conflict the media's continued fascination with fashion and clothes mystified Smith. At the height of the war with Argentina, The Fall released the single 'Look, Know' in which Smith proudly claims to not 'give a shit' what he looks like – he has 'a wash and that's enough'. It was the start of the narcissistic 'designer decade', with fashion labels from Armani to Lacoste sought-after symbols of identity for style-conscious youth encouraged by magazines such as the recently started *The Face*. Because of his healthy scepticism about fashion, Smith steered clear of this world, particularly that part which attempted to combine a wantonly consumerist message with social and political critique: 'I mistrust glossy magazines that go on about equality and oppression and all that shit,' he said. '*The Face* wouldn't cover us for years because we didn't have an image, because I wore a bloody anorak. They only cover fashion people and that to me is prejudice. Cocktail socialism I call it.'[10] The B-side, 'I'm Into CB', was equally sarcastic although this time the satirical swipe was against the UK's CB (Citizen's Band) radio enthusiasts.

Paul Du Noyer made it Single of the Week in the *NME*, saying it showed The Fall at its 'brilliant best'.[11] The reviewer for *Melody Maker*, however, was not so appreciative: 'Mickey Most could get a better sound on a Laskey's £15 cassette recorder with his toupee on backwards. Even "OTT" get pretentious about this "North", "*Coronation Street*", "Repetition-ah" (delete) consciousness. B-side has Under-23 International Smith belatedly jumping on CB band-wagon with song about some idiot who doesn't "know" who he is. "Alienating", "Repulsive", *Bury Times* Mid-Weeker.'[12] Ever his harshest critic, it was Smith reviewing himself.

Despite Smith's indifference, or maybe because of it, the band's fashionable credentials just kept on accumulating. The audiences increased, as did the number of journalists seeking pearls of Smith's wisdom: the band was in serious danger of becoming popular. 'We were everybody's darlings,' Smith complained, 'we'd had a big up-surge, big audiences that we'd never had. I'd had enough of it.' The time seemed perfect to run away from it all. How about a tour of Australia and New Zealand? 'It was good to get away for a bit,' said Smith. 'We realized the value of Britain again after that.'[13] They were invited over by Ken West and 'Helene', manager of Sydney's Stranded venue. Both were flushed with the recent success of an Australian tour with The Birthday Party. The tour started for The Fall at the end of July at West Town Hall, Geelong, Australia, and ended about a month later in Auckland, New Zealand. Two sets would eventually be released as live albums – *Live To Air In Melbourne* and *Fall In A Hole* – with both capturing a confident band and a singer unafraid of the occasional comical ad-lib. In the sleeve notes for *Fall In A Hole* Steve Hanley reported that the tour started like many tours by The Fall ended, 'with fights, black eyes and a missing drummer. Karl Burns always did have trouble trying to leave England.' Apparently Burns's passport was stolen during the last US tour and its replacement

10   Richard Lowe, 'Fall Out', *The Hit*, October 1985
11   Paul Du Noyer, 'The Fall: "Look, Know" / "I'm Into CB" ', *NME*, 24 April 1982
12   Mark E. Smith, 'Prole in Art Threat Horror', *Melody Maker*, 1 May 1982
13   Richard Cook, 'The Curse of The Fall', *NME*, 15 January 1983

was eaten by a dog, just days before setting off for Australia, thus his non-appearance at the first few gigs. Chris Knox reported on one incident where Smith turned up late for a set at the Sydney Musicians' Club: 'After some minutes of yer Oz audience chanting, "The Fall don't keep us waiting," Kay Carroll leapt on stage, saying, "Hey, hey, he's not Mick Jagger! He's Mark Smith and he's got lost!" It was true, he had. But he slouched on stage seconds after with his omnipresent bag of goodies, and conducted the evening's festivities with his back firmly and inexorably turned to the audience. Apparently, his grin was immense.'[14] Before the visit The Fall had a top-twenty hit in New Zealand with 'Totally Wired'. According to music-business wisdom the tour should have increased the band's popularity, but, said Smith, 'I think we actually had more fans before we went than after we came back.'[15]

These moaners should get a good dose of army discipline

On return from the tour The Fall went straight into another round of promotion with the October release of *Room To Live* (subtitled on the cover, 'Undilutable Slang Truth').[16] The album had been recorded just before the Antipodes tour at Cargo Studios with production by Carroll (except for 'Room To Live', which was credited to John Brierley). As happened with *Slates*, the band had only intended to record a single but had ended up with seven tracks. Another ten-inch single seemed too predictable so the result was a cut-price £3 album. Smith was determined not to make another *Hex Enduction Hour* so he recruited two new musicians to the usual line-up: Adrian Niman on saxophone and Arthur Cadman on guitar. Both were local musicians, with Cadman formerly part of Manicured Noise, Ludus and the Distractions. The plan was to return to a more spontaneous method of recording, using just one drummer at a time, and excluding some members of the band from particular tracks: 'The band weren't even familiar with some of the songs, we just went in and did them, which

14   Chris Knox, 'The Fall', *Rip It Up*, August 1982
15   Cook, op. cit., 15 January 1983
16   The album was later reissued by a German company, LINE Records GMBH, in 1983. To bring it up to standard album length, 'Lie Dream Of A Casino Soul' and 'Fantastic Life' were added.

is how we always operated in the good old days!' said Smith. 'I think it's served to stir them up a bit! I suppose I'm a contrary bastard – I like to do the opposite of what I've just done.'[17] Steve Hanley and the rest of the band were not particularly happy with the results of the experiment. On the subject of *Room To Live*, he says, 'You can tell whether the band is going through a bad time, you can tell by the music that came out.'

Room To Live has its critics but it's a long way from being a bad album. 'Joker Hysterical Face' describes a woman Smith knew who played Abba records at full blast. The second track, 'Marquis Cha Cha', was the main reason for going into the studio.[18] It was meant to be The Fall's topical comment on the Falklands War, with Smith taking on the personality of a modern-day Buenos Aires-based Lord Haw-Haw. In reality Smith's views were outspokenly in support of the Task Force's attempts to get the Islands back. 'I thought the Army did a great job,' said Smith, 'and these communists and revolutionaries in the pubs were going "Thatcher's War" and every bloody group was bringing out anti-war singles, it was fucking disgraceful. At the Labour Club I started rowing with these guys and I said if the Russians came they wouldn't let you sit here bleedin' all day on the dole drinking yourselves to death. And they say the war's costing a lot of money and I'd say what's fucking money anyway, I thought you were socialists.'[19] Maybe remembering army tales from his grandfather and father, Smith went as far as to suggest conscription as a cure for the complainers: 'I'm just sick of people wailing and moaning about it – I mean in most countries you have to join the army for a period, there's no choice, it's compulsory, some of these moaners should get a good dose of army discipline and patriotism, then they'd change their tune!'[20] Understandably, it was around this time that Smith began to acquire a reputation as a reactionary.

'Hard Life In Country' takes on the less controversial subject of the city-dweller's distrust of the country: 'It's like, semi-fun but very

---

17 Fitzgerald, op. cit., Autumn 1982
18 A 'Marquis Cha Cha' single was scheduled for release in October 1982, but was abandoned with only a handful of copies pressed. A year later two hundred copies turned up in Virgin in Manchester; by then Kamera was bust.
19 George Kay, 'The Fall of Slick, Mark E. Smith's Enduction Hour', *Rip It Up*, September 1982
20 Fitzgerald, op. cit., Autumn 1982

prophetic, I really did have feelings of paranoia about the villagers surrounding the house, and it came true. When we went to Australia I left this bloke in charge of me house, but he let all the scum of the village in and they, like, wrecked the place, broke down doors, and they attracted the police to the place, so the village did close in on me.'[21] What Smith wanted was revealed in the title of the next song, 'Room To Live'. 'Detective Instinct' is about an inept detective, while 'Solicitor in Studio' describes the doomed attempt of a solicitor to become a celebrity like Magnus Pike. The last track was the most experimental yet by The Fall. Largely improvised, it utilized distant echoing percussion, a sampled Pope John Paul II and scratchy, but effectively haunting, violin. The song commemorated the visit of the Pope to Heaton Park in Manchester earlier in 1981. Although not anti-Catholic in general, Smith was no fan of John Paul ('Biggest fucking hypocrite in the world that guy is') and his hatred was compounded when the Pope's helicopter flattened Heaton Park's magic mushroom field.[22]

The album found little commercial success and peaked at number four in the indie charts. Perhaps the group was just too productive and its audience becoming over-familiar with The Fall sound. Ian Pye complained that the group was suffering from 'inertia' and was 'beginning to sound terribly like The Fall'.[23] Amrik Rai thought the album suffered from 'art pretensions' and that it was 'becoming increasingly difficult to distinguish between the white rap and the right crap'.[24] Although Smith would never have admitted to being hurt by bad reviews he might have wondered if his work would ever be understood. In later interviews he confessed that *Hex Enduction Hour* and *Room To Live* might have been The Fall's last albums. He was fed up with the music industry and what little money the band earned was spread very thinly between the six musicians and Carroll. 'I thought it was all over for The Fall. My attitude was, "Let's do these, push things to the hilt, then it's fucking finished lads." These albums were meant to be a big "Fuck off" to the music business.'[25]

21 ibid.
22 ibid.
23 Ian Pye, 'The Cha-cha Jive and Fall-out Blues: The Fall, *Room To Live*', *Melody Maker*, 2 October 1982
24 Amrik Rai, 'White Rap or Right Crap?' *NME*, 2 October 1982
25 Roger Sabin, 'People Talking: M. E. Smith', *Speak*, 1996

Of course The Fall continued and struggled on to the end of 1982 with a mini-tour of England supported on various dates by Danse Society, Felt and Eton Crop. The group were still using gigs to trail new material, including on this tour 'Garden' and 'Pilsner Trail'. Mat Snow caught the band on the 12 December at the Lyceum in London and took up the increasingly familiar theme that The Fall was but a travesty of its former self: 'this performance was drained of colour and inspiration . . . Mark Smith's usual charismatic acerbity had slumped into distant and lacklustre self-parody.'[26] Perhaps the journalists sensed a *malaise* within the band: the fine line between Smith's provocative creative destruction and just plain destructiveness. Marc Riley, for one, decided he'd had enough and on 22 December at the Lesser Free Trade Hall played his last gig for The Fall.

Dare to dance on an Aussie dance floor

During the August 1982 tour of Australia and New Zealand differences between Smith and Riley, both musical and personal, came to a head with a fist fight in an Australian nightclub. The two temporarily patched up differences but by the end of the Christmas mini-tour it was clear they could no longer work together and Riley, after four years in the band, left. Steve Hanley and Scanlon also considered leaving, but decided against it. 'They didn't get on,' said Hanley, 'the fight in Australia in the nightclub was the beginning of the end. It was a clash of personalities, all that "sacking" was more Mark's version of it. We helped out on Marc's first single, but then we went our separate way for a good few years. There were a few rows about money. When it's your mate that you've grown up with, it's even more difficult. I came to the decision though that, "You're not responsible for them and they're not responsible for you." '

In interviews at the time Smith claimed it was Riley's constant attempts to make The Fall more melodic that split them apart. He also thought that Riley lived too much in the past: 'He kept on saying, "Ah, it's not as good as this or that we did a year ago," and that is just not the point of The Fall at all.'[27] Riley's version of events was that Smith wanted him to leave because he was too outspoken,

---

26   Mat Snow, 'The Fall of Prole Art', *NME*, 18 December 1982
27   Don Watson, 'Looking at The Fall Guise', *NME*, 1 October 1983

independent and willing to challenge Smith's authority. The rift had been growing for at least a couple of years: 'I think Mark wanted to kick me out around the time of *Grotesque*.' The subsistence level wages and Riley's interest in writing his own material meant he was no longer totally focused on the group: 'It was getting to the point where I was just doing as I was told. I'd been writing stuff by myself and I knew Mark wouldn't tolerate that, he won't have people doing things for themselves.'[28] Riley had also just married Tracy and was in the process of setting up home with a tarantula, an Indian python called Sabu and a dog called Timothy Malcolm Riley.[29] It was time for a change so he left.

The new band he started was called Marc Riley with the Creepers. His television-personality sister, Lisa Riley (of *Emmerdale* and *You've Been Framed* fame), later claimed some credit for the choice of name: 'I used to call him creep all the time and that is how he chose the name. Mind you, I thought that his singing was terrible and by the time I was a teenager I was too embarrassed to admit we were related.'[30] Riley's début single, 'Favourite Sister' / 'Carry Mi Card', was recorded with various members of The Fall and released in July 1983 on his own label, In Tape. The second single, 'Jumper Clown', contained an obviously satirical attack on Smith, with Riley singing, 'Dare to dance on an Aussie dance floor,' to a bass line remarkably similar to The Fall's 'Man Whose Head Expanded'. Not surprisingly it took some time for Riley to escape comparisons to The Fall. He had been such a big part of The Fall's sound and he wasn't going to change his style overnight. Indeed, as The Fall he had left behind became increasingly accessible and chart-friendly during the eighties, the Creepers became a kind of surrogate Fall for those fans still pining for the good old days. The Creepers knew how to thrash out a furiously good tune and Riley's lyrics, although never reaching the range or complexity of Smith's, were often as humorous, sarcastic and sneering as any Fall fan could desire. The first line-up of the Creepers included Eddie Fenn (drums), Pete Keogh (bass), Paul Fletcher (guitar) and Jim Khambatta (occasional organist, manager and co-owner of In Tape). Their first

28 Gavin Martin, 'Jeepers Creepers', *NME*, 31 March 1984
29 Jonathan Romney, 'Stand-up Creeper', *NME*, 31 August 1985
30 Lisa Riley, quoted in *Women on Top*, May 1999, reproduced in *TBLY*, no. 16, 1999

release to make an impact on the indie charts was *Creeping At Maida Vale*, an EP of a John Peel session released in March 1984. Scanlon and Hanley guested on the first album *Gross Out* (1984) with the tracks 'Teacher Travel' and 'Earwig O'Dowd'. At this time few critics gave Riley much of a chance. Johnny Waller wrote: 'Riley plays music so unsophisticated as to make Crass sound like the London Symphony Orchestra.'[31] However, by October 1984 and the release of the twelve-inch single 'Shadow Figure', Riley's reputation improved and Richard Cook was able to write: 'From souped-up stomp to observations on life that're plain nuts, Riley's sarky little band are turning out the best and most playable garage music in Britain.'[32]

Riley's activities soon spread beyond the Creepers as the In Tape label grew and included on its musically diverse roster the Birmingham skiffle band Terry and Gerry, the Janitors, the Weeds, and Leicester quintet Yeah Yeah No. A selection of tracks from the label can be found on the retrospective compilation *Just A Mish Mash* (1987), which also includes early tracks by the likes of the Membranes and Gaye Bykers on Acid. Meanwhile, the Creepers continued releasing entertaining and innovative albums – *Fancy Meeting God!* (1985) and *Miserable Sinners* (1986) – before finally disbanding with the release of *Rock 'n' Roll Liquorice Flavour* (1988).

Throughout this period Riley held no illusions about the fickleness of the music industry. In 1985 he told Jimmy Dare, 'I don't think us upstarts are ever going to make any money out of it, we'll eventually have to go and get a proper job.'[33] Riley's proper job materialized in the nineties as 'Lard', sidekick to BBC Radio One DJ Mark Radcliffe. The duo was so successful they even won the coveted breakfast-show slot for a short while in 1997. Smith wasn't bitter of course – 'It's almost exactly as I forecast. I said he'd get into astrology and the runes and end up as some floppy mong on TV' – but Riley's rise to fame did have some disturbing side-effects for Smith. One day, when he was taking a cab to a Manchester recording studio, a billboard poster gave him the shock of his life, as he told Bill Dunn: 'I was really sick – you

31 Johnny Waller, 'Marc Riley with the Creepers, *Gross Out*', *Sounds*, 23 June 1984
32 Richard Cook, 'Marc Riley with the Creepers: Shadow Figure', *NME*, 13 October 1984
33 Jimmy Dare, 'Riley', *Debris*, no. 6, January 1985

know when you're feeling so ill you think you're going to die and everything looks really big? We came over a hill and saw this big poster of Marc Riley and Mark Radcliffe, this big fuckin' head on a wall, like 1984. I thought I was going to die and all the people I'd ever known were flashing before my eyes. It was fuckin' scary.'[34]

---

34 Bill Dunn, 'Old Peculiar', *Esquire*, December 1997

8

The Man Whose Head Expanded, 1983

I worry a lot about my brain exploding in my head. I don't know why, but there's like this fear where my head will stop moving or something, y'know, where my brain will just go like 'qch-ch-ch-ch.[1]

The Fall spent the first two months of 1983 touring Switzerland and the Netherlands. While abroad, Smith was asked whether he was too old to be doing this sort of thing. He replied, 'I'm twenty-five and it's not like that with me; I don't grow out of it.'[2] If proof was needed of Smith's undiminished energy it could easily be found in the group's sixth Peel session, broadcast in March: 'Smile', 'Garden', 'Hexen Definitive Strife Knot' and 'Eat Y'self Fitter' were all brand new songs. On the same trip to London the band played two nights at the Venue. Colin Irwin of *Melody Maker* described Smith's appearance at the time: 'One hand slapped carelessly into his pocket, the faintest trace of a sneer flickering across his face, Mark E. Smith slouches across the stage in that peculiar gangling fashion of his and gingerly approaches the microphone. "Good evening, we're The Fall," he says in hollow, unemotional tones.' Irwin then listed what made The Fall so different from the prevailing music industry norm: 'When everybody else is getting drum machines, The Fall opt for two drummers. When everybody else reckons that touring is for circuses and R&B bands, The Fall hit the road with a vengeance. When everyone knows that no band can afford to make it through a gig without playing at least something recognizable, The Fall dispense with old "hits" like "Elastic Man" and "Hip Priest" and play almost entirely new material.'[3]

The Fall's output was prodigious, so much so that some tracks had

1 Smith, quoted in Judith Ammann (ed.), *Who's Been Sleeping in My Brain? Interviews Post Punk*, Frankfurt: Suhrkamp, 1987
2 ibid.
3 Colin Irwin, 'The Fall, the Venue, London', *Melody Maker*, 2 April 1983

to wait years before being commercially released. One such track, 'Words Of Expectation', was filmed live at the Venue and appeared on Cabaret Voltaire's Doublevision video magazine *TV Wipeout* in 1984. The video also featured a short interview with Smith and a clip of an irate Kay Carroll arguing on the phone with Tony Wilson about Factory using a track by The Fall on a video without the band's permission.[4] In the background of this scene lurked Geoff Travis of Rough Trade.

Travis's presence was linked to Smith and Carroll's growing dissatisfaction with Kamera. They loved Galpern but the accounts just weren't adding up. Kamera, after barely a year of trading, was about to go very bust. Apart from The Fall, its other bands – the Dancing Did, Charge, Aerial FX and the Au Pairs – never came close to covering their costs. A move into the gothic sado-masochist genre with the compilation *The Whip* (featuring Marc Almond, Dave Vanian and Blood and Roses) did little to halt the rot. 'We had to leave Kamera because we knew it was going down,' Smith recalled. 'It broke my heart. Kamera were like, Here y'are mate, what you're saying is fantastic. *Hex Enduction Hour* is brilliant, you're brilliant, here's a cheque. Ha ha. You play *Hex* to them, they go, Fuckin' brilliant, mate! Uriah Heep at its best! Ha ha. Only label I was upset to leave.'[5]

With few other labels registering an interest in the band, Smith had no option but to swallow his considerable pride and give Rough Trade one more chance. Rough Trade, driven by Travis's enthusiasm for the group and his genuine respect for Smith, knew that The Fall's substantial and loyal fan base could provide consistently high sales for the indie sector. *Hex Enduction Hour*, for example, by mid-1983 had already sold twenty thousand copies.[6] It was a marriage of mutual benefit but also of convenience and therefore all the more precarious.

4 The track 'Totally Wired' was subsequently removed from *A Factory Video* (FAC 26).
5 David Cavanagh, 'I Didn't Get Where I Am Today . . . ', Q, March/April 1994
6 Frank Worrall, 'Fall Guys', *Melody Maker*, 18 June 1983

Amphetamine and groupies just don't go together

A couple of weeks after the Peel session and the Venue gigs, The Fall
began a gruelling month-long US tour. Everything seemed to be
going fine as the tour opened in April at the Dirt Club in Bloomfield,
stopped off for a couple of dates in New York and then went on to
Boston. After a show at the the the Rathskeller, the band hit a local bar.
Inexplicably the barman took a dislike to Carroll, claimed she was
drunk and refused to serve her. She turned to Smith and the others
saying, 'Let's forget this place, the guy won't serve me.' But they
ignored her, got their drinks and sat down. 'I'm like in tears,' she
recalled. ' "C'mon, let's go!" ' But they just carried on drinking, with
Carroll reduced to surreptitiously sharing a girlfriend's beer. The
band eventually drank up and headed for the minibus. 'They all got
in, I didn't,' said Carroll. 'This was the end of the line for me, I didn't
have the stomach for it any more. I got into my girlfriend's car and
took off. They followed me back to her place. Finally I resorted to
screaming my head off: "No-more!" They got the message and left
for Canada.' That wasn't quite the end of the story because for the
next week Smith continued to call Carroll: 'I wouldn't talk to him. I
knew he just wanted to make sure I was still there. It hurt me even
more when I read in the *NME* or *Sounds* a few weeks later that the
reason I had left, Mark apparently said, was because I was ill. Not
true. However, I did find out I had cancer five months later, another
story . . . '

Although precipitated by the Boston bar humiliation, Carroll's decision to leave the band had far deeper roots. 'I had been with The
Fall almost six years,' she said, 'and had gone through a lot of abuse,
from myself, the biz and Mark. He knew my one and only Achilles'
heel, monogamy, and so let's say he used it against me too many
times, sometimes in front of my face. Talk about double binding
schizophrenia. I wanted to run and leave it all, but I loved the band so
much and, like many abusive relationships, loved the man too. I
think Mark wanted me gone. Not so much as the manager but as the
lover. Amphetamine and groupies just don't go together, Mark's scars
and mine can attest to that.'

Carroll stayed on in America, settled in Hoboken, New Jersey,
remarried and turned down many opportunities to manage other
bands: 'They had quite a healthy underground there but I was burnt

out and to be honest with you I feel there was only one band I could have ever managed and that was The Fall. I sometimes find myself having a "what if" moment. Then a voice inside me cries, no!' Carroll stayed on the East Coast until 1990, when her marriage ended and she moved on to Portland in Oregon. There in 1991 she had another daughter, Megan, and married for the third time: 'Megan is the joy of my life and I feel the universe forgives me for abandoning my older children.' By the end of the nineties she was working for a medical company that treated adults with head injuries. 'Some things never change,' she said. 'I was a facilitator and my job was to cognitively retrain people with short-term memory deficits.'

By 1983, with an already lengthy list of ex-Fall members, it's difficult to say that anyone, apart from Smith, was indispensable to The Fall, but Carroll came mighty close. When others floundered or grew hesitant she pushed through with a driving force, energetically hectoring the band to maintain its uncompromising attitude. As Steve Hanley reiterated, 'I don't think Mark'll admit to this, but Kay set the blueprint, the ideals of the band, whatever they were. She was a massive influence on how it was, "no selling out" and all that.'

Oh my God! They're like the Gods of the East Village

Laura Elisse Salenger, better known as Brix, was born 12 November 1962 in Los Angeles. Her parents divorced when she was just a year old and from then on Brix's childhood was split between her father, a Freudian psychoanalyst based in Malibu Canyon and Pacific Palisades, and her mother, a model, living in Hollywood Hills. After her modelling career ended Brix's mother became involved in politics and television as producer for CBS's *60 Minutes*. She eventually moved to Chicago to take up a job in charge of the Film Commission for the state of Illinois. It was Brix's mother that arranged for the Blues Brothers to smash their way through the Daley Plaza window. 'She was just fantastic,' Brix said, 'and she's a really smart business woman and she brought millions of dollars into the state, wonderful woman and mother, and total inspiration. I came from a background where a woman could be strong and beautiful and do this. I saw that, and I knew I could do it as well.'[7]

7 James Brown, 'Godhead!', *NME*, 4 March 1989

A babysitter started Brix on the guitar when she was just seven. She received further encouragement from her father, himself a keen amateur musician particularly interested in bluegrass. Brix's first ambition was to become an actress, but this changed when she discovered English pop culture. 'I was really obsessed,' she said, 'there was the Clash, of course, especially the "Guns of Brixton", which I used to sing and which is also where I got my name. I was into anything I could get my hands on, even Culture Club, Tears for Fears, Adam and the Ants, anything that looked English and cool. Depeche Mode, any of it, I was devouring it. I don't know why it was, it must have been because of a past life. Before all the punk stuff I was obsessed with Led Zeppelin and Jimi Hendrix. We would smoke pot after school – most of my friends were boys, all the stoner crowd – and just listen to Hendrix and Bowie and then I moved on to punk stuff.' Under age, she used to sneak into gigs by, amongst others, U2, Bow Wow Wow and her favourite, the Ramones. She also sang at local proms and parties for a band that performed cover versions of hits by the Police and Blondie.

Brix did well at high school without studying too hard: 'I got As and Bs and the odd C, but I was really stupid at maths and science. I definitely partied and I always loved boys, especially the ones at university. The majority of the girls in the school were very straight and proper and I think they saw me as a threat or like a wild animal. I was lucky because my family were quite prestigious so in a way they had to accept that I was a bit off the wall.' After she left high school, Brix's parents sent her to a famous liberal arts establishment, Bennington, in Vermont on the East Coast. Bennington catered for just around six hundred students and specialized in courses on modern dance, theatre and literature, producing such luminaries as Bret Easton Ellis and Donna Tartt. Brix described it as 'very New England colonial, the most beautiful place you have ever seen but you would go mad there. Some people called the place an insane asylum for the rich.'

Brix majored in theatre and literature, but still found time for additional experimental music courses. She formed a band with fellow students Lisa Feder and Claus Castenskiold called Banda Dratsing, *Clockwork Orange*-speak for Fighting Band. Feder played lead guitar, Castenskiold the drums and Brix played bass and sang. It wasn't long before Brix and Feder decided to take time off from Bennington to further their musical careers. They moved to

Chicago to live with Brix's mother and quickly took over the top floor of her house as a rehearsal space. In Chicago they recruited another drummer and played a few gigs but mostly they spent their time going to see other bands. One day, while hunting through the record bins at Wax Trax, Brix discovered The Fall: 'Lisa was looking through the bin and pulled out *Slates*. "Have you ever heard of them?" and I said, "No," and she said, "Oh my God! They're like the Gods of the East Village." "Oh really, let's hear it." So we took it home and I was obsessed, like I used to be with Joy Division. I was reading the sleeve notes and I couldn't understand what he was saying, it was just the weirdest lyrics I had ever heard.'

Two weeks later Brix read excitedly that The Fall was due to play at Chicago's Cabaret Metro. She almost never made it: 'I had my period and had really bad cramps. I felt like shit. But I did go and that was when fate stepped in really.' After her friend, Feder, disappeared with her boyfriend, Brix watched the band by herself, transfixed by what she saw: 'It was hypnotic and I couldn't help but rock back and forth. I remember thinking Steve Hanley was the most amazing bass player. Up until then it had been Peter Hook who was my idol, but Steve was different, in a way heavier and more brutal but still melodic. I remember thinking Mark looked troubled and mean, but at the same time there was something inside me that was slightly fascinated. I guess I was pretty cocky and it was just the thought of being able to conquer something that was frightening. Not in terms of sex, I wasn't attracted to him at all, particularly, I was just fascinated by his mind and what he was thinking, what he was saying. It was just weird.'

After the gig, rather than go home, Brix decided to have a drink in the downstairs Smart Bar. Smith literally ran into her, 'Bang! He had a bottle of beer in each hand and a line of coke running down his nose, well I assumed it was coke anyway because it was white powder. I said, "Hi," and he said, "Hi," and he said, "Do you want a drink?" and I said, "OK." Then we started chatting. He was cheeky and charming and asked me if I wanted to come to a party? I knew he fancied me instantly and we went to the party.' Brix drove and in the car, at Smith's insistence, she played him a demo tape of her band: 'Who wrote this?' he asked. 'I did,' she replied. 'Well, you're a fucking genius then!' It wasn't long before Smith was inviting her back to his place – Prestwich, England. Brix needed little persuading: 'I was like, "I'm there," but my mother was like, "You're not going anywhere!" My mother made me get a round-trip ticket because she said, "You never know if he's going to turn out to be a drunk or a wife-beater." I was like, "Oh don't be so stupid." ' Six weeks later Brix took a flight to England with just $700 in her pocket: 'I remember him saying to me, "I'm not a rich man, I've only got a thousand pounds in the bank." I was like, "That's enough!" He would describe to me where he lived, the pub, the George, which he always went to in Prestwich, and things like that and it sounded really romantic to me. Back in 1981, when I graduated from high school, the year before Bennington, my mother and stepfather took me and my two stepsisters to Europe for a holiday. We landed in London first and the minute the plane touched down I turned to my mother and said, "This is where I'm going to live." I just knew it. It was a weird thing with me and England. I'm really happy and comfortable here.'

Brix arrived in Manchester on 17 May to find that Smith was not kidding about his slender means. The year before, Smith and Carroll had moved out of the Glebelands Road flat into Flat 2, 4 Beech Tree Bank on Rectory Lane, just round the corner. The flat, unfortunately, never really lived up to its attractive name. It was bigger, with a higher ceiling and plenty of space for Smith's cats to roam around, but it was also damp and cold and none of the electric fires worked. Brix summed up her first impression of the flat with the word 'gross', but her disgust was tempered by the excitement of finally making it to England: 'There was no central heating, just a Calor gas thing. He didn't even have a refrigerator and I asked him where he kept his meat and eggs. "I keep them on the window sill." And no Hoover, just a carpet sweeper. I'd come from a house where we had a housekeeper, and sometimes a cook, because my parents worked. So it was quite different, but the thing was, I was so happy with what I was doing that I was blind to it all, it was just a minor inconvenience. I remember when my parents first came to visit – there are pictures somewhere of them sitting in the flat, springs coming out of the chairs, dirt on the wall. Mark had about six cats which peed and shat everywhere and stunk. The first thing my mother did was walk up the road to Sainsbury's and get cleaning supplies and my mother cleaned that flat. Pretty shocking.'

Just a few days after her arrival, Brix accompanied the band down to London for a gig at the Electric Ballroom in Camden Town. The support band was The Smiths and even though it was just their seventh gig the critics were falling over themselves to praise the band and their début single on Rough Trade, 'Hand In Glove'. Brix's initiation into The Fall continued in June with a brief tour of Germany and Austria and the release on Rough Trade of the single 'The Man Whose Head Expanded'. The sleeve was the slickest yet for a Fall single, without a piece of graffiti in sight, just some simple typography and a colourful sketch of Smith by Bob Pearce. Hanley's bass dominated most of the track, apart from some comic electric keyboard passages. The lyrics followed on from 'How I Wrote Elastic Man', except this time it was not a writer going mad but an ordinary bloke convinced that he was being followed by a soap-opera writer stealing his words to use in television scripts.

I think maybe he's matured

On 19 July 1983, Mark Edward Smith (26) married Laura Elisse Salenger (20) in the General Registry Office in Bury, with witnesses Karl Burns and Claude Bessy in attendance. For Brix it was quite a lonely time: 'I didn't want my mother to come because I was embarrassed. I didn't know what would happen if she met his parents. I knew she'd be horrified, it was just too much stress for me to have everyone meet each other. I knew my mother wouldn't be over the moon about it. I told her I was going to do it and she really wanted to come over and I said, "No, I don't want you to come." And then the night before I started crying on the phone, "Please come over," and she said, "No, its too late now." So at the wedding there wasn't anyone that I knew, not even one friend.'

The marriage took place between two high-profile gigs: the first on 15 July at the Ace in Brixton and the second on 27 July at the Hacienda in Manchester. Of the Brixton gig, Don Watson wrote: 'The Fall has never been so exciting. Not since the paradoxical peaks of The Birthday Party has a live performance caused such an increase in a collective heart rate, or a music blended so brilliantly the maverick dynamics of jazz and the pit-gut thrill of rock. Smith forms a nucleus of charisma around which the holocaust of rhythm revolves.'[8] What impressed Vermilion Sands was the band's culturally diverse audience: 'They manage to capture the interest of all sorts of

8 Don Watson, 'The Fall / The Box: Brixton, the Ace', *NME*, 30 July 1983

people – blacks, trendies, skins, rockabillies, punks, weirdos, cranks, bespectacled students and hippies.'[9]

The Fall continued to live up to its reputation as the hardest working bands in showbiz, with recording sessions for its next album followed immediately by a country-wide tour. New songs premièred at this time included 'C.R.E.E.P.', 'Two By Four', 'Clear Off', 'Pat Trip Dispenser' and 'Oh! Brother', all songs that showed the first signs of Brix's lightening influence. On return from America, Smith's writing style had also become less effusive. 'The songs are getting shorter,' Smith admitted. 'It used to be like self-destructing bursts of creativity. Different things spur me on now. I can look more at what I write – do it the best way I can. I've talked about it being like "work" in the past. I'm just realistic enough to spend the time behind the scenes sorting everything out. That's where a lot of Fall imitators let themselves down. They think they can just go on stage and take the piss out of people.'[10] At least one commentator, Frank Worrall, saw signs of a new mellowness in Smith. Watching the band go through its paces at the Hellfire Club, Wakefield, he felt that Smith had 'undergone a transformation'. He was no longer 'the sullen-faced depressive who treats his audience as if they didn't exist. He looks as if he's found a new meaning in life, resplendent with distinctly fresh features and even an occasional smile. I think maybe he's matured.'[11]

In October, The Fall welcomed the new football season with the single 'Kicker Conspiracy'. It formed the key element of an attractive double-seven-inch gatefold package that also included 'Wings' and, from a 1980 John Peel session, 'Container Drivers' and 'New Puritan'. Smith included the latter tracks because he thought new audiences should be reminded about the band's history: 'I do hate looking back in the sense of glorifying the past, but I do think you have to be aware of the fact that The Fall have always been ahead of their time, because it's realizing that which will give us the impetus to move forward.'[12]

9   Vermilion Sands, 'The Fall / the Box / Headhunters: Brixton Ace', *Melody Maker*, 30 July 1983
10 John Wilde, 'The Fall Guy', *Zig-Zag*, November 1983
11 Frank Worrall, 'The Fall, Hellfire Club, Wakefield', *Melody Maker*, 1 October 1983
12 Don Watson, 'Looking at The Fall Guise', *NME*, 1 October 1983

In 'Kicker Conspiracy', The Fall produced one of the greatest football songs of all time. The difference from terrace favourites like 'Ossie's Dream' or 'Three Lions' was that rather than stirring up fan fervour or patriotism, Smith detailed early signs of the corruption and greed that would almost destroy the national sport in the coming years (with disasters such as the Bradford City fire and the Heysel tragedy in 1985 and the crushing of Liverpool fans at Hillsborough in 1989). Smith blamed the 'corporate-u-lent' directors: 'They are a right load of dicks, real mongs. If you look at football stadiums here and then go to Europe you wouldn't believe it, they are real palaces. Mind you, I don't agree with this other idea that football is something for all the family to enjoy. If you want a hot dog and all your family with you then go to the park, not a football game. The great thing about soccer is that you are there with thousands of people you don't know sharing together in these great emotions. That's why I love it.'[13] Smith also bemoaned the mentality that hounded maverick talents like George Best out of the game: 'In him there's the story of British soccer,' Smith later claimed. 'Anyone with any talent was mercilessly gunned down. He never used to train or anything, but he was brilliant even when he was playing for Hibs at the end of his career. I met him once at a club and he was dead nice and dead clever. I was dead surprised. He knows one hell of a lot about soccer, you wouldn't believe it. He said to me that if he pulled forty thousand people a week he should be able to do what he wanted and he was right. He was always into entertaining the crowd.'[14]

'Kicker Conspiracy' became the first single by the band to be accompanied by a promotional video. In contrast to Duran Duran's travel-brochure locations, The Fall chose Burnley's Turf Moor football ground. The run-down stadium suited the song perfectly. Shots of the band were intercut with nostalgic footage of flat-cap crowds and the then contemporary anti-fan barbed-wire fences. The most hilarious section was a shot of Smith as he walked along the touchline, miming badly into a can of beer.

Brix played just a small part in the video but elsewhere she was beginning to draw the attention of the music press. Bleddyn Butcher photographed the couple for NME, with Don Watson describing

13 Barry McIlheney, 'Entertaining Mr Smith', *Melody Maker*, 12 October 1985
14 Mark E. Smith, 'Heroes', *Melody Maker*, 27 September 1986

Brix as 'the sultry, blonde LA punkette'.[15] Brix's glamorous image contrasted well with the rest of the band and importantly she convinced Smith that appearing on television might be a good thing. The Fall's first chance came in November when The Fall appeared on *The Tube*, a popular music show fronted by Jools Holland and Paula Yates (even though it was John Peel that introduced the group). Smith appeared in a red shirt and black jacket and with long hair that reached his shoulders – a kind of grown-out mullet. With one hand buried deep in his trouser pocket and nose screwed up in a permanent sneer, he launched into 'Smile'. For the second number, 'Two By Four', Brix joined the band, plugging in her cherry-red 63 Gretsch Corvette, a gift from a Joan Jett and the Blackhearts guitarist.[16]

The latter part of 1983 was a critical period for Brix as she slowly integrated herself into the band. 'Brix was a big change,' said Steve Hanley. 'Her coming in was very gradual. I suppose anybody outside could have seen it a mile off. She started off doing the lights, then singing on one song. She was OK, good for the band. We'd reached as far as we could with fifteen-minute songs like "And This Day" battering the audience. She did commercialize the band, she helped convince Mark to go that way. She was like a bit of fresh air for five miserable blokes from Manchester.' It helped that Brix was sociable, enthusiastic and full of musical ideas: 'The rest of the band accepted me,' she said. 'If they had any other feelings it was never made known to me. They didn't make a big deal of it. A lot of people were put off that "his wife" was in it, a kind of Linda McCartney-type backlash. But I think after a bit they accepted me as a musician. I'm sure there were moments when I was a diva, a bitch, but I think they grew to really like me and respect me. I totally respected them and it was just a pleasure working with them.'

15 Watson, op. cit., 1 October 1983
16 Apparently after the show Johnny Marr wanted to buy it from her, but she refused all offers. Unfortunately, a year later it was stolen from the tour van, but five years later it turned up in a music shop in Denmark Street and she bought it back (information from Nick Smith, 'The Fall Girl', *Guitarist*, December 1996).

Perverted By Language

A couple of weeks after *The Tube*, The Fall released its eighth studio album, *Perverted By Language*. The television appearance stimulated interest in the group and the album sold well, taking the coveted number one spot in the indie charts for Christmas 1983 and staying there for four weeks. Like the last two singles, the album was ably produced by Steve Parker despite severe restrictions in recording facilities: 'It could've been ten times better,' Smith later said, 'the songs live sounded dynamite. Because it was Rough Trade, they put us in some fucking crap studio for like four days. Some of the tapes were actually recorded too slow, things kept breaking down.'[17]

The opening track, 'Eat Y'self Fitter', takes its title from the back of a Kellogg's cornflakes packet and is filled with crunchy flakes of Smith's heightened observational humour. On 'Neighbourhood Of Infinity' Smith helpfully sings 'We are The Fall', just in case you were in any doubt. 'Garden' contains one of Smith's weirdest lines, when he incredulously screams, 'A Jew on a motorbike!' Later Smith explained where the image came from: 'Derives partly from these talks I'd have with a driver of ours who was Jewish, long talks about Judaism. I'd say to him, "Now there's one thing you never see, a Jewish person on a motorbike." Then one day I was going though Golders Green on the way to a London gig and suddenly the street was full of Jewish people on motorbikes.'[18] 'Hotel Blodel' featured Brix on vocals with music courtesy of a Banda Dratsing track, 'Everything For The Record'. At Smith's insistence, Brix reacquainted herself with a guitar after years of playing the bass (even The Fall couldn't find space for two bass players). The out-of-tune and spooky violin came courtesy of Smith. 'I remember doing the vocal,' said Brix, 'and it was just like a hand-held mike, it was really crude and recorded in one take. For years I just couldn't listen to it. I'm singing like a man. I just didn't know how to sing then, but there's something really good about that song and now it's my husband Philip's favourite Fall song. There's just something magical about that even though it was very crude.' 'Smile' is one of the strongest tracks on the album and draws once again on Smith's deep well of anti-humanism.

17 Dave Segal, 'Hip Priest in Motown', *You Can't Hide Your Love Forever*, no 3, Winter 1989

18 Steve Lake, 'After The Fall', *Melody Maker*, 21 April 1984

The last track, 'Hexen Definitive/Strife Knot', is downbeat, and Smith sounds like he's singing into a bucket. The line – 'You know nothing about it, its not your domain, don't confuse yourself with someone who's got something to say' – is one for the critics.

They, or rather Jim Shelley in particular, thought *Perverted By Language* offered little threat, 'it's The Fall plodding on, going nowhere, making do'.[19] Lynden Barber believed The Fall didn't want to be liked, but 'held in some kind of awe, like terrorists rejoicing in their power to affect events'. The album's jumble of words and phrases he likened to 'a jig-saw puzzle of language, its pieces strewn across the table; we are left to make of it what we will.'[20] The same could also be said of The Fall's first commercially available video, *Perverted By Language Bis*, produced by Ikon FCL to coincide with the release of the album.[21] It had come about chiefly through Brix's enthusiasm. Rough Trade was initially loath to get involved because of costs. 'They were going, "Aztec Camera's video cost £7,000," and we were saying that we didn't mean like that,' said Smith. 'Then they'd say, "Well you've got to have a union crew." Why have you got to have a union crew, y'know?' Brix and Smith talked about their ideas for the video with Malcolm Whitehead and Claude Bessy of Ikon and they agreed to fund the project themselves with just £500 coming from Rough Trade for 'props' (chiefly cans and pints of beer). 'I was interested in it because my lyrics are ideal, in a lot of ways, for that sort of thing,' said Smith. 'Have you seen the *Open University* programmes and they have a graph on the screen for about five minutes? I think that's fantastic, I thought it would be great to have something like that and just the music playing. Not flashing or anything, just like . . . a graph.'[22] The highlight of the video comes halfway through 'Eat Y'self Fitter' where Smith takes to the dance floor and does a spirited John Travolta impression.

19 Jim Shelley, 'Words: Fall on Stony Ground', *NME*, 10 December 1983
20 Lynden Barber, 'Speaking in Tongues', *Melody Maker*, 17 December 1983
21 The company was part of Factory Communications Limited and run by Malcolm Whitehead, Claude Bessy and Tim Chambers. The release was one of a series that also included *Pleasure Heads Must Burn* by The Birthday Party and Joy Division's *Here Are The Young Men* which sold over 6000 copies, a large figure for the still developing video market. The videos were not cheap, either, costing £14 through mail order.
22 Edwin Pouncey, 'Rough Justice', *Sounds*, 9 June 1984

News of Smith's marriage, the Christmas number one hit and the video eventually reached Kay Carroll across the Atlantic. She was not too interested, she had enough on her plate just getting used to life in America: 'I'd been in the States about six months,' she said. 'I was a nanny for a *New York Times* writer in Hoboken. One day she introduced me to her younger sister, Theresa, who happened to be home for the summer from that most prestigious and exclusive college, Bennington. Of course, like all Americans, she wanted to know how I came to the States. So I told her the story. To cut a long story short she called me about two weeks later, after she had returned to college in the fall and said: "Was the girl who ended up with your boyfriend from Chicago named Laura." I said, "No, I think it was Brix." "Yeah, yeah she called herself that after that song. She's my room-mate, she lives in my dorm at college. All the girls here are going nuts, they're saying she's not coming back and that she's gone to live in England with a rock 'n' roll singer. Do you think it's the same girl, Kay? She always said she was going to marry a British rock musician." '

9

C.R.E.E.P., 1984

> When I started out I wanted to wipe out pop music and start again
> and I thought there were some writers who felt the same way. Now
> of course it's pop, pop, pop all the way, and being a pop musician is
> supposed to be something terribly clever and smart. Grown men and
> women write this crap. Well I'm still on the other side of the fence.[1]

During March and April 1984, The Fall toured Scotland, the Netherlands and Germany.[2] Although new songs such as 'Lay Of The Land',
'God Box' and 'Copped It' showed the group still had an abrasive
edge, Smith's stage persona had mellowed just a little: 'Last year I was
doing almost the whole set with my back to the crowd and I was
thinking, "Hmmm this is very rude," so I've forced myself to turn
round again.' Another Smithism left behind was the between-songs
repartee with the audience: 'When The Fall started it was difficult to
shut me up. When you hear the earliest tapes there was more rapping
than music. I was making jokes and insults and so on. Big monologues. But I stopped it because I thought it was becoming too much
of a gimmick. It was a period where I was very much influenced by
Lenny Bruce. I like to think now that the songs say all that needs
saying.'[3]

After the tour, Smith set about leaving Rough Trade for the second
time. His latest grudge began with the recording of *Perverted By Language*: 'They booked us into this dirt-cheap studio in Manchester,'
Smith complained. 'After three days we just got out of the studio,
we'd had enough.' The problems continued into the New Year:
'We, in our minds, had left them at Christmas after *Perverted* came
out. I said no more, I'd rather not work, I'd rather retire than work

---

1   Smith, in Steve Lake, 'After The Fall', *Melody Maker*, 21 April 1984
2   For the Scotland leg of the tour they were supported by a young Del Amitri.
3   Lake, op. cit., 21 April 1984

with them again. They eat up so many groups, Rough Trade, and destroy them.' Rough Trade had persuaded Smith to sign with promises of the best studios, producers and television appearances. 'So we go back with them,' Smith said, 'and after four weeks it's the same old story, except worse this time because they were concentrating on that *one big act*.'[4]

That 'one big act' was The Smiths, then celebrating two recent hit singles, 'What Difference Does It Make?' and 'This Charming Man'. As Travis later observed: 'When The Smiths were successful, that immediately alienated Mark E. Smith. I don't think Mark was thrilled to see these upstarts pass him by and I can understand why he felt like that.'[5] Smith, at times, needed to be the centre of attention. Added to this was his mystification at Morrissey's new-found popularity. 'He just considered Steven Morrissey a twat,' said Brix. 'He used to write letters to Mark for years and years, like fawning, sycophantic letters. I think Mark has a book of them somewhere and he's threatened to publish them a few times.' Travis remembered an incident that highlighted their tense relationship. One day Morrissey came into his office to discuss business and accidentally bumped into Smith: 'Mark just fixed him with this very sardonic look and said quite clearly – "Ah, hello, Steven!" Morrissey was visibly shaken by it.'[6] Rough Trade, it seemed, just wasn't big enough for both Smith and The Smiths.

Brix believed that Rough Trade were happy to keep The Fall as a reasonably successful cult band but they lacked the foresight and ambition to promote the group to a larger audience. 'I think in their minds they never believed they could make The Fall into a pop group,' she said. 'They just wanted to keep the band because it looked good, that they had The Fall in their stable.'[7] Such a state of affairs was useless to a cash-strapped Smith, who since Carroll's departure had taken over the business side of the band with the assistance of London-based manager Richard Thomas. The band carried substantial debts, including a large and overdue tax bill. The only sure supply of income came from playing gigs. Added to the band's problems, Smith was irked by having to hear about all the

4 Edwin Pouncey, 'Rough Justice', *Sounds*, 9 June 1984
5 Travis, in Johnny Rogan, *Morrissey & Marr: The Severed Alliance*, London: Omnibus Press, 1993
6 Nick Kent, 'Dreamer in the Real World', *The Face*, no. 61, May 1985
7 Pouncey, op. cit., 9 June 1984

compromises other bands were making. 'I'm like a priest, y'know,' he said. 'A lot of bands who are now big stars, people like the Bunnymen, The Smiths and so on, lots more I could name, they all used to come and see The Fall. Now if I meet one of them they'll come into the room and sit down and next thing you know I've got this tide of confessions coming at me. I have to hear all the terrible things they've done, all the little sell-outs. And I'm sitting there like this [tight smile], saying, "Oh hey, don't worry about it, old chaps. Everybody's got to earn money." And I'm thinking GET LOST! Y'know – here's me and The Fall, practically starving for the last six years and never compromised an inch, and here they are, stinking rich, asking me for my pity!'[8] Such accusations couldn't go unanswered and Ian McCulloch responded, humorously describing Smith as, 'The most well-balanced person in the world – he's got a chip on *both* shoulders.' He continued: 'He's really bitter now and I don't know why. Maybe because he did want to be successful. He accuses us of compromising, selling out. We've never done that but I remember he used to do gigs purely for the money. And that is a sell-out.'[9]

Smith's solution to the band's troubles was to take The Fall out of the independent sector and sign-up with one of the majors. One unlikely offer came from US label Motown, where an enthusiastic A&R man had offered Smith a £46,000 advance. 'The funny thing was,' Smith said, 'this guy at Motown asked for some of our old stuff he could listen to and the only thing I had was *Hex Enduction Hour* and the first line on that is, "Where are the obligatory niggers?" I thought, "When they hear that, we've had it." ' Smith was correct. It was not long before Motown's head office contacted Smith with its verdict: 'We see no commercial potential in this band whatsoever.'[10]

With Motown out of the way it fell to Beggars Banquet to make a more feasible proposition. The label had grown out of a record shop set up by Martin Mills and Nick Austin in 1974 in the Earls Court area of London. In 1976, the duo started a promotions company, working with groups like the Stranglers and the Damned. In 1978, capitalizing on the new-wave boom, the Beggars Banquet record label launched itself with a single by the Lurkers. The company

8 Lake, op. cit., 21 April 1984
9 McCulloch, in Mat Snow, 'Warren Peace', *NME*, 4 August 1984
10 Colin Irwin, 'Perverted by Anguish', *Melody Maker*, 20 October 1984

continued to grow but it required a partnership deal with WEA and the surprise Tubeway Army hit 'Are Friends Electric?' to guarantee its survival. Other key Beggars bands in 1984 were Bauhaus, the Associates, the Icicle Works and, about to become the most successful of all, the Cult. According to music press reports The Fall signed a deal worth 'five Bauhaus singles of their choice'.[11] But joking aside, The Fall signed because Beggars recognized that poor production had held the band back. To change this they brought in John Leckie, an established producer celebrated for his work with Magazine, Simple Minds and XTC.

For The Fall, after suffering the inefficiency and neglect of Rough Trade, Martin Mills and Beggars proved to be a revelation, as Brix explains: 'Beggars was this happy family with big warm open arms and they'd had singles at number one with Gary Numan. They could make it happen. It was more money and they were great to us and in retrospect I must say it was my best label of all. Martin Mills was lovely and I still have contact with him.' Beggars at last gave Smith the opportunity to expand the band's audience base. Maybe if Carroll had stuck around his plans might have faltered but in Brix he had a more than enthusiastic collaborator. 'I was much more career orientated than he was,' she says. 'We did think about writing hit songs and about moving forward and being more successful. There are Brix haters who say I ruined the band, but the band never sold more records than the time I was there – never have, never will. I don't think I ruined it at all, I just added a hook where there wasn't one before. I didn't take away what was there, I just added a tiny bit more light. I didn't try and control. I wasn't the horrible wife that took over. I just thought that the band deserved so much more success than it was having. I was more like a big supporter and pushing it as far as it could go to reach as many people as it could reach. Mark liked that kind of enthusiasm and he listened to me.' Although Brix won the 1984 'Linda McCartney tea-towel' award in the *NME*,[12] Smith spoke enthusiastically about his marriage's positive effect on his dealings with the band: 'I'm a lot more understanding, I don't try to control every move they make. I haven't got time any more 'cos I'm

11   Anon., 'Fall, Wah! Sign On', *Sounds*, 19 May 1984
12   Mark E. Smith, 'What the Stars Foretell', *Melody Maker*, 5 January 1985

married. It's done me a lot of good though, I'd have been fucking
dead by now, dead as a post.'[13]

The first manifestation of The Fall's new partnership with Beggars
Banquet was the June single 'Oh! Brother'. An irrevocable sign of the
group's acceptance of marketing values was the release of the single in
both seven- and twelve-inch formats, a historic first for The Fall. John
Leckie, fresh out of a Rajneesh Commune, produced the record and
impressed Scanlon with the way he captured The Fall's live sound:
'We set up like we're going to be playing live and do the songs. He
gets great drum sounds, which most producers can't. Most producers
are stoned idiots who spend most of their time on the phone with their
financial advisors, seeing how their shares did . . . He's not scared of us,
either. He's not afraid to say, "I thought that was pretty boring." '[14]
Smith agreed, 'It's the first time Karl's drums sound like you're in the
same room as him.'[15] For all its fresh pop finish, Smith's lyrics for 'Oh!
Brother' remained as impenetrable and as intriguing as ever. The press
release offered little help: 'As the cover details were being finalized on
the morning of May 4th, Barbara Castle MP drove past the Fall home
in Manchester declaring through a megaphone: "Vote for FOGG!
Vote Fogg! I'm Barbara . . . " This is oddly relevant to the text of "Oh!
Brother".' The B-side, 'God Box', was more straightforwardly
inspired by Smith's visit to America at the beginning of the year and
his unsettling experience of Christian TV evangelism.

The critics mostly congratulated The Fall on producing an attractive
record without compromising on any credibility. Hugh Fielder
commended Smith on having it both ways: 'obscure enough to
maintain his cult following' while at the same time sneakily trying out
'a couple of catchy riffs'.[16] 'It's got a tune . . . of sorts. And the great
Mark E. actually *sings* . . . well, almost,' wrote Colin Irwin.[17] Mat
Snow predicted 'that very soon The Fall are going to write a tune
that Mark E. Smith will whistle'.[18]

13   Pouncey, op. cit., 9 June 1984
14   Tim Anstadt, 'Interview was with Simon Rogers and Craig Scanlon', *Offense
     Newsletter*, no. 59, 19 July 1985
15   Pouncey, op. cit., 9 June 1984
16   Hugh Fielder, 'The Fall: "Oh! Brother" ', *NME*, 16 June 1984
17   Colin Irwin, 'Single of the Week. The Fall: "Oh! Brother" ', *Melody Maker*, 28
     July 1984
18   Mat Snow, 'Elephant Fayre, Cornwall Port Eliot', *NME*, 11 August 1984

I think he's a pretty regular sort of guy really

During June the band toured and premièred the new songs 'Hey! Marc Riley', 'Elves', 'No Bulbs' and 'Craigness'. The summer brought with it a couple of outdoor festivals, the first in July at Elephant Fayre in St Germans, Cornwall, and the second in August promoted by the GLC in Brockwell Park, Brixton. At the latter, The Fall took to the stage around four o'clock under a 'GLC working for London' banner and was promptly met with a hail of half-empty beer cans, thrown by New Model Army and Spear of Destiny fans. Barry McIlheney described Smith's disdainful reaction: 'During the entire time he was on stage, he spoke to no one, acknowledged nothing, and seemed generally oblivious to the world outside. It has of course been said many times before, but this is truly the stuff of which legends are made.'[19]

Also in London in August, The Fall's music could be heard in a more surprising setting: accompanying Michael Clark & Company at the Riverside Studios in Hammersmith. Clark was no ordinary dancer, as his interest in The Fall indicated. Born in Aberdeen in 1962, Clark showed great talent as a dancer from an early age and left home at thirteen to study at the Royal Ballet School in London. Clark's rebellious spirit quickly emerged and he often sneaked out to see his favourite bands, including Throbbing Gristle and The Fall. Occasionally the school authorities threatened to expel him but they were loath to lose their star pupil. London provided contrasting experiences for the young Clark as he constantly shuttled between classical ballet's strict training and the new wave's anarchic excesses. At seventeen, he left the Royal Ballet and joined Ballet Rambert before moving to New York and studying with Karole Armitage. 'It was a real eye opener for me,' he said, 'because she knew exactly what she wanted, she was really determined and, like most Americans, she got on with it. There was no sitting around discussing why you were doing it, or what you were trying to achieve. It seemed a better way of working than what was going on over here, which is all more intellectual.'[20]

19 Barry McIlheney, 'The Damned, New Model Army, The Fall, Spear of Destiny, Brockwell Park Festival', *Melody Maker*, 18 August 1984

20 Paolo Hewitt, 'Peculiar Clark', *NME*, 17 September 1988

In 1982 he made his début as an independent choreographer and dancer at the Riverside Studios, London, with the production *Parts 1–4*. A year later he became the choreographer-in-residence at Riverside and his growing fame and notoriety prompted *Vogue* to describe him as 'the new Nureyev'. Part of Clark's uniqueness lay in his ability to bring together elements from classical ballet and London's vibrant clubbing subcultures. 'I lead a wild life for a dancer,' he confessed in 1983. 'My friends are separate from the dance world and they are shocked that I can do something so hard as dance. In the dance world they are surprised that I have the sort of friends I do, and that we can be up all night drinking. My work falls somewhere between the extremes of strict and wild.'[21]

Smith first became aware of Clark's work when he saw him perform on a local evening news television programme: 'He was dancing through a Manchester supermarket in a dress. Everyone was going, "he looks a right idiot," but I thought, "he looks pretty cool to me." That was my first impression – and first impressions are usually the best.'[22] Soon afterwards Clark contacted Smith and asked for permission to use some of The Fall's music in his work. Smith, although incredulous, gave his consent. Clark: 'I'm not sure what he thought about the idea. I don't think he was very familiar with anything I'd done, I think it was just one of those things that he basically took a chance on and hoped that something interesting would come out of it.'

Clark founded Michael Clark & Company in 1984 with dancers Ellen van Schuylenburch, Matthew Hawkins and Julie Hood. One of the Company's first shows paired The Fall with Bruce Gilbert, formerly of Wire. 'I thought Bruce and The Fall would make a good contrast, each was quite distinctive,' said Clark. 'A lot of the critical response to that show wanted me to develop the Bruce Gilbert half rather than The Fall. It was more conventional and abstract and I guess that was the direction the dance world would have liked me to have gone in.' Clark entitled The Fall section *New Puritans* and Leigh Bowery, an Australian renowned in the club world for his outrageous

21 Ann Nugent, 'Walking on the Wild Side of the Umbrella', *The Stage and Television Today*, 27 October 1983
22 Glenda Cooper, 'How We Met: Michael Clark and Mark E. Smith', *Independent on Sunday*, 16 November 1997

clothes and make-up, provided the costumes of glam-era platform boots, tights with a cheeky hole cut in the bottom, false breasts and a peaked military hat. Provocative elements of the show included Clark and Van Schuylenburch spitting on the floor and later Clark pretending to eat a live goldfish.

Clark had chosen The Fall because of its combination of stunning lyrics and rhythmic power: 'I think most lyrics today don't really say anything and I think Mark's lyrics have got a complexity that I like to think my work has as well. Things aren't black and white, life in this day and age is very complicated, and his lyrics reflect that. I can use that in the dance, juxtapose them with something, and it thickens the plot really. Also the drive of the music I find is right for what I want to do. That kind of drive is almost aggressive and you don't find that in much other dance.'[23]

Clark's interpretation of The Fall's music found favour with Smith: 'I like his piece, I was pleasantly surprised.' Asked what he thought of Clark's campness, Smith refused even to recognize it: 'No, it's not camp! It's theatrical what he does, it's just theatrical. I think he's a pretty regular sort of guy really. All that camp crap – well, I can't see it. You don't really see it like that, do you?'[24] Brix's enthusiasm was based on the new things Clark had brought out in The Fall's music: 'It was really good. So good. It added a new dimension to the music that you never saw before, even playing it, recording it, knowing it.'[25]

The first instance of Clark and The Fall working together in a live situation took place on 20 November 1984 on BBC 2's *Old Grey Whistle Test*. The national television audience enjoyed both the sight of The Fall performing 'Lay of the Land' and, more infamously, flashes of the dancers' posteriors through Bowery's bare-assed tights. Andy Kershaw, wearing a 'Marc Riley with the Creepers' T-shirt, introduced the group and dancers. The stage proved a little too cramped for the four dancers and they only meshed sporadically with the music. The performance ended with the dancers leading a panto-mime cow across the stage and force-feeding it cartons of milk.

---

23 Hewitt, op. cit., 17 September 1988
24 Dick Witts, 'The Wonderful and Frightening World of Michael Clark', *City Life*, no. 11, 11 October 1984
25 Brix, interviewed on the *Skin and Bone* tapezine, 1984

'Boom!' went Smith, then the camera cut to a momentarily speech-less Mark Ellen: ' . . . There are those that say Michael Clark is the new Nureyev, but I don't remember Nureyev having those kinds of trouser problems.' Later in the week the critics on Ludovic Kennedy's *Did You See?* review programme expressed their outrage at the bare bottoms and The Fall's 'accompanying noise'.[26]

A lot of people think it's about them

Released in August, 'C.R.E.E.P.' boasted an even shinier and brighter Leckie production than 'Oh! Brother'. Smith's lyrics still retained their vitriol, but now they followed the melody more closely and worked well with an infectiously sing-along chorus. Rumour had it that the song was aimed at Morrissey, but Smith denied this: 'It's bits of things. A lot of people think it's about them.'[27] When Richard Skinner repeated the Morrissey allegation on *Round Table*, Smith rang up Radio One and demanded an immediate retraction, which he got. Beggars, ever-pushing The Fall's marketing envelope, placed advertisements in the music press and sold the single as both a seven- and twelve-inch, with the latter's first pressing in green vinyl with a signed colour print of Claus Castenskiold's cover painting.

The music press responded well to 'C.R.E.E.P.'. Andy Coyne thought it, 'The most accessible thing that The Fall have ever done,'[28] while Richard Cook described it as 'polished indie pop with a slight Fall smear over it'.[29] Colin Irwin saw it as The Fall edging 'still closer to conventional pop music'.[30] However, no matter how close The Fall got to pop, it would never quite make it. This was just how Smith wanted it: 'I can write pop songs, but I also hold them in contempt.'[31]

In 1984 the band eased itself away from the ghetto of the John Peel Show and recorded sessions for the more mainstream Radio One DJs, Kid Jensen and Janice Long. The Fall's music reached a wider and younger audience and Smith immediately noticed the difference in

26 Push, 'Info Freak', *Melody Maker*, 15 January 1994
27 Irwin, op. cit., 20 October 1984
28 Andy Coyne, 'The Fall: "C.R.E.E.P." ', *Sounds*, 25 August 1984
29 Richard Cook, 'The Fall: "C.R.E.E.P." ', *NME*, 8 September 1984
30 Colin Irwin, 'The Fall: "C.R.E.E.P." ', *Melody Maker*, 1 September 1984
31 Frank Worrall, 'Fall Guys', *Melody Maker*, 18 June 1983

the type of fans that followed the group: 'Yesterday we were getting mithered by all these little kids, all about seven or eight. They were saying, why didn't you do "Pat-Trip Dispenser" and stuff. Wanted autographs. So I said to Craig, get those little kids away from me. It's bloody perverse. And he said they know all our names, y'know. That's what *Smash Hits* does for you. I said, Craig – there's all swear words in our songs! They shouldn't be hearing that fuckin' stuff!'[32]

As the eighties progressed, record labels increasingly used singles as loss-making marketing tools to promote the more profitable albums. In The Fall's case, Beggars was banking on the October release of *The Wonderful and Frightening World of The Fall*. Chartwise it did quite well, reaching number 62. The album – once again produced by Leckie – starts with the band chanting, 'Lay, lay, lay,' and ends with a 'boom!' 'Two By Four' chugs along nicely and 'Copped It' features the 'friendly visitor' Gavin Friday of the Virgin Prunes, who ends the song with an exuberant, 'It ain't what you do it's the way that you do it!' 'Elves' sees Smith battling with his demons ('The fantastic is in league against me') and 'Slang King' stars the latest Smith *alter ego*. 'Bug Day' is a melancholy reflection on an itchy assortment of midges, green moths, cockroaches and Tonguehorns, while 'Stephen Song', Smith later explained, is 'about competitiveness, people getting at you, imitating you and your habits'.[33] 'Craigness' follows in the vein of 'Joker Hysterical Face' and describes Scanlon's downstairs neighbour with one eye and 'a mass of blonde curls'. The album ends with 'Disney's Dream Debased', a song based on a gruesome accident witnessed by Smith and Brix at Disneyland, where a woman was decapitated after falling on to the tracks of the roller-coaster ride. When Brix asked Mickey and Goofy what was going on, they couldn't say because they were not allowed to talk to visitors when in costume.[34]

Alongside the album, The Fall released the *Call For Escape Route* EP, a combination of a twelve-inch single with three tracks – 'Draygo's Guilt',[35] 'Clear Off!' and 'No Bulbs' – plus a bonus seven-inch with 'No Bulbs 3' and 'Slang King 2'. The cover of the seven-inch featured the most awkwardly posed photograph of The

32 Richard Cook, 'The Art of Markness', *NME*, 29 June 1985
33 Phil Sutcliffe, 'Lyricists: Mark E. Smith', *Q*, no. 68, May 1992
34 Anstadt, op. cit., 19 July 1985
35 The riff is borrowed from Amon Duul II's 'Luzifers Ghilom'.

Fall since 'It's The New Thing' in 1978. To promote the album the band toured extensively around the UK, Belgium, the Netherlands and France. At a packed-out hometown gig in October at the Hacienda, a small element of the crowd baited Smith by calling the band 'lazy bastards', 'miserable fuckers' and 'a bunch of wankers' and committed the ultimate crime by requesting old songs like 'Rowche Rumble'.[36]

Brix was still getting used to life on the road on this tour and was particularly concerned about the state of the van they travelled in. 'She had a manic fear that the tour van was going to blow up,' Smith later said. 'We stopped at a petrol station once, walked around, and when we started off again Brix said she smelt petrol. No one else could. Things got worse, and she went berserk, demanding we stop the van and then running down the embankment to shelter from the impending explosion. We convinced her to get back on, but ten minutes later she was wigging out again. No one else could smell petrol. She thought she was having her first long-awaited nervous breakdown. She was losing it completely, until finally someone else smelt it. You have never seen anyone look so relieved. She wasn't crazy after all – my coat had dragged through a petrol puddle and she was sitting on it. She wouldn't speak to me for a long while afterwards.'[37]

The tour was well attended with the band playing to packed audiences everywhere. What the fans witnessed was a particularly tight line-up, with the Hanley brothers and Karl Burns providing an irresistible rhythm section. Danny Kelly caught the band at the Lyceum and provided this vivid description: 'The wall of rhythm generated by the Hanleys and the great and loyal Karl Burns is huge and brutal. Craig Scanlon and Brix Smith drill shockingly harsh metallic guitars into the heart of the beast. Where the babblings of the wordSmith used to be a constituent part of an urban guerrilla cell – mercurial, fragmented, chancy – they now find themselves riding atop Krupp's wet dream, a black, invincible war machine. The noise is crude, cruel, inescapable and authoritarian. Smith has always been a lucky bastard, chucking his writing bag of words into the music like a carcass into a set of propellers, to watch the results spin off not as gore and offal, but diamonds, a *tour de force* of inexplicable sorcery.'[38]

36 Milly Rhener, 'The Fall, Hacienda, 18th October 1984', *Debris*, no. 7, April 1985
37 Ted Mico, 'Just Like Edie', *Melody Maker*, 30 November 1985
38 Danny Kelly, 'H.E.L.P.!: The Fall, London Lyceum', *NME*, 10 November 1984

I voted Tory for a while, last year, y'know

As part of the Christmas special issue of the *NME*, Smith offered his reflections on the past year. He complained that so many people were 'in "bands" OR at home with personal computers that the motorways never got fixed'. Another of his worries concerned Britain 'contracting into an agrarian state', and the best quote of the year was, 'The BBC World Service is the Oxfam of the mind.' The best of the year's music came from 'sub-art groups' like Jim Foetus, Frank Chickens, Cabaret Voltaire and 'us'. In conclusion he said that England now resembled a 'robber state'.[39]

With Margaret Thatcher's re-election in 1983 with a 144-seat majority, workers and their unions prepared themselves for a series of battles to protect jobs and working practices. First came the dispute over the loss of union rights at the GCHQ intelligence-gathering centre in Cheltenham, but most spectacular and traumatic was the year-long strike by the National Union of Miners over pit closures and job losses that started in March 1984. Fundraisers invited The Fall to take part in a benefit for miners in London, but they refused: 'We wanted to do it in Yorkshire,' said Brix, 'where they needed it and where the miners could come, you know. But no one would put it on anywhere north so we said forget it.'[40] The IRA's terrorist campaign continued with a bomb at Harrods in December 1983 and the bombing of the Grand Hotel in Brighton during a Conservative party conference in October 1984. In November 1984, Smith talked politics with Mat Snow in the *NME*. His views reflected a general dissatisfaction with the established political parties: 'I voted Tory for a while, last year, y'know. Budget changed my mind about the Tories a lot. It was a middle-class budget; I thought it was horrific the way they put VAT on take-away food. There's a sort of strangeness about the Tories which I think is really fascinating.' Smith went on to say he thought the Labour party and its new leader Neil Kinnock 'sucked' and that he liked the Liberal party but its Alliance with the SDP made him wonder, 'What the fuck's going on there?' What he didn't like was 'knee-jerk liberalism'.[41] In another interview he was reported as saying – in ironic parody of his growing reactionary

39   Mark E. Smith, 'Thoughts on 1984', *NME*, 22/29 December 1984
40   Brix, interviewed on the *Skin and Bone* tapezine, 1984
41   Mat Snow, 'Before and after The Fall', *NME*, 3 November 1984

reputation – 'I change my politics every day. Sometimes I'm a fascist, sometimes I'm a Nazi.'[42]

Backed into a corner, Smith was, of course, going to exaggerate his already contrary persona. For a start he never understood why journalists wanted his opinion on these kinds of topics: 'I finally asked one,' he said, 'and he said that for rock journalists in England their job gets very boring after a year or so, it's more interesting for them to wind people up. I was wondering why anyone would want to know what I think – I mean, they ask me about politics and sport and all this crap.'[43] It was a fair point, but Smith was nothing if not a provocative opinion former and journalists never had to try that hard to get a quotable rant from him. The interaction of pop and politics was also just about to become unavoidable.

In November 1984, a stream of pop stars entered a London studio to record a song by Bob Geldof and Midge Ure. From December, for the next three months, you couldn't turn on the radio without hearing Band Aid's 'Do They Know It's Christmas/Feed The World'. The record eventually sold three million copies in the UK alone. The following summer was marked by the spectacular Wembley Live Aid concert. From that moment onwards no disaster or political cause could pass without its own charity event or concert. 'Half-wit philanthropists, cosy charity gigs', Smith called them in 1985.[44] With Thatcher pining for a return to Victorian values and – despite Bob Geldof's histrionics – no sign of a concerted and sustainable political effort to aid the African continent, social responsibility, for both the Conservatives and entrepreneurial philanthropists like Geldof, was thought best left a matter of individual choice and conscience. Smith demonstrated the limitations of this attitude when he explained his opposition to the Live Aid concert: 'I thought it was all a lot of old crap really and the best thing about it was Black Sabbath doing 'Paranoid'. I certainly wouldn't have done it and in fact I refuse to do anything for nothing. Why should I? . . . Ethiopia has been in a bad state for two hundred bloody years to get back to history for a moment. And sending them billions of pounds is never going to solve anything. What they need is two tons of fucking birth-control pills,

42 Jon Wilde, 'The Frightening World of The Fall', *Jamming!*, no. 22, November 1984
43 Michael Azerrad, 'The Fall of Our Discontent', *Only Music*, 1986
44 Smith, in 'Gut of the Quantifier' on *This Nation's Saving Grace*

that would be a good idea. I know it sounds horrible and it's awful to see people dying of hunger but you don't have kids if you can't afford them, not unless you are a bit mental. I smell a lot of Victorian bloody do-gooding about the whole thing. There are people in Hulme who are half-starved so why not send it to them, eh? Never in a million years.'[45]

In the latter part of 1985, Billy Bragg and assorted music industry comrades founded Red Wedge as a consciousness-raising organization uneasily allied to a Labour party desperate for a greater share of the youth vote. Outside of Red Wedge, other pop stars also joined the anti-Thatcher campaign. Frankie Goes To Hollywood, the sleazy hip rising stars of 1984, popularized Katharine Hamnett's slogan T-shirts with its own contribution – 'Frankie Say Arm The Unemployed'. With the Tory party's commitment to 'modernization', the list of contentious issues just kept on growing: there was the opposition to US military bases and the deployment of Cruise missiles; the abolition of Labour-run metropolitan councils, including the Greater London Council; the introduction of the Youth Training Scheme, forced labour for sixteen- to seventeen-year-olds; and the all-persuasive slow death of the welfare state through lack of investment in social security, the National Health Service and education. Added to this were global campaigns against apartheid in South Africa and the spread of AIDS everywhere. Asked by *Melody Maker* at the end of 1984 what he would like to see more of in 1985, Smith's reply was libertarian to an extreme: 'Twenty-four-hour TV, less toadies, pirate radio, originals ideas, friendly landlords.' Asked what he would like to see less of he replied: 'Top 20 groups with the aura of AIDS, also less careerists and more genuine purists.' What would he ban: 'All "ANTI" lunatics, i.e. Townshend, Stoppard, CND, and all that encroach on personal choice.'[46]

45 Barry McIlheney, 'Entertaining Mr Smith', *Melody Maker*, 12 October 1985
46 Smith, op. cit., 5 January 1985

10

This Nation's Saving Grace, 1985

A lot of young people nowadays, they've got no guts, have they? They're all vegetarians and CND, they're a waste of time. They're clever but they know nowt. If ever I want any material I always hang out with old people, they're very interesting. Very rude, like, a lot of them are scum like everybody else.[1]

After two years of a relatively stable line-up, The Fall suddenly lost not one but both of its Hanley brothers. Steve left temporarily when his wife Heather gave birth to their first child. Paul's departure seemed to be more permanent, especially when it was announced he'd formed his own band, Kiss the Blade, with a couple of moon-lighting Creepers and old friends from his school – Paul Keogh on bass and Paul Fletcher on guitar and vocals. The split had occurred after a massive row at Brighton Polytechnic on 3 November 1984. 'MES blamed the bands recent woes (we'd had all our gear nicked the night before) on the fact that the rest of the band was having too much say,' Hanley recalled. 'To be honest it would probably have blown over but Steve decided to take a bit of time off from The Fall for various reasons so it seemed like a good idea to stay left. I felt I could do without MES and it was time to form my own band, which would obviously be more successful than The Fall. Shows what I know!'[2]

They released just one single, 'The Party's Begun', in March 1985 on the Incision label. An impressed Helen Fitzgerald reviewed it for *Melody Maker* calling it 'winsome, fractious music, distinguished from a horde of other hopefuls by the flair of its construction'.[3] By August, Kiss the Blade had become Shout Bamalam and recruited Martin

---

1   Edwin Pouncey, 'Creek Show', *Sounds*, 28 September 1985
2   Mark Prindle, 'Paul Hanley – 2002', email interview from: http://www.mark-prindle.com/hanley-i.htm
3   Helen Fitzgerald, 'Kiss the Blade: ' "The Party's Begun" ' (Incision)', *Melody Maker*, 2 March 1985

Dulson on guitar and keyboards. In retrospect, the spokesman for the band was over-optimistic when he announced: 'The group aims to be a classic pop combo, so earnest young men might be disappointed if looking for a new Fall or Joy Division.'[4] Although not half as disappointed as anyone looking for a Shout Bamalam record – they never released one. After this Hanley decided to leave the music business and took up a job in the computer industry. 'Being in The Fall,' he later recalled, 'was a dream come true and a bit of a nightmare. I have a lot of good memories about The Fall and I'm still very proud of the records they made while I was involved. Mark Smith certainly had his moments, but contrary to what he would have you believe he isn't (or wasn't) The Fall. I didn't join The Fall to work with Mark Smith, I put up with Mark Smith to be in The Fall. Having said that, he was the best lyricist I've ever come across and on his day was certainly one of the best front men.'[5]

The remaining drummer, Burns, provided ample cover for Paul's departure, but finding Steve's replacement was potentially trickier. Fortunately, a possible candidate had already entered The Fall's orbit through a Michael Clark connection. Simon Rogers first met Clark through their work together at Ballet Rambert. When Clark needed a musician to orchestrate The Fall's 'The Classical' for his *HAIL the Classical* with the Scottish Ballet Company (because the Musicians' Union refused him permission to use recorded music), he turned to Rogers. Despite his efforts, however, it proved to be an impossible task for the celebrated Royal Scottish Orchestra, as an exasperated Smith explained: 'You're talking about two chords and about three inflections in the whole song. Simon scored the whole thing for the orchestra and they couldn't get it, they couldn't get, they couldn't play the fucker. I mean can you believe it? It's disgusting. You know, it cost a lot of money to score it for a thirty-two-piece orchestra. And I did a vocal tape that they were supposed to play along with. And they couldn't carry it. I couldn't believe it, they couldn't carry it, they couldn't play, it was too difficult.'[6] Because of the difficulties the Musicians' Union finally relented and Clark danced to the recorded version at the work's première in Glasgow in March.

4 Anon., 'Fast Forward', *Melody Maker*, 10 August 1985
5 Prindle, op. cit., 2002
6 Scott Brecker, 'Wordsmith', *Option Magazine*, July/August 1986

Clark chose the track because it fitted well with his parodic use of classical ballet forms. His irreverence shocked ballet *aficionados*, not least when he sprang on stage sporting a giant strap-on penis. Music journalists and Fall fans alike often wondered why the famously unpretentious Smith should want to work with a ballet dancer. But Smith saw clear parallels between his own long struggle with musical forms and Clark's commitment to reinterpreting modern dance: 'He is a tremendous hard worker who is completely dedicated. He had to live ballet twenty-four hours a day. I have great admiration for people like that. He was so brave to break away from the traditional expected route of ballet and create his own style and following. He is immensely popular and is, in fact, changing the course of modern dance.'[7]

By the mid-eighties Clark had gathered together many talented collaborators, including the film and video maker John Maybury, the photographer David La Chappelle and the clothes designers Bodymap. Brix particularly appreciated Bodymap and often modelled their clothes, even appearing on the catwalk for them in October. The Fall and Clark's collaborations continued in September with *our caca phoney H, our caca phoney H* at the Riverside Studios. To the soundtrack of 'An Older Lover' and in a reversal of sexual stereo-typing, Julie Hood and Ellen Van Schuylenburch came on wearing thick military jackets and monkey boots, before being joined by Clark wearing a white apron, curly-haired wig and another giant dildo. Chris Savage-King described Clark as looking like 'Dionysus on speed', before outlining the work's sticky climax: 'Regarding them alternately, Clark grasps the prosthesis and gives it a quick wank. His face is fixed in the slack-jawed expression of the callow lout, but the toughie image is undercut not only by the costume, but by the way in which he turns his attention from one woman to the other – by way of first-grade spring points. This collusion of childlike perkiness and masculine debauchery is delightfully silly, comically knowing. Julie Hood finishes the sequence by producing a knife and chopping off his willy. Clark's consistent undermining of the phallus turns literal!'[8]

7 Anon., 'Interview with The Fall', *Muze Magazine*, issue 4, October 1985
8 Chris Savage-King, 'Back to the Sixties with Michael Clark', *Dance Theatre Journal*, Winter 1985

We're The Fall and we're from the First World

Simon Rogers brought some experience of chart success to the group, albeit as a member of the 'Bolivian' folk group Incantation. A versatile and knowledgeable musician, just as capable on keyboards as on guitar, Rogers's arrival forced the reluctant retirement of a loyal piece of The Fall's hardware, the Snoopy electric piano. With its loss, though, the band took another step towards radio-friendly easier-listening. Rogers's first live appearance came in March at Hammersmith Town Hall. Supporting the band that night and for the rest of the mini-tour was Khmer Rouge, with Marcia Schofield on keyboards.[9] Richard Cook later summed up The Fall's performance that night as 'vicious heavy metal'. Smith agreed but laid the blame on Leckie's high-decibel mixing: 'He bust all the sound meters on the PA, everything full up like in a studio. A lot of people liked it, a lot thought it was the worst gig they'd seen. Leckie did us once in Essex and we were deaf for days.'[10] Rogers then accompanied the band on another gruelling American tour through to April, and helped to develop new material like 'Couldn't Get Ahead', 'Barmy', 'Petty Thief Lout' and 'Cruiser's Creek'.

By June, Hanley had returned to take part in the band's eighth Peel Session. The set included a version of the band's forthcoming single 'Couldn't Get Ahead', which would be paired on the single with 'Rollin' Dany'. The Fall had recorded the songs earlier in the year with producer Leckie in a live-in studio Smith thought far too extravagant: 'Too comfy. You'd be getting ready to do a take and somebody'd have a cup of tea on in the kitchen. You'd have to sleep in a bed which some scruffy horrible guitarist had been in two weeks before.'[11] Significantly, 'Rollin' Dany' borrowed from Gene Vincent's back catalogue and was The Fall's first cover version. Smith's choice was wilfully obscure and listeners could easily have mistaken it for an original by The Fall, a not-too-distant relation perhaps of 'Fiery Jack'. The music critics certainly rated the single. Mat Snow made it his Sound of the Week, writing: 'This sonic blitz vigorously shakes out all your loose change and sends you hyperventilating on

9 The *NME* spread a rumour that The Fall had turned down Sonic Youth as support for this tour. See Anon., 'T–zers: Hot Brix', *NME*, 16 March 1985.
10 Richard Cook, 'The Art of Markness', *NME*, 29 June 1985
11 ibid.

your way.'[12] Jack Barron in *Sounds* joked that the letter E between Mark and Smith stood for 'Elvis',[13] while Yazoo's Vince Clarke, a guest reviewer for *Melody Maker*, described 'Rollin' Dany' as 'very poppy'.[14]

In July, a week after the massive Live Aid concert at Wembley, The Fall made a headlining appearance at the WOMAD Festival on Mersea Island, Essex. The Festival was an annual celebration of music from around the world, but what excited Smith about the event was the appearance of one of his favourite English musicians, Peter Hammill, playing just before The Fall. Never one to ingratiate himself with an audience – especially a liberal one – Smith opened The Fall's set with the announcement: 'We're The Fall and we're from the First World.'[15]

A well-produced bedroom sound

Beggars announced the release of *This Nation's Saving Grace* in September with full-page advertisements in the music press, reproducing Castenskiold's moody cover drawing of Manchester's city-centre skyline. These expensive advertisements helped the album get to number 54 in the official charts, an improvement of eight places over *Wonderful and Frightening* and seventeen over *Hex Enduction Hour*.

The album opens with 'Mansion', a rare example of an instrumental by The Fall. 'Bombast', the following track, returns to more familiar territory where 'bastard idiots' come to 'feel the wrath' of Smith's bombast. 'Barmy' borrows a riff from 'Valleri' by the Monkees, while 'What You Need' borrows its title from a *Twilight Zone* episode about a man with the ability to know and give people exactly what they need. The lyrics for 'Spoilt Victorian Child' hailed from the time of *Live At The Witch Trials* but Smith could never get the group to write some 'really daft English music' for it until Rogers came on the scene. The locked groove of 'LA' provides Smith with the perfect backdrop

---

12 Mat Snow, 'Sound of the Week: "Rollin' Dany" / "Couldn't Get Ahead" ', *NME*, 29 June 1985

13 Jack Barron, 'The Fall: "Rolling Dany" ', *Sounds*, 22 June 1985

14 Vince Clarke and Paul Quinn, 'The Fall: "Rollin' Dany" / "Couldn't Get Ahead" ', *Melody Maker*, 22 June 1985

15 Gavin Martin, 'It's a WOMAD, Mad, Mad World', *NME*, 27 July 1985

to share his paranoid thoughts on that most imaginary of cities, Los Angeles: 'It's more haunted than any old place. The atmosphere's very still, I think that has a lot to do with it, so things stick a lot more.'[16]

'My New House' humorously celebrates Smith and Brix's purchase of a semi-detached house in Sedgley Park, just a couple of streets away from his parents' home. 'Paintwork' – 'Hey Mark, you're fucking up the paintwork' – continues the domestic theme both in its lyrics and style of recording (Rogers's spare room on a four-track). Smith created the song's surreal over-dubbed segment when watching television in a hotel room and accidentally hitting the record button on his cassette player: 'It fits in really good, you can't contrive something like that.'[17] The album ended with the exuberant Can tribute, 'I Am Damo Suzuki', and the throwaway 'To Nkroachment: Yarbles'.

Of the reviewers, Chris Roberts in *Sounds* wrote, 'Oh, to be thirteen, and have this be the first record one heard. Life and what you needed would never be the same again.'[18] David Quantick described it as the most accessible album yet by The Fall, but it was still 'infinitely more peculiar than almost anything else released this year'.[19] The marriage of the peculiar and the accessible at least partly derived from Leckie's production skills. Smith marvelled at his work with The Fall's sound, particularly how he separated and brought forward the drums and bass. 'It's not effects that are involved,' he said, 'it's just what's there, bringing out what's always there.' Leckie chose not to smooth out The Fall's rough edges; instead he made them a virtue. What both aspired to was a 'well-produced bedroom sound'.[20]

Accompanying the album was the single 'Cruiser's Creek' and its promotional video directed by Cerith Wyn Evans. The song and video recounted the events of a macabre office party where everybody dies after the gas is left on. 'It's a party lyric with an evil twist,' said Smith.[21] The video starred Leigh Bowery, dressed, according to Smith, 'like a clerk on acid, like he was from some alternative

16 Pouncey, op. cit., 28 September 1985
17 ibid.
18 Chris Roberts, 'Nationwide', *Sounds*, 28 September 1985
19 David Quantick, 'Fall In! The Fall: *This Nation's Saving Grace*', *NME*, 28 September 1985
20 Gary Hopkins, 'Free FALL', *One Two Testing*, June 1986
21 Andy Strickland, 'Rise & Fall', *Record Mirror*, 26 October 1985

world.'[22] Smith himself wore a less extravagant suit and tie and brandished a loud hailer bought especially for the occasion.

Smith kept the loud hailer and it accompanied him on The Fall's October and November tour. His image had changed drastically since the last live appearances. When he performed 'Bombast' and 'Cruiser's Creek' on *The Tube* in November he wore riding boots, a long black leather trench coat and his hair was cropped short, but it was his eye-liner that shocked many fans. Apart from the outfit, the performance on *The Tube* contained the full and familiar repertoire of Smith's stage mannerisms, including singing through his hand, chewing gum, pouting, endless struggles with the mike stand and rifling through a plastic bag for lyric sheets. Before the set, presenter Muriel Gray interviewed Smith and asked him about The Fall becoming accessible. Staring at his fingernails, he replied: 'When I was teenage I always thought accessibility was something to be spat upon. The problem is actually bringing stuff out that is comprehensible to the public, which is what we always manage to do.' Did success threaten to ruin Smith's anonymity? 'The people who follow The Fall are the salt of the earth, but they're not the sort of people that attack you in supermarkets.'

In 1985, Smith started to build up a working relationship with the promoter John Lennard. Since Carroll's leaving, Smith's management responsibilities had increased considerably. 'I really enjoyed it,' Smith said, 'but I became more of a clerk than writing songs. Two days a week was for filling in tax forms and shit.'[23] Over the next year Lennard became increasingly involved in both strategy and the day-to-day management of the band. 'He promoted a couple of our shows and he seemed really together,' said Brix. 'He was glamorous and handsome, upper-middle-class, very flash, drove a convertible Mercedes. Plus I liked him because he was Jewish and I'm Jewish, so on a brotherly level I trusted him, which was stupid and naïve of me. Up until he got into financial trouble he was great. We just loved him. He was so much fun and we'd stay at his house in Gospel Oak. He always had these really glamorous girlfriends, with blonde hair and big tits.'

Over the next couple of years Smith and Brix spent increasing

22 Anon., 'Lost MES interview', *TBLY*, no. 3, February 1995
23 Michael Lang, 'The Fall – Mark E. Smith Interview', *BravEar*, vol. 3, issue 5, Fall/Winter 1986

amounts of time in London, something which pleased her more than him: 'I loved going to London. It was like a big city where you could get smoked salmon, like a little bit of luxury. But Mark hated, hated, hated London – "Fuckin' Southerners!" I always wished that we could live there like all the other rock stars. The first year in Manchester I remember vomiting every week because the diet was just disgusting – fish and chips, full of grease. He would drink beer and be in the pub all the time. I didn't like the pub at all. It was just nasty old men with fags in their mouths – gross, sad, grim people. I just avoided it. He was just so anti the middle-class and so pro the working class.'

To provide an outlet for her obvious pop leanings, Brix formed her own band, Adult Net. The name came from a line – 'adult net, net of mesh' – in The Fall's 'Stephen Song'. Brix chose it because she liked the combination of 'adult' representing the illicit and 'net' with its double-meaning of trap and safety net: 'I wanted to form an unknown band with no pressure and sing and have fun and make a song that wasn't depressing or political, that was humorous – one that you felt full and satisfied at the end of.'[24]

May saw the release of her first single on Beggars Banquet, a perky cover version of Strawberry Alarm Clock's sixties hit 'Incense And Peppermints'. On the B-side was 'Searching For The Now', a thinly disguised version of The Fall's 'Rebellious Jukebox', and the experimental 'Fat Hell', with its backwards music and forwards vocals. Brix chose 'Incense And Peppermints' after hearing it on a video of Russ Meyer's *Beyond the Valley of the Dolls*. It was a song she had heard throughout her childhood: 'I think I must have heard it a lot subconsciously because when I heard it again when I was sixteen – I knew it! My mother used to take me to Sunset Strip and I saw all the hippies and freaks and things.'[25]

Various Fall-related musicians worked on the record each using a joke pseudonym: 'Ottersley Kipling' was Simon Rogers (because, Brix said, he always used to talk about 'exceedingly good cakes'); 'Mask' Aiechmann was Karl Burns ('because, you know, he's kind of a "Nazi" guy'); 'Silki Guth' was Craig Scanlon ('Silki was the name of his girlfriend at the time'); 'Count Gunther Hoalingen' was Smith ('he used to say if we ever had a child he would name it Gunther');

24   Richard Cook, 'The Girl Can't Help It!', *NME*, 25 May 1985
25   ibid.

149

and 'Cissy Williams' was a friend of Rogers's. 'Dr K. Rouge' and 'Mrs Mer Rouge', on guitar and 'spectral keyboards' respectively, were Philip and Marcia Schofield. The producer Leckie adopted the name 'Swami Anand Nagara'.

The single came out, much to Brix's dismay, in the middle of a psychedelic fashion revival, labelled by journalists as the 'Paisley Underground'. Not to be discouraged, Brix remained faithful to the sixties with her second single, 'Edie', released in the middle of November. The song commemorated the short life of Edie Sedgwick, Andy Warhol muse and star of his film *Ciao Manhattan*. Brix wrote the song at college and while there took the opportunity to play it to Sedgwick's cousin, Rob Sedgwick, a fellow student at Bennington: 'He was disgusted,' Brix recalled. 'He said, "Why would you want to write a song about that, it's a tragedy?" and we'd say, you should be proud of her, she was such a character in history.'[26] For Brix, Sedgwick epitomized the modern pop icon she wanted to become: 'She just lived life really fast and people described her as just like the most captivating and enchanting girl. Everyone would like to be like that, wouldn't they?'[27]

Because of the reverence shown to The Fall, Brix's brand of pop was always going to cause problems for the critics. Gavin Martin's comments in the *NME* typified many people's inability to judge Adult Net on its own merits: 'I could go on about the ill-advised nature of eulogizing one of Andy Warhol's long dead satellites, but instead I'll note the winsome vocalese and the regurgitated psychedelic doggerel and breathe a sigh of relief that an outlet exists for preoccupations which would otherwise blemish The Nation's Saving Grace.'[28]

Part of the fun in music is working out the lyrics

Journalists often asked Smith why he never put lyric sheets in with his records and he always answered that he wrote the lyrics to fit with particular pieces of music and never intended them to be read by themselves. Brix described the process that brought the two together:

26 Jonathan Romney, 'Alias Smith & Edie', *NME*, 7 December 1985
27 Nancy Culp, 'Just Like Edie', *Record Mirror*, 4 January 1986
28 Gavin Martin, 'The Adult Net: "Edie" ', *NME*, 23 November 1985

'Mark just had books of lyrics and certain things he had ideas for and he'd say I want it like this and he'd go "ah, ugh, ah, ugh" and I'd have to interpret it into the guitar and he'd go, "No, not, ugh, ugh, it's ah, ugh." That would be one way. If I wrote something I would write a full song, with verses and chords, and he would just add the words.' Because of his long-standing reticence at seeing his lyrics in print, it came as quite a surprise when he allowed Berlin-based David Luff to publish *The Fall Lyrik & Texte* (also known by its cover title, *The Fall Lyrics*). The pamphlet contained assorted press releases, drawings by Smith and Brix and, most importantly, the lyrics to twenty-one songs in both German and English.

Knowing the lyrics, Smith previously said, spoilt the listener's first experience of the record: 'If ever I bought an LP when I was a kid with a lyric sheet in it, I used to sit down and read the lyrics before I even played the record. So you don't really listen to the record, you're reading the lyrics. If you just want to write lyrics you should be a poet or something. Part of the fun in music is working out the lyrics, I think.'[29] This was certainly part of the fun with The Fall, where uncertainty over Smith's lyrics opened up a space for listeners to provide their own creative misunderstandings. Matters weren't helped by Smith's sometimes muddied vocals, often the result of being recorded in the same room as the group (a technique also used by Damo Suzuki in early Can).

Another reason for Smith not publishing his lyrics was the constant changes he made to them: he liked to ad-lib and definitive versions didn't exist. He also felt that lyric sheets were a 'bourgeois thing' and 'most people who print lyrics are arrogant and stupid, it's hilarious to read these lyrics that they think are good'.[30] Printed lyrics were of more interest to fans than to the writer, as Kay Carroll pointed out to Ian McCulloch when he asked about Smith's lyrics: 'We'd always tell him the same thing – that the best records, from Captain Beefheart, Lou, Iggy, whatever, meant far more to the fans than the writers.'[31]

29 Pouncey, op. cit., 28 September 1985
30 Dave Segal, 'Hip Priest in Motown', *You Can't Hide Your Love Forever*, no 3, Winter 1989
31 Carroll, in Mick Middles, *Ian McCulloch: King of Cool*, London: Independent Music Press, 1998

Smith rarely talked about the mechanics of his writing, but what little he did say was marked by a clear enthusiasm: 'Writing lyrics is what I got into rock music for. I love writing, it's me only pleasure. I'm compulsive, my problem's knowing when to shut up on a song, I can't put that bleeding pen down, so I hone it, try to get it as simple as possible.' The least of his problems was finding rhyming words: 'The funny thing is I think in rhyme all the time and a lot of the time when I'm cutting and honing lyrics what I have to do is unrhyme them. Dostoevsky's a brilliant writer, Gogol, and none of their stuff rhymes but it's pure poetry to me. It's sweet, hard, it buzzes with words.'[32] He also never worried about running out of ideas, claiming to have hundreds of songs stuffed in drawers at his home: 'It is very much a need to write that draws me on. It is something of a hunger. It's not like a masturbation exercise. I just feel that I'm missing something if I don't write about it.'[33] Smith's skill lay in his ability to combine often obscure but always compelling lyrics with simple but never bland music: 'My attitude is if you can't deliver it like a garage band, fuck it.'[34]

His sources of inspiration came from all quarters: from high literary culture, like the Russian classics mentioned above, to television and the letters page in the *Daily Mirror*, 'I'm really into the ridiculous ways people abuse the English language.'[35] The main inspiration for Smith, however, was not the media but the observation of people as they went about their day-to-day lives. Speaking in 1990 he revealed just how passionately he believed this to be his vocation: 'I think my fuckin' role in The Fall has always been, whether people fuckin' buy it or not, is to fuckin' observe people and fuckin' comment on 'em. It might sound fuckin' simplistic, but surely that should be the role of all lyric writers, and there's fuckin' none doing it . . . Most of these people who write about the world never even walk down the street.'[36]

32 Phil Sutcliffe, 'Lyricists: Mark E. Smith', *Q*, no. 68, May 1992
33 John Wilde, 'The Fall Guy', *Zig-Zag*, November 1983
34 Sean O'Hagan and James Brown, 'The Three Horsemen of the Apocalypse', *NME*, 25 February 1989
35 Barney Hoskyns, 'Hip Priest: The Mark Smith Interview', *NME*, 14 November 1981
36 Ian Gittins, 'The Fall: Funfair for the Common Man', *Melody Maker*, 3 March 1990

Not surprisingly Smith's list of what he termed 'intelligent rock writers' was short and exclusive, consisting of just Captain Beefheart, Ray Davies, Hank Williams, Lou Reed and Peter Hammill.[37] His advice for budding lyricists was simply to read more: 'Take a fucking relish in literature, not the fucking *Sunday Mirror*, they should go and read summat proper, and write down their fucking feelings. What more advice do you want? There's no fucking computer disc of fucking lyric writing that you can fucking just buy, you know what I mean?'[38]

Because of Smith's obvious way with words, publishers have occasionally approached him with book deals. But rather than the novel or autobiography the publishers ask for and think might sell, Smith has always been more interested in writing fragments of prose and short stories: 'I could write a book on a beer mat,' he once boasted.[39] While structured and sustained prose may not be his forte, he remains a master of the telling word or phrase that encapsulates a character, a scene or even a whole philosophy of life.

Smith's longest piece of text (at approximately 1,400 words) was published in the *NME* in December 1985. Entitled 'Hark the Hoaly Lunatic', it opens with an extract from another text, 'Your Publex / Transport Map of Hoalingen Station', published in '1998'. Hoalingen, Lancashire, with a population of 105, was once 'the indispensable hub of an autocracy stretching from the shores of the Baltic to the irreverent ice-bulks of Moose-Annuk'. In the story an 'obnoxious Christian family' board a train with an evil child. The conductor, Stingdorf Carthwaite, 'talks to it as if it were a budgie', while the 'sunlight dapples on the heads of the other passengers, leaf shadows portrayed briefly on their spazframes.' The Christian family eventually disembark and the conductor puts on a cassette of 'upbeat synthesizer music which, distorted thru' the unserviced Jap desk, sounds like a mocking gaggle of duck-klaxon imitators'. Intercut with the narrative is an advertisement, 'Bulletin from Dikkville House, London, February 2009', which offers 'innovatory word-processed circulars in original blue, red, and black print,

37 Sutcliffe, op. cit., May 1992
38 Paul Quinn, 'Pride and The Fall', *Making Music*, May 1991
39 Ian McCann, 'Love, Love, Love, Love, Love your Armani', NME, 29 February 1992

c. 1980–8' and the 'recently discovered writings of a "Staret" or "Hoaly Lunatic" from the 1980s'. The latter offers random observations on mini-zoos, painters and decorators, Hulme Estate, designers of motorways and the state of pavements. This is followed by Field Marshal Dashiell Wynan exclaiming, 'The Lord help us if we have that war,' and Prof. Bruce I. Shepton providing a reappraisal of British music, including a critique of Kevin Rowland's 'redick gypo-paddy look'. Then there is a poem by Zabadak Goolze entitled 'The '80s Depression and Me'. The text ends with a 'youth', next to the Copeland monument to Large-Scale Small Enterprise in Piccadilly, Manchester, picking up a handbill with the text: 'WILKOMMEN! HIYA! WELCOME! BIENVU! HOALINGEN STATION!'[40]

40   Mark E. Smith, 'Hark the Hoaly Lunatic', *NME*, 21–28 December 1985

Martin Bramah, Karl Burns, Mark E. Smith, Tony Friel,
Una Baines, Prestwich, December 1977

Karl Burns, Marc Riley, Mark E. Smith, Yvonne Pawlett,
Martin Bramah, Manchester, August 1978

Mark E. Smith, Mayflower Club, Manchester, July 1979

Steve Hanley and Mark E. Smith, Rafters Club,
Manchester, July 1980

Craig Scanlon and Mark E. Smith, Prestwich Clough, January 1981

Michael Clark and Mark E. Smith, *I Am Curious, Orange*,
Edinburgh, August 1988

Marcia Schofield, Craig Scanlon, Brix E. Smith, Steve Hanley,
Simon Wolstencroft, *I Am Curious, Orange*, Edinburgh,
August 1988

Mark E. Smith, London, March 1993

Bend Sinister, 1986

I had a computer about two years ago. I'm not against computers. But I got rid of mine after about a year 'cause I was trying to write songs on it and shit. And I wrote prose on it and stored me lyrics and stuff like that. And I just hated the way this thing'd dictate how I should paragraph things and how things should be said and punctuated. It wouldn't obey me at all. I write in a real weird way. I misspell words and I write half sentences then leave a thing and complete the sentence like I do in me songs. I like to play around with it, it's part of the fun. And this computer wouldn't have it, man. It'd fucking put it back up there, like a letter. I fucking gave it away![1]

In February 1986, at the invitation of Morrissey, The Fall formed part of a delegation of Manchester musicians dispatched across to Liverpool to help raise funds for Liverpool City Council and its 'loony left' leader Derek Hatton. The council was appealing against surcharge and disqualification proceedings brought against forty-eight councillors for delays in a 'legal' rate. Three thousand Liverpudlians paid £6 and crammed into the Royal Court Theatre to see three of Manchester's finest bands – New Order, The Fall and The Smiths. Smith later complained about the supposed illiteracy of the audience. His 'evidence' was poor sales of his lyric books. Whereas Luff had shifted about fifty copies a night at The Fall's own headlining gigs, in Liverpool he sold just three copies.[2] The declining intelligence of the nation's youth would be a recurring theme for Smith throughout the year.

The rest of February and March saw The Fall touring America and promoting the US release of *This Nation's Saving Grace* on the PVC/Jem label. In April, Karl Burns left the band for a second time, this time because Smith objected to his new girlfriend, Carrie. The two had first met during an interview at Radio Derby. They fell in love

1 Scott Brecker, 'Wordsmith', *Option Magazine*, July/August 1986
2 ibid.

and a year later in 1987 had a son called James.[3] Smith drafted in Paul Hanley as a temporary replacement. For a brief moment he also considered radically rethinking The Fall's rhythm section: 'I don't even know whether to get a drummer,' he speculated. 'I'm thinking of using Paul when he's available and using other things, like a DX7 rhythm section, a rep sort of thing. We've proved how good we are with drums and I'm sure I could do it just as well on a machine.'[4] Despite Smith's confidence, it quickly became clear that The Fall needed a new permanent drummer.

Born 19 January 1963 in Altrincham, John Simon Wolstencroft's first band was the Patrol, formed with friends Andy Couzens, Ian Brown and John Squire. The band soon split and Wolstencroft, by now also known as 'Funky Si', earned his living working in a fish shop (while Brown and Squire, of course, went on to form the Stone Roses). Between February 1981 and February 1982, he played and rehearsed at Decibel Studios, Manchester, with Andy Rourke and Johnny Marr as the Freak Party. Wolstencroft also joined the rehearsal group that included Morrissey and Marr, but turned down the opportunity to join their band, The Smiths. Next up came a stint in Terry Hall's the Colourfield, then the Weeds, and then an offer from Smith he just couldn't refuse.

Wolstencroft's first gig with The Fall came in June at Leas Cliff Hall, Folkestone. This was quickly followed by a series of high-profile dates, including in July supporting Talk Talk in Hanger T2 at the Imperial War Museum, Duxford, and the next day at the G-Mex, Manchester, as part of the 'Festival of the Tenth Summer'. The festival was Tony Wilson's way of celebrating the tenth anniversary of the beginning of punk and by extension the start of the burgeoning Manchester music scene. Appearing alongside The Fall in front of eleven thousand fans were John Cooper Clarke, The Worst, Virgin Prunes, Pete Shelley, John Cale, The Smiths and, closing the night, New Order. The Fall came on early, at about six o'clock in the evening, and played to a largely unsympathetic audience, impatient for the chart acts to follow.

A week later a similar situation arose when at Finsbury Park, London, The Fall along with Pete Shelley and New Model Army supported the Damned for their 'Tenth Anniversary Tea Party'.

3   Billy Smith, 'Thirst', *Melody Maker*, 7 February 1987
4   Gary Hopkins, 'Free FALL', *One Two Testing*, June 1986

Accepting these types of gigs signalled Smith's new willingness to make compromises, earn some cash and possibly win over new audiences for The Fall. The band's constant touring, however, carried the danger of exhausting the band and destroying some of its inventiveness, as Smith admitted: 'You get tired, really tired . . . I'm psyching myself up all the time for these live concerts and a lot of it is going through the ceiling.'[5] After almost ten years of excessive and itinerant living, perhaps Smith was beginning to feel jaded: his next single certainly invited speculation.

Give me some energy

The Fall's 'Living Too Late' appeared in early July with a front cover painting by Castenskiold of a man being tempted to his right by the devil and to his left by an angel. With lines like 'crow's feet are ingrained' and 'maybe I'm living too late', interviewers naturally asked whether the twenty-nine-year-old Smith was beginning to feel his age. He replied that the song shouldn't be taken literally and although it contained elements of his own experience he was more interested in getting inside the heads of his neighbours in Prestwich. 'I was thinking about suburbia,' Smith said, 'upper-working-class suburbia, and I was just wondering about these guys walking around the streets, whether they ever get really pissed off. All of my neighbours are like – y'know, they're all good people and that but they've all got a lot under their belt.'[6]

For all its lyrical qualities, the mournful grind of 'Living Too Late' was an unlikely choice as a single. Smith played a surer hand a couple of months later with the release of a cover 'Mr Pharmacist', originally by Texas-based garage band the Other Half. It had the lot – a pumping rock riff, a sing-along chorus and topicality. Smith's request for Mr Pharmacist to 'give me some energy' came at a time when the British government was in the midst of one of its periodic attempts to stem the use of class A drugs. Smith's attitude was consistently libertarian: 'I don't think heroin is any good, it's crap, a horrible drug. But I've got to say it – if someone wants to smoke themselves to death or drink themselves to death with whisky, jump

5   ibid.
6   Ron Rom, 'Semi-detached Suburban Mr Smith', *Sounds*, 19 July 1986

out of windows or whatever then it's their basic right.' He, personally, couldn't see the attraction of heroin: 'Have you ever seen anyone on it? They sweat and snuffle like little piglets. Imagine paying money to be like that, you'll find out what it's like when you're ninety anyway.'[7] The Fall's obscurity ensured that the guardians of public morality remained blissfully unaware of the song's controversial message. Still, some people listened and, more importantly, bought, because the single became the first by The Fall to enter the Top 100, reaching the giddy height of number 75.

Brix's Adult Net also had a productive summer on the singles front with 'White Night (Stars Say Go)' coming out in June and 'Waking Up In The Sun' in early September. The singles both benefited from the guiding hand of Ian Broudie, the first as a mixer and the second as producer. Despite the unmistakable pop credentials of the wistful 'Waking Up In The Sun', reviewers still unfairly judged Adult Net according to The Fall's unapproachable standards. Kevin Murphy thought it as summer-like 'as a bank holiday in Cleathorpes',[8] while Dele Fadele simply requested that somebody 'phone the morgue'.[9]

The whole idea of civilization is to get everybody on the dole

The Fall's next album, *Bend Sinister*, came out in early October. Despite selling well and reaching number 36 in the charts (almost 20 places higher than the last album), it disappointed some fans and even Smith himself: '*Bend Sinister* is the hardest to listen to in retrospect. It's interesting because it's the one album I can't be objective about. Did people hate it that much? Well, I only noticed it when we went on tour and thought, "must do something off that," and there was like one song I wanted to do when I thought about it.'[10]

The main bone of contention was the woolly production. The producer, John Leckie, put this down to Smith's insistence that the album be mastered from an ordinary chrome Dolby cassette. This helped Leckie decide that *Bend Sinister* would be his last album with

---

7   Gavin Martin, 'Revolting Soul', *NME*, 30 August 1986
8   Kevin Murphy, 'The Adult Net: "Waking Up In The Sun" ', *Sounds*, 13 September 1986
9   Dele Fadele, 'The Adult Net: "Waking Up In The Sun" ', *NME*, 13 September 1986
10 Jonh Wilde, 'The Mouth that Roared', *Melody Maker*, 5 March 1988

The Fall: Smith's idiosyncrasies had become too much to bear. 'They would do things like play a song once and then that would be it,' Leckie said, 'they wouldn't want to record it again. Mark was crazy. He'd do things like, you'd do all the mixing and he'd listen to them and he'd take tapes away home and he'd be very enthusiastic. But then you'd get to the cutting-room and he wouldn't like it. When we were mastering *Bend Sinister* and the guy had just cut the acetate, Mark was stomping around saying, "That's not the mixes we had in the studio," but he'd been listening to a chrome Dolby cassette he'd taken away and played on this little Walkman through a speaker that was distorting, and that was his reference. In the end, a lot of that album was cut from a cassette because that's the quality that Mark wanted.'[11] After his time with The Fall, Leckie moved on to work with the Stone Roses producing in 1989 what many consider to be his finest work, the eponymous *Stone Roses* album.

Despite the poor sound quality, *Bend Sinister* does have its highlights, such as the sprightly and self-deprecating 'Shoulder Pads' and the spiralling menace and paranoia of 'US 80's–90's' (made extra-relevant by Reagan's recent use of British airbases to bomb Libya). The most inadvertently topical song on the album was 'Terry Waite Sez', the subject of which was kidnapped just before the album came out. For Smith it confirmed his powers of precognition. 'He was very interested in witchcraft and believed himself to have powers,' recalled Brix, 'which may be a mental condition; my father would certainly say that he was delusional. There was also "The Curse of The Fall", where he would curse people and bad things would happen to them. He wasn't like a devil worshipper or anything like that, but he definitely thought of himself as an empowered person and able to control things.' Brix claims to have come up with the title for 'Terry Waite Sez' and wrote the music but not the lyrics. A couple of weeks after the release, Waite's brother rang Beggars and asked for a copy of the lyrics to see if there was any psychic clue as to where he might be held. There wasn't.

The critics were unanimously disappointed with the album. David Haslam missed Smith's 'Babel-ling monologues of eyeball-to-eyeball social comment', thinking they had been replaced by 'more occasional

---

11   T. Doyle, 'Control Zone: A Desk Job with John Leckie', *Melody Maker*, 3 June 1995

contributions:; pithy, scratchy phrases delivered in so clotted a vocal style that they undermine any potential accessibility in the music.'[12] Jack Barron blamed Brix's 'pop devices' and warned that 'the lights on the Smiths' Christmas tree are flickering.'[13] Simon Reynolds raised similar points but added that whatever criticisms could be made against The Fall it remained an enigma, something that refused to be pinned down: 'A vast body of work, around which a million words have been spilt, and still I don't feel nearer a notion of what they're about. The Fall don't represent or propose anything. They cannot be recruited to any scheme, clarified or filed away. They are this stubborn thing.'[14]

The title of the album came from a novel by Vladimir Nabokov, first published in 1947. 'Bend sinister,' he wrote, 'means a heraldic bar or band drawn from the left side (and popularly, but incorrectly, supposed to denote bastardy). This choice of title was an attempt to suggest an outline broken by refraction, a distortion in the mirror of being, a wrong turn taken by life, a sinistral and sinister world.'[15] In Nabokov's novel, the hero, Adam Krug, is persecuted, and his child tortured and murdered, for not complying with the wishes of the totalitarian party of the 'average man', run by an old school enemy, Paduk (aka the 'Toad'). This theme of antipathy to middle-class conformity recurs throughout Smith's career, from 'Middle Mass' of 1981 through to 'Bourgeois Town' of 2001. In interviews at the time of *Bend Sinister*, he repeatedly stated that the greatest threat to society did not come from political extremists but from anybody wishing to suppress individuality: 'What really annoys me is that people can't really get it into their head that there really isn't any threat from the left or the right. The threat is some kind of standardized horrible society. Run by a bunch of fucking idiots.'[16] The real danger was when the middle-class took charge, then, said Smith, 'you've got the germs for a real evil society. People forget that the SS weren't skinhead thugs, they were doctors and lawyers, guys with a grudge.'[17]

12 Dave Haslam, 'Mind Rocker', *NME*, 4 October 1986
13 Jack Barron, 'Curly Wurlies: The Fall, *Bend Sinister*', *Sounds*, 4 October 1986
14 Simon Reynolds, 'Fall Guise', *Melody Maker*, 4 October 1986
15 Vladimir Nabokov, *Bend Sinister*, London: Penguin Books, 1974
16 Michael Lang, 'The Fall – Mark E. Smith Interview', *BravEar*, vol. 3, issue 5, Fall/Winter 1986
17 Martin, op. cit., 30 August 1986

Like his attitude to drugs, Smith's take on politics was libertarian: 'The left wing has been in as much control in Britain as the right wing has and it always has been. My values are basically conservative. I don't want a fucking twat from the state telling me what to do, what to watch, it's crap.'[18]

Despite his anti-political stance, Smith ended 1986 the same way he started it – with a benefit gig. This one took place at the Free Trade Hall, Manchester, on 22 December and was billed as 'The Festival of the Millions'. The organizers intended it as a party for the unemployed and anyone with a valid unemployment-benefit card gained free entry. The one price they had to pay was listening to various local politicians give speeches about unemployment in between the bands. The organizers also subsidized the beer and by the time The Fall hit the stage the atmosphere was boisterous and some of the audience started throwing things at the band. Smith, never one to pour water on a fire, announced after a couple of tracks: 'At least we have something in common with you, for we too do nothing all day.' After more missiles Smith had to be physically restrained from jumping into the audience to remonstrate with somebody who was pestering Brix.[19] Still, for Smith, the gig advocated a cause he completely supported: 'I think it's a great system. I always think the whole idea of civilization is to get everybody on the dole, surely.'[20]

It was a nice little scene, very East Village, very druggy

When Simon Rogers announced his unavailability for an October tour of Austria, Smith turned once again to his immediate circle of friends and musicians to find a new keyboardist. Marcia Schofield as part of Khmer Rouge had already supported The Fall and helped out on Brix's Adult Net recordings: now she seemed the natural choice to replace Rogers. Born in 1962 in Flatbush, Brooklyn, her parents were both left-wing professors who later became heavily involved in the anti-Vietnam war movement. Schofield went to university, but dropped out and met her future husband, Philip Schofield, then a member of the Revolutionary Communist Party and formerly a sex-shop worker.

18 Brecker, op. cit., July/August 1986
19 Billy Smith, 'Out of the Dole-drums', *Melody Maker*, 10 January 1987
20 Stud Brothers, '*Perverted By Language*', *Melody Maker*, 4 October 1986

'Phil lived with a stripper,' said Schofield, 'and was supported by her and was completely illegal and overstayed his visa. When I met him he'd been in New York for three years and was about to be deported, so I married him. We used to belong to a group of people who met every week and wrote poetry together and plays. There were also underground film makers like Jim Jarmusch and bands like Sonic Youth and the Swans and I was particularly close friends with Alan Vega of Suicide. It was a nice little scene, very East Village, very druggy, but in some ways a lot more intellectual than the British music scene. Everybody in New York read journals like *Semiotext(e)*, everybody knew about post-modernism. We discussed ideas in a way that, when I came to London, people just didn't do here. The clubs were cheap, the drinks were cheap, no admission fees, no velvet ropes, it was very democratic. We all lived in these grungy unheated warehouses with rats. We had no money and what we did have we spent on drugs or studio time. There was no government support for the arts and there was also no dole. In New York you just got by doing whatever you could: Phil moved furniture and I worked as a bartender.'

Out of this scene Schofield formed Khmer Rouge with herself on keyboards, Philip on vocals and guitar, Ray Gange (star of the Clash film *Rude Boy*) on bass and Claus Castenskiold on drums. 'Claus is Danish, although he's German by birth,' Schofield explained. 'He was adopted by a Danish couple and they moved to America. When I met him he was living on Park Avenue in his sister and brother-in-law's apartment. They were incredibly wealthy people, his father was an investment lawyer and his sister was an art collector and they had this incredible apartment with genuine Picassos in the front room.'

In 1984, Schofield and Philip moved to London and lived in a run-down squat in Clapham North: 'It was the coldest and most miserable time I ever spent in my life,' Schofield said. 'We weren't doing anything creatively interesting. Our whole scene of like-minded collaborators had evaporated. We were stranded in London.' Help came in the form of Castenskiold and his old friend from Bennington, Brix Smith. He helped Schofield get a Khmer Rouge demo tape to Smith who then offered the band some support slots with The Fall. 'They were incredibly nice to us,' Schofield recalled. 'We had absolutely nothing and they basically fed us and paid for our petrol, they were lovely. It was really nice meeting Brix, because here

I was, this American in London and hating it. London in the mid-eighties was disgusting, nothing like it is now. Everything closed at eleven o'clock, it was cold, dirty, it was not fashionable – there were a few people like Leigh Bowery who were doing interesting things, but most of it was just foul. It was all happening in places like Manchester. It was like punk had burnt out and nothing had replaced it.' Over the next year Schofield's marriage to Philip fell apart and although they kept the band together she was keen on finding a new challenge. Enter Simon Rogers and his invitation to replace him on the Austrian tour: 'I said fine, why not? Nothing was holding me in London. So I joined initially for two weeks, then three years later . . . '

Schofield's preparation, in time-honoured Fall-fashion, was minimal and consisted of being lent a copy of *Bend Sinister*, handed a bundle of written instructions and being pushed into a rehearsal gig in Ipswich: 'It was packed and I had to walk onstage with all these scraps of paper with notes written down. The sound-check was the first time I'd played with these guys. Terrifying! For the encore they did two songs I'd never even heard before! Talk about baptism by fire. Mark always said, "That was your best gig with us." '[21] With Schofield passing the test of both the Ipswich gig and the Austrian tour, Smith invited her along for a promotional tour of the United States and then, most unlikely of all, offered her a part as an Israeli commando in his first play.

There's demonic possession, Italian fascists, ex-Nazis, a Scottish communist

During 1986 Michael Clark's notoriety continued to increase. In May, Channel 4 screened a 'fantasy documentary' on Clark entitled *Hail the New Puritan*, directed by his American friend, Charles Atlas. Atlas was part of the design team, along with Bodymap and Leigh Bowery, that won New York's 'Bessie' Award for Clark's *No Fire Escape in Hell* in 1986. This work had its critics, especially those who objected to the incorporation of a Nazi salute. But an unperturbed Clark brought it to Sadler's Wells in the autumn and it included music by The Fall plus live percussive accompaniment by Laibach.

21 Mick Mercer, 'I Married a Marcia from Outer Space', *Bitch Mental*, no. 1, February 1990

Atlas's *Hail the New Puritan* documented Clark and his company dancing, rehearsing and performing sections of *HAIL the Classical*. The film provided useful exposure for The Fall, with Clark dancing to 'Spectre vs Rector', 'Prole Art Threat', 'Copped It', 'Ludd Gang' and 'Gramme Friday' (during which Clark pretends to eat a live goldfish). Atlas also filmed Clark sitting at a table with Smith and Brix as they read prepared statements in satirical mockery of high-brow arts programmes. Smith offered observations such as: 'The refusal of genius to fulfil its destiny has been a problem of mankind's since 1911. Pap-art nor ghoulish tinkering is not science.' Later Clark added: 'Men folk were deft, but the real populist was steeped in panache. I glittered with spirits of cheap liquor and newsagent perfume. And newsagent perfume. And newsagent perfume.' The 'debate' ended with a comment by Smith: 'Mike, this is the scab you must take on. The computer hamlets, inefficient in their cock-ups, are not something to dance past.' Clark's seriousness is belied by his unlikely fashion style for a ballet dancer: a short bleached mohican, T-shirt and leather biker jacket.

Later in the year Clark introduced Smith to Charlie Hanson, the adventurous director of the Riverside Studios, and Smith told him about his idea for a play about the death in suspicious circumstances of Pope John Paul I (Albino Luciani) in 1978. The basics of the plot came from David Yallop's best-selling book *In God's Name* (1984), in which he describes Luciani's rise to office, his brief thirty-three days in power, the reforms he wished to put in place to fight corruption in the Vatican, his sudden and suspicious death from a massive heart attack and, according to Yallop, the subsequent cover-up. After reading the book, Smith wrote the song 'Hey! Luciani' for *Bend Sinister* but subsequently held it back and developed the idea for the play.

Smith wrote the bulk of the play during the American tour in October. 'The way I write is very laborious,' he said. 'I collect fragments, pieces of paper, diaries, cig packets, menus, all covered in scribbles, so when I sit down in front of the typewriter I've got this big spread of paper. I've been coming back from gigs and spending the rest of the night writing and it's been really enjoyable.'[22] What particularly interested Smith was the complex and far-reaching

---

22 James Brown, 'Papal Visit?', *Sounds*, 6 December 1986

conspiracy Yallop uncovered. But Smith had little interest in following the narrative or repeating the journalistic facts of the book and continued writing the play, including a new third act, until just days before the first performance. Speaking to Gavin Martin, Smith outlined what remained of the plot after his late-night writing sessions. Comparing it to a cross between Shakespeare and *The Prisoner*, Smith claimed that 'if you're sharp enough there's a real conspiracy to follow. There's demonic possession, Italian fascists, ex-Nazis, a Scottish communist.'[23]

The play opened on 5 December and ran for two weeks, with tickets costing £8, about double the cost of a normal gig. The dramatic medium suited Smith's ability to speak through a range of characters. Trevor Stuart, one of the few professional actors in the cast, played the older Luciani while Clark played the younger. The other main part went to Leigh Bowery as Bishop Marcinkus, head of accounts at the Vatican. Everybody in the band played a part: Smith acted as the Narrator; Wolstencroft played Cardinal Villot; Hanley took on the part of John Paul II; Scanlon was Dr Buzzonetti; Brix and Schofield played Israeli commandos; and Rogers had a backstage role as musical director. Smith also found parts for friends Lucy Burge (Rogers's wife), David Luff, Cerith Wynn Evans and even journalist James Brown, whom he press-ganged into playing a radio announcer. The scene reminded Schofield of her New York days: 'It was a nice interesting group of people who were all very talented but very much in the early stages of their careers. There was a lot of experimentation with no commercial pressure on any of us. We were all just experimenting, having fun, exploring things creatively. I'm sure a lot of what we did was very half-baked. A lot of it was cobbled together in that night-clubbing "let's stay up all night and write a play" sort of way. *Hey! Luciani* was like a school play with all your mates except you got paid to do it and people came to see it.'

Brix also has fond memories of the production and her role: 'Mark thought it was hysterical to make me and Marcia be Israeli commandos because we're Jewish. I liked it because we got to wear commando uniforms and had huge guns slung over our backs. We found Martin Boorman [played by a dummy] in the woods and I

23   Gavin Martin, 'Hip Priest for Pope of Pop?', *NME*, 13 December 1986

remember being really violent with him and Marcia had to sing "Haf Found Boorman". My line was, "The jungle has addled his desert mind and mescal screwed his nomad wits" – the most genius line! It was very interesting visually and also I remember singing "Dr Faustus" wearing this see-through red lace dress with little rubber skeletons, spray-painted red, hanging from it.'

The play lasted approximately ninety minutes and featured the songs 'Sleep Debt Snatches', 'Guest Informant' and, of course, the band's latest single 'Hey! Luciani', released to coincide with the play. Props included a papal balcony, an igloo, a deathbed and an overhead screen for projecting the 'Hey! Luciani' video, which included a particularly gruesome shot of a pair of eyes floating on a churning sea of maggots. Reviewer Len Brown's favourite lines included, 'The rear view mirror became a credit card,' 'I squeeze the leech-wondrous thingies out of the porthole,' and 'Caterpillars, full and wriggling, with translucent suckers and tail hairs about my size.' His overall assessment, however, was negative: '*Hey! Luciani* typically flaunts all the laws of theatre (and I accept that they are there to be broken) through pathetic acting and incomprehensible narration. Fall fanatics will no doubt argue that Mark's a god, much misunderstood and that insights such as, "The earth is made up of Terylene patches," have clearly sailed way over my badly permed helmet. But all I can say is that the play wot Mark E. Smith has wrote is a heap of shite. No doubt it's a metaphor for the modern world.'[24]

Roy Wilkinson, although complaining that the dialogue was 'pretty impenetrable', reluctantly admitted that it was 'a very watchable, incident-packed treatment of this fascinating piece of recent history.'[25] Adam Sweeting thought that 'the completeness, the *thoroughness*, of Smith's failure must be accounted his only achievement'. The play, he concluded, lacked any acting of note, dialogue that could at best be described as 'fragments of language' and a plot conspicuous by its absence.[26] Mark Lawson thought the material deserved better treatment and that Smith missed his targets. He also thought Smith's writing suffered from 'translation to a medium in which you can hear the words'. The evening was diverting, but 'the truth is that Kate

---

24 Len Brown, '*Hey! Luciani*', *NME*, 20/27 December 1986
25 Roy Wilkinson, 'Cardinal Sins', *Sounds*, 13 December 1986
26 Adam Sweeting, 'Gelli Babies Go Pope', *Guardian*, 12 December 1989

Bush's "Wuthering Heights" made shrewder use of its source material.'[27]

The criticism did not surprise Smith. The play contravened both literary and dramatic conventions and, of course, by the standard criteria of character and plot development the play was impenetrable. Most damaging was the red herring of the link to Yallop's book: 'People thought it was about the Pope,' Smith said, 'that was the problem. It wasn't really about the Pope at all. People got it all wrong. It was because we didn't send any press releases out. But the audience enjoyed it – old people liked it, and young people liked it, which I was very flattered with. And it was full most nights.'[28]

The trouble that reviewers and audiences had understanding the play was shared by most of the cast. Brix, for example: 'He wrote the play just like he wrote lyrics, on scraps of paper. I didn't understand anything that was happening in the play except the odd vignette. By and large The Fall fans really loved it because it was just such a bizarre experience and it was just so quintessentially Fall, but I think other, more "discerning", people thought, "What the hell? This is the weirdest thing I've ever seen." I think it was his most fertile period. He was very ambitious, a bit arrogant even, but it was a great thing that he did it. It wasn't Shakespeare but it was good.'

Schofield was slightly more perceptive in her interpretation of the play. She saw strong parallels between power struggles at the Vatican and the way Smith ran The Fall. 'Mark has always been really interested in obscure parts of history,' Schofield explained, 'and I think that the whole idea of the P2 lodge and the Vatican bank and the manoeuvrings around selecting the Pope – all of that secret conspiratorial world – in some way mirrors what it was like being in The Fall. It's a very closed world, outsiders don't really get a look in. And I think he's very attracted to stories about that kind of power dynamic. *Hey! Luciani* was not just about the power dynamic around the selection of a very unorthodox choice of Pope and the reaction to that selection, it was also in some way about Mark's control over the wonderful and frightening world of The Fall.'

27 Mark Lawson, 'Religious Farce after The Fall: *Hey! Luciani*, Riverside Studios', *Independent*, 11 December 1986
28 Smith, on BRT, Belgium Radio, broadcast 4 February 1987

12

Kurious Oranj, 1987–1988

It's a great life. Get up when I fucking like. That's the pleasure of
what I do. I've never set an alarm-clock in my life.[1]

A decade had passed since Smith and his friends played their first gig at
King Street. Since then Smith had slowly but surely guided The Fall
from its punk-scene origins, through new wave to become leaders
of its own genre-defying cult. Now with Beggars Banquet's help,
The Fall's audience had expanded enough to make it a commercially
successful group – successful enough, at least, for Smith to be able to
renegotiate the contract with Beggars and strike a potentially lucrative
publishing deal with Warner Brothers. After ten years on a sub-
sistence-level income, the time had come for the band to fulfil not just
its creative potential, but also its commercial potential. 'This is the
year we are going to do it,' Smith said. 'The Fall has always expanded
its audience anyway, the audience gets bigger every year and we sell
more records. It's not a major consideration to become commercial.
But I think it's more interesting than being your normal British art-
school group who play to students and they're big for two or three
years and then that's it. That doesn't interest me at all.'[2]

One observer, Schofield, watched as Smith sought to extend his
'sage of Manchester' persona into something much bigger. The role
model was Frank Zappa who combined what seemed to be a resolutely
uncommercial attitude with an uncanny knack of shifting units. The
strategy involved slowly expanding a loyal audience base through the
release of quality product and at the same time keeping a tight rein
on publishing and the release of material from the back catalogue.
Lowering standards to rush-release ill-considered new material and
saturating the market with inferior 'greatest hits' packages, quickly
destroyed that most elusive of commodities, credibility.

1 Smith, in Jonh Wilde, 'The Mouth that Roared', *Melody Maker*, 5 March 1988
2 Smith, on BRT, Belgium Radio, broadcast 4 February 1987

One member enjoying the band's growing celebrity and wealth was Brix. Even though Smith officially paid her only £30 a week (a figure just below the income-tax level) she still had access to plenty of cash and The Fall's credit card. 'I could spend whatever I wanted,' she recalled. 'We walked around with bags of cash, like thousands of pounds. At the end he got quite mad at me because I ran up quite a credit-card bill, but I was depressed and shopped. He didn't drive but I did, so I bought a nice car, a Mercedes, and everybody thought this was incongruous.' Along with Brix, the rest of the band also enjoyed the higher standard of living. 'Mark was very fair and generous with wages,' said Brix. 'He wasn't cheap or penny-pinching when it came to his band. He looked after everybody. Steve was able to buy a house – I think they all were able to buy a house. He paid them £250–£300 a week for as long as he could, and that wasn't terrible at the time.'

Part of The Fall's new commercial strategy included the release of carefully chosen cover versions, exemplified in April 1987 by 'There's A Ghost In My House', an old Motown standard recommended by Beggars' press officer Karen Ehlers. In keeping with Smith's horror-story aesthetic, the seven-inch version came packaged with a ghostly hologram pasted on the sleeve, courtesy of Holovision ('Making holograms part of today's world'). The combination of a classic song plus the added quirk value of Smith coming dangerously close to singing stunned the critics. Don Watson made it *NME*'s Single of the Week,[3] while James Brown in *Sounds* felt overwhelmed by the 'forceful disco inferno'.[4] The critics' positive reviews and a hilarious video of Smith and Brix pursued by poltergeists, helped it become The Fall's most successful single, reaching number 30. Normally a new entry at that level ensured an appearance on *Top of the Pops*, the premier music television show in the UK, but the call never came and Brix was left bitterly disappointed: 'The Fall were never asked, I mean that was one of the biggest crises in the history of the band . . . Me and Marcia were going, "What will we wear, what will we wear?" It was like, failure, we didn't get on.'[5]

With 'There's A Ghost In My House' following on from 'Rollin'

---

3   Don Watson, 'Single of the Week 1', *NME*, 2 May 1987
4   James Brown, 'The Fall: "Ghost In My House" ', *Sounds*, 2 May 1987
5   Brix, interviewed by Terry Christian on Key 103, broadcast 18 May 1989

Dany' and 'Mr Pharmacist', Smith's reputation as a cover-version expert led to *Sounds* inviting him to list his top 5 and explain what made them successful. First up was 'Wedding Bells' by Gene Vincent and the Bluecaps: 'Gene V totally renovates this corny song by the genuine tragedy in his vocal.' Link Wray's 'Batman' demonstrated that Wray 'knows a true cover is half not knowing it and half mutilation'. 'Incense And Peppermints' by Adult Net was improved by John Leckie's production, and 'Hit The Road Jack' by Big Youth came 'from the days when reggae was stoned, non-religious and immaculate'. 'Runnin' Scared' by Nick Cave he recommended as 'real pub stuff'.[6]

The Fall released 'There's A Ghost In My House' during a spring tour of the UK. This was followed in the summer by an unlikely support slot for U2 at Elland Road in Leeds. U2 had just released *The Joshua Tree* and could fill a stadium quicker than if the Messiah himself was in town. The Fall's appearance came about because the scheduled support act, World Party, dropped out at the last moment. Smith's memory of the gig was dominated by the image of U2 fans throwing Bibles at the band and shouting, 'Satanists! Satanists!'[7] This incongruous gig was followed by other large, high-profile concerts, supporting bands The Fall would previously have left town to avoid, such as Siouxsie and the Banshees in July at Finsbury Park and the Mission and Fields of the Nephilim in August at the Reading Festival. Smith later scornfully commented on Reading: 'It was really depressing to see twenty thousand Quo fans all aged about thirty-five and all pissed out of their heads. There were about three thousand people at the front to see us and twenty thousand behind them throwing stuff.'[8]

In between these two gigs, on 15 August, The Fall headlined an altogether more appropriate music festival, the 'Kings of Independence', promoted by Jeanette Bleeker at the Knopf Music Hall in Hamburg. The Fall appeared alongside a line-up of bands that read like a roll-call of the alternative scene at the time – Nick Cave and the Bad Seeds, Die Haut, Crime and the City Solution, the Swans, and the Butthole Surfers. 'The whole place was complete chaos,'

6 Mark E. Smith, 'Take 5', *Sounds*, 2 May 1987
7 Danny Frost, 'Grouch Rumble', *NME*, 10 July 1993
8 Mick Middles, 'The North Will Rise', *Underground*, no. 8, November 1987

Schofield recalled. 'All the bands knew each other, half of them weren't speaking to each other, half had had affairs with other people in other bands, it was just great turmoil backstage.' And front stage, and outside the venue. The Music Hall was not large and each of the bands could have sold it out by themselves. Quite early in the evening it became apparent that too many tickets had been sold, leaving hundreds of people outside trying to gain entry. To avoid a dangerous crush the venue's management took the desperate measure of locking all the doors.

As it became apparent they were going to miss the gig, the excluded ticket holders grew increasingly agitated and set fire to a pile of tyres perilously close to a local petrol station. The Fall watched all this unfold from an upstairs flat across the street from the venue. Schofield: 'We were looking out the window and I was filming it with a super eight camera: "Wow, now they're setting the tyres on fire, now they're in the petrol station, wow here come the riot police," and Brix was saying, "Oh my God! Get down, there's going to be an explosion." We hadn't even played yet. We'd been inside and left. Mark hates all that backstage stuff. Eventually the police brought it under control but there were people in the venue for hours with no music and nothing going on and they couldn't move; they were packed in like sardines, really thirsty.' At last the concert started with the Butthole Surfers. 'They were great,' Schofield recalled. 'All members of the band used to be on the same mind-altering substance – one night of this, one night of that. That night they were first to play and they smashed every piece of equipment that all the bands were supposed to use.' The Fall finally got to play at about four o'clock in the morning.

I find it easier to work with women

'Hit The North', The Fall's second single of 1987, came out in October in a variety of formats, including The Fall's first picture disc and – another first – a set of twelve-inch remixes. Accompanying music co-written by Brix and Simon Rogers, Smith's lyrics railed against 'useless MPs' and cops who 'can't catch criminals' but 'speak to God' (a reference to the then local Chief Constable James Anderton). In the song's simple chorus, Smith encapsulated his feelings about the North/ South divide: 'Hit the North,' at once a defiant cry of outrage but also a proud identification with the song's 'savages'.

Although Jack Barron made it Single of the Week in *NME*[9] and Peter Kane in *Sounds* described it as 'more accessible than ever',[10] the single stalled at a disappointing 57 in the charts. Even an appearance on ITV's rival to *Top of the Pops, The Roxy*, with cameramen and director excessively lingering on Brix and Schofield's camera-friendly glamour, could not help it break into the Top 30. Such unwelcome attention underlined for Schofield the sexism in the music industry. In fact, her most embarrassing moment with The Fall was when a *Sounds* magazine poll placed her in the top 10 of the most desirable women in music: 'I was so humiliated. I used to read these reviewers writing about "Marcia Schofield's amazing figure" and I was so angry. That wasn't why I was doing music. And Brix would be going, "Wear short skirts, wear boots!" and I'd refuse.'

Despite such arguments Brix and Schofield developed a close relationship. 'Brix was like the younger sister who borrows all your clothes and then gives them back torn and dirty,' Schofield said. 'But we had a great time. We grew up in the same era and liked the same things, like tacky sixties' television shows and Barbie dolls and make-up and clothes. But I don't think she ever got the whole Lower East Side art thing. She was always more interested in the media-friendly, fashion, side of it all. I think I was in music for a different reason. To me it was more of an artistic exercise. I never wanted to be a pop star, being a pop star should be secondary to being true to your vision and not compromising on that.'

Smith, at least for the moment, happily shared the media spotlight with Brix and Schofield: 'I find it easier to work with women than with men in the group,' he said. 'The women have got better suss, they're good; they don't get pissed and they don't take drugs.'[11] Well, not as much as he did, at least. Smith also appeared comfortable with his home life, inviting James Brown around to document the gun-metal grey Mercedes in the drive, the Castenskiold paintings on the walls and husband and wife relaxing 'in their black V-neck Armani jumper and big fun Mickey Mouse slippers respectively'.[12]

The happy domestic state of affairs was helped by Adult Net's

9 Jack Barron, 'The Fall: "Hit The North" ', *NME*, 24 October 1987
10 Peter Kane, 'The Fall: "Hit The North" ', *Sounds*, 24 October 1987
11 Dave Haslam, 'The Fall', *Debris*, no. 16, 1987
12 James Brown, 'Drunken Driver Causes Chaos – in a JCB!', *NME*, 31 October 1987

continuing development. Earlier in the year Brix's Californian sunshine smile beamed out from the cover of *Sounds* while inside Richard Cook recounted the events of her recent busy visit to Los Angeles, with its bit part in the television movie *Daddy*, its screen tests, acting agents, music agents and visits to record companies and lawyers. Naturally Brix saw America as her home market: a market where The Fall's left-field credentials would not work against Adult Net's populist ambitions. 'It'll be different in America,' she asserted optimistically. 'I want to be right in the mainstream, and it's hard when people here go, "Oh, it's just that girl from The Fall." ' [13]

Throughout 1987 Brix worked sporadically on Adult Net's début album, provisionally titled *Spin The Web*. But The Fall's punishing tour schedule and uncertainty over the best production for the album slowed progress interminably. Some much needed impetus returned with Adult Net's first (and as it turned out, last) live gig. The performance, at the ICA in London, in October represented Brix's best chance to convince US record company Geffen Records that Adult Net amounted to more than just a studio project. Her star-studded backing band for the night consisted of Mike Joyce, Andy Rourke and Craig Gannon, all ex-Smiths. Expectations were high and the gig sold out almost immediately with celebrities and record-industry figures fighting to get their names on the guest list. 'I was giving myself a test by doing it,' Brix said. 'Someone came in and said, "It's totally sold out, tickets are going outside for £22, this record company and that paper are here . . . " I was practically catatonic, I was so nervous. So I did the best that I could.'[14] And Brix's best appeared to be good enough, Myrna Minkoff describing her melodramatically as 'born to stand in front of a wind machine and bedazzlingly survey the cosmos stretched out before her', before humbly decreeing her destiny 'to take Pop Art to the Cosmos'.[15] More down-to-earth was Roy Wilkinson's assessment in *Sounds*. Unimpressed by the band, he described the rhythm section as 'leaden' and likened Brix's compositions to 'Arndale C&W' and 'gold lamé thrash'.[16]

13 Richard Cook, 'Caught in a Spider's Web', *Sounds*, 21 February 1987
14 Dave Jennings, 'Adult Net: California Dreaming', *Melody Maker*, 27 May 1989
15 Myrna Minkoff, 'Galaxies May Tremble: The Adult Net, London, ICA', *NME*, 31 October 1987
16 Roy Wilkinson, 'Marking Mrs Smith: The Adult Net, The Mall, ICA', *Sounds*, 31 October 1987

Brix's main aim, however, was not to impress the critics but rather selected representatives of the music industry. And impressed they were. The day after the show, major label Phonogram rang with an offer to transform her fledgling side-project into a mainstream pop act. But still she felt a pang of loyalty towards Beggars Banquet: 'They were particularly nice to me and encouraging with Adult Net. They suggested that I do it and put up the money and got me John Leckie. I will now admit that my biggest mistake in my career was leaving them and going to Phonogram. I didn't realize that a nurturing family is better that being a number in a system. You have to learn.'

But the lessons were still to come. For the moment the future looked bright for Mr and Mrs Smith. At the end of 1987 they posed for a *NME* photo-shoot dressed as Lord Nelson and Lady Hamilton. In the accompanying caption, Smith claimed to have much in common with the one-eyed admiral: 'Fucking clever guy, very typically British in that he was never given credit for what he did until he was twenty years dead.'[17] The media spotlight continued to fall on the indie king and queen into 1988, when *Record Mirror* made them cover stars of its 'cupid special' issue ('Brix and Mark E. Smith of The Fall say it with roses'). The photograph showed Smith theatrically presenting Brix with a bunch of red roses, the Mills and Boon connotations only slightly tempered by the bright red stage blood streaming down Smith's hands where the thorns had supposedly torn through his skin ('Happy Loving Couple Of The Year' simpered the caption). Inside Brix candidly answered questions about their relationship: 'If you have a boyfriend and you share the same interests you start grating against each other,' Brix explained. 'But with Mark and me we're such different people that it doesn't go that way.' There were arguments, of course: 'Sometimes you get frustrated trying to get your point over, because we're both quite stubborn. But there's absolutely no hate. We've never had a real fight.' Brix concluded the interview with a description of their disparate night-life: 'I go out with girlfriends, and he goes to the pub all the time.'[18]

17 Smith, in *NME*, 19/26 December 1987
18 Roger Morton, 'Falling in Love Again', *Record Mirror*, 13 February 1988

I just went Cog . . . Sinister

With a wardrobe full of designer clothes and a Mercedes safely parked in the drive, Smith now attended to other things The Fall's booming economy could provide. Never one to be overly impressed by the way record companies were run, he decided to see if he could do better. He called his label Cog Sinister Records Ltd, a half-reference to precognition, the ability to see into the future: 'I just went Cog . . . Sinister. Then I was thinking of bringing out records that were particularly good and calling them Pre-Cog Sinister.'[19]

The label's short-term mission was simply to rerelease material from The Fall's back-catalogue as it fell out of licence or as Smith acquired the rights. Operating from an office on the second floor of 48 Princess Street in Manchester, Cog Sinister released its first compilation at the end of November 1987. *In: Palace Of Swords Reversed* brought together tracks from the two Rough Trade eras of the early 1980s. 'I don't wish to exploit this,' Smith said at the time, 'it's simply a way of letting people get hold of old Fall stuff. I have all the old Fall tapes stored upstairs and all the publishing rights. This stems back to the days when I used to rip contracts up. I just didn't believe in them, which, I'm telling you, was insanity at the time. But now it's proved worth it. It was worth starving the band for.'[20] The album certainly fulfilled a need and, ironically with the help of Rough Trade's distribution, reached the top of the indie charts during the lucrative Christmas period.

Apart from distribution, Smith maintained total control over Cog Sinister, from release schedules through to marketing. The long-term plan for the label was to reinvest any profits from The Fall reissues into other acts, from older neglected geniuses to fresh new talent. Smith's magnanimous plans also accommodated local singer/song-writers exploiting the 'pool' of musicians on The Fall's pay-roll. 'If it weren't for Manchester,' a spokesman for the label explained at the time, 'he wouldn't have got very far, and this label is his way of giving something back to the city.'[21]

The first product of this strategy appeared in March 1988 in the form of the twelve-inch single 'Unsatisfied' by Smith's friend, hairdresser

19 Roy Wilkinson, 'The Bug-Eyed Pop Goblin', *Sounds*, 2 January 1988
20 Middles, op. cit., November 1987
21 Ron Rom, 'Sinister Dealings', *Sounds*, 5 December 1987

and former member of the Weeds, Andrew Berry. 'I'm a hairdresser like other people are musicians,' Berry said. 'My haircuts are like works of art to me. They're too important to fuck about with.' Optimistically, Berry expected an album to follow in the summer, but still wisely planned to keep his day job: 'Ideally I'd like to combine hairdressing with being a pop star.'[22] The problem of deciding between the two careers, however, never arose because 'Unsatisfied' made little impact, critically or commercially. Sam King in *Sounds* found it 'spectacular only for its sheer lack of any discernible hooks, bite or enthusiasm, apart from its stunningly fitting title'.[23] Berry's last, and equally unsuccessful, attempt to be a pop star came in July 1990, when Fontana released into an unresponsive market his single 'Kiss Me I'm Cold', with backing by Johnny Marr.

In July 1988 came the compilation album *The Disparate Cogscienti*. It represented the second part of Smith's plan, to showcase neglected artistes, in this case old material by the Hamsters, John the Postman, Mr A. Valler (apparently a pub organist from Prestwich) and Philip Johnson, plus recent material from Beatrice (featuring Brix's close friend Lisa Feder), the Obi Men, the Lowthers, God, the Next Step (with soon-to-be Inspiral Carpet, Martin Walsh) and, that man again, Andrew Berry. Despite variable quality, the record still has its moments, such as the manic intensity of John the Postman's 'Work' and the humour of 'Stupid Songs' by the Hamsters. Apart from these tracks, nothing suggested that Smith's precognition was in particularly good working order the day he chose this line-up. Jonh Wilde in *Melody Maker* agreed: 'Where, pray tell, is old fuckface lurking when the Quality Control Dept at Cog Sinister suck on their Woodbines, fill in their pools coupons and approve this kind of sub-amateur nonsense?'[24]

Smith followed the album with Cog Sinister's second single, Phil Shöenfelt's 'Charlotte's Room'. Phil Shöenfelt was Marcia's ex-husband, Philip Schofield. He'd changed his name because too many people confused him with the identically named children's television presenter. The low-key and mournful 'Charlotte's Room', like

22 Stuart Maconie, 'Hairdresser on Fire', *NME*, 9 April 1988
23 Sam King, 'Andrew Berry: "Unsatisfied" ', *Sounds*, 26 March 1988
24 Jonh Wilde, 'Various Artists: "The Disparate Cogscienti" ', *Melody Maker*, 9 July 1988

Berry's 'Unsatisfied', left the music press and record-buying public unstirred and thus ended Smith's attempts at pre-cog-ing talent. Cog Sinister reverted to being exclusively The Fall's label.

Gene Crime Experience

Even though 1987 was one of those rare years when The Fall failed to release a new studio album, the band still came sixth in the 'best band' poll in the *NME* (first and second were The Smiths and U2 respectively). The Fall's fans were in obvious need of some product and in 1988 they got it in spades. First up was the January single 'Victoria', a fairly literal updating of an old Kinks song, about Britain's fading empire. Beggars' marketing department came up with the idea of packaging some copies in a numbered limited-edition boxed-set, along with a tacky plastic medal, two lyric sheets and details of the new Cog Sinister fan club run by Smith's sister Caroline. The single continued the success of 'There's A Ghost In My House' with a highest chart placing of number 35. Accompanying chart success were the inevitable cries of 'sell-out'. Ralph Gibson in *Sounds* wrote that The Fall's version sounded unnervingly like 'Yellow Submarine' fed 'through a blender',[25] while David Stubbs in *Melody Maker* lamented: 'I've looked on in sadness as The Fall appeared to have gone hard and soft in all the wrong places and degenerated into something calamitously unlistenable (that is to say, "listenable").'[26]

Smith defended 'Victoria' by claiming his version, in contrast to the Kinks' nostalgic original, was profoundly relevant to the current situation in Britain: 'I don't want to labour the "Return to Victorian Values" point too much, 'cos they never really went away. I've just got a feeling that the whole Victoriana thing is due to be big again.'[27] Smith's comments came at a time when the British economy was once again drifting into recession. How would The Fall fare as mid-eighties boom became late-eighties bust?

A good indication of its continuing strength came at the end of February with the album, *The Frenz Experiment* (originally to be

25 Ralph Gibson, 'The Fall: "Victoria" ', *Sounds*, 16 January 1988
26 David Stubbs, 'The Fall: "Victoria" ', *Melody Maker*, 16 January 1988
27 Danny Kelly, 'Victoria Falls', *NME*, 13 February 1988

called *Gene Crime Experience* until Smith realized it spelt GCE).[28] Album sales were helped by promotional stunts like an unprecedented in-store appearance at HMV in Oxford Street where the band played thirty minutes of material from the album with Smith singing through his loud hailer. Later The Fall signed copies of the album, just like a real pop group.[29] Reaching number 19, it achieved the band's third highest chart position.

The album opens with 'Frenz', a low-key and deceptively simple track over which Smith bitterly reflects on his lack of friends. The mood then lightens with 'Carry Bag Man', Smith's self-mocking confession of his carrier bag fetish. 'Mark's always walking around with carrier bags,' Brix observed. 'My parents have bought him a gorgeous leather satchel and a nice briefcase but he always stuffs things in carrier bags. In the streets, to concerts, everywhere . . . He's not fussy. Liquor store, Sainsbury's, Boots. As long as it's a certain size and shape.'[30] Side one closes with 'Athlete Cured', the story of a German athletic star poisoned by exhaust fumes from his brother Gert's car. The moral of this tale is that: 'From certain facts you have to go on and further and often it is better to go around or look under.' On side two, Smith once again surveys the madness in his area with 'In These Times', while 'Bremen Nacht' takes on historical ghosts encountered during the 1987 European tour. 'I'd been to Bremen twice before on tours,' Smith recalled. 'The first time I just puked my ring up all day, spewing this black liquid. When I went back there this time I just went crazy. The gig had a really low steel roof – it was this German polytechnic with steel everywhere, metal shutters on the windows which made it real claustrophobic. The dressing-room was like a fucking gas chamber, man. We go out and play and I'm just feeling worse and worse. I just felt like a different person, I was snapping at everyone – and that's weird 'cos I'm usually very controlled on the road, a father figure. In the morning I had all these handprints on my leg, bruises from the inside that looked like a child's handprints. What I've settled on at the moment – everybody says it must be the Nazis, they must have killed somebody – is that it

28 Smith, interviewed by David Haslam on Piccadily Radio, broadcast 28 February 1988
29 Keith Cameron, 'His Master's Vice', *Sounds*, 12 March 1988
30 Wilde, op. cit., 5 March 1988

was probably the firebombing in the Second World War and it was like an air-raid shelter that had been bombed.'[31] The album ends with 'Oswald Defence Lawyer', a conspiracy theory about a 'zigzag bullet line'.

Throughout the album Smith's lyrics remained as inventive and as occasionally obscure as ever. The major difference when contrasted with earlier albums lay in the band's new-found flexibility. *The Frenz Experiment* contained a variety of tempos and musical styles. This was partly down to the number of writers in the band, all seven of whom – including Simon Rogers who produced most of the album – contributed new compositions. Schofield: 'The way we'd write was we'd come up with a groove and then everyone added their little bits and pieces and Mark would listen to the tapes a few times, and come up with some lyrics. Brix was the only person who actually wrote songs from start to finish.' Danny Kelly in the *NME* misinterpreted this diversity as 'musically chaotic' and 'undisciplined' and thought the album The Fall's *Sandinista*.[32] In contrast, *Melody Maker*'s David Stubbs accepted the smorgasbord of voices and noises as 'coincidental with the sound of the times'.[33] Only Andy Gill in *Q* recognized the album's transitional nature, 'part of the tentative move towards the mainstream, without sacrificing the peculiarities that keep them underground'.[34]

On the album's release, The Fall took off on a gruelling three-month tour of the UK, Germany, Austria, Belgium and the Netherlands. By the time the band reached the United States in May, Smith was understandably fatigued. Taking a break from gigs, he visited Cleveland with Brix to meet some of her family. A surreal encounter occurred as they walked through the downtown area of the city and a tall threatening figure jumped out at them. 'It looks like he's ready to mug us,' Smith said, 'and I go, "Uuuuurgh!" And he goes "Mark E. Smith, my maan, 'Repetition'." He'd just seen me through the bar window and turns out he'd been a fan for years. He was quoting from *Zig-Zag* in '78 and asking me about members of the band who I couldn't even remember.'[35]

31 Wilkinson, op. cit., 2 January 1988
32 Danny Kelly, 'Totally Weird', *NME*, 5 March 1988
33 David Stubbs, 'The Drama of Exile', *Melody Maker*, 27 February 1988
34 Andy Gill, 'Perverse, The Fall, *The Frenz Experiment*', *Q*, no. 18, March 1988
35 Mark E. Smith, 'Hot Dog's in the Far-out Zone', *NME*, 30 July 1988

I don't want to show anybody up, y'know, so I keep still

When the Holland Festival invited Michael Clark to produce a ballet as part of its William and Mary Tercentenary Celebrations, he turned to Smith as his musical and historical advisor. They both agreed that the 'Glorious Revolution' of 1688 would make an appropriate starting point. The bare facts of the story start in 1685 when the Protestant King of England and Scotland, Charles II, died and was succeeded by his Roman Catholic brother, James II. In 1688 a son was born to James who replaced his daughter Mary as heir. Mary was a Protestant and married to the Dutch prince William of Orange. Fearful of a Catholic dynasty, a broad alliance of Tory Anglicans and Protestant Dissenters invited William to invade England, which he did, landing in Brixham, Devon. James was allowed to escape to France and thus be judged as having vacated the throne. William and Mary were crowned King and Queen of England and Scotland.

The question was how would Clark and Smith translate these historical events into a ballet? Very loosely, came the answer. Like Smith in *Hey! Luciani*, Clark was not interested in providing a factually based account. History merely provided the raw material that could be cut-and-pasted alongside elements of the recent past, as was apparent in the title they chose, *I Am Curious, Orange* (a play on the title of the infamous Swedish porn film of the sixties, *I Am Curious, Yellow*). 'To tell you the truth,' confessed Smith, 'until I got into doing this it was a period that I knew sod all about. I'm pretty well up on the period before and after but, apart from the obvious stuff, I didn't know much about William of Orange. So I guessed a lot of it, like. And it was weird 'cos a lot of it turned out to be true.'[36] Smith's lyrical abstruseness added many interpretative layers to the most ordinary of events; an effect mirrored in Clark's conception of dance. 'The thing with movement,' Clark pointed out, 'is it's got so many different meanings for different people. You're not dealing with specific things like you are with words. That's why dance appeals to me so much, because it's got all those different levels of meaning.'[37]

The Fall's almost constant touring throughout 1988 complicated the ballet's production. Songs were written and recorded on the road

36 Stuart Maconie, 'The History Man Whose Head Expanded', *NME*, 17 September 1988

37 Clark, interviewed on *Forth Fiesta*, BBC2, broadcast 16 August 1988

and sent back to Clark in London. The problem with this arrangement became immediately apparent at rehearsals, just a couple of weeks before the June première at the Stadsschouwburg in Amsterdam. The new songs had evolved as the tour progressed and therefore the versions that Clark had choreographed to were now out of date. Schofield volunteered to listen to Clark's tapes and reteach the band the older versions. 'This was the source of much friction,' she recalled. 'I was seen as being very bossy. But I was torn between Michael's needs and The Fall's, who never did anything the same way two nights running. We had some major rows about that time. I think it was the first time I quit or Mark fired me.'

The ballet started with the simultaneous playing of the Dutch and English national anthems. Then a football match kicked off with dancers dressed in Celtic and Rangers replica kits. The match ended with an explosion killing all the footballers. All of this was performed against a giant backdrop of the modern-day House of Commons. At one point Brix entered the stage seated on a giant hamburger and Leigh Bowery made an appearance dressed as a tin of Heinz baked beans. Clark performed one section in a curly-haired wig, dancing with the aid of crutches. Other props included a large green telephone that was rushed across the stage and never seen again and an over-size carton of McDonald's fries that was later emptied over the dancers. The second half of the ballet featured more contemporary references, including an Acid House setting, complete with strobe lighting, dry ice and a 'smiley' grumpy face. And, just in case you had forgotten the work's Dutch origins, some of the dancers wore windmills on their heads. 'It was on a grand scale,' Clark recalled. 'Each member of The Fall had their own crew member. It was a combination of all the stuff we'd been doing before. It had that feeling of finally getting to a point that we'd been aiming towards for some time.'

After Amsterdam, Clark and The Fall performed the ballet at the King's Theatre during the Edinburgh Festival in August, and at Sadler's Wells at the end of September. BBC Radio One's Liz Kershaw asked Smith: 'Is it not all a bit poncey and arty farty?' 'Not particularly, no,' Smith replied. 'I like to do things a bit different than the tour-LP-tour schedule.' Asked whether he danced, Smith modestly replied, 'I don't want to show anybody up, y'know, so I keep still.'

In the reviews, the dance establishment criticized Clark's icono-clasm. Stephanie Jordan in *Dance & Dancers* described him as 'a mere shadow of what he has been' and castigated him for his 'untidy' feet,[38] while an exasperated Jann Parry in the *Observer* complained about the 'head-banging repetitiveness of The Fall's music'.[39] David Dougill in the *Sunday Times* agreed, asking why wasn't the band in the pit? The 'sum effect', he concluded, was of 'a ninety-minute rock video'.[40]

The music press was more positive, obviously enjoying the novelty of the situation. *Melody Maker*'s Caren Myers thought the collabor-ation 'a brilliant idea' because you not only got a fine performance from The Fall but you could also switch your attention to the dancers if you got bored: 'Possibly the perfect spectacle for the channel-switching generation, with something for everybody, and nothing for too long.'[41] Sean O'Hagan in the *NME* admitted to being mystified about what was going on, but judged that The Fall dominated proceedings, upstaging the dancers: 'This was The Fall in a new context – innovatory, exciting, iconoclastic – all the adjectives you'd heard applied to Michael Clark.' O'Hagan finished by recommending the ballet to his readers as better than spending another night 'staring at another band over another beer'.[42]

Beggars released the album of the ballet, *I Am Kurious, Oranj*, just as the production at Sadler's Wells was coming to an end in October. Chartwise it was a disappointment, reaching just number 54, but as The Fall's second album that year this was perhaps excusable. Ian Broudie produced the album with minimal fuss, partly at Suite 16 in Rochdale and partly live during the Edinburgh performances. Its rushed nature did little to detract from the quality of tracks like 'New Big Prinz' – 'check the guy's track record' – and the perverted reggae of the title track 'Kurious Oranj'. The highlight of the album remains 'Dog Is Life/Jerusalem' with writing credits shared between Smith and William Blake. The track starts with Smith's spluttering anti-dog

---

38 Stephanie Jordan, 'Choreography or Curiosity?', *Dance & Dancers*, November/ December 1988

39 Jann Parry, 'Insect Power', *Observer*, 25 September 1988

40 David Dougill, 'Peeling an Orange and Losing the Pith', *Sunday Times*, 25 Sep-tember 1988

41 Caren Myers, '*I Am Curious, Orange*, King's Theatre, Edinburgh', *Melody Maker*, 3 September 1988

42 Sean O'Hagan, 'M.E.S. in Tutu Draw', *NME*, 1 October 1988

rant before spiralling into The Fall's supersonic take on the familiar hymn, complete with a new middle section in which Smith recounts how he slipped on a banana skin in the street, claiming it was the government's fault.

Smith admitted to holding the greatest respect for Blake: 'I suppose my favourite work by him is "Ghost of a Flea". Ha ha ha ha! What a title! What I like about it is that it's just like a really, really grotesque painting. I like something grotesque in an artist.'[43] They had much in common: Blake, like Smith, was single-minded and eclectic, an autodidact with idiosyncratic spelling and a keen interest in occult and esoteric systems of knowledge. Both found it difficult to establish long-term relationships because of their erratic behaviour and short tempers and both were resolutely anti-commercial. Indeed Blake could almost have been quoting Smith when he described commerce as a 'spectrous fiend'.[44]

Not surprisingly Smith chose 'Jerusalem' as one of the tracks for the album's single. Once again Beggars used the box-set format but this time it included two seven-inch singles plus a postcard with a cartoon by Schofield. Jane Solanas in *NME* thought, bizarrely, that The Fall's choice of 'Jerusalem' was misguided and doubted that the majority of its fans 'even know who William Blake is'.[45] Reviews of the album made more sense. Ian Gittins in *Melody Maker* recognized the power of The Fall's 'Jerusalem', describing the new version as 'doing actual physical, violent damage to the song and its laws'.[46] Len Brown in *NME* punningly called it 'outspanding'[47] and Paul Davies in *Q* applauded the return of The Fall's rough edges.[48]

With such plaudits ringing in their ears, at the end of 1988 everything should have been more wonderful than frightening in the world of The Fall. The group had just helped attract sell-out audiences to Sadler's Wells, one of the most prestigious theatres in the world, and was supported by a record company capable of releasing and

---

43 Ted Kessler, 'Mark E. Smith: Heroes & Villains', *NME*, 11 December 1993
44 Peter Ackroyd, *Blake*, London: Vintage, 1999
45 Jane Solanas, 'The Fall: "Jerusalem" ', *NME*, 26 November 1988
46 Ian Gittins, 'Agent Oranj: The Fall, *I Am Kurious, Oranj*', *Melody Maker*, 29 October 1988
47 Len Brown, 'Outspanding: The Fall, *I Am Kurious, Oranj*', *NME*, 29 October 1988
48 Paul Davies, 'The Fall: *I Am Kurious, Oranj*', *Q*, December 1988

promoting two well-received albums in a year. In the band Smith had collected together a team of musicians at their creative prime, writing more songs than they could release. Financially secure, Smith and Brix were feted as 'Happy Loving Couple Of The Year'. What could go wrong? Well, just about everything. The first public intimation of trouble came with Smith's announcement in December that The Fall was leaving Beggars Banquet and that he was open to offers: 'After five albums in five years, we felt it was time to move on. It is an amicable split and I think it will be good for us to have a change. Beggars took us up when we were in a particularly bad way and I will always be grateful to them for that.'[49] Few people, except Smith's closest friends, realized that behind these measured words stood a man about to turn his whole world upside-down.

49 Anon., 'Beggars Fall Out', *NME*, 10 December 1988

13

Seminal Live, 1989

New Year's Resolution for 1989? Reassessment.[1]

During the run-up to Christmas 1988, Brix and Smith's relationship was deteriorating after they fell out badly during the *I Am Curious, Orange* performances at Sadler's Wells. 'It was heinous, it was vile,' admitted Brix. 'We had to go on stage pretending we were husband and wife every night. We were in separate dressing-rooms; we were not speaking at all.' When the show finished the two resolved their differences enough to spend Christmas and New Year together in Prestwich. But the reconciliation was short-lived, and on 4 January Smith told Brix he was leaving. His bags were already packed and Simon Wolstencroft was outside in a car ready to drive him to Edinburgh. Brix was in shock: 'I did not know what to do, so I called Craig Leon and Cassell Webb who were at that time the closest people to me. I was hysterical and they told me to get on a plane and come down to London. So I came down and stayed with them. They helped me find an apartment in Holland Park. It was a totally new experience. I'd never in my life had my own apartment or even my own cheque book. They helped sort me out.'

In time Brix found out that Smith was having an affair with Saffron Prior, the daughter of old friends from Prestwich. 'I don't blame Mark one hundred per cent for this,' Brix later said. 'In hindsight I'm really grateful, but at the time, when your ego takes such a bashing like that, when a man leaves his wife for somebody else – I was hardly in a wheelchair either, I was only twenty-five – I was ready to murder her.' But instead she went to see a lawyer and set about divorcing Smith on grounds of adultery. Once she'd got over the initial shock, Brix appeared to take the separation in her stride: 'Within four months I was the happiest dating girl in London and

1   Mark E. Smith, 'My Favourite Year', *Melody Maker*, 7 January 1989

having the time of my life and never looked back really. But obviously some part of me will always love Mark and he was extremely good to me in terms of nurturing me musically and inspiring me and teaching me so much. I will always be grateful for that, but the relationship ran its course and that's what happened.'

During the first half of the year Brix remained a member of The Fall, but it soon became clear it was not just Smith she would be divorcing. The crunch came in February when The Fall was booked to do a live television show in Germany. Brix dreaded the trip and on the day she simply bypassed the airport and disappeared to a luxury hotel in Sussex with her boyfriend at the time, Ian Flooks: 'Basically I just chilled out while they went to Germany without me. It was too uncomfortable for me, to be honest, to be in that situation. I had my own money at that point from Adult Net, so it wasn't like I had a gun pointed at my head.'

Throughout 1987 and 1988 Brix had been working fitfully with Simon Rogers and Ian Broudie on an album for Beggars Banquet provisionally entitled *Spin This Web*. But the results of these sessions never satisfied Brix. In particular she didn't like the drum machines and synthesisers and thought the tracks could be improved if played by a proper band: 'It was too inorganic really and it kind of lost punch. When I listen back to it now there are some things that are really good and some things that make me cringe.'

The US label Geffen's response to the tapes devastated Brix's confidence. They thought they were OK, but not good enough to release. Brix took their advice and refused to allow Beggars to release the album. After the 1987 ICA gig, Fontana, a subsidiary of Phonogram, signed her and supported her idea of turning Adult Net into a proper band. Much of Brix's advance from the resulting deal was paid to Beggars Banquet in exchange for the tapes and the rights to her back catalogue. It left her out of pocket but free to re-record and release the material she thought still salvageable.

The band she put together consisted of a variety of jobbing musicians: drummer Clem Burke (formerly of Blondie), bassist James Eller (The The and the Pretenders) and guitarist Craig Gannon (The Smiths and Aztec Camera). Craig Leon, famous for his work with the Ramones and Blondie, produced and played keyboard while his partner Cassell Webb provided the backing vocals. The first release by this new team, the single 'Take Me', appeared in March 1989.

Brix's glamorous looks may have helped her on to the front cover of the *NME* but at the same time she rebelled against pressure from her record company to promote her sex appeal more explicitly.[2] 'It's always a struggle to get people to look beyond my face and image,' she said. 'I'm into beauty from within and people looking at me for my mind and my strength. If I wanted to be a star I could've been an actress or taken my clothes off years ago. You just have to listen to the record to know it comes from the heart. I shouldn't have to justify *anything* . . . I'm living proof that a woman can be talented, intelligent, pretty and successful.'[3]

Aside from the constant pressure to exploit her sex appeal, Brix willingly accepted guidance from her record company and her personal manager, John Lennard. Much of it was advice she later regretted: 'I think I was too manipulated by the record company. They weren't allowing me to be me, they didn't have any vision. They wanted me to be something that had already been, they wanted to recreate something. I'm not Debbie Harry, I'm never going to be Debbie Harry. I'm Brix and I'm special in my own way. But I was too insecure and too overwhelmed by the huge record company machine to argue or stand up for myself. I didn't know any better.'

The follow-up single in May, 'Where Were You', reached only number 66 in the charts but received good reviews in the press. Bob Stanley in *Melody Maker* said it could become the 'summer anthem for 1989',[4] and Ralph Traitor in *Sounds* described the tune as 'God-like'.[5] A couple of months later came the single 'Waking Up In The Sun', and at last, in July, Fontana finally released Adult Net's début album, *The Honey Tangle* (named after a racehorse Brix saw on television). Utilizing vocal harmonies and jangly guitars, *The Honey Tangle* presented an updated version of the bubblegum pop close to Brix's heart and her Californian roots. She called it 'pop music with substance and feeling'.[6]

2 James Brown, 'Godhead!', *NME*, 4 March 1989
3 Tony Beard, 'The Importance of Being Brix', *Record Mirror*, 18 March 1989
4 Bob Stanley, 'The Adult Net: "Where Were You?" ', *Melody Maker*, 27 May 1989
5 Ralph Traitor, 'The Adult Net: "Where Were You?" ', *Sounds*, 27 May 1989
6 Todd Avery Shanker, 'Brix Smith: A Short Fall to Adult Net', *Illinois Entertainer*, November 1989

Once again the music press seemed unwilling to judge the album on its own merits. Simon Williams in *NME* thought it so 'sweet' it gave him a 'saccharine OD',[7] Cathi Unsworth in *Sounds* complained that Californian sunshine had 'melted everything; Brix's hairdo and brains included',[8] and Peter Kane in *Q* considered the music 'cloying' and 'a three-minute party piece that is best kept that way'.[9] With time, Brix came to agree with at least some of this criticism: 'It was over the top: sickly, shining, pure California pop. But on the good side it taught me how to sing five-part harmonies and it pulled me together as a musician and I worked with the best musicians and people in the business. It was a big jump from being in The Fall, where everything and anything goes and you don't really tune your instruments, to playing with string quartets.' Another important lesson she learnt was to trust her own instincts more and rely less on the opinion of those around her, even her new boyfriend, the violinist Nigel Kennedy. 'When he would suggest things I would listen, because I figured he was much better musically educated than me. I didn't even really know how to play the guitar. I knew, but I was self-taught. I let him take some decisions and basically released control.'

The key to Adult Net's failure, as she later admitted, was her lack of leadership qualities: 'Now in hindsight and clearer mental health, I realize that I am more happy being number two, being guitar player, contributing writing and singing now and again. I never liked being a front person, there's too much pressure. I never relaxed. I'm better playing off another person and influencing them. That's where I was most comfortable, that was my happy position. I am Mr Spock.' Brix's lack of confidence, her busy life with *Four Seasons* superstar Nigel Kennedy, the poor sales and negative press cuttings, all contributed to Phonogram's decision to drop the band in October 1990.

7 Simon Williams, 'What a Mesh! The Adult Net: *The Honey Tangle*', *NME*, 15 July 1989
8 Cathi Unsworth, 'Tangled up in Goo: Adult Net, *The Honey Tangle*', *Sounds*, 15 July 1989
9 Peter Kane, 'Adult Net, *The Honey Tangle*', *Q*, no. 35, August 1989

This is the story he told me about being in deep

The first half of 1989 proved to be a difficult few months for Smith. He had self-exiled himself in Edinburgh, many miles from his friends, family and home in Prestwich. With an absent leader and Brix concentrating solely on Adult Net, the band drifted into a state of limbo, only briefly coming together to record a handful of tracks to fulfil its contractual obligations to Beggars Banquet. Most devastating of all for Smith was the death of his father of a heart attack at the end of May, aged just fifty-nine. Shortly afterwards he wrote 'Bill Is Dead' and described this period as 'probably the worst ever'.[10]

Earlier in the year, and for the first time in his career, Smith collaborated with musicians outside The Fall. Matt Black and Jonathan More, working under the name of Coldcut, had recently achieved chart success with remixing work on pop acts Yazz and Lisa Stansfield. But they shunned the 'superstar DJ–producer' lifestyle and preferred to work instead with maverick outsiders like Smith. Black considered him one of the best rappers in Britain: 'If British rappers took more inspiration from him and less from the Sugarhill Gang and company, the world would be a happier place.'[11] The collaboration '(I'm) In Deep' can be heard on Coldcut's *What's That Noise* album released in April 1989. For the track Smith adopted the guise of a storyteller and talked about a man who 'trekked up and down the tendril wires of this haunted isle'. This man, however, could never escape 'the thing he was under' because it was 'inside him . . . in deep'. More described the song as a 'rant over a nauseating heavy-metal house groove'.[12]

The Fall's contractual obligations to Beggars disappeared with the June release of the single 'Cab It Up' and the budget-price album *Seminal Live*. The album, although obviously thrown together quickly, did have some interesting work, particularly the five studio tracks recorded in Rochdale and Edinburgh in a week with producer and former member of the Stockholm Monsters, Shan Hira. Among the highlights was a cover version of Lonnie Irving's 'Pinball Machine', an achingly sincere song about a life lost to old trucks and

10 Ian Gittins, 'The Fall: Funfair for the Common Man', *Melody Maker*, 3 March 1990
11 Sean O'Hagan, '*What's That Noise*', *NME*, 8 April 1989
12 ibid.

pinball machines. Only The Fall could follow this acoustic and mar-vellously rambling country and western song with, a couple of tracks later, the synthesizer-driven industrial hell of 'Mollusc In Tyrol'.

Despite these tracks, Schofield's judgement on the album was un-equivocal: 'The worst piece of shit I'd worked on in my life. No songs, no ideas. Done quickly and cheaply in a terrible studio that sounded awful. It was way below the standards I was used too. I was really so unhappy with it. I joined The Fall thinking it was the most amazing creative force at that time in music and I felt really lucky to be part of it but with *Seminal Live* I thought, "What are we doing? This is really crap." After *Seminal Live* I thought that's it, wow what a last album to go out on.' The circumstances of the album and its unsatisfying mix of live and studio tracks seriously compromised The Fall's credibility. Simon Reynolds in *Melody Maker* judged that The Fall had 'become the status quo',[13] and Andrew Collins in *NME* felt that the album just offered 'the sound of The Fall cruising'.[14] In retrospect, *Seminal Live* represented a band playing for time; a band determined to keep its best cards (songs such as 'Bill Is Dead' and 'I'm Frank') close to its chest.

To Smith's credit, complaints within the band about the financial situation remained minimal. 'Most of the time I was quite happy with the money situation,' said Hanley. 'It wasn't easy to find the money, I know it wasn't. Most of the time there were ten people on the pay roll and that's a lot of money to find. Some people weren't happy, just because they didn't know what was going on. They thought there was more coming in than there was. Most of the time it was shared out fairly, although Mark, obviously, kept more.'

The chief reason why Smith wanted to leave Beggars was his obsession with change for its own sake. After almost five years with the same label the relationship was jaded. Smith felt Beggars had taken The Fall as far as it could; it was time for a bigger label to have a go. The Fall's bargaining power came from its legendary status as the most innovative and relentlessly uncompromising band in Britain. The Fall would never make a label rich, but it would add lustre and status to that label's roster. Ironically it was Fontana, Brix's

13   Simon Reynolds, 'Dead Beat Descendent: The Fall, *Seminal Live*', *Melody Maker*, 24 June 1989
14   Andrew Collins, 'Frenz Again: The Fall, *Seminal Live*', *NME*, 24 June 1989

new label, which made Smith the best offer. The deal contracted The Fall to produce five albums over the next five years using the Cog Sinister imprint. Despite this purely symbolic subterfuge, signing to Phonogram saw Smith cast off the last remnants of indiedom: he was now label-mates with Elton John, Dire Straits and Status Quo and had no regrets. 'We were never an independent band really,' he claimed. 'We were an autonomous band.' Smith didn't care what label he was on as long as it didn't interfere with his plans: 'When we signed to Phonogram we said we're gonna keep on doing what we're doing, and they said, well OK, you just keep on doing what you're doing.'[15]

One of many areas outside the label's control was Smith's decision-making on hiring and firing. When The Fall took to the stage at the Cambridge Corn Exchange in July, fans were met with two line-up surprises. The first was the appearance of a young shaven-headed flautist called Charlotte Bill and the second was the return of founder member, guitarist Martin Bramah.

I was very wary when I left The Fall

It had been ten eventful years since Bramah left The Fall and formed, along with Una Baines and Eric, the Blue Orchids. The name was Eric's idea and had its origins in a misheard phrase from a John Cooper Clarke poem about a kid brought up by Alsations on a slag heap in Salford who joined the Blessed Orchids, an un-threatening gang of haemophiliacs. Drummer Ian Rogers, using the stage name Joe Kin, completed the line-up. Rogers hailed from South Manchester and according to Bramah was fresh out of Borstal: 'I liked him because I thought our name was a bit soft and precious and it was good to have a drummer who was a bit of a thug. He was quite a motivated and intelligent guy and it was him that went down to Rough Trade in London with our first demo tape. We sacked Ian after our second single because he was terrible to work with and not a very good drummer either. But I am grateful to him because he did get us the Rough Trade deal while we were all sat on our arses thinking we were great but doing nothing about it.'

The first single on Rough Trade, 'The Flood', came out in

15   Smith, on La Stampa, Holland, broadcast 5 April 1990

November 1980 and, like contemporary work by The Fall, was produced by Geoff Travis and Mayo Thompson. Bramah realized that comparisons were going to be inevitable, but he was determined to make the Blue Orchids distinct from his old group: 'I was very wary when I left The Fall of sounding too much like them, travelling on their coat-tails, etc., etc. It was genuine though, with the Orchids, that was the music I wanted to play, going back to my influences, Velvets, Stooges, etc., songs with strong melodic lines.'[16]

By this time Bramah and Baines were married and had a seven-month-old daughter called Morgan. On Bramah's own admission, they were still quite blasé about taking various mind-altering substances, like LSD and magic mushrooms. 'We were under the impression at that time that the great artists made their best stuff when they were under the influence of strong drugs: the shamanic view that other worlds were revealed through altered states of conscious-ness. But it's not true. We were misguided kids and a lot of the time when we recorded we were tripped out of our brains thinking we were making better music.' The pressures of being a mother, being in the band and taking too many hallucinogenics precipitated Baines's second serious breakdown – a breakdown complicated by chronic anorexia. 'I was completely psychotic,' she said. 'I couldn't relate to people . . . I'd just had a baby and I was in the band and even people in the band didn't approve – "How can you be a good mother and be in the band?" And that was only the beginning. I couldn't stand the sexism, the way they talked about women. It was like a nightmare being in a van for four hours with a load of people talking about women like they're nothing more than something to screw. It was just disgusting! I used to be really upset.'[17]

Baines's health deteriorated over a period of months. She wasn't eating or bathing, and her weight dropped to just under five stone. Her biggest fear was hospitalization, chiefly because of her experi-ences as a mental nurse. But the situation became so grave that social services visited and forced her to seek professional help. After five weeks of hospital care she was well enough to return home: 'I don't know why we didn't do that sooner,' said Bramah. 'They gave her

16 Anon., 'Simply Blue: Martin Bramah Interviewed', *The Hell With Poverty Fanzine*, no. 4, Autumn 1985
17 Steve Sutherland, 'The Sane Old Blues', *Melody Maker*, 1 May 1982

things to calm her down and she ate three meals a day and made a full recovery.' Baines's memories were more harrowing: 'All they were doing was shoving tranquillizers down me which were making me almost asleep on my feet. At the end of it I had to convince them I was normal by saying, "Oh, I can't wait to get back to my baby and wash the nappies and cook my husband's tea!" ' On release, Baines faced the massive challenge of getting her life back together and also rejoining the band. 'The state my mind was in when I came out – I didn't trust anybody – I was totally paranoid. I felt that getting back in the band was the biggest battle that could exist in the universe. But I was determined because my biggest fear was that I was gonna become a housewife and lose everything – nothing but dusting shelves for the rest of my life.'[18]

During Baines's illness, the Blue Orchids released its second single, 'Work', in March 1981. The song clearly demonstrated Bramah's obsession with the twisted melancholy of everyday-life situations. It also revealed his pessimistic view of society: 'I'd rather be a doom-monger than escapist, because times are bad. The way society is structured at the moment, it's founded on illusion, not reality. There are no real values there.'[19] Not long after the single, Baines returned to the band. There was also a new drummer 'Toby' (real name Philip Tolman), the replacement for Ian Rogers. The Blue Orchids soon began to attract quite a fan club in the music press. Lynn Hanna noted appreciatively the band's 'air of cool intrigue'[20] and Steve Sutherland thought them 'good enough to be destined for legend'.[21] Barney Hoskyns went as far as to call them 'one of the only worth-while groups left in the world'.[22]

Such rhetoric built up expectations for the group's début album, *The Greatest Hit (Money Mountain)*, released by Rough Trade in June 1982. Commercially it did OK, reaching the number 5 slot in the indie charts and continuing to sell steadily throughout the year. Like the previous singles, the album is full of Bramah's otherworldly and

18   ibid.
19   Lynn Hanna, 'When Reality Rears Its Orchidacious Head', *NME*, 20 June 1981
20   Lynn Hanna, 'Bunnies Wail Back: Echo and the Bunnymen, Blue Orchids, Nottingham', *NME*, 2 May 1981
21   Steve Sutherland, 'Blue Orchids / Birthday Party / Nightingales, Venue, London', *Melody Maker*, 25 July 1981
22   Barney Hoskyns, 'The Blue Orchids', *NME*, 15 May 1982

pensive lyrics, their brittle charm complementing his hesitant singing style and compelling guitar work. Baines's Yamaha organ provides the perfect accompaniment, adding a Doors-like melodic counterpoint on tracks such as 'Sun Connection' and 'A Year With No Head'.

The Greatest Hit was contemporary with The Fall's *Hex Enduction Hour* and comparisons between the two albums clearly show how far Bramah and Baines's direction differed from that of Smith's. Where the Blue Orchids followed the Velvet Underground's seductive 'Pale Blue Eyes', The Fall emulated its pile-driving 'White Light/White Heat'. There were other more fundamental differences, according to Bramah: ' . . . before you can tell anybody anything they've gotta be enjoying what you're saying or doing. The music has to be accessible and enjoyable before any of the deeper content will ever influence people and, I think, the trouble with The Fall originally was that not many people could appreciate the music.'[23]

During the spring of 1982, the Blue Orchids teamed up with former Velvet Underground singer Nico for a chaotic European tour. Nico at this time was living a heroin-addled life in Manchester, eccentrically managed by local promoter Alan Wise. Baines recalled her first meeting with Nico as being like a dream come true: 'It was just amazing that somebody you'd been listening to in a bedroom when you were sixteen or seventeen, should move, years later, to just about a hundred yards from that same spot. She was looking for a band and I remember Alan Wise introducing her to us. It felt like such a privilege. We just saw her back and her long auburn hair and when she turned round there was this incredible face.' On the tour the band played classics such as Bowie's 'Heroes', and the Velvets' 'Femme Fatale' and 'All Tomorrow's Parties'. However, the novelty of performing with a former hero quickly wore off after one too many drug-related near disasters going through the various border controls of Europe. 'We had a child at home,' Baines explained. 'We'd done all that and didn't want to get into any more danger.' On return, the Blue Orchids decided to split from the Nico scene but not before Bramah nearly died from a heroin overdose.

Bramah recovered and the Blue Orchids came back with more songs of love and loss on the *Agents Of Change* EP in November

23 Sutherland, op. cit., 1 May 1982

1982. According to Bramah, however, Rough Trade was loath to spend money on the band and barely promoted the record. The final track, 'The Long Night Out', ended with Bramah's lost and downbeat conclusion: 'Have you noticed, nothing seems built to last any more? When everything around you is fake, who do you turn to? When everything around you just stinks, where do you go?' The answer, Bramah decided, lay beyond the Blue Orchids.

While Bramah retreated from the band, Baines convinced Geoff Travis that Rough Trade should fund her solo album. The result, *Furia*, was released under the band name, the Fates, on Baines's own label, Taboo, with distribution by Rough Trade. 'It was me and a bunch of women friends who were in a band called Beyond The Glass,' said Baines. 'They were more of a jazz and soul kind of thing. We did the album at Tony Friel's basement studio in Old Trafford. It was cheap, probably the cheapest album ever made, just two grand for everything – recording, publicity, packaging. I haven't even got a copy myself.'

Not long after the record was released Baines and Bramah's marriage disintegrated. The Blue Orchids, however, kept going, just. Its twelve-inch single, 'Thirst' / 'Sleepy Town', came out on Tony Friel's Racket Records in June 1985. Then, as now, John Peel's opinion could make or break a record. He played the single but didn't like it, as Bramah recalled: 'His perception of it was, and I was too proud to put him right, that we'd spent a lot of money in a big studio. The thing was, we'd hired this synthesizer from the BBC, I'd written this simple song which was about three minutes long and we were doing a twelve-inch single so we needed another three minutes of improvisation, which was where the synthesizer came in. We used every sound we could. So John Peel played this track and said, "This is what happens when a good band goes into an expensive studio and get ruined by technology." '

Bramah didn't reappear on vinyl for another couple of years. By this time he had left Baines and was living in a council flat in Hulme. Karl Burns (recently departed from The Fall), Carrie and their son James lived nearby. Together with 'Lee' on bass, the quartet decided to form the band Thirst. Its one release, the EP *Let Go*, appeared in October 1987 on Rough Trade. Produced by John Leckie, the record drew on Burns and Bramah's enthusiasm for the Stooges. Thirst lasted just a few months more then disbanded. When Bramah heard that Brix had left The Fall he decided it was a good time to offer Smith his song-writing services. 'I was drifting at the time,' explained Bramah. 'I had no interest in wasting my time doing a manual job and I had no qualifications to do anything well paid. I casually got in touch with Mark, but with the clear intention of rejoining the band, which I did.' There were, of course, no complaints from Hanley and Scanlon about Bramah rejoining, but Schofield did need some convincing. She didn't know what to expect when Smith called her up to Manchester to rehearse with the new guitarist. 'Rather apprehensively I walked into the room and there was this sulky guy with a black leather jacket, trying to tune his guitar. I was like, "Who's that? Oh no! He's one of Mark's friends from down the pub." I had no idea who he was but Craig was so reverential. He thought Martin Bramah was God. He was like, "Martin is amazing, he's the best guitarist in the world, he taught me everything about playing guitar." "What that?" I said looking at Martin. But Martin is an amazing musician, incredible, he's so good, he is the most underrated guitarist, a fantastic song writer. He said he'd written a few songs and he played "Arms Control Poseur" and "Hilary" and I thought, "Fucking hell, this guy can actually write." At the end of the first rehearsal we all looked at each other and knew something special was happening. That period with The Fall was incredible. It was the most powerful band, it was the loudest, it was the most emotionally intensive – musically and artistically it was the best time.'

At the end of the summer and into the autumn The Fall recorded its first album for Phonogram. For Smith the year had been traumatic, but at least now he could concentrate on getting The Fall back on track. In an interview at the time he was particularly excited about the new work he was doing with Bramah: 'Creatively it's been a brilliant period, recording and writing. There's the stuff I did with Martin. The stuff we've done for Phonogram, I think it's brilliant. I've played it to people I trust and they're in tears and they're moved. The songs are more vocal, not cleaner but more straightforward; you can hear the lyrics which I've always been opposed to.'[24]

Live appearances by the band remained a rarity in 1989. However, The Fall did turn out alongside House of Love and the Wedding Present for John Peel's Fiftieth Birthday Party at the Subterrania in

24 James Brown, 'Rebellious Jukebox', *NME*, 29 July 1989

London on 29 August. To mark the occasion, Smith revived 'Mere Pseud Mag. Ed.' from 1982 and covered Gene Vincent's 'Race With The Devil', a song that Smith later said described him the best.[25] Perhaps it was the line, 'Well, I lead an evil life'?

25 Mark E. Smith, 'On the Couch: Mark E. Smith, The Fall', *NME*, 12 December 1998

14

High Tension Line, 1990–1991

> I get this fuckin' illness about once every two months, it's really
> appalling. The doctor said it's like fuckin' executive stress. He said,
> 'You've got MES.' And I said, 'I've not got MES, I am MES!'[1]

A new decade, a new label and – with the departure of Brix and the
arrival of Bramah – almost a new band. It was time for the self-
exiled 'hip priest' to return to his parish and attend to his flock. The
months in Edinburgh had provided a necessary break and the time
and space to deal with his separation from Brix and the death of his
father. But now it was time to get back to work: 'It was too good. It
was like paradise, a lovely city. In Edinburgh, I was gonna write the
next day and then I was gonna write the next day, but you don't.
You end up walking in the parks and sitting in the pub all day and
going to clubs at night – not conducive to creativity.'[2] Practically
speaking, Edinburgh was also too distant from the rest of the band in
Manchester and Phonogram in London. Still, leaving Edinburgh
was a great wrench for Smith: 'I was nearly in tears, and I went to
this pub round the corner, carrying all these plastic bags full of me
clothes and stuff, and the fuckin' green-welly brigade were there,
English, all about nineteen. They were shouting at the top of their
voices and abusing the barman and they were totally non-chippable,
y'know, no chips at all.'[3]

Smith's announced his return to music in late January with 'Tele-
phone Thing', produced and co-written with Matt Black and
Jonathan More. Along with the new label came a new cover artist,
Anthony Frost, with his abstract assemblages of wood, rope and acrylic

1 Ian Gittins, 'The Fall: Funfair for the Common Man', *Melody Maker*, 3 March
   1990
2 George Kay, 'Mancunian Caustic: An Interview with The Fall's Mark E. Smith',
   Rip It Up, issue 215, July 1995
3 Gittins, op. cit., 3 March 1990

paint on sailcloth. Born in 1951 in St Ives, Cornwall, Frost was the son of the internationally renowned artist, Terry Frost. With his studio in the cliff-top village of Rosemergy near Morvah, Frost's immediate environment could not have been more different from Smith's. The first record by The Fall he heard was *Dragnet*: 'I wrote Mark quite a long letter saying that up until then it had only been Beefheart who was doing this amazing poetry and tremendous observational stuff with incredible music. I got this letter back saying, "All I get is letters saying, 'How do you form a band and can you send me some badges?' and it was really nice to get a letter talking about the music in an intellectual way." And then we just stayed in touch through letters. Some of them are like text-messaging before text-messaging was invented. I've got some lovely titles from him like *Cool Appeals In Your Direction* which was a line he sent to me on a Christmas card.' When he eventually got to see it, Frost's work stunned Smith: 'It was by far the best stuff I'd ever been submitted in ten years, as artists write constantly, but A.F.'s work was so solid as to defy description. Also, it gets up the nose of "Art Department" jerks in record companies. Art to me is Tintoretto and Wyndham Lewis. "The Fall" are not great abstract fans!! Anthony combines both!'[4]

As well as by its sophisticated abstract cover design, the single was helped to number 58 in the charts by a rarely seen promotional video plus a live appearance on BBC2's *Late Show* (with Smith introduced by presenter Tracey McLeod as 'one of the beacons of Northern punk'). For the performance Smith sang from behind a wooden lectern – 'I I I I I . . . sense youuuuuu' – while Coldcut, heads down, controlled the decks. Adding to the group's media profile was John Peel's choice of a Fall track as one of his *Desert Island Discs* for Radio Four and the *NME*'s plastering of a smiling Smith on its front cover ('The Return of Laughing Boy Mark E. Smith'). Inside he recounted his surprise at finding out that the name 'Gretchen Franklin' in 'Telephone Thing' was the name of the actress who played 'Ethel' in *EastEnders*.[5]

The music came from Coldcut's 'My Telephone', sung by Lisa Stansfield and on their *What's That Noise?* album: 'He thought the vocals and all the rest of the stuff we did on it were shit,' said Jonathan More, 'but he really liked the guitar, bass and drums and he gave that

4 Anthony Frost, *Viva Blues*, Newlyn: Newlyn Art Gallery, 1996
5 Andrew Collins, 'Funky, Cold, Modern-ah!', *NME*, 20 January 1990

cassette to his band to learn those parts.'[6] The result was a funky Fall never heard before. Cathi Unsworth in *Sounds* likened 'Telephone Thing' to 'a bull terrier with a jaw lock, it just refuses to let go',[7] and James Brown in the *NME* welcomed the return of 'the original white rapper'.[8]

It's not very nice about women

Closely following 'Telephone Thing' came The Fall's first album with Phonogram, *Extricate*. As producers for the album, Smith worked with Adrian Sherwood, Coldcut and Craig Leon, recently relieved from his Adult Net duties. Individual tracks were recorded with the help of 'a bunch of guys in pony-tails' at an assortment of studios around the country, including Southern, Swanyard, Manor, and Woolhall.[9] Smith praised Phonogram's willingness to let him experiment with such a variety of producers and studios: 'What's great is they're being enthusiastic about it. Most record companies, they just send you a tape with all the different producers who are cheap.' What Smith brought to the studio and the mixing desk, and the reason why he always claimed producer credits, was his 'big advantage', his 'layman's ear'.[10]

On the sleeve notes Smith describes the album as 'the culmination of stuff I've/we've held back or just wrote over and through the tendril wires and chaos of the last fourteen months'. *Extricate* was therefore Smith's attempt to disentangle himself from the constraints and difficulties of the previous year. And despite the long time-frame (unique for The Fall) and the array of producers, studios and engineers, the resulting album is remarkably coherent and lean.

It opens with the pile-driving 'Sing! Harpy', co-written with Bramah, followed by 'I'm Frank', Scanlon's tribute to Frank Zappa but with Smith's ironically dumb rock lyrics, 'Gimme gimme gimme it slowly baby.' The next track, 'Bill Is Dead', offers a rare glimpse of Smith's softer, almost sentimentally romantic side. According to Smith, it started out as a parody of The Smiths: 'Me and Craig

6 Stephen Dalton, 'Ring the Noise', *NME*, 20 January 1990
7 Cathi Unsworth, 'The Fall: "Telephone Thing" ', *Sounds*, 20 January 1990
8 James Brown, 'The Fall: "Telephone Thing" ', *NME*, 20 January 1990
9 *Extricate* sleeve notes
10 Richard Cook, 'The Big E', *Sounds*, 10 June 1989

got together and Craig said let's do something Smithslike, and the original lyrics were like, "My heart is going, I'm at the bus stop, ooh ooh-ooh," all that sort of stuff. But then Craig wrote a really nice tune so I thought we can't do that, so I wrote it off the top of me head. So they're a bit more personal. Bill was my father's best friend, but that was the original piss-take title.'[11] The song's poignancy lies in the disparity between Scanlon's melancholy tune and Smith's careful delivery of the heavily ironic line: 'This is the greatest time of my life.' At the end of the year it topped John Peel's Festive Fifty and Phonogram begged Smith to let it be released as a single, but he refused. Perhaps it was a little too personal.

'Black Monk Theme Part I' borrows its music from sixties' oddities the Monks and its misogynist lyrics – 'I hate you baby' – from a role-playing Smith. As he was quick to point out: 'What I'm saying is not really what I think. It's almost as if I'm putting myself into character. When I played it to some mates they said it's not very nice about women and I said it's not me.'[12] In fact, *Extricate* is distinguished by the number of tracks it contains about women. In addition to those already mentioned there are also 'Hilary' and 'The Littlest Rebel'. The rest of the album contains the threatening atmospherics of 'Chicago, Now!' and a Bramah composition, 'And Therein . . . ', which Smith likened to a Salvation Army tune crossed with country and western. On 'Arms Control Poseur' Smith reads, as an introduction, some well-selected lines from the English writer Malcolm Lowry: 'What do you seek? Oblivion.'

After the disappointment of *Seminal Live* the music press returned to what they liked doing best – showering The Fall with superlatives. James Brown in the *NME* called it 'The Fall's most remarkable LP in five years' and gave it ten out of ten.[13] Robin Denselow noted that despite the album being 'danceable' in places, the band's credibility was 'still intact',[14] and John Robb was pleased to announce that 'just when cynics thought The Fall's sell by date was past, Mark Smith lashes back with his most direct music for ages.'[15] Jon Wilde simply

11   Smith, on La Stampa, Holland, broadcast 5 April 1990
12   John Robb, 'Cutting Loose', *Sounds*, 3 February 1990
13   James Brown, 'Fall's Gold: Top Mark', *NME*, 17 February 1990
14   Robin Denselow, 'Punks Back in the Pink', *The Guardian*, 1 March 1990
15   John Robb, 'The Fall: *Extricate*', *Sounds*, 3 February 1990

called it 'possibly their finest yet', in other words 'cooler than fuck'.[16] The chorus of approval continued for the single drawn from the album, 'Popcorn Double Feature'. It made Sam King's Single of the Week in *Sounds* – 'best single The Fall have ever released'[17] – and despite Edwin Pouncey's initial misgivings, he had to admit – 'Damn The Fall for being so sickeningly gifted.'[18] Nobody seemed to care that it was yet another cover version (this time of a Searchers' song) and also the first time that The Fall released a single straight from an already released album, just like all the other groups.

Mark is the definition of a diva

With these releases out of the way, The Fall embarked on a gruelling five-month tour of the UK, the Netherlands, Belgium, Germany and Switzerland, plus an ultra-rare excursion into France, and a couple of dates in New York and Los Angeles. Then, after a month's break, it was off again to Australia and Japan. No wonder Smith summed up the year as being one of 'continuous travel'.[19] With so much time on the road, relationships within the band became strained and during the brief break between Los Angeles and Australia Smith and Schofield fell out badly: 'I called Mark all these horrible names and he called me some too,' recalled Schofield. 'I said, "That's it I'm leaving. I'm going back to London and I want nothing to do with him. He's out of his mind, out of control." I remember saying to him, "You've got the best band you've ever had with The Fall, you're producing your best work. Why are you trying to destroy it? What can't you handle about it?" ' One of the arguments was over Schofield's working with other musicians, including Barry Adamson: 'Mark was absolutely furious,' she said. ' "You don't work for anyone! You work for me!" He just got so upset, furious and I didn't appreciate Mark Smith telling me what I could do in my own time.' It was particularly galling for Schofield because of Smith's collaborations with Coldcut and more recently with Keith Le Blanc and Adrian Sherwood's Tackhead (resulting in 'Repetition', the B-side of their 'Dangerous Sex' single). Why couldn't she do the same?

16 Jon Wilde, 'The North's Circular', *Melody Maker*, 17 February 1990
17 Sam King, 'The Fall: "Popcorn Double Feature" ', *Sounds*, 17 March 1990
18 Edwin Pouncey, 'The Fall: "Popcorn Double Feature" ', *NME*, 17 March 1990
19 Mark E. Smith, '1990, Pick of the Year', *Melody Maker*, 5 January 1991

So Schofield returned to London, determined to leave The Fall. But a few days later new manager Trevor Long contacted her and tried to persuade her to come back for the band's tour of Australia. After some urging, she relented and, against her better judgement, rejoined the group. 'Mark is the definition of diva,' she said. 'He has to have things exactly as he sees them and he gets absolutely furious if things are not the way he wants them to be. His vision is hard to understand, but it's there and if you are not conforming to it, he'll be merciless, he'll just criticize you, goad you into doing things that you probably didn't think you were capable of doing. He's not a motivator at all; he rules with a reign of terror, he's a dictator. It was like working in an office and having to look busy when the boss was around. The band was always run as a business where he was the boss and he employed the band members. You were a hired hand and worked for Mark E. Smith and you did what he said.'

The last date of The Fall's tour of Australia took place on 14 July at the Coogie Bay Hotel in Sydney. Later that night, as the band helped pack away the equipment, Long asked Schofield and Bramah if he could see them later in his hotel room. 'It was four o'clock in the morning,' recalled Schofield, 'and he said, "Here are your plane tickets, you're on a plane tomorrow morning." And that was just that. It was all very much planned, to get us out of the country before we had a chance to talk either to Mark or anybody else. I'm not sorry, but I think the way he did it was very cowardly. Martin was actually very upset about this. He loves Mark as a brother and respects him and wants to work with him. But they just can't get along, like Cain and Abel. I had plenty of history of being sacked, leaving, rejoining, etc., but I certainly didn't want Martin to get sacked on my account.'

The manner and timing of the dismissal, just before the group was about to go to Japan, could not have been crueler. During the tour she and Bramah had become lovers and she thought this riled Smith and in some way threatened his position in the band. 'It wasn't Mark's band any more,' she said. 'We'd split into different factions: Martin and Charlotte, Martin and me, Mark and Kenny, the lads, me and the lads. It was a real shame, because that was one of the best live shows that we did and to my mind *Extricate* was my favourite Fall album to work on.'

A couple of weeks later the line-up change became public

knowledge when Long issued a statement: 'They were fired because they wanted to pursue other projects and it was pointless them remaining in the band any longer.'[20] In subsequent interviews Smith rationalized the sackings by saying that the band was getting too big, he wanted it stripped down and simplified. With Bill and fiddle player Kenny Brady the band had become a seven-piece and he didn't want to end up like 'fuckin' Ian Dury and the Blockheads.'[21]

On their return to England, Schofield and Bramah retreated to a hotel in Brighton to think about their future. Schofield decided to quit music, signed on the dole and studied A levels at college: 'I could have played on, I had plenty of offers, but fuck that! I'm not going to spend the rest of my life on *Top of the Pops* with a cameraman shooting up my skirt.' She accepted a place to read medicine at Cambridge University, split up with Bramah and by 1999 was a fully qualified doctor. Bramah, meanwhile, re-formed the Blue Orchids and released two more records: the single 'Diamond Age' in March 1991 and the EP *Secret City* in November 1992.

Bramah and Schofield's departure came too late for them to be airbrushed out of a poster accompanying The Fall's *The Dredger* EP in August. The EP was a deluxe limited edition of the single 'White Lightning', yet another cover and yet another Gene Vincent song. Imperial Eye directed a promotional video for the single that recreated the famous opening shot of *The Wild Ones*, when a motorcycle gang comes over the horizon and drives over a camera placed at road level. The song's rock 'n' roll style restated Smith's aversion to the dance music craze then sweeping the nation. 'I like doing things that go against the grain,' was his understated comment.[22]

You know me, I'm a man of the suburbs

The summer outdoor-festival scene had grown beyond recognition since The Fall played the informal and often chaotic Deeply Vale festivals in the late seventies. But it was a phenomenon that had mostly bypassed the group and Smith felt this was in revenge for some anti-CND statements he'd made many years before: 'The hippies who

20 Anon., 'News', *NME*, 28 July 1990
21 David Cavanagh, 'The Fall', *Volume*, no. 4, September 1992
22 Leo Finlay, 'The Man Whose Head Expounded', *Sounds*, 25 August 1990

run Glastonbury are like the fuckin' Mafia. So we were banned from ever playing there. It's no great tragedy, apart from the fact that they're the same old fuckin' tossers who run the whole festival scene.'[23] In August 1990, The Fall played Reading as second billing behind the Pixies. In front of a crowd of thirty thousand and from behind a lectern, Smith sang his way through a set that included 'Bill Is Dead' and ended with a rousing 'Jerusalem'. Steve Lamacq described the band as 'brilliant' and a welcome relief after the 'inglorious self-promotion and unwarranted arrogance' of the earlier bands.[24]

In early November the band made another festival appearance, this time for WOMAD at the Casino L'Alianca de Poble Nou in Barcelona. Working on backline for the first time was Dave Bush. Born 4 June 1959 in Taplow, Bush was an experienced sound engineer who had worked with bands such as the Clash, Echo and the Bunnymen and Teardrop Explodes. When he first started working with The Fall Smith told him: 'Don't worry about me, you just look out for the band. If I get caught up in my mike line or anything, don't you bother, you just look after the band, make sure they're all right.' Given Smith's increasingly eccentric stage mannerisms (tangling mike leads, changing settings on amplifiers, throwing mikes into the bass drum), it was general knowledge in the business that if you could do backline for The Fall you could do it for anybody. 'I always thought The Fall was shit,' Bush later admitted. 'I thought it was Les Dawson playing piano, that's what it sounded like to me. My mate said: "If you go away with them I bet you'll love them when you come back." I said: "I'll never love The Fall, they're a pile of shite!" And he was right. They were brilliant. In Barcelona I was stood on stage and could really hear what was going on. You got all these weird harmonies. So when they finished the gig I said to Mark: "Listen, you've got to let me program for you because I was hearing noises in my head that were fuckin' brilliant." He gave me a shout and that's how it started. We were really looked after. Mark's really generous. First thing he said to me was: "Dave, I want to pay yer a good amount of money. The only thing I want you to worry about when you wake up in the morning is writing songs for The Fall." It was lots of money for Manchester.'

23 Anon., 'The Fall', Melody Maker, 25 August 1990
24 Steve Lamacq, 'Reading: Live', NME, 8 September 1990

The Fall ended 1990 with the single 'High Tension Line'. The song's title came from an obscure source, composer La Monte Young's *The Second Dream of the High Tension Line Stepdown Transformer* (1963), a piece of music with no apparent beginning, middle or ending. Because it was the band's fourth single in a year Smith had some trouble convincing Phonogram that it was a good idea: 'In my perfect world, The Fall would bring out a single every month,' he said. 'Records should still reflect what people think at the time and it's very tense in England at the moment. Everyone's worried about their mortgages and stuff. You know me, I'm a man of the suburbs.'[25]

To mitigate Phonogram's unease, The Fall included on the B-side its first Christmas song, 'Xmas With Simon' (so named because Wolstencroft provided the keyboards). 'Atrocious lyrics!' admitted Smith. 'The outside opinion of The Fall is that we have no sense of humour but someone who's into The Fall understands the humour within the songs. That's the secret of our accessibility. I find extreme sarcasm very funny indeed.' Smith didn't like Christmas in Britain, chiefly because everything closed down for a couple of weeks: 'It's disgusting. You can't get any bread or milk and that's what the song's about. Christmas is more of a family time . . . where families can beat each other up.'[26]

The 'usual brilliant whine', wrote Steven Wells,[27] while Andy Stout thought 'High Tension Line' both a 'turgid little masterpiece' and 'innocuous, inoffensive, and ultimately as bland and tasteless as a microwave chicken tikka'.[28] Despite Smith's assertion that 'High Tension Line' was topical, there was little in the lyrics that directly linked it to any particular contemporary event. The video, however, made an explicit reference to the recent reunification of Germany, with the band wearing SS uniforms: 'I just thought it would be a good crack,' said Smith. 'All these bands into shocking people are as tame as fuck. I made everybody cover up the SS symbols and swastikas. I'm very anti-Nazi, actually. What they did was criminal. They put German art back about one hundred years.'[29]

25 Andy Peart, 'Badmouth Strikes Again', *Sounds*, 8 December 1990
26 ibid.
27 Steven Wells, 'The Fall, "High Tension Line" ', *NME*, 8 December 1990
28 Andy Stout, 'The Fall, "High Tension Line" ', *Sounds*, 8 December 1990
29 Stephen Dalton, 'Not Falling, Soaring', *Vox*, June 1991

'A man of the suburbs' would also have been aware of 'high tension' in the Gulf after Iraq invaded Kuwait and operation 'Desert Storm' began. Closer to home he might have celebrated Margaret Thatcher's departure as prime minister. The year had started badly for her as fears about 'mad-cow disease' (BSE) began to grow, despite John Gummer, her agriculture minister, feeding his four-year-old daughter a beef-burger to demonstrate, 'British beef is safe.' March saw anti-poll tax rioting in Trafalgar Square and in October Thatcher was powerless to stop the EU agreeing on future monetary union. In the middle of November, Michael Heseltine challenged her leadership and by the end of the month the seemingly impossible had happened: Maggie was out, out, out.

I just love them to death. Jesuit lads, you know

The Fall's first release of 1991, the album *Shift-Work*, hit the shops at the end of April. Produced by Craig Leon, Grant Showbiz and Robert Gordon and recorded in Sheffield and Birmingham, the album drew on a large number of musicians. In addition to the four core members of the group – Smith, Hanley, Scanlon and Wolstencroft – there was Brady on fiddle, Cassell Webb on backing vocals, Dave Bush on 'machines', Craig Leon on organ and guitar and – obviously recorded before they departed – Bramah and Schofield playing guitar and keyboards on 'Rose'. With the latter two now forced out, Smith once again fell back on the writing skills of his two most loyal supporters, Scanlon and Hanley: 'They're fuckin' hard as nails, actually, them two,' enthused Smith. 'They're really far out. Freaks me out, you know. Very super-intelligent fellows, but they're really reticent. Reticent isn't even fuckin' in it, I'll tell you. They're perfect . . . They don't ask me about the lyrics, they don't ask me about anything. I just love them to death. Jesuit lads, you know. I've had people in the group and they go on about money, and give me this and give me that and I wrote half of this. What's this song about and fuckin' . . . Steve and Craig are brilliant.'[30]

Wolstencroft was also developing as a writer, creating demos at home on an old Roland 505 drum machine and a Yamaha keyboard: 'I can come out with like a bass-type synth sound over the drum

30 Cavanagh, op. cit., September 1992

machine, and then give it to Craig and he'll put a guitar on. Or we'll just mess about with riffs at rehearsals or sound-checks and stuff, and if we like it we'll go ahead and work on changes and choruses. Then we'll make a rough recording and give it to Mark. We actually did 'So What About It?' on four-track.'[31]

Other tracks on the album included 'Idiot Joy Showland', a critique of the hyped-up Manchester scene, and the touching 'Edinburgh Man', Smith's ode to his second-favourite city. The main theme of the album was captured in 'The War Against Intelligence' (the original title for the album until the Gulf War started and Smith decided to change the title to something less controversial). 'There is a war of intelligence going on at the moment,' he proclaimed. 'I do genuinely think that, and it's not because I'm particularly intelligent, I just think there is. Intelligence is actively discouraged in all walks of life, the media and all of it.'[32] In the title-track, 'Shift-Work', Smith describes a relationship that breaks down because of incompatible time-keeping, while in 'You Haven't Found It Yet' he muses on the meaning of life as he drives around London, lost. 'A Lot of Wind' has Smith complaining about daytime television and the banality of *This Morning*-like talk shows. The album's love interest came in 'Rose', which, with its references to 'Hampstead', 'wah-wah' guitars and 'freckles', was probably intended for Brix.

Smith later admitted his nervousness about how the LP would be received and even considered packing in the band. But what else could he do? 'I wouldn't mind being on the dole,' he shrugged, 'I wouldn't mind being on the buses. I don't give a shit, you know what I mean?'[33] He needn't have worried, the reception was reassuringly positive. Jon Wilde in *Melody Maker* thought it captured The Fall at its 'awkward, bloody-minded, self-respecting best'.[34] Leo Finlay in *Vox* wrote 'without doubt, this is Album of the Year,

---

31 Paul Quinn, 'Pride and The Fall', *Making Music*, May 1991. For all you guitar buffs, in the same article Wolstencroft said that Hanley used Fender Precision basses and an Ampeg SVT, and that Scanlon also used Fender guitars, with recently acquired Jazz Chorus amps. He formerly used Fender Twin Reverb and a Consorti.

32 Roger Morton, 'Time and a Half, Gentleman, Please', *NME*, 20 April 1991

33 David Cavanagh, 'Sarky Street Poet in Love-Tug Riddle!', Select, May 1991

34 Jon Wilde, 'The Sinister Waltz: The Fall, *Shift-Work*', *Melody Maker*, 20 April 1991

thus far',[35] and the *NME*'s Stephen Dalton gave it ten out of ten and considered it to be 'confident, confrontational and straightforward enough to be a strong commercial contender'.[36] And it was: with a highest chart position of 17, *Shift-Work* became The Fall's second most successful album.

The cover art for the album marked the début of Pascal le Gras. Born in 1962 in Senlis in France, Pascal claims to have attended art school from the age of seven. The first time he heard The Fall was on independent radio: 'I was stupefied and immediately ran to the record shop.' The Fall rarely visited France so Pascal made sure he was in the crowd when it played in April 1990 at the Montmartre Elysée in Paris. After the show he approached Smith: 'I showed him my work and offered him a portrait. I told him I wanted to do a cover. He came near me, looked at me and took me by the ear (like Julius Caesar with his men) and said yes.' Smith's praise for Pascal's work couldn't have been more fulsome: 'He's just like a sublime genius, all his work looks well ahead of its time. I don't have that much contact with the fella though, because he's from Normandy and he lives in Paris and I can hardly understand a word he's saying, but he's great. He never moans about me messing about with his stuff. Of course I mess about with things, change the angle and things like that. But I'm just his editor or something . . . I get a lot of stuff sent in to me from people wanting to do our covers because a lot of artists are into The Fall, you know. Oh yeah, a lot of artists. But half of it's crap, of course.'[37]

They accuse me of wearing flares, but they're parallels

At the end of January 1991, the 'Madchester' scene lampooned by Smith in 'Idiot Joy Showland' began to unravel when the Hacienda was temporarily forced to close because of gang violence and drug-dealing. For the past three years Manchester bands led by the Happy Mondays and the Stone Roses had stormed the national charts and fostered a huge E-fuelled, flared-trousered, raving youth cult. In

35 Leo Finlay, 'Working Class, The Fall, *Shift-Work*', *Vox*, May 1991
36 Stephen Dalton, 'Quiet Genius at Work: The Fall, *Shift-Work*', *NME*, 20 April 1991
37 Ted Kessler, 'Mark E. Smith: Heroes & Villains', *NME*, 11 December 1993

December 1989, when the *NME* cover story read, 'Manchester: so much to answer for', Smith named his favourite Mancunian as 'my guru Fred', the landlord of his local pub who 'grossly insults his customers'.[38] Smith's 'Madchester' ended in 1989 when he stopped taking Ecstasy, claiming it turned him into a 'bloody sex maniac'. The artificial nature of the drug also made him suspicious: 'It was very fishy the way it was invented. It was to get American middle-class kids off the street. So it was like, here's a combination of coke, speed, pot and acid, but it's the chemical equivalent . . . Ecstasy's like a CIA drug or something, like Soma, ever read *Brave New World*?'[39]

At the end of 1990, Smith despaired at the number of would-be fashionmongers swamping Manchester: 'You wouldn't believe it up here. I go out to a club, and people look at what shirt I've got on and write it down so the Happy Mondays and the Charlatans can wear one. They look at my jacket, they look at my shoes. It's horrible and I just can't cope with it.'[40] They also looked at his trousers: 'We've always worn baggies, us, we've always worn parallels. That's where they get the bleedin' idea from. They accuse me of wearing flares, but they're parallels – there's a bit of a difference.'[41]

Behind much of the brouhaha surrounding Manchester was Factory's Tony Wilson (once memorably described by Smith as 'the poor man's Richard Branson'). Smith had long since distanced himself from the 'third-rate Joy Division impersonators' of the Factory scene: 'We always keep on the other side of town,' he explained in 1980. 'Factory have got a good thing going for themselves but it's got nothing to do with us.'[42] Ten years later and Factory still caused problems for Smith: 'They say university applications have gone up twenty per cent, and I think, Thanks a lot Factory. I'm really grateful – twenty per cent more students.'[43]

The Fall's next hometown gig came in August 1991, at the Cities in the Park festival in Heaton Park – the first large-scale event to take place there since the Pope's visit in 1981. The two-day festival was

38   Mark E. Smith, '24-Hour Party People', *NME*, 2 December 1989
39   Paul Benney, 'A Quick Pint with Mark E. Smith', *Jockey Slut*, January 1996
40   Peart, op. cit., 8 December 1990
41   Paul Lester, 'The Fall: Prole Art Threat', *Melody Maker*, 1 September 1990
42   Smith, interviewed by Dave Fanning for RTE (Ireland), broadcast 18 October 1980
43   Finlay, op. cit., 25 August 1990

promoted by Alan Wise, with ten per cent of the takings intended for African Famine Relief and the Kurdish Trust Fund.[44] The Fall played as last-minute replacements for the Soup Dragons and as support for the headliners, the Wonder Stuff. Also performing that night were Cabaret Voltaire and the Buzzcocks, playing 'Ever Fallen In Love' for the millionth time. There was no such nostalgia from The Fall. 'Nothing is extraneous,' wrote Sally Margaret Joy[45] and Stuart Maconie agreed: 'The older and grouchier he gets, the better MES is at his avowed mission: to take the stupidity out of rock and leave it leaner, cleverer and uncluttered with sentiment.'[46]

Surprisingly, neither reviewer noticed the unfamiliar figure on stage behind the keyboards. In his infinite wisdom, Smith had decided that this hometown gig in front of seventeen thousand people would be a great opportunity to introduce new band member Dave Bush. 'Mark didn't turn up for rehearsals,' Bush recalled. 'I had a bit of an idea what they'd be playing because I'd been doing a bit of backlining for them. So I learnt about sixty songs in all. I'd programmed a lot of stuff up. In rehearsal we did the first three or four songs and Craig went, "Yeah, you're fuckin' great. Let's go to the pub." And I said, "No, no, we've got to polish the set up. You don't know what the rest sounds like." "No you're fine, let's go to the pub." So we then did Heaton Park and I was shitting my pants. To play in front of thousands of people for your first gig was an amazing experience. I said to myself, "Dave, this is always what you wanted to do. You can either shit out now or you'll fuckin' enjoy it." '

With just a small warm-up gig in Manchester in between, Bush's next gig for the band was even more daunting: an appearance on the main stage at Reading. The day before, the crowd had been entertained by Nirvana (riding high on the success of *Nevermind*), Sonic Youth and headline act Iggy Pop. Below The Fall on Saturday's bill were Mercury Rev, Blur and De La Soul and, above them, Carter USM and James. But still The Fall shone out: Andrew Collins

44 Two years later, in December 1993, Smith played a benefit gig at Al's Music Café to aid Alan Wise, who at the time was homeless, selling the *Big Issue* and living on the street with his dog Sly. (See Anon., 'Fall–ing on Hard Times', *NME*, 25 December 1993/1 January 1994.)

45 Sally Margaret Joy, 'Cities in the Park', *Melody Maker*, 10 August 1991

46 Stuart Maconie, 'Cities in the Park', *NME*, 10 August 1991

described the set as 'mesmerising and untouchable',[47] and Andrew Mueller thought it 'brilliant, obstinate, surly and a lovely venomous antidote to the bland complacency of what's gone before'.[48] After the gig, BBC Radio One's Mark Radcliffe interviewed Hanley and Scanlon. Asked how the gig went Scanlon replied: 'I'll just repeat a quote from Steve. I'm sorry but it's quite apt: "It sounded like the Beatles at Shea Stadium playing with one Vox amp." We were very separated but I think we played well.' Hanley confessed to being wary of playing big festivals: 'I think they're really badly organized. There's too many chiefs and not enough Indians around, and you meet too many people you know . . . I really like a bit of solitude before a gig.' Radcliffe made the point that The Fall was more associated with 'small, sweaty rooms' than with large outdoor festivals. 'Yeah, it is obviously,' Hanley replied. 'Even the equipment we've got and some of the songs are not really suitable for a place this size.'

For the rest of the autumn the band wrote and rehearsed new material and then entered the recording studio in November. Some of the new tracks were then premièred on a seven-date tour of England in December. By this time Smith's divorce from Brix was finalized and he married Saffron Prior on 27 November at the Registry Office in Manchester. At the time the twenty-two-year-old Prior described herself as a 'secretary'. She worked for her new husband's company, Cog Sinister, in an office at 23 New Mount Street, just behind Victoria Station. The large redbrick building was formerly the home of the Cooperative Printing Society Ltd, but now housed a number of small local businesses. Steve Hanley later observed that Smith's mixing of business, family and romance didn't always create the best working conditions: 'Saffron wasn't different. Every one of Mark's girlfriends was involved in some way. His personal life was always mixed up with the band . . . I can't think of anything worse really.'

47 Andrew Collins, '91 Reading', NME, 7 September 1991
48 Andrew Mueller, 'Reading 91', Melody Maker, 7 September 1991

15

Why Are People Grudgeful?, 1992–1993

I was once on a train with, among others, Mark E. Smith. Tired of
playing Pictionary, I announced that I could sense, simply by looking, whether oranges contained pips. 'I can tell people's religion just
by looking at their faces,' countered Smith. A VIP had just entered
the carriage and eager to muck in, said to Smith, 'What am I then?'
The whole carriage hushed. Smith looked him up and down.
'You're a cunt, pal,' he said.[1]

In the second half of 1991, as the Soviet Union tore itself apart and
the EEC came closer together with the Maastricht Treaty, Smith
wrote the lyrics for the single 'Free Range' with its ominous '2001
Also Sprach Zarathustra' prophesy of 'trouble' about to sweep
'Europa'. Smith's predictions rang all-to-true when the single's
March 1992 release coincided with the first harrowing news reports
of ethnic fighting in Bosnia-Herzegovina. Ironically the track came
very close to remaining unrecorded, as Dave Bush recalled: 'We tried
to record it loads of times but Mark wouldn't let me do it the way I
wanted to do it. He wouldn't let us have the click track on and said
we couldn't play with sequencers. In the end he went: "Right, I'm
going to the fuckin' pub. You've got half an hour. If you don't get it
fuckin' sorted out by then we're not doing that fuckin' song." He
went to the pub and we got it down in one go.'

'Free Range' was linked to The Fall's latest album release *Code:
Selfish*, produced by Smith, Leon and Simon Rogers. Since leaving
The Fall in 1988, Rogers had worked with Peter Murphy, Xmal
Deutschland and most recently with Ian Broudie on the Lightning
Seeds' *Sense* album. Smith brought him back, he said, to help make
the album 'harder', 'more crunchy', less melodic than the last two
albums. 'This LP's going for brute force,' Smith added. 'We've got a
keyboard player, he can't play the keyboards, know what I mean?

1 Andy Darling, *FHM*, May 1993

He's an ex-roadie of ours but he sounds good. Vicious.'[2] Bush shifted the band towards using tapes and programming, but Smith made sure it didn't shift too far: 'The Fall are still a good drummer and a good bass player basically, there's no two ways about that.'[3]

The first track, 'The Birmingham School of Business School', is strongly autobiographical and relates to Smith's recent falling-out with manager Trevor Long. Described by David Buckley as a 'lovable Brummie rogue',[4] Long had worked with Duran Duran and Dexys Midnight Runners before joining The Fall and at one point had managed Haircut 100. After five years working with The Fall, for Smith at least, his 'lovable' side had come to be eclipsed by the 'rogue' in him. During 1991, Smith became convinced that Long was fiddling money from the group and took him to court. When the case was heard in 1994 Long was fully acquitted on 'charges of stealing £5,000 and obtaining another £4,000 intended for the band by deception'. He was also found not guilty of three charges of forging Smith's signature to transfer funds from the band's account to his own.[5] Smith quoted William Blake in his summation of the affair: 'The weak in courage are strong in cunning.'[6] The song itself mocks 'scientific management', 'case-carrying' con-men, and their Stepford wives. It certainly wasn't Smith's last word on the matter as we shall see. Other tracks included 'Return', a straightforward chugging Steve Hanley composition garnished with Smith's sarcastic 'baby, baby, baby, come back to me' chorus, and 'Time Enough At Last', with its suitably laid-back melody. 'Everything Hurtz' hails from the 'Totally Wired' and 'Gramme Friday' school of Fall songs about over-indulgence and the effects of 'pursuing the fuel too long', listing side-effects such as tinnitus and Tourette's. This self-destructive bent contrasted well with the next track, 'Immortality', in which Smith, over Bush's sequencer, gently explains that there are some things you just can't buy, change or rearrange.

In 'Two-Face!' Smith self-consciously celebrates his schizophrenic

2 Ian McCann, 'Love, Love, Love, Love, Love your Armani', *NME*, 29 February 1992
3 ibid.
4 David Buckley, *No Mercy: The Authorised and Uncensored Biography of the Stranglers*, London: Hodder & Stoughton, 1997
5 Anon., 'Not Sinister', *NME*, 24/31 December 1994
6 *Code: Selfish* sleeve notes

personality as it splits in two. 'Just Waiting' is adapted from the Hank Williams original, with new lines including a description of a cretin 'waiting for U2 to come on MTV'. After the heavily sequenced 'So-Called Dangerous', with its fragments and cut-ups, including the aphorism 'the meek shall inherit the mirth', we come full circle back to the Long affair with 'Gentlemen's Agreement' and more of Smith's wallowing in the mire of broken trust. His final word on the matter comes with 'Married, 2 Kids' a song about a man who avoids risks because of wife, mortgage and kids. It includes Smith's cruel but humorous description of a man like a 'long-winded article' who smells like a goat. Smith made it pretty clear he had no plans for a middle-age of baby-rearing: 'When a bloke has kids, he goes right down the fuckin' shaft. They start fiddling, they don't concentrate on their work. I come from a family of six, I never saw my dad. But these guys with their pony-tails, they're just hanging around their kids all day. It's cruel to the kids . . . people go on about child abuse but that's child abuse.'[7] The album ends with 'Crew Filth', a low-fi album-filler that reminds listeners that just below the surface lurks a Fall just as wilfully obscure and avant-garde as the day it recorded 'W.M.C.-Blob 59' in 1980.

Reviewers of the album noted The Fall's tougher sound, with Sally Margaret Joy pronouncing it as 'unexpected and unignorable as a hornet's sting.'[8] Dele Fadele thought it 'harsh and uncompromising' and a 'triumph of the imagination'.[9] Only David Cavanagh in *Select* found it a 'disappointment', chiefly because of the 'fussy' arrangements and the industrial-style drum programming.[10] A new technological era had begun for The Fall and the record-buying public seemed enthusiastic, enabling the album to reach number 21 in the charts.

7 McCann, op. cit., 29 February 1992
8 Sally Margaret Joy, 'Cork-Ah! The Fall, *Code: Selfish*', *Melody Maker*, 14 March 1992
9 Dele Fadele, 'Tales of Cryptographic Oceans', *NME*, 14 March 1992
10 David Cavanagh, 'The Fall, *Code: Selfish*', *Select*, March 1992

Not In The City

The Fall's promotional tour for *Code: Selfish* began with up-and-coming band Levitation as support. A few dates in and Levitation dropped out, claiming Smith called them 'a bunch of fucking crusty poofs'. They also complained about having to work under Smith's 'oppressive regime'. 'We're not into character assassination, but we couldn't work under the atmosphere he was creating,' explained indignant Levitation guitarist Christian Hayes. Smith denied all allegations and counter-claimed that Levitation took over an hour each night to sound-check and used too much dry ice during their set.[11]

During May and June, The Fall toured Europe, including a trip to Halle, near Leipzig, where Smith found much to remind him of home: 'It was like one of them old films. They don't repair the windows. Bit tough audience, you know, throwing things. They remind me of North Manchester people. The toilet was overflowing, all this. I'm saying fix that bloody toilet, it's going to flow on to the stage and electrocute everybody. The promoter's going, "It's not my job," this woman – she's on steroids, bandages up her arms – she goes, "It's not my job, you stick the sign up." So I said I'll bloody do it and I'm sticking the sign up – BAND AND CREW – DON'T USE THESE TOILETS. Weird attitude. It's chaos. People driving on the pavement, lorries stopping in the middle of the road for a chat. Very like a housing estate. They'd rather moan about the windows than fix them.'[12]

After Germany, The Fall prepared itself for the festival season with the release of 'Ed's Babe', a cheerful song about DIY and promiscuity. The single also included the wonderfully named 'Pumpkin Head Xscapes', 'The Knight The Devil And Death', with its novelty female vocals, and 'Free Ranger', a remixed version of 'Free Range'. The release coincided with The Fall's first ever performance at Glastonbury, where the band appeared between the House of Love and archetypal crusties the Levellers. Luckily for the promoters, Smith saw the funny side: 'Hello, my Glastonbury muckers,' he announced to the crowd. 'We've been banned from playing Glastonbury for ten years, now you've invited us back – and we're supporting the Levellers! Marvellous, innit?'[13]

11   Anon., 'Levitation Dropped by Fall!', *Melody Maker*, 28 March 1992
12   Mark E. Smith and David Quantick, 'Singles', *NME*, 27 June 1992
13   Andrew Collins and David Quantick, 'Keep Britain Tie-Dye: Glastonbury Festival 1992', *NME*, 4 July 1992

Back at home in September, Manchester buzzed with the excitement of the first 'In The City: International Music Convention'. Organized by Yvette Livesey and Tony Wilson, the convention boasted one thousand music-industry delegates, forty debates and thirty official gigs. Just two years earlier a typically bombastic Wilson had announced at the convention's prototype, the New York New Music Seminar, 'Wake up, America. You're dead'. With a £25,000 grant from Manchester City Council he hoped to demonstrate the continuing vitality and international significance of the Manchester music scene. Smith, meanwhile, had long boycotted the New Music Seminar because, he said, it just consisted of 'fat cats' sitting around discussing how to 'steal money off artists'.[14] He was not going to get excited about its Manchester wannabe, and neither was Scanlon: 'The seminar is rubbish. It's not really international and it's certainly not representative of Manchester. It's just a PR job for Factory.'[15] A coincidental gig by The Fall at the Ritz in Manchester was quickly and defiantly re-billed as 'Not In The City'. Whatever Wilson learnt at the convention did little to stop the collapse of his Factory Records empire just a couple of months later with debts of over two million pounds.

Karaoke and nothing fucking else

A few days before Factory announced its ruin in November, Phonogram's press office released a phlegmatic statement cutting all ties with The Fall: 'Both parties felt the relationship had gone as far as it could,' it said, 'but we wish them every success in the future.'[16] The split came about during recording sessions for the next album. With the recession at its height and Phonogram jittery about the commercial potential of many of the bands on its roster, executives at the company demanded to hear demo tapes of the sessions so they could monitor progress. While this may have been normal practice for most bands, it was unprecedented for The Fall. Smith rang his A&R man at the company: 'We've given you three fuckin' Top 30 LPs in three fuckin' years, and this fuckin' kid who's fuckin' just come out of

14 Smith, interviewed by Mark Goodier, BBC Radio One, broadcast 16 September 1992. Transcript in *TBLY*, no. 6, July 1996
15 Steve Lamacq and Iestyn George, 'Pills, Thrills 'n' Belly Action', *NME*, 26 September 1992
16 Anon., 'Fontana Fall Out', *NME*, 21 November 1992

fuckin' business school wants fuckin' demo tapes of The Fall! And he goes, Man, it's the recession, mate.'[17] Phonogram had committed the ultimate *faux pas*. As Hanley explained, The Fall's simple code of conduct when it came to record companies meant that they got what they were given – 'This is what we're doing, this is how it is and this is what you get. Never any doubt.'

Smith's disappointment with Phonogram was compounded by the label's alleged reneging on its commitment to release The Fall's records in America through Mercury, if they reached the Top 30 in the British charts. With this and Phonogram's refusal to schedule a release for the next album – preferring instead merely to review the situation in April 1993 – Smith decided to act quickly.[18] He started proceedings over an alleged break of contract, but before it came to court Phonogram decided to cut its losses. The full size of the pay-off was never officially revealed although Smith did mention a figure of £20,000 in relation to the non-release of the albums in America.[19] Dave Bush remembered the final pay-off as being much higher: 'Phonogram used to phone every day. We'd be in the pub and Mark would come in and say: "They've offered us £30,000 to leave. What do you think we should do? I reckon we should hang on." The next day he came in: "They've offered us £60,000." In the end we got £120,000 to leave which was great because we knew we already had a brilliant album, they'd already paid for the studio.'

Smith took Phonogram's excuse of the recession with a pinch of salt. He thought the company was simply diverting too much energy towards promoting middle-of-the-road acts like Dire Straits and releasing superfluous but profitable Tears for Fears remixes. According to Smith, the work-shy and over-cautious executives also found it difficult to handle The Fall's relentless productivity. 'Record company people don't like doing any work,' he said. 'You'd think making two albums in a year was a bloody crime or something. That's why I left Phonogram because they want you to spend four months on it, they want to have a marketing meeting for three months and they want to plug it for three months and you've forgot what the bloody songs are like by the time they come out.'[20]

17   Andrew Perry, 'Alright?', *Select*, May 1993
18   Dave Thompson, 'Falling Forward', *Alternative Press*, September 1993
19   Anon., 'Indie vs Majors: The Great Maker Debate', *Melody Maker*, 17 April 1993
20   Paul Benney, 'A Quick Pint with Mark E. Smith', *Jockey Slut*, January 1996

For Phonogram 'hard times' meant the bottom line always came first. And despite The Fall's relative chart success, for a company that counted its turnover in the hundreds of millions, Smith and The Fall were minor irritants it could easily ignore. The corporates now adopted new tactics to deal with 'difficult' acts. Rather than invest in individual bands they started to buy up independent record labels, thus spreading the risk and casting a wider net for new talent. Smith warned that when financial departments started running things you would soon end up with just 'karaoke and nothing fucking else'.[21]

In retrospect the Fontana/Phonogram deal represented Smith's last chance to establish a conventional rock career. Rather than mellowing with age, Smith's behaviour became increasingly erratic and wilfully self-destructive. His options soon began to shrink as his notoriety as a 'difficult' character preceded him. At one point Smith considered signing to ex-Kamera boss Saul Galpern's Nude label, but both parties failed to agree over the terms of the contract. And besides, Smith had good reason to distrust Galpern, not just because of what happened at Kamera, but also because he didn't have 'any chairs in his office apart from his own'.[22] Smith eventually turned to another former business associate, John Lennard, and his cottage label Permanent Records (with its distribution deal with the corporate BMG). It was a case of 'better the devil you know' but still a risky strategy. Permanent's track record was non-existent and the only thing Smith had in common with label mates such as folk-singers John Martyn and Al Stewart was longevity.

Why are people grudgeful?

At the end of 1992, The Fall's highest entry in John Peel's Festive Fifty was at number 5 with 'The Legend of Xanadu', a track from the *NME*'s *Ruby Trax* and a follow-up to the magazine's successful *Sgt Pepper Knew My Father*. The Fall's suitably obscure choice was a 1968 chart-topper by Dave Dee, Dozy, Beaky, Mick and Tich. Almost thirty places below 'Xanadu' in the Festive Fifty was a session track, 'Kimble', recorded earlier in the year. In March 1993, the Strange Fruit label, which specialized in releasing old John Peel sessions,

21 Anon., op. cit., 17 April 1993
22 David Cavanagh, 'I Didn't Get Where I Am Today . . . ', Q, March/April 1994

released it as a single along with the bonus tracks 'C'n'C-Hassle Schmuk', 'Spoilt Victorian Child' and 'Words of Expectation' from 1981, 1985 and 1983 respectively. In 'Kimble', Lee Perry's original lyrics are squeezed through the Smith mangler. The reggae style highlighted The Fall's flexibility and, in contrast to the youthful exuberance of 'C'n'C-Hassle Schmuk', it also shows just how mature the group had become, more sure of its hand, less striving in its effects.

The reggae and Lee Perry-related theme continued with The Fall's April release of 'Why Are People Grudgeful?', the first on its new label Permanent.[23] This time the reggae roots are buried a little deeper beneath the dancier beats of Wolstencroft's drums and Bush's keyboards. Paul Mathur thought it was 'the most engaging thing [Smith]'s done for a couple of years'.[24] But, despite good reviews, a live appearance on Gary Crowley's show *The Beat* and a grainy low-budget promotional video aired on MTV, the single was only moderately successful, reaching just number 43 in the charts. It was the end of The Fall's Lee Perry period, but Smith continued to admire the Jamaican and later told a story about a visit Adrian Sherwood made to his home: 'Lee Perry was digging the back of his garden up and he said, "What are you doing?" and he said, "I'm burying all me early singles" – hahaha . . . funeral for his singles. Hahaha.'[25]

The Fall followed the single with the release in April of *The Infotainment Scan*, produced by Rex Sargeant, Smith and Rogers at Suite 16 in Rochdale.[26] Sargeant, previously an engineer at the studio, was surprised to find himself promoted to producing duties: 'They didn't start very early,' he recalled. 'Everybody'd come in about dinner time, sit there, have their cigarettes, read the paper, then five minutes later they'd all be down the pub. About two hours later they'd finally come in and set up everything properly and start on a

23 The origins of the song are unclear: either it is based on Lee Perry's 'You Crummy' (Ian McCann, 'The Fall: "Why Are People Grudgeful?" ', *NME*, 20 March 1993) or, as claimed on *A World Bewitched* (2001), a cover of Joe Gibbs's retort to Lee Perry's 'People Funny Boy'.

24 Paul Mathur, 'The Fall: "Why Are People Grudgeful?" ', *Melody Maker*, 3 April 1993

25 Smith, interviewed by Marcelle van Hoof on Another Nice Mess Radio, broadcast 11 May 1993

26 Formerly known as Cargo Studios, its new name resulted from the change of ownership from John Brierly to Chris Hewitt and New Order's Peter Hook.

piece of music, write a really good tune, then Mark'd come in, get his spanner out, throw it in the works, then a bit of fire in the studio, a bit of hostility, a bit of war, a bit of tension built up and then they'd come out with a killer tune.'[27]

The studio suited The Fall perfectly: 'It's really sort of small so you get the live feel of the band . . . But we could also use a lot of machinery. And it was better than going to a massive like Peter Gabriel sort of studio. It was a nice surprise cuz we had the best of both. So we could sound like we recorded it in my front room but also we could put the techno shit over it.'[28] The 'techno shit' came courtesy of Dave Bush, who despite what it says on the writing credits contributed a substantial amount to the album's music: 'It's not worth getting bitter about writing credits,' he later said. 'It's just the way that Mark used to dish out the credits however he felt. Some of the things I was credited for I'd never even heard and there was no keyboards on them! It's a bit of a pisser moneywise but you don't do it for the money – well not for The Fall.'

At the time Bush lived in Stockport and had his own studio at home. It was here that much of *Infotainment Scan* was written. 'All the band used to come down,' Bush said. 'On Monday I'd start knocking some tracks together with the band, then Tuesday I'd programme it all up, getting it really tight, and on Wednesday I'd get them to play their bits again on top of this track that I'd built up. Then in the afternoon after we got back from the pub we'd start on the next track. On Thursday I'd get that together then Friday they'd come in and re-record in the morning and then in the afternoon we'd start on more new ideas. We just sent Mark tapes and he'd phone up and say whether he liked them or not. When he heard 'A Past Gone Mad' he'd said: "I suppose its passable. You could've done better." We all worked hard on it and were really buzzing. Even if we were just fucking about we'd get something really good.'

The album opens innocuously enough with 'Ladybird (Green Grass)' but really takes off with the next track, a cover version of Sister Sledge's 'Lost In Music' that The Fall manage to make sound

27 Grant Showbiz, 'Falling through Time', broadcast on Resonance Radio in London, June 1998
28 Joe Silva, 'The Fall: The Curse of Paranoia Man', *QRM: The On-Line Alternative Music Magazine*, September 1993

altogether more sinister and paranoid. The joyous 'Glam-Racket' draws heavily on Smith's Gary Glitter influences, but at the same time criticizes seventies nostalgia for, amongst other things, suede clothes. Some misunderstood the song as an attack on the band Suede, but Smith refuted this. He knew Suede from way back: 'First time I met Brett he keeled over and fell on the floor. I got on with him OK but he kept following me into the toilet every time I went for a piss. I'm not making this up. It's God's honest truth. For drugs? No, no. For sex? I don't know. Maybe he just wanted to look at my underwear . . . Morrissey used to do things like that, follow me into the toilet. He used to give me dirty phonecalls too.'[29]

The second cover on the album is an affectionate version of Steve Bent's 'I'm Going To Spain'.[30] Asked if he was thinking of heading off to the sun, Smith replied. 'No, I like living here. That song's meant to be a skit on *Eldorado*. This idea of people upping and leaving a sinking ship and going somewhere sunny. It's a bit of a con.'[31] A familiarly crabby Smith returns for 'It's a Curse', complaining about 'look back bores'. The song could be taken in two ways, Smith said, life's a curse and also beware: 'I used to have this power to curse people. But I don't use it any more.'[32] 'Paranoia Man in Cheap Sh*t Room' derives some of its inspiration from a similarly titled episode of the *Twilight Zone*, 'Nervous Man in a Four-Dollar Room', in which a hired killer argues with his double about whether he should commit a murder. In 'Service', Smith melancholically reflects on 'this day's portion', while in 'The League Of Bald-Headed Men' Hanley's bass drives us on as Smith curses middle-aged men who exploit youth culture. A backing track of mad cackling laughter can be heard on 'A Past Gone Mad', as Smith pleads for somebody to cut his throat with a 'kitchen tool' if he ever ends up like Ian McShane. The album ends with the now obligatory DIY experimental cut-up track, this time entitled 'Light/Fireworks'.

The 'Infotainment' in the album's title referred, according to Smith, to the media's tendency to turn news into entertainment: 'cheap

---

29 Mark E. Smith, 'Norf vs Sarf', *Vox*, no. 53, February 1995

30 Bent's one moment of fame came in 1974 as a contestant on the television talent show *New Faces*.

31 Sam Batra, 'Falling into the Groove', *The Wire*, May 1993

32 Silva, op. cit., September 1993

thrills masquerading as hard news or information. The people in the media are middle-class people who don't have enough sex or enough cars, which is all they want.'[33] Few of the reviewers, however, picked up on the album's intended social critique. The overriding response was one of surprise at the music's new accessibility. Dave Jennings in *Melody Maker* wrote: 'What's different here is that, at last, Mark E. Smith sounds like someone you'd actually want to have at your party.'[34] Such positive reviews, good distribution and excellent timing ensured that the album entered the chart at number 9: The Fall's one and only Top 10 hit. A proud Smith felt justifiably vindicated: 'I was going to throw a brick through Phonogram's window with "9" written on it.'[35]

Shove it

The album became the first to be released in the US since 1989's *Extricate*. Two labels combined to take on the group, the hip independent Matador and the more established Atlantic Records. Matador also housed up-and-coming American groups Come, Superchunk and Fall acolytes, Pavement. At the time Smith claimed ignorance of Matador's Pavement connection and said the first time he heard the group was when somebody played him one of their tracks and he mistook it for a 1987 live performance by The Fall, it was that close: 'They say imitation is the sincerest form of flattery, but I don't hold with that. I feel sorry for them, actually. I don't get mad, I just can't see the point of forming a group if you're imitating someone else, it's like, get a life, man. Get a real job! I found this when we set up the label Cog Sinister. We used to get five to ten tapes a week, and they all sounded like New Order or The Fall. We gave up in the end. The reason I formed The Fall was because no one made the music I wanted to hear. We can't sound like anybody else. We try to but we can't. We're always contemporary, I believe. At arm's length from the mainstream, most certainly. For most bands, it's just a student hobby. In America, everybody forms a group until they reach twenty-seven and leave college. It always makes me laugh

33 Carol Clerk, '15 Years of Fame', *Melody Maker*, 1 May 1993
34 Dave Jennings, '*The Infotainment Scan*', *Melody Maker*, 24 April 1993
35 Cavanagh, op. cit., March/April 1994

when you read, "Black Flag Have Broken Up", and it just so happens they're twenty-seven and they've finished their law degrees!'[36]

After all Smith's talk of stripping down the band, new figures continued to appear or reappear, as in the case of Karl Burns who rejoined in the second half of 1993. Reviews at this time began to get a little less forgiving. Dele Fadele watched the band in May at the Cambridge Junction and described Smith's voice as possessing 'a sandpaper grain and a mighty slur that can only be achieved by coating your palate with beer and whisky'. He concluded his review with the observation, 'You can only be cantankerous and curmudgeonly for so long.'[37]

In August, The Fall travelled around America with the destination on the tour bus reading 'Shove it'. The honour of looking after Smith for at least some of the trip fell upon Spencer Gates, a publicist from Matador. It would be an unforgettable experience for him: 'Every chance he could make fun of me or be a jerk, he would take it. Once we were sharing a cab to the Matador office and Mark insisted on smoking. Our very nice Iranian cab driver kept asking him to stop, which made Mark scream obscenities at the guy. After a rather excruciating ride, Mark gets out yelling that the guy should go back to his country to kill babies. From then on, he referred to me as Cagney, of *Cagney and Lacy*, for some reason. Maybe he just sees all publicists as cops?'[38]

Smith wasn't the only one behaving badly. 'JC', a member of the road crew for the tour, recounted the events that led to Burns's umpteenth sacking: 'He'd lost a letter with some money in it that he was sending to his mum and he was convinced somebody at the hotel had stolen it. He was smashing up mirrors and stuff. Then, later, the place got busted by the FBI because they thought there was some major drug deal going down. They had us all out in the corridor and one of Mark's friends, who was doing the T-shirts, had loads of cash stashed in his bag. Mark ended up having to pay about a thousand dollars for the damage and he sent Karl home.' But Burns didn't go

36 Simon Price, 'Counter Culture', *Melody Maker*, 18 December 1993
37 Dele Fadele, 'Fallen from Grace: The Fall, Cambridge Junction', *NME*, 22 May 1993
38 Spencer Gates, 'What's Your Worst Matador Experience?' *Escandolo!*, April 1997; Matador Records' newsletter, posted on Fallnet, 15 October 2000

home. A few weeks later he hooked up again with the band, telling them tales about his American adventures. 'Karl was an animal,' Bush explained, 'but he was funny. One time we were going away for a six-week tour of America and we get to the airport and Karl turns up with a plastic bag with just a Walkman and a packet of fags in it. That was his whole baggage for the six weeks! He's a drummer so he sweats like a pig, no one would share a room with him.'

The tour manager also received his marching orders a few dates into the tour. At the Cabaret Metro in Chicago, the same club at which Smith had played ten years before and met Brix, Smith came on stage and went straight for Bush and smashed all the keys off his keyboard and threw the microphone at him: 'You do the fuckin' set.' Never one to decline a challenge Bush started screaming nonsense into the mike. 'He didn't like that so he came back out,' Bush recalled. 'He once said to me: "If I come over and smash your keyboards up it's only showbiz. We'll get 'em mended the next day." We had money in them days. Anyway it was a great gig and we come off and the crowd were going mad and everyone's going, "Where's Mark? We've gotta do an encore." But we couldn't find him and eventually we lost the crowd, they thought we weren't coming back. And then we found Mark asleep. He'd come straight off stage after this brilliant gig and fallen asleep by the fire exit backstage.'

By this time Smith's stage antics were legendary. 'It was always impossible to get him to go on stage on time,' JC said. 'He would even take the band's name off the dressing-room door so nobody could find him. The band would always come on stage directly from the dressing-room, but Mark would like to come on differently, like from behind the curtains, making his own appearance. It used to backfire on him, though, because at the end of the gig he'd amble off first and he'd forget where the dressing-room was and end up stranded down some dead end. You'd find him sitting by the fire escape, because he couldn't make a tit of himself by coming back on, going, "Have yah got a cigarette?" '

On return to England, Smith's increasingly erratic performances continued to draw attention. Johnny Cigarettes wrote of a below-par performance in October at the Forum in Kentish Town. He thought Smith's bad-tempered stage exit after one song was the action of a man who had 'started to believe his own press'. Most damaging was the impression that Smith just didn't care any more:

'And the band can't be arsed to save the day: without any spanners in the works like Brix, Martin Bramah or Marcia, they've settled into a terminally workmanlike R&B rumble, with the dynamics and spark removed.'[39]

God help us if there's a war

Smith clearly understood the potential of the massive US market for The Fall, but what he didn't appreciate was those aspects of American culture currently being imported into Britain, particularly the drug, gang and gun culture infesting the streets of Manchester. 'I've seen it in Chicago,' he observed. 'All the rich people live on one side of town and all the poor on another and there's a great barbed-wire fence down the middle. The police can't even go where the poor live. On one side everyone's in mansions, on the other no one's got windows in their flats and no shoes on their feet. People blame Thatcher and all these people and that's nonsense. It's just Americanization.'[40]

And European influence was not much better: just as we only imported the bad things from America, all we got from Europe was the 'regulations'.[41] Smith also perceived Europe as a potential battle-field and had first-hand experience of the spiralling enmity of the various factions in the former Yugoslavia. The group had passed through the area just before the fighting began and he recalled picking up 'two lovely couples' in Ljubljana and giving them a lift to Zagreb. 'These were cultured people, talking about Shakespeare and George Bernard Shaw – which the band would know nothing about; y'know, does he play rhythm guitar, or what? – and they're going, "We do not like the people in Zagreb. We'd like to kill them." And we're going, "Yeah, we're like that, we make jokes about Southerners and all those people." And they go, "No, we want to kill them and their families, the women and the children." Blood in their eyes, I tell ya.'[42] While in Greece in November 1992 the band drove up into the hills and saw military aircraft flying overhead on bombing missions, 'It's on our

39 Johnny Cigarettes, 'The Fall, London, Kentish Town Forum', *NME*, 30 October 1993
40 McCann, op. cit., 29 February 1992
41 Silva, op. cit., September 1993
42 Perry, op. cit., May 1993

fuckin' doorstep.'[43] John Major, the prime minister, reminded Smith of Neville Chamberlain just before the Second World War. With Europe completely unstable what does Major do? 'He cuts the army by half and closes the coal mines down,' said Smith. 'He should remember we're an island.'[44] And with the nation's youth fawning over records by the likes of Verve, 'God help us if there's a war.'[45]

In 1993, Mike Leigh's compelling film *Naked* was released. Of the main character, Johnny, Mark Morris of *The Observer* wrote: 'He wanders the capital like the ancient mariner, buttonholing anyone he can find and ranting sprawling, compelling millennial nonsense at them.'[46] It could easily have been a description of Smith. The actor David Thewlis must have had him in mind when he constructed Johnny's rain-coated character, preaching expletive-riddled sermons filled with half-baked prophesies of doom and destruction.

Just like in the movies, this golden age of Smith tirades left few issues unscathed, including the monarchy and unemployment. Smith may have been protective of his English national identity but he was no monarchist, dismissing the royal family as German, middle-class and mean: 'Elvis lived like a king. Charles frightens me to death. You can't have a vegetarian as a king. They haven't got the style, even the Queen. Charles is in fuckin' London and he goes, "Look at the way people are living, summat must be done about the inner cities." And the cunt owns fuckin' Cornwall! He could do summat about it tomorrow.'[47] On the unemployed: 'I walk through town, me, going, "Get a fucking job, you cunt." ' What people needed was a job not state hand-outs: 'Give him £5 a week, and as long as he's got his occupation he's happy, he's got his pride. Give him £300 and he's just gonna be nagged and dragged round the shops by his wife. I know this from employing musicians. You can give 'em £1,000 a week and they'll still be skint by Friday. Just open a few fuckin' factories and chuck people in 'em.'[48]

43 John Harris, 'Mark E. Moan', *NME*, 3 April 1993
44 ibid.
45 Smith and Quantick, op. cit., 27 June 1992
46 Mark Morris, 'At the Movies, It's So Tough at the Top', *Observer*, 12 December 1999
47 Perry, op. cit., May 1993
48 Price, op. cit., 18 December 1993

Further tales of Smith's dissatisfaction with the world can be found on the *Behind The Counter* EP released at the end of the year. On the title track Smith takes on the persona of a lowly shop-worker and moans about everyone always picking on him. A spirited cover of Henry Cow and Slapp Happy's 'War' from their 1975 album *In Praise Of Learning* and the whispered 'Cab Driver' made up the rest of the EP. 'War' developed further the military theme of 'High Tension Line' and 'Free Range'. As Smith admitted, The Fall's version strayed slightly from the original because he could not find the record, just the empty sleeve with the lyrics. When he eventually heard the original he realized how different The Fall's version was: 'Same lyrics, you know, but the arrangement is completely different, not even the same notes.'[49] Despite being The Fall's first single to get on to the BBC Radio One playlist, 'Behind the Counter' only reached a disappointing number 75 in the charts. Maybe this was just one of the reasons why, in answer to a *Melody Maker* end-of-year questionnaire, he summed up 1993 with the phrase 'pure cack'.[50]

49 Tim Midgett, 'Interview with Mark E. Smith', *Rocket*, September 1994
50 Mark E. Smith, '1993: The Agony and the Ecstacy', *Melody Maker*, 8 January 1994

16

Chiselers, 1994–1996

I've cut the liquor out. You're right in saying I was going off the rails
a bit – I was drinkin' a lot of whisky. I hate all that confessional shit,
but I must admit I was losing friends and family because of it. People
were stopping talking to me. I was just going for the jugular all the
time, being gratuitously obnoxious with people. I could handle it,
mentally and physically, but you don't wanna be like that. Besides,
you become a caricature, dead predictable.[1]

Smith made just one appearance on *Top of the Pops* and it came not
with The Fall but with the Inspiral Carpets. Their single 'I Want
You', with a contribution from Smith, had impudently barged its
way to number 18 in the charts in March 1994. In front of the
teenage screamers, the thirty-seven-year-old Smith – his shoulders
hunched under a black leather jacket – took to the stage holding a
microphone in one hand and a lyric sheet in the other. Ambling
around to the side of the animated lead singer, Tom Hingley, he
shouted against the grain of the song: 'It's about time you decided
which side you're on. You said you lost two stone in weight, so why
are you so fat?' At the song's conclusion, the camera cut to the
disconcerted announcer Simon Mayo, 'Right, OK . . . thank you,
boys.' Smith remembered the event as 'a bit strange', but was amazed
at the effect it had on people: 'You get served quicker in the shops.
Surprising how many people watch it. I haven't for ten years.'[2]

The collaboration came about after a speculative phonecall from
the group to Smith. At a loose-end, Smith immediately caught a taxi
to the studio and recorded his part in just one afternoon. The
Inspirals were lucky, Smith was normally extremely choosy about
whom he worked with: 'People ask me to work with them all the
time. Bowie. Lou Reed. People get desperate and want some help.

1 Johnny Cigarettes, 'One Man and his Grog', *NME*, 7 May 1994
2 ibid.

Or they want credibility, some seriousness, 'cos their young fans are growing up. Blow Monkeys. Boy George. I tell 'em all fucking no. Nirvana have asked me. Dinosaur Jr. They all want me to sing or produce 'em. John Cale. I get millionaire bassists phoning me up saying they'll play guitar on my LP, they'll do it for nothing, they'll roadie for me. Madonna's session men. Mick Jagger's. I tell 'em fuck off, right? The last thing The Fall need is another fucking guitarist!'[3]

Another thing Smith didn't need in March was to be questioned about his work at London's ICA. Billed as a discussion between Smith and the novelist Michael Bracewell about Smith's 'ideas and work as a "self-taught artist" ' the audience spent the first hour talking among themselves and looking at two empty chairs. Eventually Smith and Bracewell appeared, Smith armed with five bottles of beer, Bracewell with his questions. Despite the alcohol, Smith's mood was far from expansive: 'Mark, can you remember what those early working-men's club gigs were like?' ' 'Course I can remember, d'you think I'm bloody retarded or something?'[4]

A pearled isle will be destroyed by a man from the circus

Smith and Prior's marriage officially ended in February 1995. Their break-up through 1994, plus the stress of suing Trevor Long, the usual money problems and seventeen years of living the rock 'n' roll lifestyle all began to take their toll on Smith's health. In particular, Smith's drinking habits could no longer be dismissed as youthful over-indulgence. Few interviews or press reports from this period onwards failed to mention either Smith's apparent state of inebriation or his prematurely aged appearance. Smith, predictably, refused to acknowledge the problem: 'If you can hold your drink and you're civilized, there's nowt wrong with it. I've got nothing to hide. I drink beer all day and I always have. The problem is when you start getting ashamed of it – secret drinking.'[5]

Some of Smith's domestic problems were hinted at in the April single release '15 Ways'. Intended partly as a sardonic rejoinder to Paul Simon's '50 Ways To Leave Your Lover', Smith took the opportunity to criticize women's magazines, especially those 'that go on about

3 Ian Gittins, 'Manchester United', *Melody Maker*, 26 February 1994
4 Taylor Parkes, 'Prole Art Threat', *Melody Maker*, 23 April 1994
5 Stephen Dalton, 'Not Falling, Soaring', *Vox*, June 1991

how to tell if your old man's having an affair and how to subsequently screw him up. Heh heh heh! Can't say any more than that, I really can't. Sorry.'[6] Along with '15 Ways', the single included 'The $500 Bottle Of Wine' and 'Hey! Student', an updated version of one of The Fall's earliest and most furious of songs (at one time known as 'Hey! Fascist').

These three tracks plus another three from last year's *Behind the Counter* EP appeared on The Fall's *Middle Class Revolt* album released in May. Rex Sargeant once again produced the album at both Suite 16 and the Windings Studio in Wrexham. Prior exposure to some of the best tracks meant the album lacked much in the way of revelations. Of the new tracks, 'The Reckoning' lacked focus and 'Symbol Of Morgen' – a recording of Scanlon phoning in a Manchester City match report to John Peel's radio show – was little more than a private joke made public. The covers 'Junk Man' (an old Groundhogs song) and 'Shut Up!' (originally by Smith's favourite dome heads, the Monks) were spirited enough but inevitably derivative. The album only really livened up with 'You're Not Up To Much', a witty character study of an underachieving acquaintance of Smith's whose 'mind's in pieces'.

Of the rest of the album, three tracks stand out for their superb music and ambitious lyrics: 'M5#1', 'City Dweller' and 'Middle Class Revolt!'. 'M5#1' found 'city born and bred' Smith in best prophetic spirit, travelling along the M5 motorway through the English countryside with a head full of car-fumes. In 'City Dweller' Smith poked fun at Manchester's parvenu ambitions to host the next Olympic Games, while the title track, 'Middle Class Revolt!', celebrated the middle class's confused reaction to the recession and the floundering end-game of Tory rule. Smith had it all figured out: 'John Major is the Antichrist. There's something in Nostradamus about him: "A pearled isle will be destroyed by a man from the circus who has turned to politics." It's a bit like *The Omen*, innit?'[7]

The most obvious difference musically from *Infotainment Scan* was Bush's dwindling contribution. 'I wasn't happy with *Middle Class Revolt* because I had a smaller role and I never really listen to it now,' said Bush. 'We recorded the album in a week and we'd done no

6 Ted Kessler, 'Mark E. Smith: Heroes & Villains', *NME*, 11 December 1993
7 Cigarettes, op. cit., 7 May 1994

prior writing for it. We just went in and made it up in the studio. That was amazing really, even though it was a shit album.' The music press agreed. Ian McCann in the *NME*, for example, believed it was 'nothing special' and that 'we've been here before'.[8] Poor record sales mirrored the critical response. Just one year after *Infotainment Scan* had reached number 9, the highest *Middle Class Revolt* could manage was 48. The Fall was once more out of joint with its time as the record charts filled with Britpop and its chief exponents, Blur and Oasis. Smith thought he'd heard it all before, on Rough Trade in 1982 – and he'd not liked it then either.[9]

He just didn't look well

After Smith's almost twenty years in the music business and despite many upheavals his own yearly schedule must have assumed at times a grinding predictability. Dave Bush outlined the routine for much of the 1990s: 'During the spring we'd tour, then the summer we'd do the festivals, then in September/October we'd be writing, then November/December we'd be in the studio recording, then around March the album would come out and we'd start touring again.' In 1994 it was business as usual, with a UK tour through late May and early June and summer festival dates in Lithuania and Stratford-on-Avon. What the band needed, thought Smith, was some new input – then he got a phonecall.

Not long after Brix left The Fall in 1989, her new boyfriend, Nigel Kennedy, hit the commercial jackpot with his phenomenally successful classical album *The Four Seasons*. Kennedy became a national celebrity and Brix initially enjoyed the media attention: 'I was out of the scum-pit area and was back into my normal middle-class upbringing. It was a really good time.' But the relationship with Kennedy eventually floundered and Brix left England for LA to share an apartment with her old friend Lisa Feder. Taking a rest from music, she enrolled for acting classes and found work in television commercials and the theatre, and when 'between jobs' she waitressed.

The chance to return to music came through ex-Bangles star

---

8   Ian McCann, 'Revolting Cock: The Fall, *Middle Class Revolt*', *NME*, 7 May 1994
9   Sylvia Patterson, 'Git Pop Now!', *NME*, 3 February 1996

Susannah Hoffs. She wanted to tour and invited Brix along as bass player. Playing with Hoffs rekindled Brix's love of music and when she heard in the summer of 1994 that Courtney Love was looking for a bass player she auditioned, but was rejected. Around this time Brix dug out her old Fall albums and realized how special they were. She phoned Smith: 'I said, "I'm just calling to say that I've been listening to all the old stuff we did, and I think you're great, you're a fucking genius, there's nobody like you. And I just wanted to call you and tell you." And he was like, "Thanks." And that was it. And then I went out and I came home and there was a message saying: "Brix, it's weird that you called me and said that because I've been thinking about getting you back in the band. Would you come back and play? We're playing in Edinburgh and Glasgow, I'll fly you over." '[10] It was their first conversation since the divorce in 1991. This time Brix was determined to join the band on her own terms: 'I wouldn't be his wife, I would be there as a musician. He couldn't push me around, I had learned and gone through so much. I'd went through therapy, had the lot, and emerged a stronger person – the same but more together.'

The first thing that struck Brix when she saw Smith was his markedly aged appearance: 'He had physically deteriorated. You know, everybody ages, but he just didn't look well. Bad diet, shocking lifestyle.' When Brix left the group in 1990 it was relatively well managed and still signed to Beggars, now Smith's business affairs were in chaos. 'The organization had fallen to shit,' she said. 'When he wanted to be difficult he could be bloody pig-headed and very difficult. He had strong opinions about how things should be and I suppose he'd had clashes and burnt bridges with figures of authority, so he was running the band by himself.' Most disturbing, though, was Smith's increasingly volatile behaviour. She experienced this first hand in Edinburgh at only her second gig back with the band, when Smith, frustrated by sound problems, jumped from the stage and stormed through the crowd to remonstrate with Rex Sargeant on the mixing desk. Once back on stage, he turned on Burns and the show faltered for ten minutes before order was restored. Later a spokeswoman for The Fall described the incident as 'just a friendly skirmish between old friends'.[11]

10 Anon., 'It's Brix', *TBLY*, no. 4, July 1995
11 Anon., 'In Love with Melissa', *Melody Maker*, 27 August 1994

The bust-ups continued as the band staggered through a September tour of the US and Canada. 'It was just chronic,' recalled Brix. 'He was having fights with everyone all the time. He had a list, the torment list, and certain people would be at the top and he would just torment them endlessly until they left, were sacked, or until somebody else was picked on. I started off at the bottom, but I grew to be very high up the list by the end. Usually the monitor man was at the top of the list. Every tour manager ever was at the top of the list. Dave Bush was at the top of the list when I came back. Craig got to the top of the list. It was all chaos really but the band as a core was still tight and good.'

After a couple of weeks recovering from the tour the band reassembled in London to record material for the next album. During these sessions they stayed in the Columbia Hotel, the notorious rock musicians haunt near Lancaster Gate. It was the first time Smith had been allowed back since he was banned in 1990 for flooding a room. It turned out to be a brief reunion, however, because Burns bought some airbomb repeaters and proceeded to fire them out of his hotel-room window across the road into Hyde Park. A spokesman for the band told *Melody Maker*: 'They had to pay for the damage in the morning. They'd been in the recording studio for days on end and were naturally a little frazzled. And also, being allowed back into the Columbia after a four-year ban was a great reason for celebration.'[12]

It wasn't a nice time for me personally

The album they were recording in London, *Cerebral Caustic*, was released at the end of February 1995. Like *Middle Class Revolt* it was recorded quickly – in just seven days according to Brix,[13] in just three weeks in a 'small disco studio in London' according to Smith. Locked in the studio with the group was new producer, Mike Bennett. Smith claimed Bennett used to work with Sweet when he was about seventeen, 'so he knew what I wanted, he could get the drum sounds'.[14]

12 Anon., 'Fall's Fireworks Spark Ban', *Melody Maker*, 26 November 1994
13 Anon., op. cit., July 1995
14 Lucy Nation, 'Northern Soul', *The Lizard*, no. 4, April–May 1995

Brix's backlog of recently written tunes supplied Smith and the band with just the impetus they needed. Her influence is immediately apparent in the first four tracks – 'The Joke', 'Don't Call Me Darling', 'Rainmaster' and 'Feeling Numb' – with their relatively conventional structures and direct and hooky guitar work. Burns wrote the music for 'Pearl City' and Smith's lyrics take their inspiration from a visit to the Pearl City Chinese restaurant in Manchester. Hanley and Scanlon wrote the catchy 'Life Just Bounces' while Frank Zappa provided 'I'm Not Satisfied'. Smith thought 'The Aphid' resembled a sixties' style dance track, 'a bit like the Twist but a lot more surreal'.[15] 'Bonkers In Phoenix' started out as a love song by Brix, but Smith added various electronic effects and extra vocals and turned it into a song about music festivals and, according to Brix, 'tripping on acid and being in between the indie tent, the rock tent and the folk psychedelic tent and how it all sounds'.[16] The album quicky runs out of steam despite the frenetic 'One Day', the piss-taking 'North West Fashion Show' and the melancholy 'Pine Leaves', with its whisperings of ghosts and historical atrocities.

'To be honest,' said Smith, 'it was very diaryish, and it wasn't a nice time for me personally.'[17] These traces of autobiography could be heard most obviously in 'Feeling Numb' – the effect of 'remedies and Prozac' – and 'Life Just Bounces', where Smith confessed he was in a 'vortex', heading 'for a Fall'. Also falling were record sales, as the album reached just 67 in the chart. The group's audience had become polarized between those who thought the group could do no wrong, like Jamie T. Conway in *Melody Maker* – 'destined never to suffer from the creative fatigue which has plagued his peers'[18] – and those who thought they had heard it all before, like John Harris in *NME* – 'moments that are worryingly generic'.[19]

One man definitely jaded by the whole experience was Dave Bush. The album contained little of his keyboards and programming because Smith had wiped it all away at the mixing stage. 'Using less technology was very conscious,' Smith explained, 'because it was getting a bit sludgy, with the process we were using and that. As you

15   ibid.
16   Anon., op. cit., July 1995
17   Alaister Mabbott, 'Fall Guy', *The Scotsman*, 15 March 1995
18   Jamie T. Conway, 'The Fall: *Cerebral Caustic*', *Melody Maker*, 18 March 1995
19   John Harris, 'Carp Life! The Fall: *Cerebral Caustic*', *NME*, 4 March 1995

probably know, its all computers in studios now, and they're always losing the plot really. You can't get people like Craig and Steve and myself to play to drum machines, so . . . '[20] So Bush had to go.

Up until the time of *Middle Class Revolt*, Bush's keyboard work had made him an *almost* indispensable member of the group. 'I think Mark thought I was a bit too powerful and it was time to get some control back,' said Bush. 'Also the money was running out and he had to pare the band down. I remember going out for a drink one night and he said: "Are you happy?" I said: "I get a little bit pissed off when I don't get my chance." We did *Cerebral Caustic* after that, and then I got a really nice letter from him which said: "Thanks for your playing and your professionalism, but we can't work together any more." In a way it was one of the best things that ever happened to me but it was quite stressful at the time. I'd done five years and when he said "that's it" it was like a huge weight was lifted off my shoulders. It absolutely drains you. When you leave it's a mixture of relief and fear about what you're going to do next.' What Bush did next was spend five years with Justine Frischman's Elastica. Brix and the rest of the band missed him immensely: 'He was great to be on tour with,' she said, 'because he had a great attitude. He wasn't miserable and crabby, and, I'm sorry to say, The Fall is miserable and crabby on the whole.'[21]

I was er . . . terrified

Typically, when Smith sacked Bush he already had a replacement lined up. Born in Peterborough in Canada on 30 September 1960, Julia Nagle emigrated to Manchester with her parents (originally from Preston in Lancashire) when she was just six. She went to St Winifred's Catholic School ('yes I was in the choir, and was on the first album they recorded, doing a duet with the school bully, but it was before they were famous for anything fortunately') and then to Peel Moat Comprehensive. She began piano lessons at the age of eight and quickly learnt to read music. She described herself as a 'tomboy' who liked swimming and hiking. But it was seeing punk bands at the Russell Club that really excited her: 'I fell in love with

---

20 Nation, op. cit., April–May 1995
21 Brix, interviewed by Grant Showbiz in 'Falling through Time', broadcast on Resonance Radio, London, June 1998

music and that's when I considered a career in it. It was a difficult decision, because it's not a job with long-term prospects.'

Nagle studied art and graphic design at Stockport College and then worked in advertising for a few years. In her spare time she taught herself to play guitar and joined a local punk band called Blackout. Nagle's next band, Illustration, signed to Some Bizarre, the New Romantic label, and appeared alongside Depeche Mode, Soft Cell, The The and Blancmange on the label's showcase release, *Some Bizarre Album*. Unfortunately the group disbanded soon afterwards, but Nagle found work with the legendary record producer, Martin Hannett. After a couple of years of his mentoring, Nagle moved on to Yellow 2 Studios and Strawberry as a tape op and sound engineer. During the eighties she worked with the cream of the Manchester music scene, including New Order and The Fall (for the *Bend Sinister* album).

She married Chris Nagle, the producer, and had a son, Basil, in 1987. The couple formed their own group, What? Noise, and recorded an album for One Little Indian in 1989 entitled *Fat*. In 1993 they separated and Nagle briefly joined the notoriously riotous all-girl punk group, the Thrush Puppies. In her search for perhaps more suitable work she sent a speculative CV to Cog Sinister and offered her services as a computer programmer, keyboard player and guitarist. Smith interviewed her in November 1994 at the Cornerhouse, an arts centre on Oxford Road. The sessions for *Cerebral Caustic* had just been completed so he gave her an acetate of the album and asked her to learn the songs, then he dealt with Dave Bush (i.e. sacked him).

Her first gig with the band came on 10 March 1995 at the Forum in Kentish Town. The line-up consisted of Wolstencroft and Burns on drums, Brix and Scanlon on guitar, Hanley on bass and Nagle on keyboards. Smith wore the same James Bond-style white cocktail jacket he wore for the *Cerebral Caustic* insert photographs. Brix's performance that night was particularly exuberant: just before 'Bonkers' she advised the audience to, 'Close your eyes and imagine you've all dropped acid.' Nagle was understandably more subdued: 'I was er . . . terrified. I'd done some television recording with them but was still learning the songs. I'd got a tape from Fat Alex, a known bootlegger, of all the songs they'd done live over the past two years. I transcribed them into my songbook/file, and remember reading this all the way to London, because they only decided on the set lists at the last minute. We went on stage to an audience of around two thousand people, the largest I've ever done in a headline group. I was promptly sick after the show, which they all found very amusing.'

Nagle soon integrated herself with the group and she was more confident by the time The Fall played the Phoenix Festival in July, alongside such rock legends as Bob Dylan and Van Morrison. The next month saw Permanent release the double CD album *The Twenty-Seven Points*.[22] The album collected together live tracks from the past three years, home recordings and lost studio gems such as 'Cloud Of Black' and 'Noel's Chemical Effluence'. At first Smith was sceptical about John Lennard's suggestion to do the compilation album but he eventually came round to the idea: 'I could sit down with this one and work on it for a couple of weeks. It was great because we used this studio in Manchester called Dreamtime which only does black acts, mainly just drums and vocals, so it went straight down the middle, suited us fine. I think this LP is one of the best we've done, really fascinating. I don't usually listen to my stuff too much, but I like this one.'[23] Highlights on the album included: an energetic cover of the Sonics' 'Strychnine'; 'Idiot – Walk Out', which documents Smith halting the band and leading them offstage for a pep talk – 'back in two minutes' he reassured the audience; the spoken-word recordings 'Ten Points', 'Three Points' and 'Glasgow Advice'; and a handful of live tracks enhanced by the full industrial might of Bush's keyboards, namely 'The League Of Bald-Headed Men', 'Life Just Bounces' and 'Passable'. Any such positive points, however, were uniformly ignored by the music critics. Ian Watson in *Melody Maker* thought Smith was 'taking the piss' and the album was little more than 'a pointless exercise'.[24] Leo Finlay in *Vox* saw it only as a document of 'the decline of The Fall',[25] and John Robinson in *NME* said it proved 'that Smith is quite possibly madder than ever'.[26]

---

22 Smith later explained his choice of title: 'The twenty-seven points are what the Nazis brought in to take away everybody's freedom in Germany. And they're all contradictory points as well' (Smith, in David Cavanagh, 'Cash For Questions', *Q*, no. 173, February 2001).

23 Anon., 'Prole Art Threat on the Internet', *Deadline*, August 1995

24 Ian Watson, 'The Fall, *Twenty-Seven Points*', *Melody Maker*, 2 September 1995

25 Leo Finlay, 'The Fall, *Twenty-Seven Points*', *Vox*, no. 60. October 1995

26 John Robinson, 'Frowning by Numbers: The Fall, *Twenty-Seven Points*', *NME*, 12 August 1995

The bad reviews continued for a series of live dates at the end of the year. *Melody Maker*'s Jamie T. Conway wrote: 'More and more, they seem like a quaint anachronism, endearingly cantankerous pensioners hell-bent on aggravating patronizing relatives.'[27] Mark Sutherland in the *NME* was even more damning, feeling the group was caught up in 'a desperate, doomed attempt to recapture former glories'.[28] It was unlikely that the poor reviews affected Smith too much, but still when Paul Benney of *Jockey Slut* asked him whether 1995 had been a good year, Smith – after a few long seconds of staring at his pint – answered, 'Nah.'[29]

It was a bad decision

Smith started 1996 by walking out on both his record company, Permanent, and his publisher, SGO Music. Both, he claimed, found it difficult to deal with the volume of material he was releasing.[30] As if to demonstrate the point, Smith quickly signed a deal with Mike Bennett's Receiver Records and in the first four months of 1996 released three CDs featuring alternative mixes and new tracks but mostly uninspired live material. First came *Sinister Waltz*, then *Fiend With A Violin*, and then, the *coup de grâce*, *Oswald Defence Lawyer*. All together, perhaps, there was just enough interesting and new material for one album, but not for three. The fans were being exploited and The Fall's credibility took a nose dive. It represented a lowering of standards and, more worryingly, poor judgement on Smith's part. Compilation albums obviously have their place, especially for a band of The Fall's longevity, but rather than introduce new listeners to the best of The Fall, or document in detail the band's development, these compilations, and the many that followed them, merely represented The Fall as inconsistent and exploitative. Sleeve notes (when they existed) were minimal or inaccurate and artwork and packaging un-inspired. It was as if Smith had taken to bootlegging his own material. Few were fooled. Mike Goldsmith recommended the albums only

27 Jamie T. Conway, 'The Fall, Asylum, Glasgow', *Melody Maker*, 4 November 1995
28 Mark Sutherland, 'The Fall, London Astoria', *NME*, 4 November 1995
29 Paul Benney, 'A Quick Pint with Mark E. Smith', *Jockey Slut*, January 1996
30 Patterson, op. cit., 3 February 1996

for The Fall's 'trainspotter zone',[31] and Mark Luffman in *Melody Maker* used The Fall against itself to pass judgement: 'That clan has got away with twenty-one years of sheer brilliance . . . until now.'[32] Steve Dalton in *NME* dismissed the albums as proving little more than: 'The Fall have had rather a lot of off days during the last decade.'[33]

In his defence Smith did later regret sanctioning the releases: 'I don't get any money for them,' he said. 'It's just daft deals I signed when I shouldn't have done. And I do apologize to my fans for that. But I make a point of trying to show which records are genuine product as opposed to cash-in stuff. Unless I'm going to spend fifty per cent of my day doing legal stuff, I've got to make a choice in life. I could pursue it legally, but I also look at it the Elvis Presley way: if people can't differentiate between the real stuff and the cash-ins, that's their lookout.'[34]

Work on the 'real stuff' at this time was also not proceeding smoothly. The band had grown to become an unwieldy seven-piece (an eight-piece, if you included Lucy Rimmer, Smith's new girlfriend, backing vocalist and organizer of The Fall's fan club). Somehow, Craig Scanlon, one of the loyal 'Jesuit lads', now found himself at the top of Smith's torment list, with the antagonism between them peaking during the long and drawn-out recording of 'The Chiselers'/ 'Chilinist'. Grant Showbiz became involved and he looked on in dismay at Smith's behaviour: 'What you see is people going over their peak. Certainly with Mark E. Smith I was thinking, "Well you're not making any sense any more." It came to a head for me when we made "Chilinist". I was up there working on it and Craig Scanlon, who was one of the great guitarists of The Fall, had gotten a clarinet and we tried really hard to get it to work, to get a good sound. Then Mark heard it and said, "What the fuck is there a clarinet on this song for?" He told us to wipe it off the track. We played the mix again and Mark was like, "This is shit. Where is the clarinet? That was the best thing on the track." '[35]

31 Mike Goldsmith, 'The Fall, *Sinister Waltz*', *NME*, 3 February 1996
32 Mark Luffman, 'The Fall, *Sinister Waltz*', *Melody Maker*, 10 February 1996
33 Stephen Dalton, 'The Fall, *Fiend With A Violin, Oswald Defense Lawyer*', *NME*, 6 April 1996
34 Cavanagh, op. cit., February 2001
35 Grant Showbiz, 'Interview', *Tape Op*, no. 16, 2000

After more poor treatment Scanlon just simply appeared to give up on the group. 'You'd go round his house to rehearse and it'd be difficult to get him to pick up a guitar,' Hanley said. 'He was getting pushed out a bit as well. Which always happened. If you put your guitar down for five minutes there was always somebody ready to pick it up. And at that time Karl was playing a bit of guitar. Brix was back in and Julia, also, was playing a bit of guitar. So he was getting pushed out and he was sort of letting it happen. I don't know whether he'd say this or not. I just don't know. I haven't spoken to him for a couple of years.' At the time Smith said he sacked Scanlon for 'trying to play jazz or Sonic Youth-style stuff over good simple songs that he'd written himself.'[36] With the benefit of hindsight, he later admitted that Scanlon's sacking was his worst mistake: 'It was a bad decision. And he hasn't picked up a guitar since. I still see him actually, knocking about in Manchester. I do miss him.'[37]

'The Chiselers' came out in February 1996 on Jet Records, a subsidiary of Trojan Records. When Paul Benney in *Jockey Slut* asked what the song was about, Smith replied ' . . . errr . . . chisellers – yer fuckin' twat.'[38] When Sylvia Patterson in the *NME* asked the same question she fared a little better: the song, he said, was about 'people who rip me off'.[39] Altogether, 'The Chiselers' consisted of three parts: 'The Chiselers', 'Chilinist' and 'Interlude/Chilinism'. The work's convoluted structure and complicated arrangements perhaps serve best as an illustration of Smith's state of mind at the time. He later described the single as 'a pain in the arse': it took 'eight bloody months' and had 'nine parts, twelve different speeds and eight different vocal arrangements'.[40] It was The Fall's 'Bohemian Rhapsody'.

Equally epic in its variations if not its theme was the March 1996 release of 'Plug Myself In', a collaboration between Smith and the Manchester-based production team of Simon Spencer and Jason Barron, known as DOSE. The single came out on Coliseum Records, part of Pete Waterman's PWL group, in a slew of different big-beat mixes with names such as the 'Nero Mix', 'Pointblanc Intensive Care Mix', 'Disco Hospital Casualty Mix' and 'Monty's Full Up Pompeii

36 Stewart Lee, 'Leader of the Pack', *Sunday Times*, 23 June 1996
37 Cavanagh, op. cit., February 2001
38 Benney, op. cit., January 1996
39 Patterson, op. cit., 3 February 1996
40 ibid.

Mix'. Smith's opinion of Waterman was surprisingly positive but typically contrary: 'I've always liked him – we're from the same background – Northern soul, Wigan and all that. I think it's very brave of him to do this record. People always laugh at him, and call him a trash merchant but he does put money into young talent.'[41] At thirty-nine, Smith was probably too old to become Waterman's latest protégé, and the song's lyrics – especially the affected impotence of the repeated phrase, 'I just can't seem to plug myself in' – were unlikely to win fans from Kylie, but still, it sold better than Smith's latest efforts with The Fall, reaching number 50 in the singles chart.

I think it adds to the effect

The Fall's first and last album with Jet, *The Light User Syndrome*, appeared in June 1996 and used the same production team of Bennett and Smith as *Cerebral Caustic*. One surprise was the cover design with Pete Cronin's sepia-toned photographs of the group. The last time band members had appeared on the cover was *The Frenz Experiment* in 1989. From the front the group look out apprehensively over Smith's shoulder, while on the reverse they line up behind him like soldiers about to be inspected by a particularly short-tempered corporal.

Brix remembers the recording of the album as being 'so difficult'. The group quickly produced the backing tracks but Smith found it impossible to provide the vocals: 'He just, for whatever reason, couldn't get it together. He had a sore throat, he couldn't get up, he was depressed. Basically he was frustrated and fed up and because of that he would berate us. It came to the last day and Mark had to do all the vocals. Even Superman couldn't do that. It was just a shame really and I felt awful, but there was absolutely nothing I could do to help him. He really wasn't well and he wasn't happy in himself which showed.'

Smith explained away the poor vocals as a trick by the producer who told him he was just laying down guide vocals: 'When it was mixed, I went up the wall. But, in retrospect, I think it works.'[42] Further rationalization of the album's unimaginative and muddled production followed: 'Normally I'd be shouting and standing over

41 Benney, op. cit., January, 1996
42 Lee, op. cit., 23 June 1996

the producer during the recording, but I didn't bother so much this time. So if I sound a bit dopey or sloppy I think it adds to the effect.'[43] And that effect can be heard immediately on 'DIY Meat', with its slurred delivery, and on 'Das Vulture Ans Ein Nutter-Wain', when even singing in German cannot disguise a lack of ideas. However, on the bad-tempered 'He Pep!', Smith's obvious poor health and frustrations actually help the track, as it also does on 'Oxymoron', with Smith repeating – surely self-referentially – 'Mr Moody's scruffed up.' Smith gives up singing altogether on 'Hostile', and talks his way through a tale about gangsters, and the same goes for 'The Ballad Of J. Drummer' with its moralistic ending, 'Don't ever follow the path of being hard and tough when your heart is soft.' Brix sings most of 'Spinetrak', and surely the question, 'Where is the captain?' on 'Oleano' is another self-conscious reference to The Fall's situation.

The album is momentarily lifted by the unintentional topicality of 'Powder Keg'. In the song Smith sings about Enniskillen and describes Manchester as a 'powder keg' – all of which provided an uncanny presentiment of the IRA bomb that devastated the city the same month the album was released. 'Cheetham Hill' has its humorous moments, but 'The Coliseum' and 'Secession Man' lack bite and the album is concluded with two very missable cover versions – Johnny Paycheck's 'Stay Away (Old White Train)' and Gene Pitney's 'Last Chance To Turn Around'.

He was running the band on fear

Maybe it was a reflection of the weaknesses of both Smith and the album that no tour took place to promote it, apart from just three separate dates in May and June in Manchester, London and Sheffield. At the second of these, at the Astoria, Smith left the stage on three separate occasions: 'Of course,' he said, 'the audience think, "Oh, he's pissed again, old Mark." But then the music gets tighter and tighter and I can come back.'[44] Sam Taylor in the *Observer* failed to see any improvement. She described Hanley as playing bass with the 'remorseless concentration of a communist factory operative', while Nagle should be fired 'for the tuneless cacophony she wreaks from

---

43 Julian Taylor, 'Tripping the Light Fantastic', *Bigwig*, July 1996
44 Lee, op. cit., 23 June 1996

her little instrument'. She compared listening to The Fall to having 'an enema'.[45]

Smith's moods continued to cause problems for the band and the road crew. Brix, in particular, was shocked at the way he treated people. 'I realized he was running the band on fear,' she said. 'He was a big bully and he was a cowardly bully, but still, at this point, he had a major ego. He was Mark E. Smith. After years of being told he was a genius and brilliant – which I will not dispute that he was and is – it might have gone to his head a bit and he became very pushy, irate. You can't run a band on fear. People don't work for you. They need encouragement and camaraderie. Before he was truly inspiring and everyone wanted to do it, because he was amazing, but things had shifted.'

Smith's problem was that because record sales were in decline, live dates became an increasingly important source of cash income. However, being on the road caused stress and fatigue and provided many opportunities for violent clashes. At the end of June, at the Roskilde Festival in Denmark, he broke his finger in a fight. He also became increasingly antagonistic to Brix: 'I was a little bit cocky,' she admitted, 'because I was going out with Philip and I was living in a lovely house and I was being looked after. I didn't need all the stress and angst and anxiety of what was going on. I was getting to a point in my life where I was really ready to settle down once and for all and have a comfortable life. I deserved it as well. It was quite difficult to leave your comfortable house and go into a very disgusting environment where you're screamed at and called a whore, a bitch, a tramp and a cunt and really you haven't done anything except stand up for things you believed in.'

Fearing more abuse, Brix attempted to lay down some ground rules before she agreed to tour with Smith in September and October. One of her demands was to be paid in cash each night. This worked for the first night but then the excuses started. According to Brix, Smith claimed the promoters had sent the advance cheque to Manchester and she would have to wait. 'I started to throw up a real stink,' she said, 'so he handed me a cheque for my full amount, post-dated to the end of the tour, so I couldn't leave. And it was a lot of

---

45   Sam Taylor, 'Obergrumpenführers', *Observer*, 30 June 1996

money. Then he began to misbehave and each day it got worse. It was just a nightmare.'

At the Town Hall in Cheltenham on 4 October, Smith sacked Brix, Hanley and Wolstencroft *during* the set, although he reinstated them again during a meeting back-stage. After the gig the quarrels continued: 'He was picking on us,' Brix recalled. 'I don't know why. Either the songs were too long or too short. Terrible.' The next morning the group intended to leave early for the long drive up to Motherwell in Scotland. Come the morning, the band was ready, but Smith didn't appear until midday: 'He was not in a good state,' said Brix. 'There was a lot of weird stuff going on.'

Smith's bad mood, cranked up a few notches by the long journey in the bus, exploded into violence during the sound-check in Motherwell. 'Nothing was right,' said Brix, 'everything was wrong, everything was fucked up, although it wasn't. The monitor man, who'd been the brunt of everything the night before, well, Mark took the mike stand and threw it like a spear at the man's head. And I just lost it because you just can't do that. You can't hit people and be violent. Obviously Mark was in some dreadful state, and in retrospect I should have been more empathetic to him about what was going on with him, but at that point I was tired and fed up. He just threw this spear at him and I said, "That is it!" I lost my rag right there and then. He picked up my handbag and threw it across the stage, spilling everything, and started screaming at me. I was a "cunt", a "tramp", a "motherfucker", a "slut", this, that, the other. And I was like, "That's it, I'm leaving." He came at me as well and I picked up my guitar and threatened to hit him with it – I didn't hit him, I would never hit anybody – "If you come anywhere near me I'll fucking turn your head into a watermelon." I was really furious and I just took all my things and stormed off, went and sat in the corner, crying. Steve Hanley came and sat with me. Mark meanwhile had gone back to the bus, vomited and passed out. I was determined to carry on because I was a professional and I wasn't going to let the rest of them down, even though he was an asshole.'

Brix tried to keep out of Smith's way before the gig, but he returned and accused her of hitting him with a guitar and giving him concussion, and he was going to call the police. Brix replied: 'Good let's call the police. Let's have your blood tested and see what they find in there.' By now Smith was so angry Hanley and Wolstencroft had to restrain him. 'He was snarling, foaming and swinging and I was hysterically crying and I told the tour manger, "Get me out of here now. I'm fearing for my own safety. The man's going to kill me. Get me to a different hotel from them. I don't want anybody to know where I am. I want to get on the next flight out of here." ' So they took me to another hotel and I spent the rest of the night crying. With red eyes, I got on the first plane home and came back to London.'

The next day, fortunately, was a rest day, then they played the Customs House in South Shields. Smith's behaviour continued in its downward spiral and after he told the venue's management to 'fuck off' when they asked him to start the gig, because of a strict curfew they summarily cancelled the show. The police had to be called to help disperse the disappointed and angry crowd. The next day the increasingly macabre pantomime rolled into Worthing Assembly Rooms. According to reports Smith arrived very late and had great difficulty keeping his balance. Just fifteen minutes into the set he threw the mike into the crowd and the mike stand at a roadie.[46] He then disappeared backstage. The band pressed on and a few minutes later Smith re-emerged, this time naked to the waist apart from Nagle's anorak. The band soldiered on through a couple more songs before Smith finally collapsed and Hanley and Wolstencroft carried him off the stage.

The show so appalled Worthing Council, the owner of the venue, that it refused to pay the band's fee. Trevor Gray, the council's spokesman, later said: 'We have spoken to the band's management company and we are not paying the band for their show, due to the state of Mark E. Smith. Some of the audience, mostly good-natured, asked about a refund after the show. If they show their ticket at the point of purchase, they will receive a full refund.'[47] After the gig the PA company withdrew its equipment and the promoters also abandoned the group. Mike Doherty of Roy Hastings International Management told reporters: 'We've never come across anything like this before and we've dealt with everyone from Motorhead to Julio Iglesias.'[48]

---

46 Anon., 'Falling: The Fall's Mark E. Smith', *Guardian*, 12 October 1996
47 Anon., 'Falling Over', *Melody Maker*, 19 October 1996
48 Gary Edwards, 'Mark E. Smith: A Fallen Idol', *Brighton Evening Argus*, 10 October 1996

After such a mass desertion, The Fall had no alternative but to cancel the next day's gig at Folkestone's Leas Cliff Hall. Luckily there was just one more date to get through on the tour. Unluckily it was a high-profile gig at the Forum in London. Brix now came under pressure from booking agent and friend Pete Nash to do the show: 'He called me and said, "If you don't come and do the London show its over for Mark and I know you're a professional, I know you can do it." So I just turned up again and Mark said, "What are you doing here?" and I said, "I've come to do the show." ' Remarkably the show ran smoothly and without any apparent hitches, although the air of weariness and apprehension hanging over the band was palpable.

Brix knew it was her last gig with The Fall: 'As a human being, I could not watch what was going on any more, it was a sinking ship and I was a rat deserting it. The thing was I didn't want to go down as well. I just couldn't take it any more. And it wasn't fun.' Since leaving, Brix has worked on a variety of music projects, started writing a book on her experiences in The Fall, presented television shows and written fashion features for the *Daily Telegraph*. 'I'm quite happy in my life,' she said. 'I'm married and my husband's super successful. I have a home and a dog, Gromit, and I'm grounded for the first time. I'm with somebody who I really love and who loves me. And he's not mean to me.'

The remaining members of The Fall played just one more gig in 1996, on Christmas Eve at the Volksbühne Theatre in Berlin. Smith seemed back to some kind of form and included in the set 'Hark The Herald Angels Sing' and a revival of 'Kicker Conspiracy'. Smith and Rimmer also performed a duet on 'The City Never Sleeps' before Smith ended the concert with a heart-warming, 'Happy Christmas everybody.'[49] Once again Smith had brought The Fall back from the brink of self-destruction. How many more times could he manage it?

49 Stephen Dalton, 'Jungle All the Way: The Fall, Berlin Volksbuhne Theatre', *NME*, 18 January 1997

17

Godlike Genius, 1997–1998

If it's me and your granny on bongos, then it's a Fall gig.[1]

The Fall started 1997 with the 'The Farmlands Brief Tour', a three-date excursion through Bristol, Swindon and Gloucester.[2] New tracks premièred included 'Ten Houses of Eve', 'Ol' Gang' and 'Masquerade'. To replace Brix, Smith brought in guitarist Adrian Flanagan. After the mini-tour, Smith spent the weekend in London with Edwyn Collins working on a funky spoof disco track entitled 'Seventies Night'. Smith enjoyed the experience so much he asked Collins to produce The Fall's next album, but he declined. In February, The Fall headlined a memorial gig for music journalist Leo Finlay at Astoria 2, with support acts including Ash and Travis. As a special tribute, because it was Finlay's favourite song, The Fall performed 'And This Day'. They also performed the first live version of 'Plug Myself In', with Keir Stewart.

After the gig Adrian Flanagan left and was replaced by Tommy Crooks in time for a series of gigs in May. Crooks was an artist and a Jimi Hendrix and Iggy Pop fanatic living in West Lothian. By chance, one day he bumped into Smith and later sent him a postcard and some photographs of his artwork. A year later he received a letter from Smith that said, 'Sorry for not crediting you on the album cover.' With the letter was a copy of *Twenty-Seven Points* and its reproduction of Crooks's painting. When Crooks heard of Scanlon's departure in mid-1996, he phoned Cog Sinister and offered his services. After a gap of a few months he received another letter: 'Can you play in Manchester in two weeks time? Here's a list of the songs we'll be playing.' Crooks learnt the songs but by the time of the gig Smith had

---

1 Smith quoted in John Robertson, 'Narky Mark', *NME*, 7 February 1998
2 Smith, in The Fall's *Newsletter*, March 1997

decided on a completely different set list. Being in The Fall, Crooks immediately discovered, was like being thrown 'into the trenches'.[3]

In July the band went into the studio with DOSE to record the next album. It wasn't long, however, before they parted company. DOSE's Simon Spencer found it difficult to deal with Smith's unorthodox working methods: 'He'd be staggering around, kicking things over and shouting stuff down the drum mikes.' However, it was the old cliché of 'artistic differences' that provided the main reason for leaving: 'We wanted to go one way and he wanted to go another. Bloody pain it was. So we scarpered.'[4] Smith's interpretation of events was typically contrary: 'They went dead rocky. I felt like a real corrupter. I had to fire them. They obviously read a book on how to be a rock producer, or how to behave. I said, if I wanted a bad rock producer, I'd have got one.'[5]

To add to his woes, Smith also lost his drummer of the past ten years, Simon Wolstencroft. 'He wasn't really happy with what other people were doing with his songs,' Hanley recalled. 'He wrote "Everybody But Myself" and he wanted it to be a poppy single – he thought it was going to be a big hit single. But generally, I think he'd had enough.'[6] For Smith, Wolstencroft's biggest crime was telling him how he should sing: 'The fucking drummer! That sometimes happens to musicians. They will take themselves too seriously and want to write "real songs". A drummer should play drums and nothing more. I'm sometimes ashamed of the behaviour of musicians. I don't dislike musicians, but I don't like them either.'[7]

Karl Burns returned as Wolstencroft's replacement for summer dates in Cardiff, Bangor, Edinburgh and London. At this last gig the band was joined on stage by Michael Clark. Since his last appearance with The Fall in 1988 he had been struggling with injury, depression and heroin addiction and for the previous couple of years had been recuperating in Scotland. By chance his return to London coincided with The Fall's gig at Dingwalls. He called Smith and asked him if he

3 Tom Lappin, 'Falling on His Feet', *Scotland on Sunday*, 3 August 1997
4 Toby Manning, 'Mark & Spencer', *NME*, 4 July 1998
5 Smith, interviewed by Tony Herrington, London, April 1999
6 David I. Williams, 'Interview with S. Hanley', *TBLY*, no. 10, January 1998
7 Marcella van Hoof, 'The Fall – 20 Years and Still an Own Opinion', *Opscene*, no. 62, December/January 1997–1998

could help out in some way: 'At the start I was meant to be just pressing tapes on and off with a stop-watch in my hand,' Clark said. 'But as the day progressed and I spent more time with Mark, he was giving me pieces of paper and saying, "Read this out at the end of the song," and it turned into something a bit more than we'd anticipated.' Clark was understandably nervous: 'I thought, "Oh my God, I haven't been on stage for two years," so I was completely terrified. But to be just thrown in like that was the most generous thing he could have done for me. It was the spontaneity of the situation Mark put me in that finally unleashed something and freed my spirit.' Smith also remembered the gig: 'Actually he did try to get off the stage half-way through, and I stopped him. He needs a kick up the arse, like most creative people. But it's part of our friendship, pushing each other to achieve.'[8]

Despite Clark's presence, the music press continued to be sceptical about the strength of Smith's motivation. In the *NME*, Jim Wirth wrote that Smith appeared to be a man 'who really couldn't give a shit',[9] while Mark Roland in *Melody Maker* described the performance as 'the most dazzling display of ineptitude since they were slogging around working-men's clubs in 1978'.[10] Only Ryan Gilbey in the *Independent* saw beyond the apparent chaos: 'They may appear to be drunken brickies having a stab at performance art but their ramshackle stage manner cannot conceal a muscular musical prowess tight as a drumskin.'[11]

I looked at *Levitate* as a new start

Throughout 1997 record shops groaned under the weight of substandard compilation albums by The Fall. The main culprit remained Receiver Records and its releases *The Other Side Of The Fall*, *Archive Series – The Fall*, *The More You Seek The Less You Find*, *Oxymoron*, *Cheetham Hill* and the live album *15 Ways To Leave Your Man* recorded in London in 1996. These 'new' compilation albums consisted

---

8 Glenda Cooper, 'How We Met: Michael Clark and Mark E. Smith', *Independent on Sunday*, 16 November 1997

9 Jim Wirth, 'The Fall, London Camden Dingwalls', *NME*, 4 October 1997

10 Mark Roland, 'The Fall, Dingwalls', *Melody Maker*, 25 October 1997

11 Ryan Gilbey, 'The Unsettling World of Mark E. Smith', *Independent*, 26 September 1997

primarily of material already released on last year's compilations: all Receiver Records had done was juggle the tracks. Material under Smith's direct control fared just as badly. The CD version of *Fall In A Hole*, released on Cog Sinister, was mastered from scratched vinyl, with all original skips retained. Elsewhere Artful Records, the latest venture of John Lennard, released the live album *The Fall In The City* . . . recorded at the Roadhouse in Manchester in 1995. The inferior sound quality and below-par performance disappointed many. As Stewart Lee in *Q* observed 'many have made Walkman tapes of Fall shows at some stage in their lives, but only Artful Records ever saw fit to release one as an album'.[12]

Smith's reunion with Lennard had been forced upon him after he had fallen out with Mike Bennett and Jet Records. Apart from Lennard, all the other label bosses were wary of taking on Smith and The Fall. 'I thought it would be easy to find a new one,' he complained, 'but all those fucking Britpop-labels don't have any notion at all. A few asked me to send them a tape. They would like to know how we sound. Go figure, The Fall exists for twenty years and those creeps wanted to know how we sound!' Allegedly Creation offered to sign the group, but only on the condition they would not have to deal with Smith directly: 'And those are the so-called rebellious, hot labels. They're afraid even to sit in the same room with me!'[13]

So it was Artful, aided by a distribution deal with Pinnacle, that brought out the *Levitate* album at the end of September 1997. After the problems with DOSE, Smith decided to produce the album himself. The results show a major improvement on the guitar-dominated *The Light User Syndrome*. The breakbeat-powered opener, 'Ten Houses Of Eve', closely followed by the keyboard beeps and insistent bass of 'Masquerade', indicate Smith's determination to explore new territory. 'Hurricane Edward' is drum-heavy and almost free-form with its out-of-tune guitar and confused whistles. The next track, 'I'm A Mummy', finds The Fall on more familiar terrain with a version of Bob McFadden and Rod 'Dor' McKuen's 1958 novelty hit 'The Mummy'. The band rattle through it with zest as Nagle recreates some classic one-finger keyboard and Smith wonders why people run away from him.

12 Stewart Lee, '*The Fall In The City*', Q, no. 127, April 1997
13 Hoof, op. cit., December/January 1997–1998

'The Quartet Of Doc Shanley' is suitably dominated by Hanley's bass, with most of the lyrics spoken by Nagle. Nagle returns to keyboard duties for the elegiac instrumental 'Jap Kid'. The same music later turns up on the track 'I Come And Stand At Your Door', this time accompanied by Smith reading a sombre anti-war poem by the Turkish poet Natzim Hikmet (also famous for being performed by, amongst others, Pete Seeger and the Byrds). Following 'Jap Kid' is the crashing '4½ Inch', so-named because it half-reminded Smith of industrial rockers, Nine Inch Nails. Continuing the theme of bad weather introduced in 'Hurricane Edward', Smith calls out in confusion as his house falls in. The storm effect is heightened by Hanley's pummelling and brutish bass, and the cacophony of Smith's panic-mongering. The storm subsides and is replaced by the calming swing-beat and bass of 'Spencer Must Die'.

'Jungle Rock', a cover of a Hank Mizell track, misfires on all cylinders, as Hanley confessed: 'We were really trying to do a jungle version of that and it really didn't come off . . . but we had a go.'[14] 'Ol' Gang' follows and finds Smith turning the corner 'into a fist fight' accompanied by more single-finger electric piano, discordant guitar and feedback. After 'Tragic Days', a missable home-recorded jam session, the album comes to a close with 'Levitate', and its laconic, almost off-hand but infectious, guitar melody, and the optimistic against-the-odds song, 'Everybody But Myself'.

The critical response was positive. Steven Wells in *NME* described it as 'art without the wank',[15] and Anthony Thornton in *Q* called it 'the finest Fall album since *Extricate*'.[16] Ian Harrison in *Select* felt confounded by the group's ability 'to come back sounding vital just when you least expect it'.[17] A large part of the album's success could be attributed to Nagle's growing confidence and influence within the band. Smith also seemed to have rekindled his interest in sonic montage and experimenting with sound levels and pushing instruments beyond their normal boundaries. 'If you have a straight tune,' explained Hanley, 'he'll throw something in that throws it right off . . . Sometimes it can just be thrown in there for the sake of it.

14 Billy Bob Hargus, 'Interview with Steve Hanley and Tommy Crooks', *Perfect Sound Forever: The Online Music Magazine*, April 1998

15 Steven Wells, 'The Fall, *Levitate*', *NME*, 11 October 1997

16 Anthony Thornton, 'The Fall, *Levitate*', *Q*, no. 135, December 1997

17 Ian Harrison, '*Levitate*', *Select*, November 1997

Sometimes it works and sometimes it doesn't. But I don't think albums should be perfect. You don't want to do a perfect album because then you've got nowhere to go.'[18]

People smell a bit of weakness

With the release of *Levitate* safely behind them the group travelled to Ireland for a few dates at the beginning of November. The first two gigs in Cork and Dublin passed without too many problems – then came Belfast's Empire Music Hall and calamity. A backstage argument between Smith and the band, just moments before they were due on stage, led to him issuing summary dismissals for everybody. Mark Erskine, stage manager at the Hall, described what happened in the *Belfast Telegraph*: 'He walked off the tour bus, straight on to the stage, and started kicking stuff about. He sacked the band and they went away.' Smith was also reported to have upset staff by throwing a bottle of tomato sauce against an office door. Among those trying to calm him down was Terri Hooley, founder of Belfast's Good Vibrations record label. 'After renewing their friendship,' the *Belfast Telegraph* reported, 'the singer and the record boss entertained the idea of performing without music. Mark E. Smith would sing Beach Boys songs, while Hooley and his friend Angus Daye would provide backing vocals. This plan was eventually shelved.'[19] The *NME* reported that at one point Hooley grabbed Smith round the neck to restrain him: 'The singer thought he was about to get punched, and asked if he could remove his false teeth first. Hooley removed his own glass eye instead. "I'm not gonna hit you," Hooley insisted.' The *NME* also reported that Smith called the Hall the next day to apologize and to ask if anybody had found his passport and some demo tapes. A spokesman for The Fall said: 'This has surprised us as much as it probably surprised Mark. This might end up being resolved although I'm sure he did sack them at the time. As long as he regains his passport the tour will continue in typically maverick Fall fashion, even as a solo acoustic show!'[20] Inevitably, rumours about The Fall's demise started

18 Hargus, op. cit., April 1998

19 Staff Reporter, 'Punk's Fall was Anarchy in the Empire', *Belfast Telegraph*, 10 November 1997

20 Anon., 'Smith Sacks Fall Guys', *NME*, 15 November 1997

circulating and with a UK tour already booked this could have proved very damaging financially. A statement was therefore quickly issued by The Fall's publicity company Circus: 'Contrary to erroneous reports, The Fall tour is definitely going ahead. The Belfast show on November 8 was cancelled by the promoter rather than the band, and the group are looking to perform a replacement show in the near future.'[21]

As tempers subsided, Smith offered his side of what went wrong in Belfast: 'Someone kicked a guitar stand over at rehearsal, and it was like . . . open rebellion! And I was very poorly at the time, I had the flu badly. Which they all got a week later, which says something. But I couldn't hear what anyone was saying, and the moment you relax they're all going, "We want this, we want that." People smell a bit of weakness.'[22] Hanley was more diplomatic, calling it 'just something and nothing'. Once everybody had cooled off and talked about things they just decided 'to get on with it'. The Fall, Hanley said, 'never just go through the motions . . . So there's bound to be friction isn't there?'[23]

On 13 November, five days after the Belfast débâcle, The Fall played Sankey's Soap in Manchester without mishap. The UK tour was on again, but Smith increasingly became the subject of spiteful criticism. Describing a gig at the Forum, the NME's April Long wrote that Smith resembled a 'disgruntled troll' and that he staggered about the stage 'barking like a demented seal'.[24] The problem was that Smith's behaviour had become more newsworthy in the eyes of some editors than his music. A clear example of this was Smith's appearance in archetypal lads' mag Loaded. Placed in the 'Rogue' section, the interview with John Perry quickly degenerated into a slanging match. In his first paragraph Perry made clear his disrespect by describing Smith as looking like 'a melted muppet in Man At C&A'. Maybe he was upset at Smith summing up Loaded with salutary conciseness as 'Fantasy life. Bungee jumping, paratrooping. Birds in hotel rooms.' The interview ended with Smith yelling at Perry: 'You're a fucking dead-leg cunt and I'm not talking to you.'[25]

21 Anon., 'News', Melody Maker, 22 November 1997
22 Robertson, op. cit., 7 February 1998
23 Williams, op. cit., January 1998
24 April Long, 'The Fall/Foil, London Kentish Town Forum', NME, 10 January 1998
25 John Perry, 'North & Mouth', Loaded, no. 44, December 1997

For unique services to music

In 1995, in answer to a question about the *NME* 'Brat' awards, Smith replied: 'It's a waste of time and money.' If they awarded him a prize he wouldn't even bother to turn up: 'They can send it through the fucking post, can't they?'[26] Three years later, on 31 January 1998, he found himself at the awards ceremony after apparently being tricked into attending by Nagle. He used to go to these kinds of events all the time, she confided in the *NME*, but only to buttonhole people from his former record labels 'and demand money'.[27]

Channel Four screened the ceremony with presenter, the comedian Eddie Izzard, announcing winners from a stage set constructed to look like a toilet, complete with its own set of urinal bowls. Award winners that night included Beck as best solo artist, Prodigy as best dance act and Radiohead's *OK Computer* as best album. The best radio show award went to Mark Radcliffe and Marc Riley. Eventually Izzard started to announce the 'Godlike Genius Award for unique services to music'. 'For twenty years he and his group have stood outside the mainstream of popular music,' Izzard began, 'sustained by innovation, genius and a stern command of the Protestant work ethic. They have been everything from amphetamine rockabillies to mithering techno-futurists – their one constant has been their leader. Easy to impersonate but impossible to emulate, his style is hugely influential. A generation of stream-of-consciousness mumblers from Pavement to Prolapse, from Happy Mondays to Lo-Fidelity Allstars have all felt his power . . . '

At this point Smith, already having heard enough, reached the podium and Izzard, a little disconcerted, handed Smith the award (a gold cast of a clenched fist with its middle finger extended). He looked at it disdainfully and placed it back on the podium. Then came his acceptance speech: 'Not like you to be funny, Eddie! Thank you very much for this award. Eh . . . it's all due to erm . . . John Lennard, Stephen Hanley . . . without eh . . . which eh . . . and Caroline an' emm . . . Irene and Julia. What's it mean? . . . I think the achievement should go to those who read the *NME* who can read it from cover to cover, all right.' At that Smith briefly glanced at the trophy, made no move to pick it up and left the stage to applause.

26 Lucy Nation, 'Northern Soul', *The Lizard*, no. 4, April–May 1995
27 Robertson, op. cit., 7 February 1998

Never one to rest on his laurels, the Godlike Genius was soon back at work in February promoting The Fall's latest single, 'Masquerade', taken from *Levitate*. Released in various formats in one of its CD versions it was combined with a new track, 'Calendar', featuring the guitar work of Damon Gough, later known as Badly Drawn Boy. The story of how Smith and Gough first met is now legendary. According to Gough he was waiting for Andy Votel, the Twisted Nerve label boss, outside the Night & Day bar in Manchester when Smith staggered out, opened his car door thinking it was a taxi, got in and asked Gough to take him to Stockport. 'So I did, for a laugh,' recalled Gough. 'When he got out, I realized he'd left his jacket in there. I offered to give it back, but he didn't want it. And as for the teeth, I cleaned out my car the day after. When I was clawing out all the empty McDonald's packets and crisp wrappers I found this set of teeth, which I kept in the glove compartment for a couple of years, but no, I was never tempted to hang them off the rear-view mirror.'[28] Smith's version of events included the detail that it was 'a Lakeland leather jacket worth about a hundred and ten quid', and as for the teeth, 'he could keep them, the fat little get'.[29]

If the first three get shot you have another three behind them

At the end of 1997, Hanley was asked by Fall fan David I. Williams if he ever thought about 'chucking it in?' 'Every day!' he answered half-jokingly. 'Well, it does sound weird to say you've been in a job, or a band, for eighteen years. The Fall could end tomorrow . . . it could carry on for years.'[30] Hanley, more than anybody was aware of the precarious nature of being in The Fall. For many years he must have observed countless instances of Smith's ruthless attitude to hiring and firing musicians. Smith's latest boast was of a reserve army of musicians he kept ready to step into the breach when needed: 'Anyone gets stroppy with me, I've always got subs. Every time, I take no musician for granted. I don't like musicians. They elevate themselves, which is detrimental to the name of The Fall. I don't hold auditions, and it's a nasty thing to say, but it's like a

28 Badly Drawn Boy, 'Cash for Questions', Q, July 2002
29 David Cavanagh, 'Cash for Questions', Q, February 2001
30 Williams, op. cit., January 1998

platoon sort of thing. If the first three get shot you have another three behind them.'[31]

With these reassuring words ringing in their ears, Hanley, Burns, Nagle and Crooks accompanied Smith on The Fall's first US tour for four years. Organized by Hanley without any record company support, it opened with two dates, 30 and 31 March, at Coney Island High in New York City. The bad omens were plain for all to see when Smith walked on stage with a black eye, the result, allegedly, of an altercation between him, Nagle and a telephone receiver.[32] After this first night, Billy Bob Hargus of *Perfect Sound Forever* asked Hanley about the 'creative tension' that seemed to keep the band focused: 'If you're in The Fall, you've got four people pushing you on. If I make a mistake, I've got four people on my neck, and if Karl makes a mistake, he's got four people on him. That does tend to keep you on your toes. Sometimes it can get a bit out of hand.'[33]

Gigs followed at the tiny Loop Lounge in Passaic, the Middle East in Boston and a half-full Trocadero in Philadelphia. During the latter, an obviously drunk Smith caused a walk-off when he gave up singing and handed the microphone to a member of the audience. After a brief backstage discussion, the band returned but Smith continued to show little interest in singing and instead fiddled with Hanley's amp. Hanley tried to push him away but he persisted. Giving up, Hanley unplugged his bass, threw it down and left the stage, closely followed by Crooks and Burns. Smith and Nagle finished the set alone, performing a necessarily stripped-down version of 'Cheetham Hill'. There was no encore. Deepop, of the support act the Bush Tetras, recalled that after the set, the members of The Fall drove off without Smith. Deepop then spotted Smith walking down the back alley of the Trocadero: 'He's drunk and I find him a very sad figure. Mark gets put into a hotel in Philly. I wonder if there will be a show in DC the next night.'[34]

The show at the Black Cat in Washington DC, did go ahead, and although subdued, remained spat free. But to add to the band's woes,

31 Mark E. Smith, 'The Think Tank: Mark E. Smith', *Select*, January 1998
32 Anon., 'Mark E. Smith: This Nation's Misbehaving Disgrace', *NME*, 25 April 1998
33 Hargus, op. cit., April 1998
34 Deepop, email posted on Fallnet, 6 April 1998

earlier in the day thieves had stolen equipment from the tour van, including Nagle's keyboards, her precious yellow Washburn guitar (previously owned by Martin Hannett) and a bag of Burns's cymbals. The band recovered all the equipment a couple of days later (except for the guitar) when Deepop discovered it for sale in a music store in New York, just in time for The Fall's last two scheduled gigs on the tour.

The first of these on 7 April at Brownies in New York started just around midnight with an instrumental version of 'Spencer'. A dishevelled looking Smith appeared during 'Masquerade' and as he walked on stage he purposely knocked over part of Burns's drum-kit. During the break, while Burns reset his kit, Smith told the audience: 'And this lot are going to beat me up like the big men they are.' Upon the band's resumption, Smith retreated to the drum riser and squatted down to sort through a plastic bag full of lyric sheets. The rest of the band looked seriously pissed off but concentrated on playing and ignoring Smith. During 'Hip Priest', Smith handed the microphone to the audience and annoyed Crooks by backing into him. Picking up his coat, he laid it over Nagle's keyboards and made a 'wind it up' signal to the band, which they ignored. Taking a couple of Burns's spare drum sticks he nonchalantly threw them on the floor. That was the last straw for Burns and he angrily climbed over his kit and grabbed Smith and tried to drag him backstage. Smith and Burns careered across the stage and crashed into the keyboards and bass amp. Hanley intervened and yelled at Burns to get back behind the drums, which he did, reluctantly. Smith looked on apparently nonplussed by the commotion.

Amazingly the band reformed and started playing again. But Smith hadn't finished. He now baited Crooks with his mike wire and Crooks retaliated by swinging at Smith with his guitar. Once again the band stopped and Smith took refuge behind Nagle, speaking into the microphone. 'That man is a Scottish man, a fucking animal on drugs and a fucking idiot.' Burns shouted back, 'And where's the fucking singer, you cock!' Smith continued, 'I've been assaulted in public here by two people or three people, you be witness to this, bear witness, laddies. They're very big. I tell you what, these three. I got a taxi and some fucker pulled a gun out on me, from fucking Pakistan or somewhere. These three were fucking cowering in the fucking dressing-room – as usual – they're nowhere to be seen. They're very hard . . . all together.'

After that the band continued to ignore Smith and ran quickly through 'Levitate', 'Lie Dream' and 'He Pep', at the conclusion of which Crooks, Hanley and Burns simply walked off stage. It was the end for them. Nagle stayed on stage and started up the tape for 'Powderkeg' while Smith picked up Hanley's bass and threw it into the drum-kit. Improvising, Smith said his farewells: 'The owner of the Brownie Club was real glad to see three comedians turn up, but what he didn't realize was *that the town was a powder keg*! . . . And the owner of the Brownie Club just hoped it made three figures . . . see you.' As the lights came up Crooks jumped back on stage and took a couple of photographs of the audience. Hanley also appeared and leant down at the front of the stage to smile and shout to a friend: 'Who's going to play me in the movie?' 'Sting!' he exclaimed, 'Sting!'

Limited order of protection

After the gig the band returned to the Quality Hotel Eastside in Manhattan's Gramercy Park. Smith's behaviour remained fractious and reports described him running 'topless through the lobby threatening other members of The Fall'.[35] The next day, Wednesday, at a quarter past three in the morning the police arrested Smith at the hotel and charged him with third-degree assault and harassment charges relating to Nagle. They took him to the 17th Precinct headquarters and held him there until 10 April, Good Friday, when his $1000 bail was finally posted. 'I was only meant to be in for a night,' Smith claimed, 'but they kept stopping my bail because they got the forms mixed up, that was just my fucking luck.'[36]

He appeared in court on Tuesday 14 April where, according to Wayne Brison, a criminal-court spokesperson, Smith was ordered to undergo an alcohol-treatment programme and anger-management counselling. Smith agreed to submit monthly reports and observe a 'limited order of protection' with regards to Nagle. It was limited in the sense that it only allowed them to continue working together. He finally left New York on 18 April but was ordered to return for a

---

35 Anon., op. cit., 25 April 1998
36 Edwin Pouncey, 'Invisible Jukebox: Mark E. Smith', *The Wire*, no. 203, January 2001

hearing on 30 September, when the charges would be dropped if he had followed the court's Adjournment Contemplating Dismissal programme.

Smith's lawyer, Steve Saporito, told the *NME* that there was actually no physical injury: 'It escalated through the course of the night and finally the hotel called the police . . . Julia was in the room with Mark and they sort of had it at each other. I saw them last night and he and Julia were both in pretty good spirits. She stood by him, she's been telling the prosecutor, "I wanna drop the charge." She was like, "This is completely out of proportion to what happened." '[37] Later reports in *Mojo* had Saporito claiming that he thought the police response was so heavy-handed because the hotel identified Nagle as Smith's girlfriend: 'In post-O.J. America, domestic violence is taken a lot more seriously – no one takes any chances.'[38]

When he returned to England, Smith wasted little time in telling his side of the story. He described Crooks as 'just a hired guitar' and losing him was just the same as 'if the triangle player out of Phil Collins' band had left'. Burns was 'out' and if Hanley had left 'we'll just get another bassist'. He speculated that the bust-up might have been related to 'late-thirties syndrome or something, the male menopause'. The whole episode had left him exasperated: 'It's all arse about tit. Everything you read, the opposite is true. It's like one of those films where a fellow's minding his own business and he gets attacked . . . If you shout in New York, you get locked up. In New York, it's an offence to drink a beer and smoke a cigarette and raise your voice. Even the judge was flabbergasted.'[39]

Hanley's recollection of events, not surprisingly, differed from Smith's: 'He said we abandoned him in jail, but it's rubbish. I arranged for his lawyer to sort it out, made sure he had enough money. The last time I saw him was in the back of a police car. He wanted me to go to the police station with him. I wouldn't. I got a flight home.'[40] Hanley had simply had enough: 'I just thought, because I'd put so much time and effort into the tour, Mark should have supported it. Whatever he

37 Anon., op. cit., 25 April 1998
38 Anon., 'Three Falls and a Submission: Mark E. Smith Disqualified on a Technicality', *Mojo*, no. 55, June 1998
39 Anon., 'Smith: Fall Will Continue', *NME*, 9 May 1998
40 Mark Kendall, 'Hello, Goodbye: Steve Hanley and The Fall', *Mojo*, no. 75, February 2000

was feeling, whether he thought the band was shite at the time, which he did – he didn't like Tommy and Karl – I think he should have backed me up. Which he didn't. He was walking off, pissing about, knocking the gear over, messing about with the amps, fighting with Julia in the hotel. That was the final straw. I'd put three months effort into it and the least he could do was get up and sing. Promoters were paying us half the money because we didn't have a singer. There was like no agents involved and no record company, so it was a bit more personal.'

Despite the increasing ill-feeling during the tour, on the day of the last gig Smith and Hanley had spent the afternoon together discussing the group: its finances, music and future. 'He seemed quite happy,' recalled Hanley, but that made what happened that night all the more difficult to forgive. 'The worst thing was the Americans were lapping it up – the entire front row had video cameras. I'm sure seeing a band fighting on-stage is entertaining but it's not nice to be part of.'[41] Hanley thought the group had become like a freak show: 'People were just going to see whether Mark was going to kick off. Music was becoming less and less important, which is, you know, fair enough, but I think he's worth more than that. There's no place for me in that anyway.'

Crooks told reporters that the band split from Smith because he was 'impossible to work with'. 'We're not going back,' he announced to the NME. 'The tour was a bloody nightmare, just one police incident after another. It was unbelievable at the end, just fighting all the time. It was an ugly, ugly situation. Mind you, none of us got hurt. He couldn't beat himself up, let alone beat any of us up! All we were interested in was going on and playing as hard as we could, but he [Smith]) was just hitting us, or going offstage, or messing around and knocking things over, sabotaging the whole thing. I think it might be the natural end to The Fall after twenty years.'[42]

Looking back on his many years in The Fall, Hanley said he felt differently about it every day: 'Some days I think it was great, some days I think why did I ever want to be in it? It's only because it's coloured by the way it ended. It wasn't perfect, it was ups and downs all the time, but it was a good thing for me. Good to be in. It was just

41 ibid.
42 Anon., 'Fall Over?', NME, 2 May 1998

the last few years that clouded the good times really. I'd probably do it all again if I could. There was always a distance between the band members and Mark, he was never going to be your close friend if he's your boss as well. He was running The Fall before I joined. And if people didn't like it . . . well they always seemed to come back. Sad as it sounds, this is always what I didn't want to be, an ex-Fall member. I wanted to see it through to the end. There are millions of ex-Fall members out there; I just didn't want to be another one.'[43]

With Hanley leaving Smith lost his longest serving musician and, for many fans, the most innovative and compelling element of The Fall's music. The effect of his departure could not be underestimated. As Smith had admitted fifteen years before, 'The most original aspect of The Fall is Steve on the bass. I've never heard a bass player like him in my life. I don't have to tell him what to play, he just knows. He is The Fall sound.'[44]

Like I give a fuck

Smith's immediate dilemma after the New York bust-up was to figure out what to do about prearranged dates at Dingwalls in London and at the Alleycat in Reading. To cancel these shows would have hurt his pride. So, with just a week to go, he recruited and rehearsed Kate Methen, a drummer from the band Polythene, to accompany himself and Nagle. He also invited Michael Clark to play bass, but Clark sensibly declined, having no knowledge at all of playing guitar. The audience at Dingwalls must have been anticipating just the kind of freak show mentioned by Hanley, but, despite constant heckling (including a persistent shout of, 'Where's the band?'), Nagle and Methen coped well and, with plenty of help from the backing tapes, the gig proceeded without too much embarrassment. It even included a surprising and welcome revival of 'Industrial Estate', as if Smith was determined to re-establish a link with The Fall's founding spirit of '77. The second night at Dingwalls also passed by without any major

43 On their return to England, Hanley, Burns and Crooks formed Ark, with Pete Nakamura as lead singer. Later in the year Burns left and was replaced by Paul Hanley and the band recorded an album *Brainsold* that was eventually released in 2002 on Voiceprint. In 2002, the Hanley brothers could still be found performing with the Lovers, a band fronted by ex-Inspiral Carpets singer Tom Hingley.
44 Frank Worrall, 'Fall Guys', *Melody Maker*, 18 June 1983

hitches. When Smith came on stage and uttered the traditional, 'Good evening, we are The Fall,' someone in the audience corrected him, 'Good evening, we are Mark Smith!' And at one point during the set Smith asked, 'So what's people's opinions then?' He paused and turned away, muttering, 'Like I give a fuck.'

Once the Reading gig was out of the way, Smith had three months to reconsider his options. 'I am broke,' he admitted, 'there's no two ways about it. But I've got two choices: I could do a book, because I know all the scam on everybody. I've worked with everyone: Branson, Miles Copeland . . . Or I could do this.'[45] The decision was never in any real doubt. Karen Leatham came in as the new bass player and Thomas Patrick Murphy (aka Tom Head) took over the drum stool recently vacated by Methen. Murphy had been recommended to Smith by Steve Evets. 'Mark told him he was looking for a drummer,' Murphy explained, 'so he gave him this crappy old demo tape I did six years ago and Mark took it from there. I've got loads of better more recent stuff on CD I've done with bands, but Mark wasn't bothered, he just said he'd train me to play The Fall way. I asked when he'd like me to do an audition, but he told me he doesn't do auditions. He just likes to keep things simple, he joked that he'd fine me for putting drum rolls and stuff in, but it turns out he wasn't joking!' Murphy was also an actor, and could be seen as an occasional extra on *Emmerdale* and *Coronation Street* and as a 'dolie' in *The League of Gentlemen*. He adopted the stage name Tom Head to distinguish his playing career from his acting. Asked about his playing style, it was clear he'd quickly adapted to The Fall's way of doing things: 'I play the songs exactly how Mark asks me to.'[46]

Leatham and Head débuted for The Fall at Manchester University in August. The set included few surprises, being taken mostly from *Levitate*, but it did include two new cover versions; another old rockabilly song, 'F-'oldin' Money' by Tommy Blake, and from the new-wave days of 1978 'This Perfect Day' by the Saints. At the end of October, the group played two nights at the St Bernadette's Club, a small Catholic social club just north of Prestwich in Whitefield. Some people in the sparse audience took the opportunity once more to goad Smith. 'They were calling me pathetic,' he said, 'saying I was trying to

45 John Robinson, 'The E Regeneration', *NME*, 5 September 1998
46 Rob Waite, 'Tom Head', *TBLY*, no. 16, 1999

take music back to the days of the working-man's club. Trying to get them to accept what I'd done was so exciting. It's what most bands do when they start out, not twenty years into their career. Even friends who have worked for me for years can't understand why I would, for example, employ a country and western drummer. The reason is that I can mould them. I can make them a member of The Fall.'[47]

Dissolute Singer

At the same time as he slowly rebuilt The Fall, Smith put together a spoken-word album, *The Post Nearly Man* for Artful Records. He later claimed it was John Lennard's idea to do the album: 'They'd done one by Gordon Banks (ex-England goalkeeper) on fishing and it was really good.'[48] Although according to Smith it was much in demand 'in Manchester dance stores' it was meant to be sold 'in W.H. Smith with Pam Ayres'.[49] Even before the album reached the shops, the production process was fraught with difficulties and Smith feared the album might be cursed: 'At the record plant the lacquer went missing. They did a cut of it and it came out all hiss. There was a demo of it and it was sent to record shops and it came out backwards.' When operatives at the pressing plant heard the master tape they sent it back saying there had been a mistake: 'They say this track just stops here. There's this screeching sound and then it stops. Yeah, what's it got to do with you? What you doing listening to it, just do it, that's your job.'[50]

Released at the end of August, the album opens with 'The Horror in Clay', an adaptation of 'The Call of Cthulhu' by H. P. Lovecraft. The piece sets the tone for most of the album, with its fragmented narrative and dialogue. On 'I'm Bobby', Smith rants without punctuation about 'half-realized birdlike thoughts clogging the solo seventies or new intellectual skinhead morass'. The longest and most realized track was 'Visit of an American Poet', where a poet visits Smith's home and takes him hostage. It includes a segment where a female voice asks, 'Why are there so many shit people in music?' 'Dissolute Singer' deals obliquely with the events in New York, with Smith wandering lost through the city.

47   Lisa Verrico, 'Are You Talking to Me?', *Dazed & Confused*, December 1998
48   Anon., 'Mark: My Words', *NME*, 18 July 1998
49   Jonathan Romney, 'Fall Guy', *Guardian*, 23 April 1999
50   Smith, interviewed by Tony Herrington, London, April 1999

The album revealed a side to Smith free from the restrictions of working with a band. But despite the resulting emphasis on words there were too few moments when they coalesced into a forceful image or sharp observation. The album was unconventional to say the least and the music press either ignored it or treated it with disdain. Johnny Cigarettes in the *NME* called Smith 'The post any good man' and compared him to 'one of those loonies that send tapes of themselves reading poetry and singing Shakin' Stevens songs to major record labels'.[51]

Maybe Smith was too distracted by his problems with the American courts. When he failed to turn up for a hearing on the 30 September, the *NME* dramatically announced that a warrant had been issued for his arrest.[52] What had actually happened was that Judge Suzanne Mondo had rescheduled the hearing for 4 November to coincide with a proposed American tour. The bad news for Smith was her decision that his state attorney could be relieved on the grounds that Smith's income was sufficiently high for him to pay for his own defence. When Smith did turn up at Manhattan Criminal Court in November nothing was resolved because Judge Mondo adjourned the case till 12 January 1999, when Smith could present letters from his doctors and relations 'to say I'm a nice fella'.[53] This he did and with Smith having fulfilled his obligations the case was closed.

One-Take Willy

Along with his spoken-word projects, Smith also branched out into the world of acting. His first cameo appearance was as a social worker in *Diary of a Madman*, a ten-minute film broadcast on BBC2 in October 1997. Adapted from a short story by the Russian writer Gogol, it starred Steve Evets as an Elvis-obsessed office worker who becomes infatuated with his boss and thinks he can talk to dogs. In the film Smith attempts to interrogate Evets, repeatedly asking him his name. But Evets just kept repeating, 'Elvis Aaron Presley'. Smith's next role was 'The Caterer' in Mark Aerial Waller's *Glow Boys*, a

51 Johnny Cigarettes, 'Mark E. Smith: *The Post Nearly Man*', *NME*, 5 September 1998

52 Anon., 'Mark E. Smith "Wanted" in the US', *NME*, 10 October 1998

53 Anon., 'News', *Melody Maker*, 21 November 1998

fourteen-minute film set in a nuclear laboratory in Oldbury.[54] Speaking to *Melody Maker*, Smith described his involvement: 'They got in touch with me. I went and did my song and went home again. "One-Take Willy", as they call me. It's all right. It's like doing videos, really.'[55] Waller described Smith's Caterer as 'someone who has seen people come in and out of the reactor for many years and he's heard all the stories. His character is immortal.'[56] Smith's second film with Waller, *Midwatch*, also dealt with nuclear issues, this time Operation Mosaic, the first nuclear tests carried out by the British in the 1950s. The film also starred Evets and was set in a kitchen (purportedly a warship's galley) and filmed using an infra-red camera in total darkness on midsummer's night, the longest day.

Meanwhile, back at The Fall, Smith continued with his reformation project with the recruitment of two new musicians: guitarist Neville Wilding and bass player Adam Helal. Wilding joined first, playing on 14 December at the Fleece and Firkin in Bristol. Two days later Leatham resigned, or was sacked, and Wilding's friend Helal was recruited just in time for a gig on 16 December at the Astoria 2 in London. Smith explained his press-gang technique to Jonathan Romney in the *Guardian*: 'I can walk down the street in Glasgow and get nineteen-year-olds. I don't audition people, I just go and say, "You're the guitarist." . . . I'm lucky, it's a gift. A lot of people try and imitate the way I get groups together. I don't give any secrets away, you know. I don't go through the chords with them, I just brainwash 'em.'[57]

Only time would tell if Smith's 'gift' still worked well enough for him to spot and recruit musicians of the calibre of Burns, Hanley, Schofield, Scanlon and Wolstencroft. He must have had his doubts because at one point during the autumn he renewed contact with Martin Bramah. 'We were supposed to do a London gig,' recalled Bramah, 'and I'd met the bass player, Karen, and we went through some stuff without Mark being present because we couldn't get hold of him. It came to the situation when there was a week to go to the

54   'The Caterer', the song that Smith performs in the film, can be found on *The Post Nearly Man* (1998).

55   Anon., 'News', *Melody Maker*, 8 August 1998

56   Tim Wesley, *'Glow Boys'*, *TBLY*, no. 19, 2000

57   Romney, op. cit., 23 April 1999

gig and I'd still not rehearsed with the band. He was supposed to come down with a tape of their last gig and I was supposed to learn the parts from that. Well he never turned up and it turned out he'd been on a three-day bender. So I thought, "Oh, that's that then." ' Smith later promised Bramah a role on the next album but again he let him down. Having Bramah in reserve, as it were, suited Smith as he checked out the suitability of his new recruits. Bramah became superfluous when his new charges proved more than adequate. 'I recorded four new songs last week and they just might be the best I've ever done,' Smith told Lisa Verrico at the end of 1998. 'I listened back to them and heard this driving beat down the centre of each song. I've waited twenty years to hear that sound. Now I feel like the possibilities for The Fall are endless.'

When asked if anything in particular had helped him get back on track, Smith replied: 'Probably having my ears syringed. You're laughing, but it's true. I can hear everything now. It's great. I thought I was going deaf from being on stage. I was shouting at everyone. I was also very unhappy with the sound of the band. I knew something was wrong, but I couldn't hear what it was. The nurse freaked over my ears. She had to pump them out two or three times. She said she'd never seen so much wax. Apparently, I had enough for three seventy-year-old blokes. Getting it done changed my life. The other day, I was sat in my front room and I could hear these voices outside. Before, I would have thought it was people standing outside my front door, talking about me. Suddenly, I could hear what they were saying. It was only the neighbours having a chat. They didn't even mention my name.'[58]

58 Verrico, op. cit., December 1998

18

Rude All The Time, 1999–

The thing about The Fall is it might be fun to you but it isn't fun for me. I'm forty-years-old, man. I've had times when I wished I'd been a plumber like my dad. I'd have earned a lot more money and been a lot happier. But . . . there's something about rock music that hasn't been explored yet. When I feel like packing it in, there's so much crap about you have to carry on . . . What I'm trying to do is, like, keep a fucking cultural thing going.'[1]

In the middle of February 1999, the Regal (UK) label released 'Inch' with music by Keir Stewart and Simon Spencer and words by Smith. The original track had been recorded back in 1997 during the sessions for *Levitate* at West Heath Studios, just before Smith and the producers had parted ways. 'We didn't really get on with Mark as well as we'd hoped,' said Spencer, 'and once we'd got the vocals for "Inch" we ran off back to Manchester with the tapes. Then we cut about twenty CDs of the finished mix, sent it to Peel, *NME*, other radio stations, etc., which was a bit naughty really, but Mark was all right about it and agreed to us putting it out on another label. Eventually, after months of being fucked around by one label, it came out on another – Regal.'[2] The most distinctive and hilarious feature of 'Inch' is Smith's spoken 'intro' as he tells Stewart and Wolstencroft exactly how he wants the drums and keyboards to start. The rest of the track reverberates with crunching beats and Smith shouting that the house is 'falling in'.

Accompanying 'Inch' in February was The Fall's triumphant comeback single, 'Touch Sensitive'. Opening with an exuberant twangy guitar and a chanted, 'Hey! Hey! Hey! Hey!' (reminiscent of Gary Glitter's, 'Hello, it's good to be back'), Smith announced his

---

1 Ian Harrison, 'You Can Laugh If You Want', *Select*, May 2000. Smith was in fact forty-three at the time of the interview.
2 Odran Smith, 'Interview with Simon Spencer of DOSE', *Fall News* (www.visi.com/fall), 12 September 2000

return, his complaints still unanswered, his indignation still intact. The single provided a preview for the release in April of *The Marshall Suite* on Artful Records. Produced by Steve Hitchcock and Smith at Battery Studios in London, the album was recorded at the same time as new recruits joined the group. At the start of the sessions there was just Smith, Nagle and Head, with the occasional help of Leatham. Eventually Helal and Wilding arrived to join in the fun. 'I'm very lucky at the moment, touch wood, to have the people I've got,' admitted Smith. 'I've never ever believed in session musicians or being solo, etc. That is why I'm broke. It is not a hire-and-fire policy I've got, or ever have had. I cannot create with people who're doing it for 1 money, 2 ego - sex, etc., or 3 being in The Fall. Julia, Tom, Neville, Adam, *et al.* all have their own projects which I will gradually brainwash them out of.'[3]

Smith conceived the record as a three-sided album with a 'straight-forward' side, an 'opening up' side and a 'really off the wall' side.[4] The straightforward side opens with the previously released 'Touch Sensitive' and is followed by 'F-'oldin' Money', an old rockabilly song from the late 1950s originally performed by Tommy Blake.[5] 'Shake-off' touches on Smith's twin obsession with drugs (injecting eyeballs with Domestos) and plumbing (the replacement of a toilet cistern). 'Bound' derives from the Audio Arts Northern Soul favourite, 'Love Bound', while 'This Perfect Day' is an uncomplicated cover of the Saints' 1977 hit single of the same name.[6] The 'opening up' side kicks in with '(Jung Nev's) Antidotes' and closes with 'Anecdotes + Antidotes In B#'. These two tracks share heavy industrial tones and provide an oppressive and nightmarish backdrop as Smith complains about a 'second-rate' country where you can't chew gum or smoke.[7] Sandwiched between these tracks is the lighter 'Inevitable' and its celebration of 'the calling' and Saturday-night dancing. The 'really off

---

3 Rob Waite, 'Mark E. Smith Interview', *TBLY*, no. 15, 1999

4 Sietse Meijer, 'Transcript of an interview with M.E. Smith for an article in NRC Handelsblad, *Cultureel Supplement*', 10 September 1999

5 In August, 'F-'oldin' Money' became the second CD single to be released from the album. It was released in two versions, each with different additional tracks.

6 There is a hilarious falsetto version of this song on one of the 'F-'oldin' Money' CD singles.

7 The line 'If chewing gum is chewed / The chewer is pursued' comes from the Marx Brothers' film *Duck Soup*.

the wall' side starts with a short tape montage by Hitchcock while the next track, 'The Crying Marshal', started life as 'The Real Life of the Crying Marshal' recorded by Smith with the Filthy Three (including Jason Barron) at PWL.[8] For Smith, the Marshal represented the type of man who lived on the border: 'a marshal isn't anything really, is he. He's sort of in the middle of, mainly, the people and the police, and he doesn't really know where he's going really. It's got nothing to do with me, really!'[9] 'Birthday Song' is dominated by Nagle's dreamy and haunting keyboard as Smith addresses his 'darling', telling her that there exists 'another side' she never sees. On 'Mad.Men-Eng.Dog' Smith's ramblings are accompanied by insect-like screeches and pig-like grunts.[10] The last track, 'On My Own', is a revised version of 'Everybody But Myself' from *Levitate*.[11]

As a transitional work, the album was understandably patchy, and Smith's lyrics, with the odd exception, such as on 'Touch Sensitive', had become increasingly abstract. Those vivid descriptions of everyday life that had characterized earlier work were now being replaced by more personal and impenetrable lyrics. The Marshal concept also seemed confused and lacked the archetypal qualities of past inventions, such as Fiery Jack, Roman Totale and the Hip Priest. The critical response was subdued, although many still admired Smith's staying power. The *Guardian*'s Caroline Sullivan, for example, thought the new band had 'sparked a creative renaissance of sorts' and provided 'a sense of purpose that has long been missing'.[12] Despite such positive responses, The Fall's fan base continued to shrink and the album, after charting briefly at number 84, soon drifted off into sub-chart space.

---

8   This track was also included on one of the 'F-'oldin' Money' CD singles.

9   Meijer, op. cit., 10 September 1999

10 Spencer Marsden, who co-wrote this track, also collaborated with Smith on the June 2000 limited-edition seven-inch single 'Fistful Of Credits', under the name of Mild Man Jan.

11 The vinyl version of the album included 'Tom Raggazzi', which is rumoured to have Smith playing the bass guitar (it was also included on one of the 'F-'oldin' Money' CD singles).

12 Caroline Sullivan, 'The Fall, *The Marshall Suite*', *Guardian*, 30 April 1999

They don't have to, like, be my slaves or anything

The new line-up promoted the album with a May UK tour. Along with tracks drawn from *The Marshall Suite,* the set also included cover versions of 'Jet Boy' by the New York Dolls and 'Ketamine Sun', a reworking of Lou Reed's 'Kill Your Sons'. A series of summer dates included two fractious appearances at festivals in Reading and Leeds. At the first in Reading, Smith sacked Tom Head just before going on stage. His temporary replacement was Nick Dewey, formerly of the band Revolver but then part of the Chemical Brothers' management team. Head was then reinstated in time for the Leeds Festival on the next day, but further signs of tension were apparent when Smith and Wilding both appeared on stage in blood-stained clothes, the result, apparently, of a backstage fight.

Being in The Fall was definitely a unique experience, as Smith explained to Sietse Meijer: 'They think they're gonna be treated like Blur or something, but people just treat them like lepers!' Smith's attitude to musicians didn't help matters and it had even hardened, if possible, since the 1998 New York débâcle. The mistake he made in the past, he said, was 'getting a bit too close to them . . . They don't have to, like, be my slaves or anything, [just] be a bit more professional about it, really.'[13] Amongst other things this entailed learning to appreciate Smith's taste in music: 'On my tour bus you have to sit and listen to everything I play. You're not allowed to speak. If I play a cassette or whatever, you sit down, shut up and listen. If you argue, you get kicked out of the bus. I especially like to make a lot of guitarists and drummers listen to stuff like Boney M, because of the discipline of it. And lots of rockabilly. They all laugh and sneer, but they still can't play in time.'[14]

Despite Smith's animosity to them, in his line of business working with musicians was obviously unavoidable. And despite statements to the contrary, he was not above helping them out when the whim took him; like the time he made a guest appearance at a Clint Boon gig at the Camden Falcon. Invited on stage, Smith sang along to a cover version of the Stooges' 'Now I Wanna Be Your Dog'. 'They won't let me go home,' he cried at the start, before launching into an

13 Meijer, op. cit., 10 September 1999
14 Mark E. Smith, 'Songs in the Key of Mark', *NME*, 11 April 1999

unforgettably ferocious vocal performance.[15] More subdued but equally impromptu was Smith's appearance on Elastica's *Deceptive* EP.[16] Down in London for a series of interviews, Smith was spotted in a local bar by Elastica's Dave Bush: 'His publicity people were in the same studio complex that we were recording the Elastica album. So we were in the pub and we started talking and got on really well. I knew Justine loved him and would be really made up if he came down so I got some drinks and stuff and brought him down.' He helped record two tracks, 'How He Wrote Elastica Man' and 'KB' but then the beer ran out and Smith was gone: 'I think you've got enough there, cock,' he told Bush.

No Place Like It

Smith's literary ambitions, previously manifested in *The Post Nearly Man*, were further confirmed in 1999 with a short story published in *The City Life Book of Manchester Short Stories* edited by Ra Page. Smith entitled his contribution 'No Place Like It'. The story – at just three pages, the shortest in the book – records the thoughts of three characters, Frank, Joe and Stewart as they make their way around Manchester.[17] Familiar Smith themes are represented: gentrification, corrupt local government and the bad behaviour of the indigenous gross peasantry. The three characters' supposedly aimless thoughts and meandering journeys draw them inevitably to a moment in a pub, the Mitre Arms, next to the Cathedral, where they share a table and Frank says, 'Let's form a Party.' Smith's years of lyric-writing had helped him develop writing skills well suited to the short-story form, but unfortunately it's also one of the most unprofitable genres and when publishers offered to do books with him they wanted 'autobiographies, suicide notes, etc., etc.', not two-and-a-half-page short stories.[18]

For all these literary distractions, The Fall remained Smith's main

---

15   In August 1999 a recording of the song made it on to the B-side of the Clint Boon Experience's 'You Can't Keep A Good Man Down' single.

16   released in August 1999

17   Mark E. Smith, 'No Place Like It', in Ra Page (ed.), *The City Life Book of Manchester Short Stories*, London: Penguin, 1999, pp. 254–6

18   Waite, op. cit., 1999

creative outlet. To see in the new millennium, the group embarked on yet another mini-tour of northern towns and cities: Wrexham, Doncaster, York and Leeds. After a year together the band was more competent, if still a little unimaginative. Helal and Head played solidly and unobtrusively while Wilding's performances sometimes suffered from the odd moment of 'showing off'. Smith's vocals had also deteriorated over the years, and were now whittled down to a gripey drawl. The new band members were kept on a tight rein, almost to the level of becoming an anonymous trio of hired hands. A gig by The Fall carried no guarantees and only occasionally provided something special. One such occasion was a gig at the Royal Festival Hall in London on 22 September 2000. It was the last night of a series of John Peel Live sessions and supporting The Fall were Terry Edwards and the Scapegoats and the legendary 'surf' guitarist Dick Dale. The Fall played with great spirit and enthusiasm, and Smith remained concentrated throughout, but still it wasn't good enough for Nick Hasted in the *Independent*: 'He seems like a man no longer in command of his powers, and unaware that this matters. He's just carrying on, in ever-diminishing circles, to the uncritical faithful.'[19] Few fans of The Fall would identify themselves as the 'uncritical faithful', but still, for many people going to a gig by The Fall had inevitably become routine, a habitual pilgrimage offering diminishing returns.

I walk a dark corridor of my heart

Doubts about the abilities of the new line-up were cast aside, however, with the release in November 2000 of *The Unutterable*.[20] Produced by Grant Showbiz, it took just a month of studio time to put together, with tracks recorded at Helal and Wilding's Sonic Surgery, Testa Rossa in Longsight, Manchester, and Showbiz's Street Level 2 in London.

The first track, 'Cyber Insekt', exemplifies the sci-fi pop that distinguishes *The Unutterable* from previous Fall albums. Another standout track, 'Two Librans', features Wilding's power chords

19 Nick Hasted, 'Twangs for the Memory', *Independent*, 26 September 2000
20 The album came out under licence from Cog Sinister on the new label, Eagle Records. Cog Sinister was by now part of the Voiceprint group run by Rob Ayling. Voiceprint counted among its labels Resurgence and Blueprint and boasted a catalogue of over four hundred albums by the likes of Asia, Phil Manzanera, Gong, John Martyn and Robert Wyatt.

accompanying Smith as he reflects on Librans, Oprah Winfrey and historical conflicts (with specific reference to Chechnya and East Timor). 'W.B.' stands for William Blake and incorporates lines from his poem 'A Song of Liberty': 'The fire, the fire is falling! / Look up! Look up! O citizen of London, enlarge thy countenance!'[21] A throbbing bass synth underpins 'Sons of Temperance', and Smith dwells on his worst nightmare – a 'crypto-moralist nation' where drink is banned. 'Dr Bucks' Letter' also employs a looped bass to create a menacing backdrop as Smith takes a walk down the 'dark corridor' of his 'heart' and provides a list of things a celebrity DJ just can't leave home without: sunglasses, CDs, Palm Pilot, mobile phone and Amex card. On 'Octo Realm / Ketamine Sun' Smith introduces himself as 'speed 'ed', Showbiz as 'spliff head', Ayling as 'cynical' and Nagle as 'skooly' and 'skunk lad.' 'Unutterable' provides a lo-fi introduction to the swinging dinner jazz of 'Pumpkin Soup and Mashed Potatoes', complete with lounge-lizard style crooning from smoothie Smith. The most energized moment on the album is Wilding's party piece, 'Hands Up Billy'.

The Unutterable succeeded in refreshing many a jaded fan. The array of musical styles, the inventiveness and clarity of the production, and Smith's rediscovery of singing ensured a marked reversal of The Fall's recent critical reception. Dave Simpson in the *Guardian* said that after sacking his band in 1998 Smith had been in danger of entering an institution rather than being one, but that this album constituted a 'career peak'.[22] Simon Goddard in *Uncut* thought it 'tight, witty and deliriously catchy' and 'high on Smith's barometer of all-time best',[23] and John Mullen in *Mojo* considered it 'the most musically exciting LP since 1990's *Extricate*'.[24] Of course, Smith had heard such praise before, but the general critical consensus was undeniable: The Fall was back on track. Those close to the band also felt excited, Showbiz in particular. 'If they're smart and they're clever they'll stay together,' he said, 'they've got a great thing going on.'[25]

21   The poem was included in Blake's *The Marriage of Heaven and Hell* (1790). The Fall's track was used as trailer music in 2001 for *Two Thousand Acres of Skye*, the popular comedy drama on BBC1 starring Paul Kaye and Pauline Collins.

22   Dave Simpson, 'The Fall, *The Unutterable*', *Guardian*, 3 November 2000

23   Simon Goddard, 'The Fall: *The Unutterable*', *Uncut*, December 2000

24   John Mullen, 'The Fall: *The Unutterable*', *Mojo*, January 2001

25   *The Unutterable* press release

Like watching motor racing purely for the crashes

One of the weirder places to see The Fall in 2000 was in the aisles at HMV in London's Oxford Street. The Fall played there in mid-November to promote the new album to a slightly bemused but patient crowd of about two hundred fans. The short set lacked a drummer, the official reason being Head's prior acting commitments. But by the time of the full promotional tour at the end of November, Head had been replaced by Spencer Birtwistle (previously drummer for Interstella). In time-honoured fashion Birtwistle's first rehearsal with the band came in Nottingham at the sound-check to his first gig. By the time the band reached Dingwalls, Birtwistle had settled in and re-established something of The Fall's garage-band dynamic. Overall, however, the band was finding it difficult to reproduce *The Unutterable*'s studio sound in a live situation and increasingly resorted to tired standards like 'The Joke', 'And Therein' and 'F-'oldin' Money'.

Reviewers of these shows were not impressed. Julian Marshall in *NME* said that watching The Fall nowadays was 'more about voyeurism than entertainment, like watching motor racing purely for the crashes'.[26] Jonathan Romney in the *Guardian* complained that Smith 'has almost entirely dispensed with consonants and mostly sounds like a half-hearted W. C. Fields impersonator trying to dislodge a fishbone from his throat'.[27] Chris Horrie for BBC News Online decided that the audience also deserved some stick: 'About half of the blokes are bald, intellectual types, generally wearing leather jackets. The other half, the younger ones, just look scruffy beyond belief. The impression is of a national convention of Michel Foucault impersonators which has been mistakenly gate-crashed by a gang of Kwik Save shelf-stackers.'[28]

Despite such critical comments there were some highlights during the tour, such as the exhilarating ninety-minute set at Jilly's Rock World in Manchester (where the hometown audience affectionately sang along to 'Paintwork' – 'Hey Mark, you're fucking up the

26 Julian Marshall, 'The Fall: London Camden Dingwalls', NME.COM, accessed 25 November 2000.

27 Jonathan Romney, 'The Fall, Dingwalls, London', *The Guardian*, 24 November 2000

28 Chris Horrie, 'Falling Back in Time', BBC News Online, accessed 24 November 2000

paintwork!'). With most of the set now comprised of songs written by Nagle, Helal and Wilding, the band's commitment and pride was much in evidence. Smith also appeared rejuvenated, enjoying sets that regularly extended well beyond the hour mark. It was a good time to see this particular line-up, but inevitably its days were numbered.

Over the Christmas period a dispute between Helal, Wilding and Smith developed over how much money the pair were owed for their work on *The Unutterable*. Subsequently they refused to play any more gigs until the claim was sorted out and effectively left the band. For replacements Smith turned to a reserve force of under-rehearsed stand-ins, Ben Pritchard on guitar and Jim Watts on bass. Both performed with him in February 2001 at the Red Box in Dublin and in April on a short European and UK tour, ending on 25 April at Bar Cuba in Macclesfield.[29]

In May, Smith broke his shin-bone while attending a rockabilly festival in Great Yarmouth. He reportedly slipped down a slope and jammed his leg against a concrete post. An ambulance took him to hospital where he stayed for the next three days. Despite the fact he was now on crutches, Smith was determined that the band appear at the pre-booked Rockwaves outdoor festival in Athens in early July. With some difficulty the group made it to Greece but a massive thunderstorm followed by torrential rain forced the gig to be cancelled.

The Fall's next live date came in August in front of twenty thousand bikers and Hell's Angels at the Bulldog Bash at Avon Park Raceway near Stratford-on-Avon. As an attraction, The Fall had to compete with strip shows, wet-T-shirt contests and the biggest-beer-gut competition. One person to miss such delights was Julia Nagle. After almost seven years in the group she had also refused to play because of the continuing contract problems (i.e. the lack of one) relating to *The Unutterable* and the mistreatment of Helal and Wilding. She also had little stomach for the hard slog of breaking-in another transitional

29 Q magazine later published the details of The Fall's rider for the night: '14 clean, lint-free full-size towels / 48 large cans of lager / 4 litres of pure orange juice / 2 litres of pure apple juice / 10 litres of still mineral water / 1 bottle of Scotch whisky / 1 bottle of vodka / 2 bottles of Moet et Chandon champagne / 2 bottles of good white wine / A large bowl of fresh fruit / A selection of sandwiches, crisps, peanuts, snacks and chocolate / A supply of ice or a working fridge must also be provided.' Anon., 'Rider of the Month: No. 39 The Fall, Bar Cuba, Macclesfield, 25 April 2001', Q, no. 178, July 2001

line-up. To add to these problems she also needed time off to recover from an operation. As she wryly observed: 'Unfortunately there's no sick leave with The Fall.'

Rude All The Time

The first release by The 'new' Fall came in August 2001 and was a limited edition seven-inch single on Flitwick Records. The record was given away to members of the Flitwick Records club and never went on general sale. Its two pretty uninspiring tracks, 'Rude (All The Time) Acoustic' and 'Wake Up In The City', were recorded and produced by the drummer Spencer Birtwistle in Salford.[30] Over the summer the new recruits continued to write and record new tracks and these were eventually collected together on the *Are You Are Missing Winner* album. A clear sign that the band was in pretty dire straits was the decision to sell the new album at gigs before it was available in the shops. Released on Cog Sinister via Voiceprint, with its obligatory typos and incorrect track-listing, the cover featured a negative colour photograph of Smith and his new wife, Eleni Poulou (also known as Eli and Elenore).[31] The two had first met in December 2000 when Smith was in Berlin helping Michael Clark with a performance at the Pro qm bookshop.

The album was produced by Smith, Birtwistle, Watts and his new managerial side-kick, Ed Blaney. Smith was not wrong when he said: '*The Unutterable* was a bit too polished, this is . . . very raw.'[32] For raw, read exceptionally lo-fi, fluctuating sound levels and eccentric editing. Such elements, in the past, have not necessarily stood in the way of a good Fall record but *Are You Are Missing Winner*, featured few redeeming qualities. The Stooges-style thrash on the opening track 'Jim's "The Fall" ' may have sounded unapologetic, but bore little comparison after a few listens. Those tracks that did work, or were workmanlike, included a cover of Robert Johnson's 'Bourgeois

---

30 'Rude (All The Time) Acoustic' originated as 'Rude All The Time', an old Trigger Happy song from the 1997 EP, *The Lots Gone*. The Fall's manager at the time, Ed Blaney, used to be lead singer of Trigger Happy.

31 Her own musical background includes recordings with Zen Faschisten and Shizuo.

32 Penny Broadhurst, 'Mark E. Smith', Studybees.com, accessed 12 October 2001

Town', 'My Ex-Classmates' Kids' with its 'Sister Ray' groove and hooky chorus, and 'The Acute'. The obligatory experimental track, 'Reprise: Jane – Prof Mick – Ey Bastardo', started off humorously enough with Smith singing in a cod Latin-American accent, 'Spen is a bastardo', but it soon deteriorated into a patched together *mélange* of out-takes from earlier tracks.

Edwin Pouncey in *The Wire* wrote generously that the album only made sense when played 'loud enough to wake the dead',[33] but few listeners were convinced. The album, at best, could be considered another transitional effort and maybe, hopefully, another *Unutterable* was on its way. This appeared unlikely, however, as one of the main figures behind it, Spencer Birtwistle, was sacked just before a gig at the Manchester Footage and Firkin at the end of November. Almost exactly a year after The Fall's stunning performances at Jilly's, Smith had completely changed the line-up of the group once again. This was a fast turnover even by his standards. After twenty-five years of spinning, The Fall's revolving door showed no sign of slowing down.

The note of E

There is no obvious way to end a book on The Fall. Like watching Zeno's Arrow, however patiently you follow its flight you'll never see it reach its target. For many people this persistence is Smith's greatest achievement. How does he manage it? How could somebody so dysfunctional have such a long career? To those that know him well, however, The Fall's continued existence comes as no surprise: 'He was born to do it,' said Brix. 'It's all he knows. He is a total and utter survivor, and you know what, maybe the bad patch will be a bad patch and maybe he'll resurrect himself again. The Fall is always reborn again and again. I have hopes that I'll hear something on the radio by The Fall that will be so good that I'll be foaming with jealousy that I'm not on it!'

The self-styled renegade genius's biggest challenge has been to maintain autonomy and control within an industry where so much is dependent upon co-operation and the uncontrollable whims of fragile egos. Smith's moments of arrogance originate from his need to maintain this myth of control and autonomy. When he said, 'If it's me

---

33 Edwin Pouncey, 'The Fall, *Are You Are Missing Winner*', *The Wire*, February 2002

and your granny on bongos, then it's a Fall gig,'[34] you can be sure the granny was on a fixed fee and that if she misbehaved she'd be back knitting scarves in sheltered accommodation before you could say 'Mr Pharmacist'. It makes him difficult to work with but it also makes working with him a unique experience. Smith's explanation for this is shockingly callous but precise: 'You've only got to hear people who have been in The Fall when they make their own records,' he said, 'there's like something seriously missing there. And, "It's Mark Smith's Fall, it's his lyrics" – it's not that at all. It's the last thing I think is missing. What's missing is that actual oppression that sort of gives rise to freedom in a funny sort of way.'[35]

In recent years there have been many manifestations of this oppression but fewer moments of freedom. But how could it be any other way? As a well-managed, predictable and financially secure band, The Fall would just not be the same. Rather than remaining a living, groaning, gasping mortal being it would become ossified, a museum piece that still draws a crowd, but on the basis of past glories alone. Smith, one suspects, could never submit to such a fate. Martin Bramah feels that he would always find a way to escape such attention: 'His own will stops him from being more famous then he is. Whenever people get too interested in him he goes out of his way to destroy that interest. He thinks longevity lies in obscurity, if he peaks too soon it will be all over.'

Such a strategy has ensured the cultural legacy of The Fall grows slowly but surely. Legions of musicians have confessed to a formative crush on The Fall, from Echo and the Bunnymen and The Smiths, through to Blur, Sonic Youth and Pavement, and into the present day with Badly Drawn Boy. Ryan Gilbey described well the extraordinary influence of the band: 'It's widely accepted that if you marshalled all the musicians who have ever been influenced by The Fall into a field and dropped a bomb on them, the industry would be left with only Céline Dion and a session guitarist from Pinner called Kevin.'[36] Despite so many admirers, Smith remains inimitable. There is no set of stylistic clichés that you can buy off the shelf. It took a lifetime of

34 John Robertson, 'Narky Mark', NME, 7 February 1998
35 Smith, in Charles Neal, Tape Delay, Wembley: SAF Publishing, 1987
36 Ryan Gilbey, 'The Unsettling World of Mark E. Smith', Independent, 26 September 1997

defiance and self-abuse for Smith to develop those particular round shoulders, that skinny frame with its sallow covering of wizened skin, the gap-toothed mouth that spits out both grating truths and downright nonsense, and the ultra-normal dress sense that makes him practically invisible but also instantly recognizable. What other musicians would do for a shard of his attitude or a gram of his credibility!

'Basically my attitude to life is to live,' Smith once said. 'It's more important to be a man than an artist. I don't believe in the artist syndrome.'[37] The Fall, he hoped, would always escape analysis: 'I don't think established high-art theories apply to The Fall. I'd much rather be seen as a failed pop singer, to be honest.'[38] And Smith is nothing if not a wonderfully failed pop singer. A failure of such matchless quality that it has enabled him and this book to veer from the usual trajectory of the classic rock biography: the rise and fall, the live fast, die young, the Jim Morrison and Kurt Cobain, the whole self-destructive artist routine: 'It's like you can only get an A+ if you top yourself,' Smith said shortly after Cobain's suicide. 'It's fuckin' bullshit. You can't create like that. If you can't go out and talk to the dustbin man or sweep your own floor, yer screwed pal.'[39]

After all this, however, can we say we're any closer yet to understanding Smith's character? Are we as close, for instance, as graphology expert Kriss Wellington in 1990, when he analysed Smith's spindly scrawl for the *NME*? 'There's a lot going on here. This person has many facets to his character. He's a bit edgy . . . and not keen on letting people get to him . . . or the real him anyway. He's slightly two-faced and can be somewhat cold. There's a lot going on mentally, he needs a lot of intellectual stimulation. He's inclined to keep you at arm's length. He's very blunt, very matter of fact, he's very good at rubbing people up the wrong way and I wouldn't be surprised if he doesn't run the risk of getting smacked. He has difficulty connecting with people from the heart, although he does have a certain sex appeal. Women like him. I think he might be a bit of a sweetie under all this "the big I am"!'[40]

37 Michael Bracewell and Jon Wilde, 'Mark E. Smith', *Frieze*, September–October 1992
38 Johnny Cigarettes, 'One Man and his Grog', *NME*, 7 May 1994
39 ibid.
40 Stuart Maconie and Kriss Wellington, 'Scrawl Together Now', *NME*, 22/29 December 1990

Smith indeed has 'many facets to his character', some of which have been documented in this book. But for such a public figure – in terms of performance (there can't be many that have spent more time on stage) and writing (thousands of words, a stream of consciousness of some twenty-odd years duration) – Smith remains, as he wants it, an enigma. 'I'm sure he's going to hate some of this book,' Kay Carroll told me. 'He was one of the most paranoiac people I have ever met who could both socially and creatively still function. He would get really pissed off with me for saying it as I saw it. I think he basically rewrites events to fit the Mark E. character, just like an author in a novel. Mark is the writer, Mark E. is something totally different.'

At his funeral, Smith revealed to the *NME*, he would like something short to be played, something like the first march of Elgar's *Pomp and Circumstance*. Or alternatively, 'I'll just get the bloody church organ player to do his job. Have him hold the note of E. But it has to be on a wind-powered organ. With pedals.'[41] Between these two wildly diverse choices, creating an amalgam of the populist and nationalistic swagger of Elgar and the inscrutability of avant-gardism, something of Smith's character is encapsulated. Beyond this only one thing remains certain, Smith's and The Fall's music will outlast us all, the Hip Priest's lessons blasting out from rebellious jukeboxes everywhere, for ever and ever, amen.

41 Mark E. Smith, op. cit., *NME*, 1 May 1999

Selected Discography

Included here are just the main studio albums and singles. For a full discography in all its convoluted glory see Jeff Higgott's monumental work available at http://www.visi.com/fall/discography.html.

Short Circuit – Live at the Electric Circus (June 1978), includes The Fall's 'Stepping Out' and 'Last Orders'
Bingo-Master's Break-Out! EP (August 1978)
'It's The New Thing' (November 1978)
Live At The Witch Trials (January 1979)
'Rowche Rumble' / 'In My Area' (July 1979)
Dragnet (October 1979)
'Fiery Jack' (January 1980)
Totale's Turns (It's Now Or Never) (May 1980)
'How I Wrote Elastic Man' / 'City Hobgoblins' (July 1980)
'Totally Wired' (September 1980)
Grotesque (After The Gramme) (November 1980)
Slates (May 1981)
'Lie Dream Of A Casino Soul' (November 1981)
Hex Enduction Hour (March 1982)
'Look, Know' (April 1982)
Room To Live (Undilutable Slang Truth) (October 1982)
'The Man Whose Head Expanded' (June 1983)
'Kicker Conspiracy' (October 1983)
Perverted By Language (December 1983)
'Oh! Brother' (June 1984)
'C.R.E.E.P.' (August 1984)
Call For Escape Route EP (October 1984)
The Wonderful And Frightening World of The Fall (October 1984)
'Couldn't Get Ahead' / 'Rollin' Dany' (June 1985)
This Nation's Saving Grace (September 1985)
'Cruiser's Creek' (October 1985)

'Living Too Late' (July 1986)

'Mr Pharmacist' (September 1986)

Bend Sinister (October 1986)

'Hey! Luciani' (December 1986)

'There's A Ghost In My House' (April 1987)

'Hit The North' (October 1987)

'Victoria' (January 1988)

The Frenz Experiment (February 1988)

I Am Kurious, Oranj (October 1988)

'Jerusalem' (November 1988)

Seminal Live (June 1989)

'Cab It Up' (June 1989)

'Telephone Thing' (January 1990)

Extricate (February 1990)

'Popcorn Double Feature' (March 1990)

'White Lightning' / 'Blood Outta Stone' (August 1990)

The Dredger EP (August 1990)

'High Tension Line' (December 1990)

Shift-Work (April 1991)

Code: Selfish (March 1992)

'Free Range' (March 1992)

'Ed's Babe' (June 1992)

'Kimble' (March 1993)

The Infotainment Scan (April 1993)

'Why Are People Grudgeful?' / 'Glam Racket' (April 1993)

'Behind The Counter' / 'War' / 'Cab Driver' (December 1993)

'15 Ways' / 'Hey! Student' / 'The $500 Bottle Of Wine' (April 1994)

Middle Class Revolt (May 1994)

Cerebral Caustic (February 1995)

The Twenty-Seven Points (August 1995)

'The Chiselers' / 'Chilinist' (February 1996)

DOSE, featuring Mark E. Smith 'Plug Myself In' (March 1996)

The Light User Syndrome (June 1996)

Levitate (September 1997)

'Masquerade' (February 1998)

SELECTED DISCOGRAPHY

The Post Nearly Man (September 1998)
Inch, featuring Mark E. Smith, 'Inch' (February 1999)
'Touch Sensitive' (February 1999)
The Marshall Suite (April 1999)
'F-'oldin' Money' (August 1999)
The Unutterable (November 2000)
Are You Are Missing Winner (November 2001)
Pander, Panda, Panzer (September 2002)
'The Fall vs 2003' (December 2002)

Index

Clark, Alvin 60
Clark, Michael 11, 133–6, 143–4,
    163–5, 180–2, 249–50, 262,
    277
Clarke, John Cooper 17, 29, 33,
    38, 41, 44, 46, 54, 95, 156, 191
Clarke, Vince 146
Clash 20, 31, 36, 54, 96, 118,
    162, 205
class 26–7, 44, 66, 86, 89, 91,
    93, 101, 139, 160, 227
'The Classical' 102–3, 143
'Clear Off' 122, 137
Clive of Plassey, Lord 4
'Cloud Of Black' 238
'C'n'C-Hassle Schmuk' 220
'C'n'C's Mithering' 86
Cocker, Jarvis 63
Code: Selfish 213–6
Cog Sinister 38, 175–7, 191, 212,
    223, 237, 248, 251, 273, 277
Coldcut 189, 199–200, 202
Coleman, Tony 5–6
'The Coliseum' 243
Collins, Andrew 190, 211
Collins, Edwyn 248
Collins, Jimmy 63
Colourfield 156
Columbia Hotel 234
Communist Party 26
Contact 39
Contact Theatre 37
'Container Drivers' 84, 87, 122
Conway, Jamie T. 235, 239
Cook, Richard 104, 112, 136,
    145, 173
Cope, Julian 35–6, 98
Copeland, Miles 47–9, 74, 78–80,
    154

Copeland, Stewart 47
'Copped It' 128, 137, 164
Corbijn, Anton 101
Cortinas 48
'Couldn't Get Ahead' 145
Couzens, Andy 156
Cox, Bernie 66
Coyne, Andy 136
'Craigness' 133, 137
Cramps 78–9
'Crap Rap 2' 60
Creation Records 251
'C.R.E.E.P.' 122, 136
'Crew Filth' 215
Crime and the City Solution
    170
Cronin, Pete 242
Crooks, Tommy 248–9, 257–62
Crucial Three 36
'Cruiser's Creek' 145, 147–8
'The Crying Marshal' xi, 270
Culture Club 118
Cummins, Kevin 25
Curious Yellows 41
Curtis, Deborah 24
Curtis, Ian 99
Cutler, Ivor 36
'Cyber Insekt' 273

Dalton, Stephen 209, 240
Damned 130, 156
Danse Society 110
Dare, Jimmy 112
Darling, Andy 213
'Das Vulture Ans Ein Nutter-
    Wain' 243
Davies, Paul 183
Davies, Ray 153
Davies, Steve 45, 81–2